CHUCK D

PRESENTS

THIS DAY IN RAP AND HIP-HOP HISTORY

An Hachette UK Company
www.hachette.co.uk

Originally published by Black Dog & Leventhal Publishers
Hachette Book Group
1290 Avenue of the Americas
New York, NY 10104
www.hachettebookgroup.com
www.blackdogandleventhal.com

First published in Great Britain in 2017 by Cassell
a division of Octopus Publishing Group Ltd
Carmelite House
50 Victoria Embankment
London EC4Y 0DZ
www.octopusbooks.co.uk

Published by arrangement with Black Dog & Leventhal Publishers, an imprint of Hachette Books, a division of Hachette Book Group, Inc.

Cover design by Amanda Kain.
Cover illustration by Kelvin Fonville.

ISBN 978-1-84403-958-6

A CIP catalogue record for this book is available from the British Library.

Print book interior design by Michael Gregoire,
laid out by Red Herring Design.

Printed in China

10 9 8 7 6 5 4 3 2 1

Commissioning Editors Hannah Knowles and Romilly Morgan
Editorial Assistant Ellie Corbett
Senior Designer Jaz Bahra
Production Controller Meskerem Berhane

CHUCK D
PRESENTS
THIS DAY IN RAP AND HIP-HOP HISTORY

WITH DUKE EATMON, RON MASKELL,
LORRIE BOULA, AND JONATHAN BERNSTEIN

FOREWORD BY SHEPARD FAIREY

CASSELL ILLUSTRATED

CONTENTS

FOREWORD

Shepard Fairey

Hip-hop is without a doubt the most influential and, at its greatest moments, the most creative musical and cultural movement of the last thirty-five years. Today the influence of hip-hop permeates virtually every form of pop music and fashion. At age eleven or twelve I didn't exactly see the future clearly, but hip-hop pushed its way into my life. It may seem strange now, but in the early '80s I didn't think hip-hop wanted me, a white middle-class kid from the South. Images of the South Bronx on fire and the media coverage of breakdancing and rapping made me feel hip-hop culture was off-limits to me as a cracker from the South with zero street cred. I loved Run-D.M.C. and the Sugarhill Gang, even though "Rapper's Delight" was the only song of theirs I knew. Eventually I noticed hip-hop's influence on groups like Blondie with their song "Rapture" and the Tom Tom Club with "Genius of Love." Ironically, it would be punk rock, the music culture that initially made me think I had to abandon all else, that later brought me back to hip-hop.

I started skateboarding in 1984 as an escape from team sports conformity. At that time, if you skateboarded it was compulsory to dive into punk and hardcore music. I quickly discovered bands like the Sex Pistols, Black Flag, the Clash, the Dead Kennedys, the Misfits, and Bad Brains. As a frustrated teen, I loved the punk bands because they all had energy and attitude, plus a lot of them had social and political things to say. The Clash and the Dead Kennedys especially demonstrated to me that musical virtuosity was less important than passion, style, and a message that connects with the disenfranchised underdog. I usually describe 1984–1986 as my "punk rock orthodoxy phase" where I refused to listen to anything else, though I did discover and love Bob Marley. Since Bad Brains played hardcore and reggae, I was open to Marley and loved his messages against oppression. A friend of mine had a New York City hardcore compilation tape called *New York Thrash* that had songs by Bad Brains and some fast low-fi songs by a band called the Beastie Boys. When the Beasties released *Licensed to Ill* I was intrigued, and it turned out to be the album that brought me back to hip-hop and helped me overcome my fear of being a cultural interloper. I loved *Licensed to Ill*, and I knew a lot of the Led Zeppelin and other classic rock samples, which inspired me to take an interest in how hip-hop songs are creatively constructed. The Beastie Boys were gigging with people like LL Cool J, and Run-D.M.C. had written "Slow and Low" for them, so they seemed credible and legit. The impact of the Beastie Boys juggernaut and their collision of punk rock and hip-hop, made me want to dig deeper into the hip-hop of that year, 1986.

Sometimes the right words in the right place at the right time achieve a lot, and no, I'm not talking about the driving premise of the art of rhyme, I'm talking about the *Thrasher* magazine review of the first Public Enemy album *Yo! Bum Rush the Show*. *Thrasher* magazine, which was the closest thing to a Bible in my life at the time, described Public Enemy's music as "the new punk rock." By '87, '88 I felt punk and hardcore had become a bit formulaic, and I was ready for some new raw power. I picked up Public Enemy's *Yo! Bum Rush the Show* and I was floored by the heaviness and defiant swagger of the music.

OBEY

Songs like "Public Enemy No. 1" and "Right Starter" have booming delivery and immediate but razor-sharp lyrics from Chuck D, the man who was soon to become a hero of mine. *Yo! Bum Rush the Show* was a powerful debut statement for Public Enemy, but it was only the warm-up for the sonic and lyrical firestorm of their follow-ups *It Takes a Nation of Millions to Hold Us Back* and *Fear of a Black Planet*. With *It Takes a Nation of Millions to Hold Us Back* Public Enemy rose to an artistic level not seen before in hip-hop and set a standard for musical, lyrical, and image genius that has rarely been achieved by any other artist. They dealt with politics and race in a supremely sophisticated yet visceral way, over a backdrop of densely collaged and diverse samples. The tension between melody and dissonance resides not only in the music, but Chuck's lyrics as well. His lyrics are the precise reason I took a deeper interest in black movements, the Black Panther Party, and leaders like Malcolm X. Chuck's ability to turn historical black figures into superheroes spoke to teenagers everywhere.

Fear of a Black Planet once again demonstrated the wizardry of Public Enemy's Bomb Squad production team, with intensely layered tracks like "Welcome to the Terrordome" and "Fight the Power," which was the anthem for Spike Lee's masterpiece *Do the Right Thing*, and has since become a protest anthem for the ages. Public Enemy proved it was possible to reach the bourgeoisie and rock the boulevard...to make you shake your rump and pump your fist. Those records showed Public Enemy to be one of the most outspoken forces in music, politics, and culture. The influence on their peers was evident as the golden age of hip-hop of the late '80s, mid '90s was filled with social commentary and gritty storytelling that some called "the CNN of the streets," and others "gangsta rap."

Public Enemy was not the only creative innovator in the golden age. The sampling laws had not yet been solidified in the late '80s, so there was a wealth of raw material for hip-hop acts and DJs to pull from. A few of the main corollaries I see between punk rock and hip-hop are their shared street roots, a defiance of the status quo, and an emphasis on attitude and creativity rather than musical virtuosity. Hip-hop was a new "do-it-yourself" movement that rewarded those who may not have had traditional music training but simply had a great ear and could remix, reinterpret, and transform samples from the vast musical universe, while also using drum machine beats and some live instruments. Musical and narrative progression in hip-hop seemed to be happening on a daily basis in the late '80s and landmark albums redefining possibilities within the genre were emerging from both New York and the West Coast. New York hip-hop was going off—Eric B. & Rakim dropping *Paid in Full*, Boogie Down Productions fronted by KRS-One put out *Criminal Minded* and *By All Means Necessary*, Slick Rick put out *The Great Adventures of Slick Rick*, LL Cool J crushed several styles with the release of *Mama Said Knock You Out*. From Long Island, De La Soul brought the sampling masterpiece *3 Feet High and Rising*, which pushed the idea of what samples could be used to construct a hip-hop track into a more diverse territory. Fellow members of the Native Tongues collective A Tribe Called Quest released several lyrically witty and musically progressive classic albums during the golden age and later put out the amazing album *We Got It from Here...Thank You 4 Your Service* in late 2016, proving great artists only get better with time.

The West Coast also brought the fire in the late '80s and early '90s with artists like Ice-T and N.W.A pioneering gangsta rap. Ice-T's *Rhyme Pays*, *Power*, and *O.G. Original Gangster* all brought tales of street crime and hustling but with some cautionary warnings about the consequences of that lifestyle. N.W.A's *Straight Outta Compton* took confrontation and irreverence to new levels, but according to main lyricist Ice Cube, they were only reflecting the world of South Central they lived in. N.W.A may have been controversial with songs like "Fuck tha Police," but along with the antagonism, the members had talent and charisma to back up their attitudes. Cypress Hill brought a Latin flavor, weed culture, and bilingual rhymes into the mix. While East Coast hip-hop acts were sampling a lot of James Brown and a bit of Parliament-Funkadelic, West Coast acts were leaning heavily on P-Funk and a little on James Brown. The N.W.A-related artists like Dr. Dre, Ice Cube, Eazy-E, and Snoop Dogg all sampled Parliament-Funkadelic, with Dr. Dre credited as pioneering the laid-back but sinister G-funk sound. I think it is safe to say that the samples used in great hip-hop songs led to a massive surge in interest in the funk and soul artists who were featured prominently. I know that hip-hop inspired me to pick up records by James Brown, the Meters, the Isley Brothers, Parliament-Funkadelic, Isaac Hayes, Booker T. & the M.G.'s, and many others. In 1989 the Beastie Boys moved to LA to record the album *Paul's Boutique* with production team the Dust Brothers and Matt Dike. For me, *Paul's Boutique* is the pinnacle of the art of sampling with more than one hundred samples from across the musical spectrum on the album. Funk, soul, disco, glam rock, punk, reggae, and film scores are all sampled to make an eclectic but electrifying album.

In the early '90s, not long after masterpieces of sample collage such as *Fear of a Black Planet, 3 Feet High and Rising*, and *Paul's Boutique* came out, copyright infringement lawsuits over samples began to make artists and labels more hesitant to take risks associated with sampling without clearance. Sampling continued but using a large number of samples per song became financially prohibitive. Nevertheless, innovators rise above limitations, and a lot of great hip-hop emerged in the '90s. Nas released *Illmatic*, the Notorious B.I.G. and Tupac put out several classic albums, Mos Def and Talib Kweli helped fuel the rise of Rawkus Records, and the Wu-Tang Clan brought the noise and their members seemed to put out new solo projects every few weeks. Missy Elliott and Jay Z became dominant hip-hop forces in the late '90s and well into the 2000s. During the same time frame a white Detroit MC named Eminem burst onto the scene with a unique verbal dexterity and the production help of Dr. Dre.

By the 2000s hip-hop proved itself to be a mainstream commercial success and an influence woven into every corner of the cultural fabric. On the one hand, I was happy the critics who said hip-hop "wasn't real music" or "was just a novelty fad" had been proven wrong, but I missed the outsider grit hip-hop had when it was still finding its footing. Early hip-hop had an aspirational charm to its bragging about money, cars, and girls, which seemed more like a defiant statement against a class system that said "people of color don't get the same access to luxuries." However, when hip-hop became more commercial, and luxury became a reality rather than an aspiration, the focus on status symbols began to dampen my enthusiasm for the genre.

One thing I've learned is that evolution can't be stopped. Hip-hop has evolved and mutated in so many different ways that it now has many subgenres. I still see ingenuity and possibility in hip-hop that reminds me why I felt it was the most vibrant and creative art form of music back when I first fell in love in the late '80s. There are amazing newer acts like Run the Jewels and Kendrick Lamar who carry on the tradition of social commentary in their music. Whether it is detractors who still see hip-hop as "not real music by no-talent hoodlums," or champions who see hip-hop as "a bottom-up revolution of empowerment that stretches from the streets to the elites," both opinions are entitled. A few groups have stood the test of time—Public Enemy, De La Soul, and Tribe Called Quest— and continue to put out great work while touring the world. In the end it is only the participants and innovators who can define what hip-hop means now and in the future. I'll be keeping my eyes, ears, and mind open for the next episode.

INTRODUCTION

Even as the sound of music grips our daily lives in its power, and as the connection to the story of music seems to get obscured and pushed to the back; I remain a cheerleader for the arts—especially in the midst of the blizzard of sports. Think about it: in a sports-driven US society, the facts and the figures—not to mention the games behind the game—take up gigantic amounts of space in our lives. This is also reflected internationally, where big biz sports is revered equally as much as the culture.

In this so-called progressive era, the duty of knowing information about modern culture has regressed in my opinion. Once upon a time, the fanatics who loved a particular recording would probably also know all the facts and information about it as well. This applied to every genre and crossed over genres habitually as listeners "discovered" music beyond their typical liking. The "dig" for content led to the "digging" of more of it, so to speak. The radio DJs of the 1950s, 1960s, and 1970s had a lot to do with forming this fan-based research, and thus helped create, and then quench, this thirst. Knowing that Jeff Skunk Baxter played with Steely Dan and The Doobie Brothers was key to any 1970s "rock head," just as a basketball fan would know the steal assist stats of New York Knicks Hall of Famer, Walt Clyde Frazier.

In rap music and hip-hop, the first 15–20 years started off like that. Once again, tip this habit to the DJs who carried, transported, and played (long before Serato) thick record crates full of wax. They had to know thoroughly the labels, the producers, and studios who had that particular "sound" that made best beat-digging possible—first for in-house playing and then for sample uses in their own record productions.

By the late 1980s/early 1990s the emergence of the rap and hip-hop journalists and documentarians helped form the importance of the fact alongside the written opinion. Magazines like *The Source*, *Rap Sheet*, *RAPpages,* and others put the fact to the words while filtering and processing the myths from the real. The thirst was always there but the info falloff was dramatic at the turn of the twenty-first century. Mergers, particularly in the technology region's programming sector, sold itself out and got paranoid. Black radio DJ rap shows—including the Awesome Two, Mr. Magic, Lady B, Greg MACK, Pinkhouse & Ramone Ski, Chicago Chuck Chill Out, Red Alert, and Tim Westwood in London with a slew of international shows; as well as the college Hip-Hop Jocks Wildman Steve, BARRY Benson, Mr. Bill Stephney, and later on 1990s shows like "Stretch & Bobbito" to name a few—all had dialogue about the records and artists they played. This fed the audience alongside the mags, which then started to have even multi-regional readers writing debates on the art form and genre.

Once brought into US law, the 1996 Clinton Powell Telecommunications Act allowed corporations to soak up and buy out individual independent regional radio stations. That was a nail struck deep into the hip-hop coffin of startups and Indies. "Indie" meaning Independent radio shows, promoters, record labels, and regional goods and services that could humbly build some rap real estate on the airwaves. The second blast was the World Wide Web, which many claimed as the death knell for record companies as we knew it. I agree yet disagree with that theory because it all ain't that simple. The turn of the century signaled a redirection of what business heads called "content." Technology took it all in and started reconfiguring it all as metadata. It was still a step up from the late 1990s CD, which reduced titles and musicians to "*track whatever by what's its name.*" Mixtapes made their mark in hip-hop as identifiers with over-the-top, CD-sized cover art.

With gadgets galore, and especially during these past Obama years, the thirst for the stone-cold facts behind the music folks love is now evident in social media. Everyone has an opinion, voiced through the power of their text. That also means mass amounts of misinformation, in this so-called communication era, is prevalent. This is exactly what made me follow up the idea of *This Day in Rap and Hip-Hop History*, first as a radio show idea in 2009.

Backtracking to that year, after being approached by Andrea Clarke of the legendary WBAI 99.5 progressive radio station in New York City, I contemplated doing a different kind of rap show broadcast. I had just finished up a four-year stint with Air America Network 2004–2008 doing a talk interview show with Gia'na Garel. Andrea had been approaching me since 2007 about doing a hip-hop show. I couldn't see how. Most hip-hop shows were stuck in the same rut format of endless mixes, and slapping the audience with records containing little or no spoken communication. This pattern across an hour (much less two), deterred and bored the avid fans and kept the non-fans out. Rap and hip-hop, regardless of its financial-*WSJ* hype, was killing itself in the diminishing returns of non-curation.

A light bulb hit me when I watched Bryant Gumbel's *Real Sports* on HBO. I saw that he moderated a show about putting a show together, along with a group of contributors. It was really the *60 Minutes* concept, I later found out. This gave me the idea of what kind of radio show to put on WBAI, one that would make sense over a two-hour period. I came up with and wrote out a recruitment plan to attract skilled hip-hop radio heads in key positions, to contribute segment blocks. WildMan Steve Adams was a standout legend who continued the hip-hop legacy on 90.3 WBAU, post Mr. Bill Stephney and André, Doctor Dré Brown. Steve had continued into the 1990s ushering in many artists and doing various voice-overs for record projects. "Songs in the Right Direction" was a perfect fit after my "Songs That Mean Something" block. Mikko Kapanen and Amkelwa Mbekeni delivered eloquently "Planet Earth Planet Rap," the only show in the hip-hop world that played the music and acts of hip-hop across the world. There was an opening for some mixes by various DJs—something Public Enemy Hall of Fame founding member DJ Terminator X does with his partner DJ DVS today. Tim Einenkel came over from Air America to supply songs, scripts, and a great interview segment called "The Library." Raven The Blazin Eurasian I met at a Club Classic event and since then she has dutifully projected women's contributions in hip-hop in a segment called "Hip-Hop Queenz."

From there I knew a chief editor would be necessary, as I would do an intro/outro as well as my "Songs That Mean Something" segment. Veteran DJ Johnny Juice was that guy to seamlessly do a few segments himself, measuring the blocks to do 1:55 minutes of blast casting, with all segments emailed in to him in MP3 form. Which leads into the segment that spurred this book, *This Day in Rap and Hip-Hop History*: I'd known Duke Eatmon and Ron Maskell for about a decade at that time, having met them before that in concerts. Diligent to the T as documentarians and hip-hop DJs from Montreal Canada (or Mount Real as we say) just an international car drive north from New York City. They were the most astute in explaining, and hence breaking down, the Public Enemy discography of words, reason, and music. With the details of every song, every member, and the track's meaning and purpose, all broken down into documentary radio broadcasts, again the common theme here being they evolved from the Rap Radio realm. Their "This Is Not A Test" and Soul Experience Shows on Podamatic and Canadian station 101.9 FM CHAI offer amazing, never-to-be-forgotten CLASSICK Material.

With their outstanding dedication to this specific research, I proposed they could approach "This Week in Hip-Hop and Rap" as a segment on the "AndYouDontStop!" show. We had also launched the radio RAPstation.com at the same time, in 2010, that we would program. We proposed how they could approach "This Day in Hip-Hop and Rap" as a daily segment. They would research, write, record, and upload. The plans early on were a calendar, book, and application. Although there are a few books out there that deal with these "This Day" themes in music, this is the first that attempts to enter as a chronological read.

So, in full-circle recognition, this book would not be possible without that Mount Everest–level dedication of Duke and Ron. Adding in the extra notes of Baird "Flatline" Warnick, putting his endless fact work into RAPstation and HipHopGods. Along with Gia'na Garel, who has been so diligent in working to make this street work edited and presentable outside its stereotypical bag. And my former assistant, Kate Gammell, for getting the ball rolling on this, as well as manager Lorrie Boula for getting it going. Along with those at BTNE Garlyn and Gary G Wiz for the other technology that this book will thrive on.

The time is NOW regarding the official start time for this project, as a book, to enter hip-hop's 44th year and rap recorded music and song's 38th season. The facts, trivia, events, quotes, and notes make this book a mandatory must-have to dispel the myths about the most powerful genres the recent world has known.

—Chuck D

1973-1983

DJ KOOL HERC

1973

AUGUST 11

DJ Kool Herc invents hip-hop at 1520 Sedgwick Avenue.

Clive Campbell, aka DJ Kool Herc, hosted a party in the rec room of his apartment building at 1520 Sedgwick Avenue in the Bronx. The party, billed as a "Back to School Jam" for Kool Herc's little sister, is seen by many as the precise birthplace of hip-hop.

The party was the first time an audience heard the results of Kool Herc's turntable experimentation, in which the up-and-coming DJ pioneered a technique of isolating the rhythm sections from '60s and '70s records, known as "the break," and looping them on repeat or together to create something new.

During Kool Herc's set, his friend Coke La Rock spontaneously grabbed a microphone and began calling out his friends' names and rapping improvised lyrics over the DJ's breakbeat.

NOVEMBER 12

Ex-gang member Afrika Bambaataa forms the Universal Zulu Nation in the Bronx, New York.

Inspired by DJ Kool Herc and Kool DJ Dee, Bambaataa wanted to form an organization that would inspire gang members and disenfranchised youth all over the world to utilize creative forces as a means to turn their lives around. Bambaataa used hip-hop culture as the vehicle to realize that goal.

By the 1980s, the Universal Zulu Nation had branches in the UK, Japan, France, Australia, and South Korea.

1977

JULY 13

New York City blackout provides a generation of New York DJs with equipment.

The New York City blackout of 1977 resulted in widespread looting and arson in many of the poorest neighborhoods throughout the city.

Pioneering hip-hop artists like DJ Kool Herc and Grandmaster Caz have both attributed the rise of an entire generation of hip-hop DJs to mass looting of equipment like mixers, turntables, and speakers that took place throughout Brooklyn and the Bronx on the night of July 13.

1978

JULY 1

Robert Ford's *Billboard* article tells the world about the rush for "B-beats" in NYC record stores.

Ford's story, titled, "B-Beats Bombarding Bronx" was one of the earliest mentions of the emerging musical genre in national media.

The article includes quotes from DJ Kool Herc, and describes the trend of DJs sifting through record bins at stores throughout New York looking for specific albums to sample.

"The requests, for the most part," Ford writes, "come from young black disco DJ's from the Bronx who are buying the records just to play the 30 seconds or so or rhythm breaks that each disk contains."

DECEMBER 23

Grandmaster Flash & the Furious 4 MC's perform a now-historic show at the Audubon Ballroom in Harlem, New York.

The crew at that point consisted of Flash, Melle Mel, the Kidd Creole, Cowboy, and Scorpio. A year later, Rahiem of the Funky 4 + 1 would join and they would become known as Grandmaster Flash & the Furious Five.

1979

MAY 5

Robert Ford writes a *Billboard* article titled "Jive Talking N.Y. DJs Rapping Away in Black Discos."

Chronicling the rising trend of "attracting followings with their slick raps," it is the first story appearing in a mainstream publication to discuss the growing phenomena of rapping.

Pioneering DJs and rappers Eddie Cheeba, DJ Hollywood, and Kurtis Blow are all mentioned in the story.

SEPTEMBER 16

The Sugarhill Gang releases their classic and groundbreaking hit, "Rapper's Delight," on Sugar Hill.

Sugar Hill Records owner Sylvia Robinson was looking for rappers near their New Jersey recording studio. Her son came across Henry "Big Bank Hank" Jackson who was flipping pizzas at a local shop. Hank was managing the legendary Grandmaster Caz, who later claimed Hank borrowed his notebook filled with rhymes for the song. The lyrics back up Caz's claim of theft, as his original rapping name, Casanova Fly, is even spelled out by Hank on the classic track.

The balance of the Sugarhill Gang was Jersey's Michael "Wonder Mike" Wright and Guy "Master Gee" O'Brien.

The song begins with an interpolation of "Here Comes That Sound Again" by Love De-Luxe, and is followed by the bass line and main groove of Chic's hit single "Good Times," both released on Atlantic that same year. The interpolations were played by the funk band Positive Force.

Chic members threatened to sue until they were added to the credits as co-songwriters and received compensation.

The fifteen-minute, ten-verse song has sold more than two million copies and is credited with bringing rap music on the mainstream. On January 5, 1980, it was the first hip-hop record to enter *Billboard*'s Hot 100 chart, reaching #36.

DECEMBER 7

Kurtis Blow releases "Christmas Rappin'" on Mercury.

Kurtis Blow became the first rapper to be signed to a major label when he released his debut single at the age of twenty. Blow's song was an instant commercial success, selling more than 400,000 copies.

The initial idea for "Christmas Rappin'" came from Blow's producers, J. B. Moore and *Billboard* writer Robert Ford.

THE SUGARHILL GANG

GRANDMASTER FLASH

1980

FEBRUARY 7

The Sugarhill Gang release their self-titled debut album on Sugar Hill.

The set featured "Rapper's Delight" as well as cult favorites like "Sugarhill Groove" and "Rapper's Reprise (Jam-Jam)," featuring the Sequence. The album peaked at #32 on the *Billboard* R&B chart.

SEPTEMBER 27

Kurtis Blow performs "The Breaks" on *Soul Train*.

Blow's performance of "The Breaks" on *Soul Train* was the first time a rapper performed on national TV. The breakthrough moment introducing the twenty-one-year-old artist to the rest of the country. He had to beg *Soul Train* host Don Cornelius to let him rap live, with the show typically relying on lip-synching for most all of its performances.

Cornelius told Blow off air that he didn't "really understand what you guys are talking about, but everybody seems to love it."

SEPTEMBER 29

Kurtis Blow releases his self-titled debut on Mercury.

Blow's debut album, the first rap record to be released on a major label, featured his second hit single "The Breaks," which was released during the summer of 1980. It was the first hip-hop record to go gold, selling close to 700,000 copies in 1980.

The album's final song, "Takin' Care of Business," was a hip-hop rendition of Bachman-Turner Overdrive's 1973 hit. The song was released six years before Run-D.M.C. would receive credit for merging rock 'n' roll and rap with their hit single "Walk This Way."

1981

JANUARY 12

Blondie release the classic smash hit single "Rapture" on Chrysalis.

The hit song from Blondie's fifth album, *Autoamerican*, was an ode to the early New York hip-hop scene.

"Rapture," which was the first rap record to top the charts, featured vocals from the group's lead singer Debbie Harry, who included a shout-out to Fab Five Freddy and Grandmaster Flash on the classic track.

1981

The single "The Adventures of Grandmaster Flash on the Wheels of Steel" is released on Sugar Hill.

The recording captured Flash mixing and scratching songs using three turntables live in the studio. Songs included Chic's "Good Times," Blondie's "Rapture," and Queen's "Another One Bites the Dust."

FEBRUARY 14

The Funky 4 + 1 perform their 1980 hit "That's the Joint" on NBC's *Saturday Night Live.*

The Bronx group featured Sha Rock, one of the first female MCs. They performed their song on the Debbie Harry–hosted show, becoming the first hip-hop act to perform on national television.

JULY 4

The Fantastic Five beat the Cold Crush Brothers in the first hip-hop MC battle at the Harlem World disco in New York City.

The prize was $1,000 cash. A staged battle between the two legendary early school New York crews can be seen in the 1983 First Run Features film *Wild Style*.

JULY 9

***20/20* airs a story on hip-hop titled "Rappin' to the Beat."**

20/20's story on the musical genre was the first in-depth national TV spotlight on hip-hop. The story, which explored the growing "overnight phenomenon" of hip-hop, featured artists such as the Sugarhill Gang, Kurtis Blow, and Blondie, whose chart-topping 1981 single "Rapture" featured lead singer Debbie Harry rapping.

The story investigated the phenomenon of break-dancing and described hip-hop as an "all beat and all talk" genre that "tells you a story and makes you want to dance."

Unlike much of hip-hop's earliest press coverage, the *20/20* piece suggested that the music might have long-term longevity. "Rap is likely to influence popular music for years to come," the show proclaimed. "It has tremendous staying power because it lets ordinary people express ideas they care about in language they can relate to put to music they can dance to."

FALL 1981

Captain Rapp and Disco Daddy release "The Gigolo Rapp" on Rappers Rapp Disco Company.

Captain Rapp's "The Gigolo Rapp," the first ever West Coast hip-hop single to be released on vinyl, was a minor hit in Los Angeles, where the party rap based on Rick James's "Give It to Me" received some airplay on the city's urban radio stations.

The single was the inaugural release from Rappers Rapp, which served as LA's first ever rap label. Captain Rapp would earn the biggest single of his career two years later when he released "Bad Times (I Can't Stand It)," a socially conscious single released in the wake of Grandmaster Flash's "The Message."

DECEMBER 30

Kool Moe Dee and Busy Bee go head to head at the Harlem World club in Manhattan.

One of the earliest high-profile rap battles went down between Kool Moe Dee and Busy Bee Starski. Each rapper freestyled for about six minutes. Busy Bee performed first and was roasted later in the evening when Kool Moe Dee took the stage and killed it.

1982

APRIL 17

Afrika Bambaataa and Soulsonic Force release the groundbreaking single "Planet Rock" on Tommy Boy.

The futuristic electronic gold-selling single off the pioneering *Planet Rock* album borrows heavily from the underground techno classic "Trans-Europe Express" by Germany's Kraftwerk.

Produced by Arthur Baker and the first to use the Roland TR-808 beat in hip-hop, it entered the *Billboard* Hot 100 chart three months after release, peaking at #48, as well as #4 on the R&B charts.

AFRIKA BAMBAATAA

MELLE MEL

CHUCK D:

I remember the entire NYC area electrified by this record. Lines surrounding Bonds International in Times Square and the *E.T.* dance went perfect to it. It was only fitting that the master of records, DJ Afrika Bambaataa and Soulsonic Force, ushered in the current legacy of what the Zulu Nation brought to the rap-recording scene. This combo of Arthur Baker and Bam are the seeds of the Miami bass hip-hop south and from this dirty and crunk.

JULY 1

Grandmaster Flash & the Furious Five release "The Message" on Sugar Hill.

After releasing a series of party singles, Grandmaster Flash & the Furious Five put out "The Message," which is considered one of the first socially conscious hip-hop songs.

The song, which combined elements of R&B, disco, funk, and hip-hop with lyrics that painted a clear picture of inner-city life, would end up serving as a template for scores of hip-hop groups to come, including Public Enemy, N.W.A, and the Notorious B.I.G. In 2012, *Rolling Stone* named "The Message" the greatest hip-hop song of all time.

The song, which reached #4 on the R&B/Hip-Hop chart, would serve as the title track to the group's debut album, released that October.

NOVEMBER 24

The Sugarhill Gang release their sophomore album *8 Wonder* on Sugar Hill.

Produced by James Cullimore and label founder Sylvia Robinson, the set would feature hits like the title track, "Showdown," featuring Grandmaster Flash and the Furious Five, which reached #13 on the R&B/Hip-Hop chart and their remake of the Incredible Bongo Band's "Apache," one of the earliest classic hip-hop breakbeats, which reached #49 on the R&B/Hip-Hop chart.

NOVEMBER 1982

Melle Mel releases "White Lines (Don't Don't Do It)" on Sugar Hill.

"White Lines," which depicted cycles of drug addiction, cocaine-fueled partying, and drug dealing, was cowritten by Melle Mel and Sylvia Robinson, the head of Sugar Hill Records. The song's sample is taken from the Sugar Hill house band's rendition of Liquid Liquid's "Cavern."

The song was originally released under "Grandmaster Flash and Melle Mel," even though the former had nothing to do with the recording of the song. The song charted at #9 on the Dance charts and #47 on the R&B/Hip-Hop chart, and then again in 1995 when Duran Duran released a remake with Melle Mel.

A young Spike Lee made an unofficial music video featuring Laurence Fishburne. Ultimately rejected by Sugar Hill Records, it remains widely available and is the song's unofficial music video.

1983

MARCH 12

Run-D.M.C. release their debut single "It's Like That" on Profile.

The hard-hitting "It's Like That" and its rap battle B-side "Sucker M.C.'s," which is thought to be one of the first "diss" records, would be on their self-titled debut album released the following year. The spare, unique-sounding single hit the top twenty of the R&B/Hip-Hop chart and is considered the first "new school" hip-hop recording.

MARCH 18

The first hip-hop film *Wild Style* opens in US theaters.

The First Run Features film, written and directed by Charlie Ahearn, starred graffiti artist Lee Quiñones as the fictional graffiti artist Zoro. A celebration of New York's hip-hop culture, the movie included appearances by some of the earliest pioneers including Grandmaster Flash, Fab Five Freddy, Grandmixer D.ST., Chief Rocker Busy Bee, Rammellzee, the Cold Crush Brothers, featuring Grandmaster Caz, Fantastic Freaks, featuring DJ Grand Wizard Theodore, the Rock Steady Crew, and Double Trouble (formerly of Funky 4 + 1).

APRIL 15

Paramount Pictures releases *Flashdance* in US theaters.

The highest-grossing movie in the US in 1983, about a struggling dancer by night who works in a Pittsburgh steel mill by day, starred Jennifer Beals and was directed by Adrian Lyne. It was the first major film release to feature B-boying with the Rock Steady Crew in a couple of dance sequences, one of which was performed to "It's Just Begun" by the Jimmy Castor Bunch, an original breakbeat classic.

MAY 23

The Disco 3 win first prize at the Tin Pan Apple After Dark Dance & Rap Contest, cosponsored by Coca-Cola and WBLS, at Radio City Music Hall in New York City.

The hefty three-man squad, comprised of Mark "Prince Markie Dee" Morales, Damon "Kool Rock-Ski" Wimbley, and Darren "the Human Beat Box" Robinson, would win stereo equipment as well as a one-off record deal, which resulted in a twelve-inch single called "Reality."

After the release failed to make any significant noise in the industry, their managers Charles Stettler and Linda West brought them to rap legend Kurtis Blow who produced their self-titled debut album, released the following year, and renamed them the Fat Boys.

JULY 8

Whodini release their self-titled debut album on Jive.

The Brooklyn rap group was one of the first to incorporate straight R&B into their music. Although the album is considered a bona fide hip-hop classic, Jalil Hutchins of the group said he was a little frustrated that the group had very little musical input into the direction of the album.

Some of the music on the album was produced by British electro-soul man Thomas Dolby, who had never met the group but sent the New York group rhythm tracks from the UK.

The set featured the hit singles "Magic's Wand," which reached #45 on the R&B/Hip-Hop chart, "The Haunted House of Rock," and "Rap Machine," which spawned a groundbreaking music video that featured appearances by members of UTFO.

DECEMBER 11

Run-D.M.C. release their single "Hard Times" on Profile Records.

"Hard Times," backed by the classic B-side "Jam-Master Jay," an ode to their DJ, was the second single from their self-titled debut album, which would be released the following year. The song was originally recorded by Kurtis Blow for his 1980 self-titled debut album.

"Hard Times," with lyrics fueled by Reaganomics and the growing sentiment of the 1980s "Me Generation," was produced by Larry Smith, Run's brother Russell Simmons, and the group's Jam Master Jay. It reached #11 on the R&B/Hip-Hop chart.

WHODINI

1984

1984

KDAY 1580 AM begins broadcasting hip-hop 24/7.

The longtime black AM radio station in Los Angeles, which served as a prominent disco and R&B station throughout the 1970s, began broadcasting hip-hop 24/7 in early 1984.

The station began transitioning to its hip-hop format in the summer of 1983, when legendary LA rap DJ Greg Mack took over as the station's musical director.

The radio station proved to be an immediate catalyst for West Coast rap, hosting a widely popular Saturday night show hosted by a young Dr. Dre and spinning early records from Ice-T. The station also helped jumpstart the career of pioneering West Coast rap groups like N.W.A and Above the Law.

1984

UTFO release the single "Roxanne, Roxanne" on Select.

The Brooklyn hip-hop group, comprised of Kangol Kid (Shaun Shiller Fequiere), the Educated Rapper (Jeffrey Campbell, also known as EMD), Doctor Ice (Fred Reeves), and Mix Master Ice (Maurice Bailey), released the single "Hangin' Out," but the song's B-side, "Roxanne, Roxanne," ended up becoming far more popular.

The song resulted in a series of dozens of "Roxanne" response records from New York hip-hop artists after Roxanne Shanté first responded to the song with "Roxanne's Revenge," which was produced by Marley Marl.

Artists that recorded "Roxanne" records included Sparky D, Blowfly, Dr. Freshh, Gigolo Tony and Lacey Lace, and the East Coast Crew.

FEBRUARY 28

Herbie Hancock performs "Rockit" at the Grammys.

Playing a keytar, the legendary jazz musician performed his Grammy-nominated single "Rockit" with Stevie Wonder, Thomas Dolby, and Howard Jones.

With Grand Mixer D.ST. scratching turntables, this performance put an unprecedented spotlight on hip-hop, especially considering 1984 Grammys viewership was forty-four million people, the highest ratings in the show's history.

Later that night, Hancock and D.ST. won the Grammy for best R&B/instrumental performance for the song.

MARCH 27

Run-D.M.C. release their self-titled debut album on Profile.

Although the album was more of a collection of the group's many twelve-inch single hits from the previous year, it nonetheless contained early Run-D.M.C. classics that would remain a staple of their live shows for decades to come, including "It's Like That," "Sucker M.C.'s (Krush-Groove 1)," "Rock Box," "Hard Times," and "Hollis Crew (Krush-Groove 2)."

The album featured production by Larry Smith, Orange Krush, Rod Hui, and Run's brother, Russell Simmons. It reached #53 on the *Billboard* 200 and #14 on the R&B chart.

1984

RUN-D.M.C.

Obey

APRIL 16

Run-D.M.C. release their hit single, "Rock Box," on Profile.

The rock-rap fusion track featured guitar work from legendary session man Eddie Martinez. The track would directly or indirectly influence future groups such as Rage Against the Machine, Limp Bizkit, the Beastie Boys, Korn, and others.

Reaching #26 on the charts, the song's memorable music video featured an appearance by comedic actor Irwin Corey and was the first video from a rap act to get put into MTV rotation.

CHUCK D:

The rap scene clearly migrates to Queens with this album. Mr. Bill Stephney was among the first to interview this trio in March 1983 on Adelphi University radio WBAU 90.3. Harry Allen took pictures. All of the station's shows played every single from that point on. They all made the final album, and the big beat was in effect. The album's cover and back were rather crude—like it was catching Profile Records by surprise—but eventually the label realized the group was edging in on rock status as much as rap.

MAY 29

The Fat Boys release their self-titled debut album on Sutra.

The Brooklyn trio (originally called the Disco 3) were discovered by Kurtis Blow at a talent competition. Prince Markie Dee, Kool Rock-Ski, and the Human Beat Box, who were sometimes looked at as a novelty act, proved they had rhyme skills on their debut set. It reached #200 on the *Billboard* 200 and #6 on the R&B chart.

The Human Beat Box had an uncanny ability to mimic the Roland TR-808 drum machine with thunderous results as opposed to the other beatbox pioneer, Doug E. Fresh, whose equally capable skills were more sound-effects oriented.

Produced by Kurtis Blow, the album contained some of the all-time biggest Fat Boys classics like "Can You Feel It?," "Jail House Rap," and the unforgettable title track. The set also featured the track "Human Beat Box" which is still today one of the all-time greatest exhibitions of the art form.

JUNE 4

***Breakin'* is released by MGM.**

The hip-hop breakdancing comedy grossed close to forty million dollars and was number one at the box office upon its release.

Breakin' was directed by Joel Silberg, and starred Shabba Doo, Lucinda Dickey, and Boogaloo Shrimp. The film is also known as Ice-T's first-ever appearance on film. The rapper appears briefly as an MC.

JUNE 8

Orion Pictures release *Beat Street.*

Following 1983's *Wild Style, Beat Street* featured the classic four elements of hip-hop: rapping, turntablism, graffiti, and breakdancing.

The film, directed by Stan Lathan, was coproduced by Harry Belafonte and David V. Picker. It starred Rae Dawn Chong and Guy Davis and featured cameo appearances by hip-hop founder DJ Kool Herc, as well as pioneers like the Treacherous Three, Doug E. Fresh, Grandmaster Melle Mel, Afrika Bambaataa and the Soulsonic Force, and Jazzy Jay. The film also included a classic B-boy battle between the New York City Breakers and the Rock Steady Crew.

SEPTEMBER 1

The twenty-seven-date Swatch Watch New York City Fresh Fest, said to be the first hip-hop arena tour, kicks off in Greensboro, North Carolina, on Labor Day weekend.

Featuring the Fat Boys, Whodini, Newcleus, Kurtis Blow, the Dynamic Breakers, and Run-D.M.C., the sold-out tour grossed more than $3.5 million and brought rap music to listeners who had never seen it performed live.

OCTOBER 17

Whodini release their sophomore album *Escape* on Jive.

Produced by Larry Smith, the album featured instrumentation by UK funkster Thomas Dolby, who also provided backing tracks on their 1983 self-titled debut album.

The platinum-selling *Escape* contained hit singles and classic Whodini tracks including the title song, "Big Mouth," "Friends," and "Five Minutes of Funk." It was the first rap album to go platinum and the first to break into the top forty of *Billboard*'s singles and reached the Album chart at #35.

NOVEMBER 1984

LL Cool J releases debut single "I Need a Beat" on Def Jam.

LL Cool J's debut single was one of the earliest releases for Def Jam, a label started in 1983 by Rick Rubin, and joined soon after by Russell Simmons. The song was the first to be released with an official Def Jam catalog number.

The hard-hitting single, which sold more than 100,000 copies, was released a year before LL Cool J's debut album, *Radio*, was released in the fall of 1985, which was the first full-length album to be released on Def Jam. A different, remixed version of the song would wind up on *Radio*.

1985

1985

Schoolly D releases "PSK (What Does It Mean?)."

Released independently by Philadelphia rapper Schoolly D, the single is considered to be the first gangsta rap, which took its name from a local gang, the Park Side Killers. The song would inspire many West Coast rappers, most importantly Ice-T on his landmark track "6 in the Mornin'."

JANUARY 15

Run-D.M.C. release the single "King of Rock" on Profile.

The hit single, and title track from their sophomore album released a week later, followed in the rap-rock fusion mode of their hit single "Rock Box." It reached #14 on the R&B chart.

"King of Rock" featured a popular music video, which became a fan favorite on MTV. It featured Calvert DeForest, aka Larry "Bud" Melman of NBC's *Late Night with David Letterman* fame.

JANUARY 1985

Run-D.M.C. release their sophomore album *King of Rock* on Profile.

The album featured a collaboration with dancehall-reggae toaster Yellowman called "Roots, Rap, Reggae," as well as the hit "Can You Rock It Like This" written by a sixteen-year-old LL Cool J. The song was also featured in the 1985 Warner Bros. film *Krush Groove*.

The album also included Run-D.M.C. cult favorites like "You're Blind" and "Jam-Master Jammin'," the hit single "You Talk Too Much," and the smash title track. The album spent fifty-six weeks on the charts, reaching #52 on the *Billboard* 200 and #12 on the R&B chart, and sold more than two million copies for Profile.

JULY 13

Run-D.M.C. perform at Live Aid at JFK Stadium in Philadelphia.

In an event to aid Ethiopian famine victims held simultaneously in Philadelphia and in London, at Wembley Stadium, Run-D.M.C. performed "King of Rock" and "Jam-Master Jammin'."

Viewed by thousands of concert attendees and by two billion people via television broadcasts and satellite linkups, this historical bill included a reunited Led Zeppelin, Tina Turner, Teddy Pendergrass, Phil Collins, Paul McCartney, U2, the Rolling Stones, Bob Dylan, and Sade, just to name a few.

AUGUST 13

Doug E. Fresh and the Get Fresh Crew featuring Slick Rick release "The Show/La Di Da Di" on Reality.

The now-classic single from the beatbox aficionado was recorded with his Get Fresh Crew, which included MC Ricky D (later known as Slick Rick), Barry Bee, and Chill Will. "The Show" reached #4 on the R&B chart and sold more than a half million copies in the US. It went top five in the UK and became the bestselling rap single in Europe. In 1987, it would appear remixed on Fresh's first album *Oh, My God!* in 1986.

SCHOOLLY D

OCTOBER 25

Krush Groove is released in US theaters.

The film, directed and produced by Michael Schultz, was a semiautobiographical account of the life of rap mogul Russell Simmons with Blair Underwood playing the Def Jam Recordings founder.

The film also starred Sheila E., as well as future rap legends like Run-D.M.C., the Fat Boys, Kurtis Blow, the Beastie Boys, Dr. Jeckyll & Mr. Hyde, as well as a sixteen-year-old LL Cool J. The soundtrack reached #79 on the *Billboard* 200 and #14 on the R&B chart.

NOVEMBER 18

LL Cool J releases his debut _Radio_ as the first album on Def Jam.

LL's platinum-selling debut set featured hip-hop classics like "I Need a Beat," "Dear Yvette," "You'll Rock," "I Can Give You More," and "I Can't Live Without My Radio," which LL also performed in the 1985 film *Krush Groove*.

LL's clear, articulate, wordy rhymes were heavily influenced by T La Rock's rap style. Def Jam cofounder Rick Rubin was responsible for *Radio*'s sparse stripped down scratch production style, so much so that the album's credits read "Reduced by Rick Rubin." Legendary DJ Jazzy Jay did some additional production on the album as well.

The platinum-selling *Radio* reach #46 on the *Billboard* 100 chart and #6 on the R&B chart. LL Cool J was the first hip-hop artist to appear on Dick Clark's *American Bandstand,* when he performed singles from *Radio*.

CHUCK D:

This was the first time a solo rapper posed a threat to hip-hop groups, stage- and record-wise. Hank Shocklee and Harry Allen went to get a number on T La Rock at Ben Franklin High School in Manhattan. They got his number but kept saying the opening act's name: "Yeah 'T' was great but LL, LL, LL." And I was like "What is an 'LL'?"

Working on WBAU, program directors like Bill "Mr. Bill" Stephney and André "Doctor Dré" Brown built a pipeline for Spectrum City to play the first records by Def Jam in 1984— the purple label discs—and the singles that led the way for LL Cool J to be solid enough to demand rap's first true label deal with CBS. *Radio* moved rap into being more album oriented when it came to promoting music, taking it from merely being about singles.

1986

1986

Ice-T releases the single "6 in the Mornin'" on Techno Hop.

The defining moment of gangsta rap was released as the B-side to the single "Dog'n the Wax." Inspired by the flow and lyrics of Schoolly D's "P.S.K.," Ice-T delivered a first-person account of inner-city life. An extended version of the single appeared on Ice-T's debut album, which was put out by Madonna's Sire Records in 1987.

APRIL 29

Whodini release their third album *Back in Black* on Jive.

The platinum-selling *Back in Black*, which was produced by Larry Smith, contains classic cuts like "Fugitive" and "Last Night (I Had a Talk with Myself)" and hits such as "One Love," "Growing Up," and "Funky Beat," which also marked the vocal debut of the group's DJ, Grandmaster Dee. The album spent forty weeks on the R&B chart, peaking at #4.

MAY 15

Run-D.M.C. release their groundbreaking album *Raising Hell* on Profile.

The multi-platinum selling album was chiefly responsible for breaking rap music and hip-hop culture into the mainstream. It spawned the singles "It's Tricky," "My Adidas," "You Be Illin'," and the smash "Walk This Way," a cover of the 1975 Aerosmith classic.

Considered one of the most important rap albums of all time, it was the first rap album to reach #1 on the R&B chart, to chart in the pop top ten, and to go platinum.

JULY 4

Run-D.M.C. release their single "Walk This Way" featuring Aerosmith.

"Walk This Way," originally a 1975 hit for Boston's Aerosmith from their album *Toys in the Attic*, was a remake produced by Def Jam founders Rick Rubin and Russell Simmons.

The drum-break intro for "Walk This Way" had been a hip-hop breakbeat favorite of New York City DJs for years, with Run-D.M.C.'s Jam Master Jay among them.

In interviews, Run said he knew nothing about the legendary Boston group and had initially thought they were called Toys in the Attic, based on their album cover. This single marked the resurrection of Aerosmith, who also claimed at the time to know nothing about rap music. However when they met in the studio, the song came together.

"Walk This Way," with its now classic MTV video, became the first rap song to enter the top five on the pop charts.

CHUCK D:

Run-D.M.C. changed the rap and rock world with this one. The story of Rick Rubin rubbing his Long Beach, Long Island, rock roots into Run-D.M.C./JMJ hip-hop rap is a legend. The video broke across the USA via MTV, but the song set off many alarms familiar to fanatics of both genres. The album *Raising Hell* stunned me while staring at it in a record store. The singles "Peter Piper" and "My Adidas" set rap fans off for accepting anything Run-D.M.C./JMJ would further deliver. The record had also come off two prep years of meshing rap and rock, with D.M.C.'s voice echoed he was the "King of Rock" all throughout 1985 from the album of the same name.

Although I wouldn't say this song brought Aerosmith back into the limelight (because the rock world is deeper than one thinks) but this hybrid made it possible for MTV to set the band in a popular glow. And Steven Tyler and Joe Perry are beasts, artist wise, whereas Run-D.M.C./JMJ got them out of whatever haze they were stuck in.

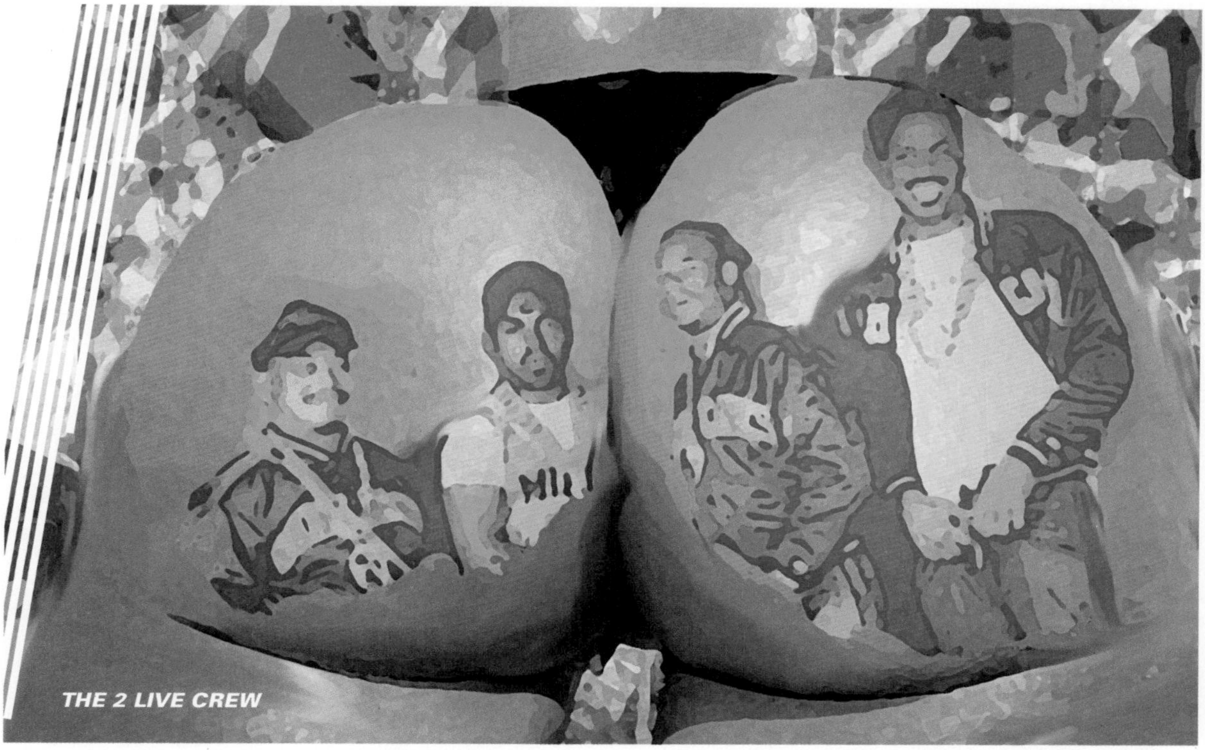

THE 2 LIVE CREW

JULY 7

Doug E. Fresh releases his debut album *Oh, My God!* on Fantasy.

Doug E. Fresh's debut, produced by Dennis Bell and Ollie Cotton, incorporated elements of funk, reggae, and gospel. The album's title was a reference to the lyrics in the Barbadian-American New York rapper's 1985 breakthrough single "The Show."

The album peaked at #21 on the R&B chart in 1986 and would eventually be regarded as one of the most important hip-hop albums of the '80s.

JULY 25

The 2 Live Crew release *The 2 Live Crew Is What We Are* on Luke Skyywalker.

The 2 Live Crew shocked listeners with an unprecedented degree of explicit sexual imagery in songs like "We Want Some Pussy" and "Throw the 'D.'"

The nasty album was a prime example of the Miami sound, a bass-driven, hip-hop subgenre reliant on drum machines that can be traced to Afrika Bambaataa's 1982 song "Planet Rock."

The debut album from the controversial California rap group was eventually certified gold, selling more than half a million records in the two years after its release, and reaching #128 on the *Billboard* 200 and #24 on the R&B chart.

CHUCK D:

When the Beastie Boys emerged from their pop beginnings in 1983, we at WBAU radio with program director Mr. Bill Stephney had already played their punk tracks from as early as 1983, and from there played their Def Jam label releases and singles in 1984, '85. Then came the Def Jam purple label indie days—banging beats. The beginnings of the rap-rock mix. Rubin-Simmons. The result was opening for Run-D.M.C. across the United States in 1985. André "Dr. Dré" Brown was their tour DJ, followed by DJ Hurricane.

We got their month-by-month news first hand. "Hold It Now Hit" is a very significant groundbreaker. Then Def Jam went CBS major. Explosion. LL Cool J's *Radio* helped build a path. Run-D.M.C. touring built another. By 1986, *Raising Hell* was the platform to launch. The album was supposed to come out summer 1986, but with big labels especially back then; acts got pushed back for proper market setup.

A Bruce Springsteen release pushed *License to Ill* into October, which pushed new act Public Enemy's *Yo! Bum Rush the Show* into March 1987. *License to Ill* exploded like no other rap record that fall and winter, and the Beasties were powerful to set up their own tour of the world. Murphy's Law and Fishbone opened from January to April 1987. Public Enemy opened and replaced Fishbone April 1 to 15, 1987. The Beastie Boys ushered in two revolutions at the same time diametrically opposed but fused in the realm of hip-hop and rap music. #Fact

NOVEMBER 15

The Beastie Boys release *Licensed to Ill* on Def Jam.

The Beastie Boys' debut album, with its punk-rock, frat-boy vibe, was the first rap album to top the *Billboard* 200, where it stayed for seven weeks. The album featured seven singles, including smash hits "Brass Monkey" and "(You Gotta) Fight for Your Right (to Party!)."

Licensed to Ill went on to sell more than four million copies in its first year. Currently, the album has sold more than ten million copies, certifying it diamond.

The Brooklyn rap trio's debut served as a major mainstream crossover moment for hip-hop. The Beastie Boys sampled a wide range of artists on the album, including Led Zeppelin, Run-D.M.C., Jazzy Jay, Kurtis Blow, Slick Rick, AC/DC, the Sugarhill Gang, the Clash, and Kool & the Gang.

DECEMBER 8

Salt-N-Pepa release their debut album *Hot, Cool, & Vicious* on Next Plateau.

The group had been previously known as Super Nature when they released their debut single, the underground cult hit "The Showstopper," an answer song to the 1985 classic "The Show" by Doug E. Fresh and the Get Fresh Crew.

Changing their name to Salt-N-Pepa (a lyric from "The Showstopper"), they released their platinum-selling debut album after Deidra Roper replaced Latoya Hanson as the new DJ Spinderella.

The platinum-selling album, produced by Salt's boyfriend at the time, Hurby "Luv Bug" Azor, who also doubled as the group's manager, had moderate success on the R&B charts with the singles "Tramp," "Chick on the Side," and "My Mic Sounds Nice."

However, the album gained its worldwide notoriety with the release of the Grammy-nominated "Push It." Originally a B-side to the album's "Tramp" single, the hit was not featured on the album's original pressing until it was remixed by Cameron Paul, and went ballistic on the charts, going platinum in the process, a first for female rap artists.

1987

KRS-ONE

FEBRUARY 8

Run-D.M.C. release the single "It's Tricky" on Profile.

"It's Tricky," the final single from the Hollis Crew's classic multi-platinum third album, reached #57 on the *Billboard* 100 and #21 on the R&B chart.

Produced by Rick Rubin and Run-D.M.C., the song featured a guitar riff from the Knack's "My Sharona," who later filed a lawsuit for its use that was settled out of court.

The classic hip-hop track's music video featured popular illusionists Penn & Teller as three-card monte street hustlers.

FEBRUARY 10

Public Enemy releases *Yo! Bum Rush the Show* on Def Jam.

Yo! Bum Rush the Show, which ushered in the golden era of socially conscious hip-hop, was produced by the legendary Bomb Squad production team, which consisted of Hank and Keith Shocklee, Eric "Vietnam" Sadler, and Chuck D. The set featured early PE classics like "Public Enemy No.1," "You're Gonna Get Yours," "Miuzi Weighs a Ton," "Sophisticated Bitch," and "Timebomb."

The album was executively produced by Def Jam cofounder Rick Rubin, who was also responsible for convincing Chuck D to pursue a music career at age twenty-six.

Yo! Bum Rush the Show featured turntable work by Terminator X and Johnny "Juice" Rosado and musical contributions by Stephen Linsley and Bill Stephney. The album featured Living Colour guitarist Vernon Reid on the track "Sophisticated Bitch."

The album reached #125 on the *Billboard* 200 and #28 on the R&B chart. The debut album by the now legendary political hip-hop group, with its spare beats and powerful rhetoric, was named album of the year by *NME* magazine in its critics poll.

MARCH 3

Boogie Down Productions release their debut album *Criminal Minded* on B-Boy.

Boogie Down's groundbreaking *Criminal Minded's* lyrics told tales of the violent side of the South Bronx, making this album a precursor to gangsta rap. The album also dealt heavily with the crew's ongoing feud with the Juice Crew from Queens, especially on songs like "The Bridge Is Over" and "South Bronx."

The original BDP crew, KRS-One (Lawrence Krisna Parker) and DJ Scott La Rock (Scott Sterling), was from the South Bronx and crafted their sound to reveal the different musical elements that made up hip-hop: funk, rock, and reggae.

La Rock was shot and killed soon after the album's release, which reached #73 on the R&B chart and is now considered a classic of the genre.

CHUCK D:

When Boogie Down Productions' first album emerged in 1987 it was a seismic shift in the way rap records were heard, along with Eric B. & Rakim's *Paid in Full.* These albums pushed a new style out of what was previously considered a singles genre. They were strongly independent, fearless, and laced with musical references in sample form, topped with dark street realities. The album cover paralleled the look of Public Enemy's *Yo! Bum Rush the Show.* Darkened in a hideaway, ready to emerge with a brand-new game of hip-hop, Blastmaster KRS-One and DJ Scott La Rock singlehandedly predicted the next twenty years of rap, like Nirvana did for rock four years later with *Nevermind.*

MARCH 19

DJ Jazzy Jeff & the Fresh Prince release their debut album *Rock the House* on Jive.

Produced by the Philly duo as well as by Pete Harris, Dana Goodman, and Lawrence Goodman, one of hip-hop's first comedic albums since those of the Fat Boys, *Rock the House* featured the hilarious hit single "Girls Ain't Nothing but Trouble," which sampled the theme song from TV's *I Dream of Jeannie*.

The certified-gold album also featured the turntable wizardry of Jazzy Jeff as evidenced on the cult hit singles "The Magnificent Jazzy Jeff" and "A Touch of Jazz."

Reaching #83 on the *Billboard* charts and #24 on the R&B chart, the lighthearted album is a classic of its kind.

MAY 22

Dana Dane releases his debut solo album *Dana Dane with Fame* on Profile.

The classic debut album by the Brooklyn native, who often rapped with a British accent, featured the hits "This Be the Def Beat," "Delancey Street," "Cinderfella Dana Dane" (later covered by Snoop Dogg), and the smash "Nightmares." The album was produced by Hurby "Luv Bug" Azor, best known for his work with Salt-N-Pepa and Kid 'N Play.

The onetime member of the Kangol Crew duo, along with Slick Rick, took the entertaining *Dana Dane with Fame* all the way to #46 on the *Billboard* 200 and #2 on R&B chart.

MAY 29

LL Cool J releases his sophomore album *Bigger and Deffer* on Def Jam.

Bigger and Deffer featured the legendary hits "I'm Bad," "Go Cut Creator Go," and the "quiet storm" crossover smash "I Need Love," rap's first hit love song. It also featured classic album cuts like "Kanday," "Get Down," "The Do Wop," and "The Bristol Hotel."

The word "BAD" (for *Bigger and Deffer*) scrawled at the bottom of the cover caused many to think that it was the album name.

The album's cover featured LL standing atop a luxury car in front of Andrew Jackson High School in Queens, New York, where LL attended as a teen. The back cover featured LL Cool J wearing boxing gloves and hitting a heavy bag flanked by DJ Cut Creator and his hype man E Love, whose silhouette Chuck D used in designing Public Enemy's logo.

Produced by DJ Pooh and the L.A. Posse, the multi-platinum album is considered by many to be the legendary MC's finest ever, reaching #3 on the *Billboard* 200 and #1 on the R&B chart.

JUNE 13

LL Cool J releases the single "I'm Bad" on Def Jam.

The leadoff single from *Bigger and Deffer*, the song sampled "Theme from *S.W.A.T.*" by Rhythm Heritage, from the 1970s ABC television police drama *S.W.A.T.* The music video for "I'm Bad" was an action crime caper with an antidrug message.

The single hit #84 on the *Billboard* Hot 100 chart and #4 on the R&B chart.

JULY 20

Too $hort releases *Born to Mack* on Dangerous Music.

After years of selling tapes out of the trunk of his car, Todd "Too $hort" Shaw began releasing albums with Oakland's 75 Girls Records and Tapes, including *Born to Mack*.

Filled with booming bass, nasty rhymes, and glorification of the pimp lifestyle, the album eventually grew to be considered one of the most influential Bay Area hip-hop albums of all time.

Born to Mack was rereleased on Jive Records a year later in 1988, after Too $hort signed with the label. The first album to be released nationally from the Oakland rapper reached #50 on the Hip-Hop/R&B chart and was eventually certified gold.

ICE-T

1987

JULY 28

Ice-T releases his debut album *Rhyme Pays* on Sire.

The groundbreaking album, which set the stage for West Coast gangsta rap, featured the classic "6 in the Mornin'" and other songs that painted a violent picture of life on the streets of Los Angeles.

Produced entirely by Zulu Nation member Afrika Islam, *Rhyme Pays* was the first album by a hip-hop artist to be released on the Sire and Warner Bros. labels. Peaking at #93 on the *Billboard* 200 and #26 on the R&B chart, it sold more than 300,000 copies, which was a feat considering it was rarely played on radio due to its explicit lyrics.

AUGUST 8

MC Shan releases *Down by Law* on Warner Bros.

The New York rapper came to prominence with his 1986 single "The Bridge," which resulted in a series of response tracks between KRS-One's Boogie Down Productions and MC Shan's Queensbridge-based Juice Crew, which debated where hip-hop originated.

MC Shan's debut album, produced by his cousin Marley Marl, featured the songs "Left Me Lonely," which reached #71 on the R&B chart, "The Bridge," and another response song, "Kill That Noise."

AUGUST 12

MC Shy D releases *Got to Be Tough* on Luke Skyywalker Records.

The rapper's hard-edged debut album was a landmark for Atlanta rap and became a hit on the independent record charts. Afrika Bambaataa's cousin, MC Shy D was born Peter Jones in the Bronx and is considered to have helped bring the early New York rap tradition to Atlanta.

AUGUST 25

Eric B. & Rakim release *Paid in Full* on Island.

Written hastily and recorded in just a week at Marley Marl's home studio and at Power Play Studios in Manhattan, the Long Island rap duo's debut album went on to sell more than a million records and would become one of the most revered hip-hop albums of the '80s.

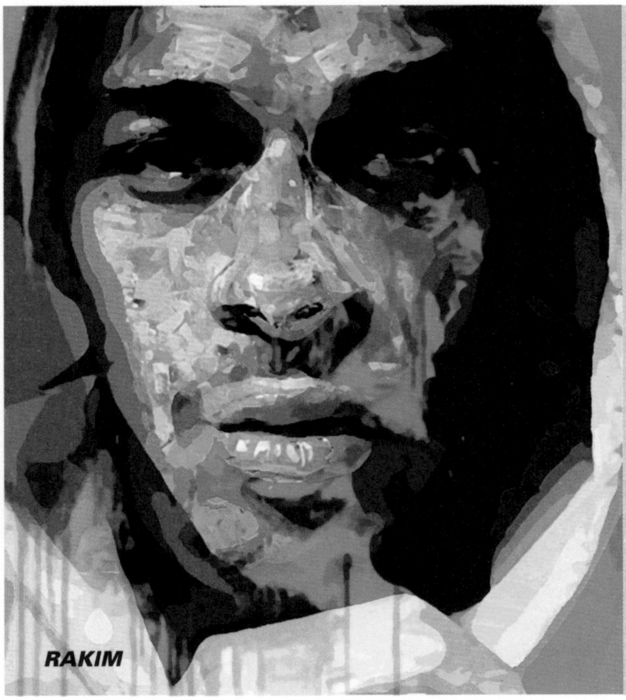

RAKIM

CHUCK D:

Eric B. & Rakim had parallel beginnings with Public Enemy. Golden era indeed. However, 1986 was the freshman year for Eric and Rakim as with KRS Scott and BDP. These two acts singlehandedly changed the Hip-Hop Rap Music game in 1986 via singles. Once Run-D.M.C., post Whodini, smashed the singles-only concept, Eric B. & Rakim had something to fit in between, so to speak. Hard for the streets, smooth for the radio clubs and dance floors.

Paid in Full blasted through the planet. Although initially Eric was known to dislike the remix at the time, the UK version took a style and video that propelled it into a worldwide thing. The world is still waiting for a necessary Eric B. & Rakim performance reunion. Me too. Front seat.

Due in large part to Rakim's laid-back lyricism and free-rhyme style and Eric B.'s flawless production and fondness for soul samples, the album spawned five singles, including the now-classic "I Ain't No Joke," which gave Eric B. & Rakim their highest-charting single to date after it reached the top forty on the R&B chart. The platinum-selling disc reached #58 on the *Billboard* 200 chart.

NOVEMBER 3

Kool Moe Dee releases *How Ya Like Me Now* on Jive.

Kool Moe Dee's longstanding feud with LL Cool J, who he felt was mediocre, began with the title track of this album. The diss is also evident on the album cover, which featured Kool Moe Dee in front of a Jeep that is driving over a replica of LL Cool J's signature red Kangol hat.

The platinum-selling album, which sampled James Brown, Paul Simon, Aretha Franklin, and Cameo, would go on to become the best selling of his career.

How Ya Like Me Now spawned two singles, "How Ya Like Me Now" and "Wild Wild West." The latter, which crossed over to the *Billboard* Hot 100 and reached #4 on the R&B chart, would top the charts again in 1999 when Will Smith covered the song.

1988

JANUARY 27

LL Cool J releases the single "Going Back to Cali" on Def Jam.

The Miami bass–influenced hit single was produced and cowritten by Rick Rubin for the soundtrack of the 20th Century Fox film *Less Than Zero*.

"Going Back to Cali" can also be found on LL's third album *Walking with a Panther*, released on Def Jam in 1989. The gold-selling single reached #31 on the *Billboard* 200 and #12 on the R&B chart.

FEBRUARY 17

DJ Jazzy Jeff & the Fresh Prince release the single "Parents Just Don't Understand" on Jive.

The gold-selling single, which was produced by Jazzy Jeff, was from the duo's multi-platinum selling sophomore album *He's the DJ, I'm the Rapper*.

"Parents Just Don't Understand" is often credited with introducing rap music to the younger set, as the song's playful lyrics and lighthearted music video offered a different perspective of hip-hop culture. It won a Grammy for best rap performance and reached #12 on the *Billboard* Hot 100 and #10 on the R&B chart.

FEBRUARY 17

The Geto Boys release their debut album *Making Trouble* on Rap-A-Lot.

Originally spelled "Ghetto Boys," the founding members of the Houston-based group consisted of Bushwick Bill, DJ Ready Red, Sire Jukebox, and Prince Johnny C.

After the release of *Making Trouble*, the label dropped Sire Jukebox and Prince Johnny C from the group and added Scarface and Willie D who along with Bushwick Bill and DJ Ready Red would become the new Geto Boys, with Ready Red eventually leaving the group.

The track "Assassins" was covered by the Insane Clown Posse ten years later on their album *The Amazing Jeckel Brothers*.

FEBRUARY 23

Biz Markie releases his debut album *Goin' Off* on Cold Chillin'.

Praised for its humor, *Goin' Off* was produced by Marley Marl and cowritten by Big Daddy Kane, who along with Biz was a part of Marl's Juice Crew.

Biz scored on *Goin' Off* with the classic hits, "Vapors," "This Is Something for the Radio," "Nobody Beats the Biz," "Pickin' Boogers," "Biz Is Goin' Off," and "Make the Music with Your Mouth Biz." The album reached #90 on the *Billboard* 200 and #19 on the R&B chart.

MARCH 29

Philly's DJ Jazzy Jeff & the Fresh Prince release their sophomore album *He's the DJ, I'm the Rapper* on Jive.

The triple-platinum album's mostly G-rated language and themes made it one of the first rap albums to cross over to younger audiences and bring the playful and comedic side of hip-hop to the mainstream.

The first rap double album, it contained the smash hit "Parents Just Don't Understand," which won the first-ever Grammy Award for best rap performance, and reached #4 on the *Billboard* 200 and #5 on the R&B chart. This was the first year the Grammys had a rap category but did not televise the award, so Jazzy Jeff & the Fresh Prince, along with a slew of other performers, boycotted the show in protest. The next year the rap category was televised.

APRIL 12

Boogie Down Productions release their sophomore album *By All Means Necessary* on Jive.

BDP's first set for Jive was also their first after the tragic murder of group cofounder Scott La Rock the previous year. The album, which takes its title from a famed Malcolm X speech, shows KRS-One looking out of a window while holding an Uzi. This image is similar to a 1965 photo of Malcolm X.

Along with Public Enemy's *It Takes a Nation of Millions to Hold Us Back*, released the same year, the KRS-One–produced album ushered in the golden era of political rap.

CHUCK D:

I first met Jazzy Jeff & the Fresh Prince in 1987 at a WNYU radio show in New York City with legendary hip-hop broadcaster P Fine and Livio G. Jeff had created the transformer style and already copped a New Music Seminar DJ title. Dude held his head high in utmost confidence. His rhyme partner, from my favorite city of Philadelphia, simply could rhyme all damn day long like a raptronome. Together these cats were flawless with routines fun as well as lethal. We toured in 1987 together on the Def Jam tour with LL Cool J, Doug E. Fresh and the Get Fresh Crew, Whodini, Stetsasonic, and Eric B. & Rakim. We were rookies together and enjoyed each other's competition and camaraderie.

We all had no problem celebrating Jeff, Will, and the crew's Grammy Award the following year. We were family, as we rolled together on the Run's House Tour in 1988 with Run-D.M.C./JMJ, EPMD, J. J. Fad, and our Philly people. We ran throughout the USA and gained respect and momentum playing alongside the Dope Jam Tour that summer, the first time two rap tours trekked in tandem. Jazzy Jeff & the Fresh Prince were 100 percent of who they were. That honesty galvanized us all and paved roads ahead for many.

A 180-degree turn from the group's hardcore debut *Criminal Minded*, the socially conscious gold-selling album spawned the hit singles "Stop the Violence" and "My Philosophy." *By All Means Necessary* contained classic album cuts like "Illegal Business," "Ya Slippin'," and "I'm Still #1," which referenced KRS's battle with Melle Mel the previous year at the Latin Quarter. The album reached #75 on the *Billboard* 200 and #18 on the R&B chart.

MAY 17

Run-D.M.C. release their fourth album *Tougher Than Leather* on Profile.

The platinum-selling album, a follow-up to the group's big commercial breakthrough album 1986's *Raising Hell*, featured some of the group's classics like "Run's House," "Beats to the Rhyme," and a cover of the Monkees' "Mary, Mary." It reached #9 on the *Billboard* 200 and #2 on the R&B chart.

The album was an accompaniment of sorts to the New Line Cinema crime film of the same name directed by Rick Rubin and starring Run-D.M.C.

JUNE 21

EPMD release their debut *Strictly Business* on Fresh/Sleeping Bag.

The gold-selling debut album from the Long Island rap duo of Erick Sermon and Parrish Smith topped the R&B chart and reached #80 on the *Billboard* 200. Filled with '70s funk grooves and cool, laid-back flow, the album sampled a variety of artists including Eric Clapton, Rick James, Joe Tex, Aretha Franklin, Kool & the Gang, Otis Redding, the Steve Miller Band, and the Beastie Boys.

The album spawned three singles, "Strictly Business," "You Gots to Chill," and "I'm Housin'," which all charted.

JUNE 28

Big Daddy Kane releases his debut album *Long Live the Kane* on Cold Chillin'.

Cold Chillin' Records was launched by the album's producer Marley Marl, who also headed up the Juice Crew collective, which Kane was a part of, along with Roxanne Shanté, Biz Markie, Mr. Magic, Kool G Rap & DJ Polo, Glamorous, MC Shan, Grand Daddy I.U., Masta Ace, Craig G, and Intelligent Hoodlum.

The classic gold-selling *Long Live the Kane* established Marley Marl as one of hip-hop's premier producers and the charismatic Kane, with his often breakneck pace delivery fueled by witty rhymes and Five-Percent references, as one of the finest MCs of the day.

Long Live the Kane contained the hit singles "I'll Take You There," "Set It Off," "Ain't No Half-Steppin'," and "Raw," as well as album classics like "Word to the Mother (Land)," "Mister Cee's Master Plan," featuring Mister Cee, and "Just Rhymin' with Biz" featuring Biz Markie. The album spent thirty-eight weeks on the R&B chart, peaking at #5.

CHUCK D:

The most skilled MC ever. Have all the tools: versatility, strength, wordplay, voice, and movement on stage. I met Kane at a DJ Chuck Chill Out party in the Bronx, as fellow Cold Chillin' artist Roxanne Shanté's DJ. Kane said he was about to emerge with some groundbreaking work. Sure enough, "Just Rhymin' with Biz" was that blowout debut. Kane was a leader in his demeanor and often he would remind me in a conversation that he wasn't as old as I was. I often forgot Kane was ten years younger than me because he seemed a throwback to the Blaxploitation film era rather than golden age hip-hop. From knocking BPMs down while speed rhyming, to jamming to the ladies—like when I saw this emotional girl in Gary, Indiana, at a record store signing scream and cry after getting his autograph, then need medical help.

However, this album is best captured onstage in a live Apollo Theater performance recording in 1989 (that I play often on my RAPstation.com ... *And You Don't Stop!* radio show). Keith Shocklee and I recently inducted Big Daddy Kane into the LI Music Hall of Fame. Only the beginning.

JUNE 28

Public Enemy release their sophomore album *It Takes a Nation of Millions to Hold Us Back* on Def Jam.

Considered by many to be the greatest hip-hop album of all time, the multi-platinum *It Takes a Nation of Millions to Hold Us Back* ushered in the golden era of hip-hop and the birth of politically and socially conscious rap music.

Produced by Chuck D, Rick Rubin, and Hank Shocklee, the album contained a potpourri of musical samples that created a melting pot of new hip-hop musical styles. It also featured speech clips by Minister Malcolm X, Dr. Khalid Muhammad, Minister Ava Muhammad, and the Honorable Minister Louis Farrakhan, showing the influence of the Nation of Islam on the album. It also broke from traditional hip-hop by escalating the tempos at times to 108 beats per minute.

The album produced five classic anthem singles, "Rebel Without a Pause," "Don't Believe the Hype," "Black Steel in the Hour of Chaos," "Night of the Living Baseheads," and "Bring the Noise," which was featured in the 1987 film *Less Than Zero*.

It Takes a Nation of Millions to Hold Us Back also contained bona fide fan favorites like, "She Watch Channel Zero?!," "Terminator X to the Edge of Panic," "Party for Your Right to Fight," "Prophets of Rage," and "Cold Lampin' with Flavor," as well as the instrumental "Security of the First World," sampled by Madonna on her 1990 smash hit "Justify My Love."

Songs from *It Takes a Nation of Millions to Hold Us Back* have been covered by Tricky, Rage Against the Machine, Staind, featuring Fred Durst, Sepultura, and Delaney's Rhythm Section. The iconic album reached #42 on the *Billboard* 200, staying on the chart for fifty-one weeks, and topped the R&B chart.

JULY 10

N.W.A release *Straight Outta Compton* on Ruthless.

At the time of their studio debut, N.W.A was comprised of Dr. Dre, Eazy-E, MC Ren, Ice Cube, DJ Yella, and Arabian Prince—the latter would soon leave the group.

The album was executive produced by Eazy-E, and coproduced by Dr. Dre and DJ Yella. The album samples a wide range of artists, including Funkadelic, James Brown, the Honeydrippers, Public Enemy, Marvin Gaye, Big Daddy Kane, and the Ohio Players.

Challenging racist attitudes, the album spawned three singles, "Straight Outta Compton," "Gangsta Gangsta," and "Express Yourself," which reached the top twenty of the Rap chart. "Straight Outta Compton" also hit the *Billboard* Hot 100 in 2015, after the release of the biopic of the same name, a first for N.W.A.

The classic protest song "Fuck tha Police" contributed greatly to N.W.A earning a reputation in the late '80s as "the world's most dangerous group."

Straight Outta Compton was key in establishing West Coast gangsta rap, and is consistently considered one of the single greatest hip-hop albums of all time. Hitting #37 on the *Billboard* 200 with little airplay, it has sold more than three million records and has been certified triple platinum.

PUBLIC ENEMY

N.W.A

JULY 26

Eric B. & Rakim release their sophomore album *Follow the Leader* on Uni.

The gold-selling *Follow the Leader*, produced by Eric B. & Rakim and Stevie Blass Griffin (Rakim's brother), spawned hits including the lyrically fierce "Microphone Fiend," "The R," and the James Bond–sounding title track. The certified-gold album also contained classic cuts like "Musical Massacre" and "Lyrics of Fury."

Follow the Leader was the legendary duo's first album for Uni (a subsidiary of MCA) after leaving 4th & B'way Records, which had released their game-changing debut album, *Paid in Full*. The album reached #22 on the *Billboard* 200 and #9 on the R&B charts.

AUGUST 2

Rob Base and DJ E-Z Rock release their debut album *It Takes Two* on Profile.

The platinum-selling album's title track—one of the most famous singles in hip-hop history—borrowed heavily from the James Brown–produced Lyn Collins single "Think (About It)."

The album also featured the smash hit "Joy and Pain," which sampled the classic Frankie Beverly & Maze song of the same name and jump-started the

CHUCK D:

A fact. *Yo! MTV Raps* was first a UK show hosted by a woman named Sophie. We were the hot item in what became our base in the world—London and the UK. Word spread to the United States that a rap show would be big. Filmmaker Jonathan Demme's nephew Ted Demme gave me a call one day asking me about my WBAU schoolmate/crew alliance André "Doctor Dré" Brown. Doctor Dré was still at the station, but had already ushered in the beginnings of Def Jam with Original Concept and a Beastie Boys tour DJ.

For the pilot, I clearly remember playing on the Run's House Tour show in Austin, Texas, where they flew in to shoot it. It was an immediate success. The choice of Fab Five Freddy of Change the Beat Celluloid Records fame fit perfectly as legit. When they went daily, I knew it would work because the thirst was across the United States and world by 1988. It made record companies look at their rap artists as album makers and justified video budgets.

Now many fans could finally see their formerly only heard favorites—just like American Bandstand and Soul Train had previously done.

hip-house genre with "Get on the Dance Floor," which sampled "Shake Your Body (Down to the Ground)" by the Jacksons. The album spent fifty-eight weeks on the R&B chart, peaking at #4.

AUGUST 6

Yo! MTV Raps makes its debut on MTV.

Run-D.M.C. hosted the pilot episode, with guests DJ Jazzy Jeff & the Fresh Prince. The first music video shown was "Follow the Leader" by Eric B. & Rakim. The pilot was one of the highest rated programs in MTV history, after Live Aid and the MTV Video Music Awards.

The weekday edition of the rap music video show was originally hosted by Fab Five Freddy, who eventually took over weekend duties, while Doctor Dré and Ed Lover took over the weekday show.

Yo! MTV Raps took its name from Public Enemy's 1987 debut album *Yo! Bum Rush the Show* and the logo was created by early graffiti writer Dr. Revolt.

Guests on *Yo! MTV Raps*, over the years, included Tupac Shakur, N.W.A, Public Enemy, Boogie Down Productions, MC Hammer, Leaders of the New School, featuring a young Busta Rhymes, Ice Cube, and the Wu-Tang Clan.

Yo! MTV Raps aired its last episode on August 17, 1995, with an all-star freestyle that included KRS-One, Rakim, Chubb Rock, Erick Sermon, MC Serch of 3rd Bass, Craig Mack, Method Man, Redman, Large Professor, and Special Ed.

SEPTEMBER 1

Sir Mix-A-Lot releases his debut album *Swass* on his label Nastymix.

Self-produced by the Seattle MC and released on his own label, the humorous platinum-selling album featured the hit singles "Posse on Broadway," which sampled David Bowie's "Fame"; "Gold"; "Rippin" featuring Kid Sensation; and a hip-hop remake of the Black Sabbath metal classic "Iron Man," featuring Metal Church. The title track's hook would later be used for the 2005 Pussycat Dolls chart topper "Don't Cha" (featuring Busta Rhymes).

The album spent fifty-eight weeks on the *Billboard* 200, peaking at #82 and #20 on the R&B chart.

SEPTEMBER 13

MC Lyte releases her debut album *Lyte as a Rock* on First Priority.

Produced by Alliance, King of Chill, Prince Paul, and Audio Two (Lyte's older brothers Milk Dee and Gizmo), the thoughtful album featured such Lyte classics like "Paper Thin," "10% Dis," and "I Cram to Understand U (Sam)." Revered as a classic, Lyte's outspoken debut reached #50 on the R&B chart.

SEPTEMBER 13

Ice-T releases his sophomore album *Power* on Sire.

Produced with Afrika Islam, the platinum album took a hard look at criminal life with the classic hits "High Rollers" and the unforgettable "I'm Your Pusher," which interpolates Curtis Mayfield's "Pusherman" from *Super Fly*, which also influenced the cover design. Guests on *Power* included Donald D, Hen Gee, and Pimpin' Rex.

Reaching #35 on the *Billboard* 200 and #6 on the R&B chart, it was the first rap record to be stickered with a parental advisory warning label.

OCTOBER 4

Ultramagnetic MC's release *Critical Beatdown* on Next Plateau.

The Bronx rap crew of Ced-Gee, TR Love, and Moe Love founded by Kool Keith released their debut album after releasing singles for years.

Primarily produced by Ced-Gee, the album featured an adventurous blend of electronic music, minimalist production, and extensive funk sampling.

Although a modest success at its release, hitting #57 on the R&B chart, *Critical Beatdown* is considered an influential and universally lauded example of New York rap from hip-hop's late '80s golden era.

SLICK RICK

NOVEMBER 1

Slick Rick releases his debut solo album *The Great Adventures of Slick Rick* on Def Jam.

After releasing a couple classic tracks with Doug E. Fresh and the Get Fresh Crew like "The Show" and "La Di Da Di" in 1985, Rick finally released his own debut solo album three years later and it was an instant classic.

His fluid storytelling spawned three hits: "Teenage Love," "Hey Young World," and "Children's Story." The beat of the latter fueled Montell Jordan's classic mid-1990s R&B smash "This Is How We Do It." The album also featured such cult classic album cuts like "Treat Her Like a Prostitute," "Indian Girl (An Adult Story)," "Mona Lisa," and "The Ruler's Back."

Produced by Rick, the Bomb Squad, and Jam Master Jay, the platinum album reached #31 on the *Billboard* 200 and #1 on the R&B chart.

1989

JANUARY 15

Led by KRS-One, the Stop the Violence Movement releases the single "Self-Destruction" on Jive.

"Self-Destruction" was released as a charity single to benefit the National Urban League, a New York–based civil rights organization that fights racial discrimination.

The benefit single was recorded after several shootings in New York's hip-hop community, including Scott La Rock, who was one of the original members of KRS-One's Bronx-based Boogie Down Productions. It featured Kool Moe Dee, MC Lyte, Chuck D and Flavor Flav of Public Enemy, and Doug E. Fresh. Reaching #76 on the R&B charts, it raised awareness and more than $600,000 for the organization.

KRS-One would revisit the song several times in later years, enlisting rappers like Method Man, Talib Kweli, The Game, and 50 Cent to rerecord the song in 2008.

FEBRUARY 7

The 2 Live Crew release their controversial third album *As Nasty as They Wanna Be* on Skyywalker.

The sexually explicit double-platinum album, produced by the band, became the first ever deemed obscene by the United States district court for the southern district of Florida. This ruling would later be overturned by the United States Court of Appeals for the 11th Circuit.

In 1990, three members of the 2 Live Crew were arrested for performing material from the controversial album at an adult club in Broward County, Florida. They were eventually acquitted after a much publicized obscenity trial in which famed scholar and historian Henry Louis Gates Jr. testified on behalf of the defendants.

Album sales flourished with the attention, spending eighty-one weeks on the *Billboard* 200 charts, peaking at #29, and hitting #3 on the R&B chart. An edited version of the album was later released, called *As Clean as They Wanna Be.*

FEBRUARY 18

Tone Lōc releases the single "Wild Thing" on Delicious Vinyl.

Employing a hook from Van Halen's "Jamie's Cryin'" with lyrics mostly written by Young MC, this dance-club anthem off Los Angeles native Tone Lōc's album *Lōc-ed After Dark* was a worldwide hit.

Produced by Matt Dike, the song peaked at #2 on the *Billboard* Hot 100, #2 on the Rap chart, and #3 on the R&B chart, selling more than two million copies in the process. The album was the first by a black rap artist to reach #1 on the *Billboard* 200, fueled by the additional hits "Funky Cold Medina" and "I Got It Goin' On."

MARCH 3

De La Soul release their debut album *3 Feet High and Rising* on Tommy Boy.

Along with producer Prince Paul, the Long Island trio, made up of Trugoy the Dove, Posdnuos, and Maseo, crafted a revolutionary sonic landscape of sampled songs, sounds, and snippets unheard of before in the hip-hop genre.

At that point, most hip-hop producers usually sampled artists like James Brown or P-Funk. De La Soul and producer Paul borrowed from recordings by an unlikely host of artists usually not affiliated with hip-hop sampling, such as Johnny Cash, Hall & Oates, Otis Redding, the Turtles, and a French language instructional record. The album also introduced the "skit" concept, which is now almost too prevalent on rap albums. The groovy 1960s and 1970s attitude, coupled with the group's concept of "The D.A.I.S.Y. Age," an acronym for "Da Inner Sound Y'all," caused people to inaccurately refer to the group as "hippies."

3 Feet High and Rising spawned hits and rap classics like the chart-topping "Me Myself and I," "Potholes in My Lawn," "Plug Tunin'," "Buddy," "Say No Go," "The Magic Number," and "Eye Know." The song "Transmitting Live from Mars" led to a lawsuit with 1960s psychedelic group the Turtles over an uncleared sample. The inventive album featured guest appearances by members of their musical collective the Native Tongues, including Q-Tip of A Tribe Called Quest and the Jungle Brothers.

1989

The album's diverse subject matter tackled things like poverty, individualism, drug abuse, love, materialism, commercialism and hip-hop clichés, as spoken about on the track "Take It Off." Featured on many "best albums of all time" lists, *3 Feet High and Rising* reached #1 on the R&B chart and #24 on the *Billboard* 200.

MARCH 14

Kool G Rap and DJ Polo release their debut album *Road to the Riches* on Cold Chillin'.

Produced by Marley Marl, the album showcases G Rap's lyrical acumen on underground hits such as "Poison" and "It's a Demo." Other titles on this hip-hop masterpiece include "Men at Work," "Cars," "Rhymes I Express," "Trilogy of Terror," and the title track, which popularized mafioso rap.

Peaking at #78 on the R&B chart, the album's crime-related themes had a major influence on Nas, Raekwon of the Wu-Tang Clan, 50 Cent, and Jay Z, to name a few.

MARCH 27

N.W.A release the classic single "Express Yourself" on Ruthless.

"Express Yourself," from the legendary group's 1988 classic multi-platinum album *Straight Outta Compton* was produced by Dr. Dre and DJ Yella.

"Express Yourself" is notable as a free speech manifesto devoid of profanity, a rarity for the controversial group. It reached #2 on the Rap chart and #45 on the R&B.

MARCH 27

De La Soul release the hit single "Me Myself and I" on Tommy Boy.

"Me Myself and I," from De La's groundbreaking album *3 Feet High and Rising*, made it to #1 on the R&B and Rap charts.

De La Soul produced the track along with Prince Paul, which featured a unique array of samples not ordinarily used at the time by artists such as the Ohio Players and Edwin Birdsong.

CHUCK D:

Prince Paul has long been a genius. Also from Strong Island—Amityville, the same town famous for the haunted house movie. The black neighborhood was the second black population of Long Island towns east of the area where we evolved. That area always had great DJs; Paul was from the next generation. He was one of the DJs with the legendary group Stetsasonic. We traveled together on the '87 Def Jam Tour sharing a bus. In 1988, PE's *Nation* record and *In Full Gear* by Stet emerged. *3 Feet High and Rising* culminated from the seeds of that bus. The combination of Paul and his hungry protégés, Pos, Trugoy, and Maseo, set a platform that lifted them into hip-hop orbit forever. And they ain't never came down.

APRIL 4

Slick Rick releases "Children's Story" on Def Jam.

"Children's Story" told the story of a young man's trouble with the law that resulted in getting shot by the police, and was a breakthrough moment in hip-hop storytelling. The second single from Slick Rick's 1988 debut album became a top five hit on both the R&B and Rap charts.

"Children's Story" has been covered by Eminem, Talib Kweli, and Mos Def, Everlast, and Tricky, among others. Slick Rick's single has also become one of the most sampled hip-hop songs of all time. A variety of artists have sampled the song, including the Black Eyed Peas, Lupe Fiasco, Missy Elliott, and Will Smith.

MAY 2

The Jaz (aka Jaz-O) releases his debut album *Word to the Jaz* on EMI.

Recorded in London, *Word to the Jaz* featured production by Pete Q. Harris, Bryan "Chuck" New, as well as the Jaz.

The Brooklyn MC's debut is most notable for featuring a young Jay-Zee (how he spelled it at the time) on a few tracks on the album, including the hit single "Hawaiian Sophie."

MAY 12

Kool Moe Dee releases his third solo album *Knowledge Is King* on Jive.

The legendary New York MC and former Treacherous Three member produced the gold-selling *Knowledge Is King*. It contained the hit single "I Go to Work," which reached #13 on the R&B chart. The action-packed accompanying music video had Moe Dee playing a James Bond–like character.

To support the album, Moe Dee became the first rapper ever to perform at the Grammy Awards. The album reached #25 on the *Billboard* 200 and #2 on the R&B chart.

MAY 16

Special Ed releases his debut album *Youngest in Charge* on Profile.

Howie Tee produced the tremendous debut by the sixteen-year-old Brooklyn MC, which reached #8 on the R&B chart.

The gold-selling *Youngest in Charge* contained the boast-filled hits "Think About It," "I'm the Magnificent," and the masterpiece "I Got It Made."

MAY 16

Nice & Smooth release their self-titled debut on Fresh/Sleeping Bag.

The New York hip-hop duo of Greg Nice and Smooth B released their debut album after appearing on Big Daddy Kane's "Pimpin' Ain't Easy." Their album spawned several singles, including "Early to Rise" and "Funky for You" and sampled Prince, Joe Cocker, Barry White, and Parliament.

Nice & Smooth spent thirty-four weeks on the R&B chart, peaking at #75.

MAY 19

The Flavor Unit's Chill Rob G releases his debut solo album *Ride the Rhythm* on Wild Pitch.

Produced by Mark "the 45 King" James, Prince Paul of Stetsasonic, Pasemaster Mase of De La Soul, and Nephie Centeno, it contained the hits, "Court Is Now in Session," "Let Me Show You," "The Power" (featuring Kim Davis), and "Let the Words Flow."

The a cappella version of "Let the Words Flow," specifically Chill's line "it's getting kinda hectic" were illegally sampled by German dance producers Snap! on their platinum-selling international chart-topper "The Power." After Chill's label Wild Pitch took legal action, a settlement was reached where Snap! allowed Wild Pitch to use the rhythm track of "The Power" for a new Chill Rob G version of the song called "The Power Jam, Featuring Chill Rob G."

MAY 22

Young MC releases the hit single "Bust a Move," on Delicious Vinyl.

The dance floor anthem was the lead single from Young MC's debut album *Stone Cold Rhymin'*, which would be released four months later.

One of the early hits produced by the Dust Brothers, "Bust a Move" was the British-born MC's biggest hit and featured vocals by Crystal Blake and bass playing by Flea of the Red Hot Chili Peppers.

The single spent thirty-nine weeks on the *Billboard* Hot 100, peaking at #7, hit #2 on the Rap chart, and won a Grammy for best rap performance.

JUNE 5

King Sun releases his debut album *XL* on Profile.

One of the earliest socially conscious rappers, King Sun was one of the first MCs to incorporate the beliefs of the Five-Percent Nation of God and Earth in his music.

Taking its title from the MC's imposing six-foot-seven frame, *XL* was produced by Cut Master DC, Anthony Moody, the Hollywood Impact, Mark the 45 King, and King Sun himself. This golden age classic contains the singles "Hey Love," "It's a Heat Up," "Mythological Rapper," and "On the Club Tip."

JUNE 6

Gang Starr release their debut album *No More Mr. Nice Guy* on Wild Pitch.

The album was produced by Gang Starr's DJ Premier and Guru, as well as Mark the 45 King, and reached #83 on the R&B chart. It contained the classic singles "Manifest" and "Positivity," which peaked at #19 on the Rap chart.

JUNE 9

LL Cool J releases his third album *Walking with a Panther* on Def Jam.

The eighteen-track, chart-topping *Walking with a Panther* was produced by LL with the Bomb Squad, Rick Rubin, DJ Cut Creator, and Dwayne Simon, a former member of the L.A. Posse production team, which, due to contractual disputes, did not work on this album.

Walking with a Panther produced several huge hits such as "I'm That Type of Guy," "Big Ole Butt," "One Shot at Love," and the classic "Going Back to Cali," which was also featured in the film *Less Than Zero*.

Despite platinum sales and reaching #6 on the *Billboard* 200 and #1 on the R&B chart, *Walking with a Panther* received criticism from rap fans and music critics alike for its "love ballads" and the fact that hip-hop was moving into a more political and socially conscious phase.

JUNE 13

Heavy D & the Boyz release their sophomore album *Big Tyme* on Uptown.

Big Tyme, which topped the *Billboard*'s Rap and R&B charts, featured production by DJ Eddie F, Teddy Riley, Marley Marl, and Heavy's cousin, the legendary Pete Rock.

One of the pioneering albums of hip-hop–reggae fusion, the platinum-selling *Big Tyme* featured the smash hits "We Got Our Own Thang," "Somebody for Me," and "Gyrlz, They Love Me."

HEAVY D

JUNE 19

Breeze releases his debut album *T.Y.S.O.N.* on Atlantic.

Breeze was a protégé of production team the L.A. Posse, best known for handling production on LL Cool J's first two albums. The title *T.Y.S.O.N.* was an acronym for "The Young Son of No One."

With a vocal style influenced by Big Daddy Kane, Breeze featured different musical influences on his album from both the New York and Cali style of hip-hop, as well as DC's go-go sound. *T.Y.S.O.N.* contained the singles "Great Big Freak" and "L.A. Posse," an ode to his production team.

JULY 4

Boogie Down Productions release their third album *Ghetto Music: The Blueprint of Hip-Hop* on Jive.

The certified gold album included BDP classic hit singles like, "You Must Learn," "Why Is That?," and "Jack of Spades," which KRS-One performed in the 1988 United Artists comedy *I'm Gonna Git You Sucka.*

Produced by D-Nice, Sidney Mills, D-Square, Spaceman, Rebekah Foster, and BDP leader KRS-One, the socially conscious album reached #36 on the *Billboard* 200 and #7 on the R&B chart.

JULY 10

Tuff Crew release their sophomore album *Back to Wreck Shop* on Warlock.

The five-man Philly crew of Tone Love, Monty G, L.A. Kid, Ice Dog, and DJ Too Tuff produced this classic, which contained the hit single "My Part of Town." The album reached #23 on the R&B chart and the title track reached #73 on the R&B Singles chart.

JULY 21

Spike Lee's film *Do the Right Thing* opens in the United States.

Spike Lee's acclaimed film about racial tensions in Brooklyn's Bed-Stuy neighborhood served as the film debuts for actors Martin Lawrence and Rosie Perez. *Do the Right Thing* was nominated for two Academy Awards.

The movie's eclectic hip-hop infused soundtrack was most notable for its inclusion of Public Enemy's "Fight the Power," which was commissioned for the film and first released on the soundtrack, before becoming a cornerstone on the group's 1990 classic album *Fear of a Black Planet*. The soundtrack reached #11 on the R&B chart and #68 on the *Billboard* 200.

JULY 25

The Beastie Boys release their sophomore album *Paul's Boutique* on Capitol.

The multi-platinum *Paul's Boutique*, produced by the Dust Brothers, Mario Caldato Jr., and the Beasties, contained the hit singles "Shadrach" and "Hey Ladies," which landed on the rock, Rap, and Dance charts.

The album's dense sample layering (it contained more than a hundred samples) by the Dust Brothers and its unique arrangement made it groundbreaking and innovative. Initially commercially unsuccessful compared to *Licensed to Ill*, it eventually reached #14 on the *Billboard* 200, and its critical standing has grown over the years, making many "best of" lists.

CHUCK D:

In 1988 in Soho, Spike Lee sat down with Bill Stephney, Hank Shocklee, and me to request an anthem for his 1989 movie based on the pressure-cooker racial tension in New York at the time. The first time myself and Hank Shocklee saw a prescreening in Brooklyn, I was appalled by how many times I saw it used in the film. The film had woven Public Enemy "Fight the Power" throughout it. I kept sinking in my seat because Spike Lee had to use a very unfinished version that sounded nothing like it would finally end up sounding. When the movie came out in the summer of 1989, it had two videos, which people often forget. The anthem, while created for the film, has resonated exponentially throughout society.

JULY 26

3rd Bass release their debut single "Steppin' to the A.M." on Def Jam.

"Steppin' to the A.M.," from the trio's gold-selling debut set *The Cactus Al/bum*, released the same year, was produced by the Public Enemy production team the Bomb Squad. It reached #5 on the Rap chart.

EPMD

AUGUST 1

EPMD release their classic sophomore album *Unfinished Business* on Fresh/Sleeping Bag Records.

Produced by the band, the gold-selling album topped the R&B chart and contained the hit single "So What Cha Sayin'" and cult favorites "Please Listen to My Demo," "The Big Payback," "Strictly Snappin' Necks," "Jane II," and "It Wasn't Me, It Was the Fame." Frank B guested on the classic "You Had Too Much to Drink" and K-Solo appeared on the fan favorite cut "Knick Knack Patty Wack."

AUGUST 1

The D.O.C. release their debut album *No One Can Do It Better* on Atlantic.

The D.O.C., who worked closely with N.W.A and cowrote several of the group's songs, enlisted longtime collaborators Dr. Dre and Eazy-E to produce and executive produce the album, respectively.

The funky and thoughtful debut album from the Dallas native topped the R&B/Hip-Hop chart for two weeks, and reached #20 on the *Billboard* 200.

The album spawned four singles: "The D.O.C. & the Doctor," "It's Funky Enough," "The Formula," and "Mind Blowin'" and featured guest appearances by N.W.A, MC Ren, and Michel'le.

Months after the release of the album, a car accident severely injured his throat, which put the D.O.C.'s rap career on hold.

AUGUST 8

Cool C releases his debut album *I Gotta Habit* on Atlantic.

The Philly MC's first set, produced by Steady B and Lawrence Goodman, reached #51 on the R&B chart. The influential album produced the hit single "Glamorous Life," which reached #11 on the Rap chart.

SEPTEMBER 1

Wreckx-N-Effect release their self-titled full-length debut album on Motown.

Originally a four-man group from Harlem when they released their self-titled EP the previous year, Wreckx-N-Effect now consisted of Aqil "A-Plus" Davidson, Brandon Mitchell, and Markell Riley, brother of famed producer Teddy Riley.

Hit singles from the album included "Juicy" and the Rap chart–topping "New Jack Swing," the musical style founded by Teddy Riley that combined New York style hip-hop, funk, R&B, and DC's go-go sound.

Guests on the album included Scoop Rock, Teddy Riley, and David Guppy, known as the Redhead Kingpin, who also produced the album with Markell Riley. The album reached #16 on the R&B chart.

Tragedy would hit the group less than a year after the release of their hit album when Wreckx-N-Effect member Brandon Mitchell was shot to death.

SEPTEMBER 5

Young MC releases his debut album *Stone Cold Rhymin'* on Delicious Vinyl.

Production on the London-born rapper's debut set was handled by the Dust Brothers, Matt Dike, and Michael Ross. *Stone Cold Rhymin'* contained the hit singles "I Come Off," featuring N'Dea Davenport of the Brand New Heavies, "Pick Up the Pace," "I Let 'Em Know," "Know How," "The Principal's Office," and the Grammy Award–winning smash "Bust a Move."

The catchy album spent forty-eight weeks on the *Billboard* 200, peaking at #9 and #8 on the R&B chart.

OCTOBER 3

MC Lyte releases her sophomore album *Eyes on This* on Atlantic.

Produced by the King of Chill, Grand Puba, Marley Marl, PMD, Nat Robinson, and Lyte's brothers known as Audio Two, the raw and honest *Eyes on This* contained the chart-topping hit single "Cha Cha Cha," "Stop, Look, Listen," and the antiviolence classic "Cappucino."

Peaking at #86 on the *Billboard* 200 and #6 on the R&B chart, *Eyes on This* helped to establish Lyte as one of the top female MCs of the day.

OCTOBER 10

Biz Markie releases his sophomore album *The Biz Never Sleeps* on Cold Chillin'.

The gold-selling album, produced by Cool V, Paul C, and Biz Markie, contains Markie's biggest hit ever, the giddy classic "Just a Friend," which reached #9 on the *Billboard* Hot 100 and #5 on the Rap chart. Beloved by many, Velvet Underground's Lou Reed called it one of his favorite albums of the year.

OCTOBER 10

Ice-T releases his third album *The Iceberg/ Freedom of Speech...Just Watch What You Say* on Sire.

Produced by Afrika Islam and Ice-T, the gritty album was released after Ice-T encountered censorship issues on tour. The first part of the album's title was a reference to Iceberg Slim (aka Robert Beck), a hustler turned author and poet who Ice-T admired. The latter part referred to an incident that happened to Ice while on tour in Columbus, Georgia, where he was told what profanities he could say on stage as well as what subject matter he could rap about.

Ice-T's Rhyme Syndicate, which included future House of Pain member as well as solo superstar Everlast, guested on the album. A spoken-word performance by Jello Biafra called "Words from Our Sponsors" was sampled for the album's opening track called "Shut Up, Be Happy," which also sampled Black Sabbath, a precursor of Ice-T's future metal band Body Count.

The hard-hitting album reached #37 on the *Billboard* 200 and #11 on the R&B chart and had three singles: "Lethal Weapon," "What Ya Wanna Do?," and "You Played Yourself."

OCTOBER 13

Freddie Foxxx releases his debut album *Freddie Foxxx Is Here* on MCA.

The debut set by the MC, also known as Bumpy Knuckles, was produced by Eric B. and Foxxx and contained the single "The Master."

Foxxx was originally slated to team up with Eric B. in the mid-1980s to form a duo. His failure to make a meeting with Eric B. resulted in the latter hooking up with Rakim and releasing classic records that changed the course of music history.

Foxxx, a onetime member of Supreme Force, would go on to also become a member of Queen Latifah's Flavor Unit and the Gang Starr Foundation.

OCTOBER 17

Philly's Steady B releases his fourth album *Going Steady* on Jive.

Going Steady, self-produced with Lawrence Goodman, contained cuts like "Analogy of a Black Man," "New Breed," and "Ego Trippin'" and had a socially conscious bent, influenced by groups at the time like Boogie Down Productions and Public Enemy.

The album, which featured the turntable work of DJ Tat Money, reached #51 on the R&B chart.

OCTOBER 23

Divine Styler releases his debut album *Word Power* on Ice-T's Rhyme Syndicate.

The debut set by the Brooklyn MC was heavily influenced by the socially conscious and politically charged hip-hop at the time, as evidenced on tracks like, "It's a Black Thing," "Koxistin U4ria," and "The Last Black House on the Left."

Produced by Styler with Bilal Bashir and Lawrence A. Duhart, the critically appreciated album spawned the underground favorite "Ain't Sayin' Nothin'."

OCTOBER 31

DJ Jazzy Jeff & the Fresh Prince release their third album *And in This Corner...* on Jive.

The self-produced *And in This Corner...* contained the hit single "Jazzy's Groove" and the classic "I Think I Can Beat Mike Tyson."

While it was not as successful as their previous release, the gold-selling album reached #39 on *Billboard* 200, #19 on the R&B chart, and received two Grammy nominations.

NOVEMBER 7

Queen Latifah releases her debut album *All Hail the Queen* on Tommy Boy.

Latifah's Afrocentric lyrics of positivity and black consciousness on this debut album helped usher in the golden age of hip-hop.

Handling production on Latifah's manifesto of soul sister pride was Prince Paul, Mark the 45 King, KRS-One, Little Louie Vega, and Daddy-O of Stetsasonic.

Classic hit singles from *All Hail the Queen* include "Wrath of My Madness" and "Mama Gave Birth to the Soul Children," which featured De La Soul and her anthem "Ladies First," featuring Monie Love. The gold-certified album reached #124 on the *Billboard* 200 and #6 on the R&B chart.

QUEEN LATIFAH

CHUCK D:

The Queen got her beginnings picking up notes as we toured together from her start in '88, '89. This Jerseyite was a leader from the hilt. Eventually putting together her Flavor Unit Company with her partner Shakim Compere. Her label Tommy Boy had great vision to propel her vision into a foundation for which she is respected to this very second.

Along with MC Lyte, Queen Latifah is the groundbreaker that made the world respect the women in rap perspective. Monie Love and De La Native Tongued the alliance with strong "peace and peoplehood" so to speak. *All Hail the Queen* was the blueprint for the woman MC soloist as an album artist. Her background as a singer/actress/ dancer in school plays as well as being a state basketball champion made these songs come to life on a tour stage and made her quite reachable.

NOVEMBER 7

The Jungle Brothers release their classic sophomore album *Done by the Forces of Nature* on Warner Bros.

Done by the Forces of Nature, produced by the duo and Kool DJ Red Alert, was universally acclaimed for its musical diversity that included hip-hop styles as well as house, soul, jazz, and African music.

The cult classic contained the high point "Doin' Our Own Dang," featuring De La Soul, Monie Love, Queen Latifah, and Q-Tip of A Tribe Called Quest, who were all part of the Native Tongues Posse with the Jungle Brothers. Other guests on the album included Towa Tei of Deee-Lite, Caron Wheeler of Soul II Soul, and Vinia Mojica.

CHUCK D:

Out of a very special time, the JBs came in affiliated with a few moments of the era: Native Tongues, the Afrocentric movement, and also the club sound going on at the time. Being managed by Kool DJ Red Alert didn't hurt either, as the JBs immediately had an international rap following. Their *Done by the Forces of Nature* was one of the most slept on of all time. The JBs is probably one of my favorite hooks choruses ever.

NOVEMBER 14

3rd Bass release their debut album *The Cactus Al/bum* on Def Jam.

The gold-selling set by the white three-man crew of MC Serch, Prime Minister Pete Nice, and DJ Richie Rich, who were born in Queens, Long Island, and Jamaica respectively, is considered a rap classic.

Produced by the Bomb Squad, Prince Paul, Sam Sever and the group as well, the New York–flavored album spawned the singles "Brooklyn-Queens" and "Product of the Enviroment," as well as the hits "Steppin' to the A.M." and "The Gas Face," both of which reached #5 on the Rap chart.

NOVEMBER 14

Def Jef releases his debut album *Just a Poet with Soul* on Delicious Vinyl.

Def Jef self-produced most of this articulate set, which fit right in with the Afrocentric and socially conscious themes in that period of hip-hop music. Other producers included the Dust Brothers, Michael Ross, and DJ Erick Vaan.

Guests on the set included N'Dea Davenport of Brand New Heavies, Julio G, and R&B legend Etta James. The album featured cult favorites like "God Made Me Funky" and "Droppin' Rhymes on Drums."

1990

FEBRUARY 12

MC Hammer releases his third album *Please Hammer Don't Hurt 'Em* on Capitol.

The double diamond set by the Oakland rapper was single-handedly responsible for bringing hip-hop culture and rap music to the mainstream unlike any other album preceding it.

His worldwide influence would be off the strength of smash-hit singles that borrowed heavily from classic R&B tracks. Among these hits were "Pray," which sampled "When Doves Cry" by Prince and the Revolution; "Have You Seen Her," a cover of the Chi-Lites smash of the same name; "Yo!! Sweetness," which borrowed from the Barry White hit "Your Sweetness Is My Weakness"; and "Here Comes the Hammer," which sampled "Super Bad" by James Brown for the remix single version. The blockbuster classic "U Can't Touch This" sampled Rick James's "Super Freak" and spent weeks on the charts, eventually winning two Grammys. Other album cuts sampled classics by the Jackson 5, Earth, Wind & Fire, Marvin Gaye, and others.

Producers on *Please Hammer Don't Hurt 'Em* included Felton Pilate of Con Funk Shun, James Earley, Scott Folks, Hammer's brother Big Louis Burrell, as well as MC Hammer.

Please Hammer Don't Hurt 'Em, which spent 108 weeks on the pop charts, peaking at #1 on the *Billboard* 200, catapulted rap music to the mainstream masses and made Hammer a household name. He had successful world tours, a Mattel action figure, a Saturday morning cartoon *Hammerman*, lunchboxes, and various endorsements, including Pepsi and British Knights running shoes.

FEBRUARY 19

A Tribe Called Quest release their hit song "Bonita Applebum" on Jive.

"Bonita Applebum" is the second single from the group's gold-selling debut album *People's Instinctive Travels and the Paths of Rhythm* released the same year.

The track was produced by the group and is a consistent fan favorite. "Bonita Applebum" also launched Tribe frontman Q-Tip on his road to stardom as well as establishing him as a sex symbol with female listeners.

CHUCK D:

MC Hammer was a tsunami on the rap stage. We were one of the few acts fortunate to play after Hammer tore the stage up and still survive. Hammer attitude to the very minute has never dipped below the confident line. James Brown, Cab Calloway, Little Richard all in a rap thing. The girl squad Oaktown's 3.5.7. was his Ikettes and made some great records in their own right. Too Bigg MC was his hype man, second in that category only after Flavor Flav.

I was invited to cover Hammer on tour in Florida in '92 for a magazine. It was a traveling circus complete with plenty of buses and show trucks outside and a helluva show. Hence there was a lot of jealousy and lawsuits coming at him from the business—just for being greater. He gave a lotta people jobs for a long time. Backlash followed as people read about related financial issues that are understood by many today. Before Diddy, Jay Z, et cetera, Hammer's empire was one unprecedented and to learn from.

FEBRUARY 22

Pomona, California's Above the Law release their debut album *Livin' Like Hustlers* on Ruthless.

The four-man crew from Pomona, California, consisted of Cold 187um, Go Mack, KMG the Illustrator, and DJ Total K-Oss. The debut album was split into violence- and sex-filled sides and featured production by Dr. Dre, Laylaw, as well as Above the Law and was executively produced by Eazy-E.

Livin' Like Hustlers contained the singles "Untouchable" and "Murder Rap" and N.W.A were featured on the track "The Last Song."

1990

MC HAMMER

A TRIBE CALLED QUEST

MARCH 27

Digital Underground release their debut album *Sex Packets* on Tommy Boy.

The Oakland-based crew released the platinum-selling *Sex Packets*, which held on for thirty-one weeks on the *Billboard* 200, peaking at #24, fueled by smash hits such as "Doowutchyalike" and Grammy-nominated "The Humpty Dance," the latter sampling from P-Funk and Sly & the Family Stone. The group's leader and founder Shock G also used an alter ego called Humpty Hump, who appeared in the video for "The Humpty Dance."

"The Humpty Dance" itself was sampled more than twenty-five times by a variety of artists including Public Enemy, BWP, Da Lench Mob, Redman, the Spice Girls, Joe Public, and Aaron Hall.

APRIL 10

A Tribe Called Quest release their debut album *People's Instinctive Travels and the Paths of Rhythm* on Jive.

The gold-selling set, produced by Tribe with help from the Jungle Brothers, introduced the world to Tribe's introspective and Afrocentric style, which followed in the footsteps of fellow Native Tongue musical collective members De La Soul and the Jungle Brothers. The music was intellectual and challenging as well as musically progressive and unique.

CHUCK D:

Out of the Native Tongues and humble Queens, New York, beginnings, these brothers were on point and serious on making history and carving their own niche on hip-hop. Q-Tip, Jarobi, Ali Shaheed Muhammad, and the B-boy of life Phife Dawg were the Fantastic Four Horsemen of consciousness in their debut. Their record label Jive was also acute enough to release a home video of their first European tour around this album.

Combining the talents of Q-Tip, Phife Dawg, and Ali Shaheed Muhammad, the album also featured appearances by fourth member Jarobi White before he left the group soon after the release of their debut.

Critically acclaimed (it received the perfect five-mic rating in *The Source* magazine), the alternative favorite featured the singles "I Left My Wallet in El Segundo" and "Bonita Applebum."

APRIL 10

Public Enemy release their third album *Fear of a Black Planet* on Def Jam.

Considered by many to be the magnum opus of hip-hop recordings, the sonically adventurous, chart-topping, platinum album sold one million copies in its first week.

Fueled by numerous hit singles, the twenty-track album contained "Fight the Power" (featured in the classic Spike Lee film *Do the Right Thing* released the previous summer), "Welcome to the Terrordome," "911 Is a Joke," "Brothers Gonna Work It Out," "Can't Do Nuttin' for Ya Man" (featured in the films *House Party* and *Jungle Fever*), "Burn Hollywood Burn" (featuring Ice Cube and Big Daddy Kane), "Anti 'N' Machine," and "Revolutionary Generation."

Fear of a Black Planet was the last album produced solely by the original Bomb Squad team consisting of Hank and Keith Shocklee, Eric "Vietnam" Sadler, and Public Enemy leader Chuck D.

Influenced by Dr. Frances Cress Welsing's 1970 essay "The Cress Theory of Color—Confrontation and Racism (White Supremacy)," the album was added to the National Recording Registry in the Library of Congress in 2004.

MAY 15

X Clan release their debut album *To the East, Backwards* on Island.

The themes in this Brooklyn hip-hop group's self-produced debut revolved around the group's politically fueled Afrocentrism.

The hard-hitting album reached #11 on the R&B chart and #97 on the *Billboard* 200. The album spawned several singles, most notably the lead "Raise the Flag," which became a hit in both the UK and the United States.

MAY 16

Ice Cube releases his debut solo album *AmeriKKKa's Most Wanted* on Priority.

The album, partially produced by Public Enemy production team the Bomb Squad along with California producer Sir Jinx, was Cube's first solo project after leaving LA's notorious N.W.A, and marked a historical melding of West Coast and East Coast hip-hop.

In this platinum-selling groundbreaking album, Ice Cube addressed subjects like poverty, crime, gang violence, and racism that prophetically predated what was to come a year later with the Rodney King beating and the subsequent LA riots. Peaking at #19 on the *Billboard* 200 and #6 on the R&B chart, the album spawned the hit singles "Who's the Mack," "Endangered Species," featuring Public Enemy's Chuck D, and the title track, which reached #1 on the Rap chart. Other guests on *AmeriKKKa's Most Wanted* included Public Enemy's Flavor Flav, Lil' Russ, and Da Lench Mob.

CHUCK D:

During the 1989 season, N.W.A had emerged with their *Straight Outta Compton* album. How the West was one. From that year forward, Ice Cube and I developed a friendship. He wanted to explore solo work for better financial reasons. His camp was telling him 1991, and he considered it a lifetime in rap street life. After trying to steer him to producers, like Sam Sever, Hank Shocklee, Eric "Vietnam" Sadler, Keith Shocklee, and I surrounded Ice Cube in a discussion—not long after recording his verse on Public Enemy's "Burn Hollywood Burn."

Immediately he and Sir Jinx came east to dig for sounds and arrange ideas. My time with Cube was more prerecording and philosophical, starting with a eighty-nine-cent notebook to organize his ideas. Every technique we were able to teach, Cube and Jinx absorbed. Along with the education they got with Dr. Dre, they were flying and never had to look back. *AmeriKKKa's Most Wanted* was like the transcontinental railroad of rap.

MAY 29

The Poor Righteous Teachers release their debut album *Holy Intellect* on Profile.

The hip-hop trio from Trenton, New Jersey, consisted of Wise Intelligent, Culture Freedom, and Father Shaheed and were one of the pioneers of socially conscious hip-hop and Afrocentric rap music.

Produced by Tony D and Eric "IQ" Gray, *Holy Intellect* reached #142 on the *Billboard* 200 and #17 on the R&B chart and contained the hit singles "Rock Dis Funky Joint," "Time to Say Peace," and the title track.

MAY 29

"We're All in the Same Gang" by the West Coast Rap All-Stars goes to the top of *Billboard's* Rap Singles chart.

The anti–gang violence anthem was produced by Dr. Dre and featured some of the biggest names in West Coast hip-hop, including Ice-T, Tone Lōc, Young MC, Digital Underground, MC Hammer, J. J. Fad, Above the Law, Def Jef, Eazy-E, and MC Ren of N.W.A as well as several others. Nominated for a Grammy, the song set the stage for a gang truce in Los Angeles.

JULY 17

Boogie Down Productions release their fourth album *Edutainment* on Jive.

The critically acclaimed album featured BDP leader KRS-One, at what many called his lyrical finest, tackling such issues as materialism, racism, police corruption, violence, black unity, and even the benefits of vegetarianism. KRS produced the album with D-Nice and Pal Joey.

Edutainment featured skits as interludes between the songs called "exhibits" (one featured Civil Rights activist Kwame Ture aka Stokely Carmichael) as well as cult classics such as "Blackman in Effect," "100

ICE CUBE

Guns," "Breath Control II," and the hit "Love's Gonna Get'cha (Material Love)." The album reached #9 on the R&B chart and #32 on the *Billboard* 200.

SEPTEMBER 3

Vanilla Ice releases his classic debut album *To the Extreme* on SBK.

Originally released in 1989 on the indie label Ichiban Records, the chart-topping, multi-platinum album was rereleased when Vanilla Ice's contract was bought out by SBK. He would go on to sell more than fifteen million copies of *To the Extreme* worldwide, making it the biggest-selling rap album at the time.

Produced by Vanilla Ice along with Darryl Williams, Kim Sharp, and Khayree, *To the Extreme* contained the singles "I Love You" and a reworking of Wild Cherry's "Play That Funky Music." However it was the massive hit "Ice Ice Baby," which helped keep the album on the top of the *Billboard* 200 for sixteen weeks.

SEPTEMBER 14

LL Cool J releases his fourth album *Mama Said Knock You Out* on Def Jam.

Produced by Marley Marl, the multi-platinum album was recorded at his home studio where LL lived during the recording process. Bobby "Bobcat" Ervin coproduced the classic title track, which was a chart-topping, gold-selling single that also earned LL a Grammy Award for best rap solo performance.

Mama Said Knock You Out also spawned another

BIG DADDY KANE

four hit singles: "The Boomin' System," "6 Minutes of Pleasure," "To da Break of Dawn," and "Around the Way Girl."

One of LL Cool J's most popular albums, it reached #2 on the R&B chart and #16 on the *Billboard* 200.

OCTOBER 30

Big Daddy Kane releases his third album *Taste of Chocolate* on Cold Chillin'.

Self-produced with Cool V, Mister Cee, Andre Booth, the eclectic *Taste of Chocolate* was Kane's first album to go gold, reaching #33 on the *Billboard* 200 and #1 on the R&B chart.

Guests on the album included Barry White, Rudy Ray Moore (aka Dolemite), the former lead singer of Atlantic Starr Barbara Weathers, and Gamilah Shabazz, the daughter of Malcolm X. It produced three singles: "It's Hard Being the Kane," "All of Me," and "Cause I Can Do It Right."

OCTOBER 30

Monie Love releases her debut album *Down to Earth* on Warner Bros.

Monie Love was a member of the Native Tongues Posse, which also consisted of De La Soul, A Tribe Called Quest, the Jungle Brothers, and several others. This is evidenced in the visual similarity of her cover to that of De La Soul's debut album *3 Feet High and Rising*.

Down to Earth, which reached #26 on the R&B charts, was produced by Jerry Callendar, Andy Cox, Richie Fermie, David Steele, Dancin' Danny D as well as by the Beatnuts and Afrika Baby Bam of the Jungle Brothers, both from the Native Tongues. It contained a slew of singles in addition to the title track, including "Ring My Bell," "Grandpa's Party," "I Can Do This," and the Grammy-nominated hits, "Monie in the Middle" and "It's a Shame (My Sister)," which reached #26 on the *Billboard* Hot 100.

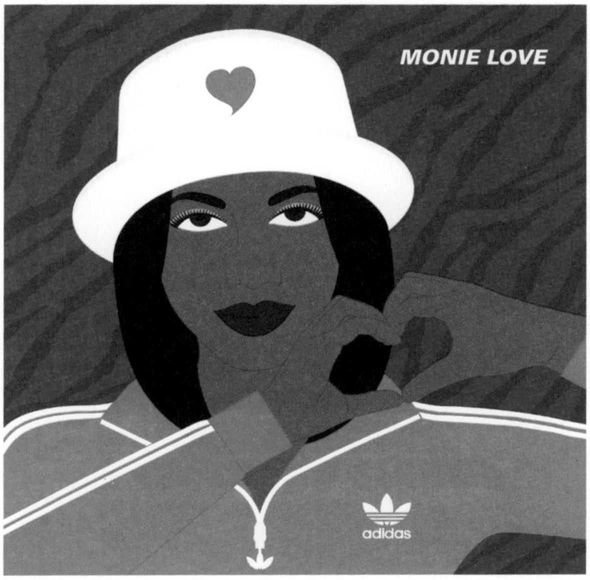

DECEMBER 4

Brand Nubian release their debut album *One for All* on Elektra.

The socially conscious *One for All* garnered attention for its politically charged lyrics steeped in Five-Percent Nation theology, as well as its musicality.

CHUCK D:

These brothers will always be my favorites. They had a solid blend of conscious street and Five-Percent Nation that earned great respect in New York, and radiated from there. To this day Lord Jamar, Sadat X, and Grand Puba Maxwell are solid go-to brothers for the math and science, and ones to raise 'em up right and teach. Beyond their solid breakthrough, one should peep forward a few years later and hear "I'm Black and I'm Proud."

In addition to the title track, *One for All* produced the classic hit single "Wake Up" and the smash "Slow Down," a tale about drug abuse that brilliantly samples the late 1980s hit "What I Am" by Edie Brickell & New Bohemians. Positive K guested on the track "Grand Puba, Positive and L.G." Critically acclaimed, the album peaked at #130 on *Billboard* 200 and #34 on the R&B chart.

DECEMBER 15

EPMD release their third studio album *Business as Usual* on Def Jam.

The group's gold-selling album, their first on Def Jam, yielded three singles: "Gold Digger," "Give the People," and "Rampage (Slow Down Baby)" which featured LL Cool J. The hard-edged album reached #36 on the *Billboard* 200 and topped the R&B chart.

"Gold Digger" and "Rampage" gave EPMD two of the biggest hits of their career, with the songs charting at #1 and #2, respectively, on the Rap Singles chart. *Business as Usual* featured the recording debut of Redman, who guested on the songs "Hardcore" and "Brothers on My Jock."

DECEMBER 18

Former N.W.A member Ice Cube releases the EP *Kill at Will* on Priority.

Ice Cube released the platinum-selling EP soon after the success of *AmeriKKKa's Most Wanted*. The seven-track set employed some recordings from the album sessions, which was primarily produced by the Public Enemy production team the Bomb Squad the previous year.

Kill at Will contained such Cube classics as "Jackin' for Beats," "Dead Homiez," and the hit single "Endangered Species (Tales from the Dark Side) (Remix)," featuring Chuck D of Public Enemy. It reached #34 on the *Billboard* 200 and #5 on the R&B chart.

1991

JANUARY 15

DJ Quik releases his debut album *Quik Is the Name* on Profile.

The talented Compton, California, producer and artist was the most expensive signee at the independent Profile Records at the time, reportedly netting a six-figure deal. He lived up to the hype with the platinum-selling *Quik Is the Name*, which spawned the chart-climbing singles "Born and Raised in Compton" and the title track.

The critically acclaimed album reached #29 on the *Billboard* 200 and #9 on the R&B chart. While still recording on his own, DJ Quik would also go on to become a highly sought after producer in hip-hop and R&B.

JANUARY 15

Gang Starr release *Step in the Arena* on EMI.

The second album from the duo of Guru and DJ Premier featured samples from artists like Big Daddy Kane, the Band, LL Cool J, the Ohio Players, the Meters, and Marvin Gaye. DJ Premier began experimenting more and more with jazz samples during the recording of this album. Self-described as "dedicated minister of underground sound," their album reached #121 on the *Billboard* 200 and #19 on the R&B chart.

The influential album spawned several singles, including "Just to Get a Rep," "Step in the Arena," and "Check the Technique."

JANUARY 15

Digital Underground release *This Is an EP Release* on Warner Bros.

The California hip-hop group released this gold-selling EP following the critical and commercial success of their debut album *Sex Packets*.

The set featured the recording debut from Tupac Shakur, who guested on the opener "Same Song." Tupac also appeared in the song's music video.

This Is an EP Release sold half a million copies in its first two months and peaked at #29 on the *Billboard* 200 and #7 on the R&B chart.

GURU

FEBRUARY 12

Master P releases his debut album *Get Away Clean* and first for his label, No Limit.

This fourteen-track self-produced album was the rough beginning of a successful slew of hard-edged gangsta albums for P's label that would eventually sell in the millions.

Apart from P's own recordings, No Limit would enjoy platinum success with P's brothers Silkk the Shocker and C-Murder as well as Mystikal, Mia X, Soulja Slim, Fiend, Kane and Abel, Mr. Serv-On, Tre-8, and Snoop Dogg among many others.

CHUCK D:

This brother was systematically moved by corporations. Master P followed in Luther Campbell's entrepreneurial footsteps, going deep in a marketplace few ever wanted. The Southeast and mid-South USA proved to be a big financial base for the No Limit Record empire. His recordings, videos, films, and magazine ads were the real empire. Universal wanted that territory rumor had it.

Master P turned them down and away. It's no big surprise how Cash Money Records came into the game, well financed to also sprout from Louisiana with force. Master P is the orchestrator of DIY independence in the record biz and his pushing of Pen & Pixel's artwork and endless magazine ads about southern slanged street life drew instant attention inside and out.

FEBRUARY 26

LL Cool J releases the hit single "Mama Said Knock You Out" from his album of the same name.

"Mama Said Knock You Out," whose opening line "Don't call it a comeback, I've been here for years," is one of the most famous rap lyrics ever.

Produced by Marley Marl, the gold-selling, Grammy-winning, chart-topping hit was included in the Rock & Roll Hall of Fame's "500 Songs That Shaped Rock and Roll."

MARLEY MARL

MARCH 12

Boogie Down Productions release their fifth album *Live Hardcore Worldwide* on Jive.

The high-energy album is considered by some to be the most acclaimed live rap album of all times. It featured BDP performing their classics like "South Bronx," "Jack of Spades," and "I'm Still No.1," in New York, London, and Paris. A fan favorite, it reached #25 on the R&B chart.

MARCH 19

California rapper Yo-Yo releases her debut album *Make Way for the Motherlode* on East West.

With production handled by Sir Jinx, Del the Funky Homosapien, and her mentor Ice Cube, *Make Way for the Motherlode* spawned the singles "Ain't Nobody Better," "You Can't Play with My Yo-Yo," and "What Can I Do?" It reached #74 on the *Billboard* 200 and #5 on the R&B chart.

APRIL 23

Toronto's Dream Warriors release their debut album *And Now the Legacy Begins* on Island.

The two-man crew of King Lou and Capital Q were heavily influenced by De La Soul and the Native Tongues Posse as evidenced in the album's eclectic musical direction which melded hip-hop with reggae, funk, jazz, and pop.

The album's four Canadian hit singles included the jazzy Juno Award–winning "My Definition of a Boombastic Jazz Style," the R&B influenced "Follow Me Not," the reggaesque "Ludi" and "Wash Your Face in My Sink."

MAY 7

DJ Terminator X of Public Enemy releases his first solo album *Terminator X & the Valley of the Jeep Beets* on Def Jam.

Aside from featuring fellow PE members Chuck D and Sister Souljah on the popular single "Buck Whylin'," *Jeep Beets* also featured X's fellow Long Island hip-hop compatriots Andreaus 13 and Juvenile Delinquintz. The Cincinnati-based female duo Bonnie 'N' Clyde appear on the hit "Homey Don't Play Dat."

Coproduced by X and the Bomb Squad, the record reached #97 on the *Billboard* 200 and #19 on the R&B chart.

MAY 14

De La Soul release their much-anticipated sophomore album *De La Soul Is Dead* on Tommy Boy.

Following up on the visuals of the 1989 groundbreaking debut *3 Feet High and Rising,* the cover for *De La Soul Is Dead* depicts a broken flowerpot, expressing the group's desire to escape the "hippie" image pinned on them.

Musically, De La Soul went darker, again pushing the boundaries with songs like "Millie Pulled a Pistol on Santa," a song about incest, and "Fanatic of the B Word," a tune about police brutality. The album contained the hits "Ring Ring Ring (Ha Ha Hey)," "A Roller Skating Jam Named 'Saturdays'," and "Keepin' the Faith." Guests on *De La Soul Is Dead* included Q-Tip, Black Sheep, and hip-hop mogul Russell Simmons.

Reaching #26 on the *Billboard* 200 and #24 on the R&B chart, *De La Soul Is Dead* received five mics from *The Source* magazine and is considered a classic by critics and fans alike.

MAY 14

Ice-T releases his fourth album *O.G. Original Gangster* on Sire.

Thought by many to be his best work, the album contained the hit title track as well as "New Jack Hustler (Nino's Theme)" from the Warner Bros. film *New Jack City* released the same year, which Ice-T also costarred in. The album also featured the hit single "Mind Over Matter," and the fan favorite "Pulse of the Rhyme." Reaching #9 on the R&B chart, the set introduced his controversial heavy metal band Body Count on an album track of the same name. They would tour the following year, including an appearance at the first Lollapalooza musical festival.

CHUCK D:

The greatest storytelling MC usually always goes to Slick Rick; I counter with that throne being shared by the Iceberg. Ice-T is simply the Johnny Cash of hip-hop—a philosophical mastermind of the active word. This album was the epitome of LA street culture broken down by the doctor philosopher himself of storied word. Personally, I have always looked up to the Iceberg, as I call him. He's one of the few that have age seniority over me. The first to put out a book. First artist to actually head a documentary and festival: *The Art of Rap*. Playing the Art of Rap most recently bears witness to probably one of the most engaging stage rap performers ever. Iceberg is also like the Alice Cooper of rap; very forward in presenting a stage atmosphere fitting his words. On the *OG* performance, he was the first MC to go handless mic, and had the Rhyme Syndicate bring the LA streets to every city—stage-wise, I might add.

MAY 18

Chubb Rock releases the single "Treat 'Em Right" on Select.

The New York rapper scored his first big hit with the title track to his *Treat 'Em Right* EP, reaching #22 on the *Billboard* R&B chart and #73 on the *Billboard* 200.

Rock rereleased the song as his 1991 album *The One's* lead single, where the song became a blockbuster hit again the spring of 1991, spending three weeks on top of the Rap chart that March, as well as appearing on the *Billboard* Hot 100 and R&B chart. The song has since been sampled by numerous artists including Mary J. Blige and K'naan.

MAY 20

DJ Jazzy Jeff & the Fresh Prince release the single "Summertime," from their fourth album *Homebase*.

Produced by Hula & K. Fingers, the worldwide hit samples "Summer Madness" by Kool & the Gang. The song won a Grammy Award in 1992 and reached #4 on the *Billboard* Hot 100 and topped the R&B chart.

MAY 28

N.W.A release *Efil4zaggin* on Ruthless.

N.W.A's final studio album, which is "Niggaz4life" spelled backward, debuted at #2 on the *Billboard* Top 200, moved to #1 the following week, and was certified platinum by August.

The ferocious album, which featured Dr. Dre, DJ Yella, MC Ren, Eazy-E, as well as the D.O.C., spawned two singles: "Alwayz into Somethin" and "Appetite for Destruction."

The gangsta classic sampled a wide range of artists including Bootsy Collins, the Sugarhill Gang, Black Flag, Little Feat, and Rufus Thomas.

JUNE 2

The Geto Boys release *We Can't Be Stopped* on Rap-A-Lot.

The Texas rap group's raw and twisted lyrics helped propel the platinum-selling album to reach #24 on the *Billboard* 200 and #5 on the R&B chart. The infamous album cover photo was taken in the hospital shortly after Bushwick Bill was shot in the eye.

We Can't Be Stopped gave the group the biggest crossover hit of their career with "Mind Playing Tricks on Me," which sampled "Hung Up on My Baby" by Isaac Hayes. The certified-gold single peaked at #23 on the *Billboard* Hot 100, #10 on the R&B chart, and topped the rap charts. It is widely considered to be one of the greatest hip-hop songs of all time.

JUNE 11

Kool Moe Dee releases *Funke Funke Wisdom* on RCA.

The album, which reached #72 on the *Billboard* 200, spawned the hit single "Rise 'N' Shine," which featured Chuck D and KRS-One and sampled Billy Preston and Sly & the Family Stone and topped the Rap chart.

JUNE 18

3rd Bass release *Derelicts of Dialect* on Def Jam.

The last studio album from the Queens hip-hop trio was certified gold and reached #19 on the *Billboard* 200 and #10 on the R&B chart. *Derelicts of Dialect* samples artists like Al Green, Blue Öyster Cult, LL Cool J, Steely Dan, and Stevie Wonder.

The album featured the group's crossover hit single "Pop Goes the Weasel," a diss track aimed at Vanilla Ice that reached #29 on the *Billboard* Hot 100, #26 on the R&B chart, and topped the Rap chart.

THE GETO BOYS

JULY 1

Stetsasonic release their third and final album together, *Blood, Sweat & No Tears,* on Tommy Boy.

Produced by Stetsasonic, one of hip-hop's first live bands, the musically diverse *Blood, Sweat & No Tears* spawned the acclaimed singles "Speaking of a Girl Named Suzy" and "No B.S. Allowed."

Members of Stetsasonic continued to have successful careers after its dissolution, most notably Prince Paul, who has become a legendary producer, especially for his work with De La Soul.

JULY 9

Quincy Jones's Qwest Records releases the soundtrack to the 1991 John Singleton–directed Columbia Pictures film *Boyz n the Hood.*

The gold-selling soundtrack from the coming-of-age movie set in South Central LA featured hip-hop artists Kam, Too $hort, 2 Live Crew, Monie Love, Main Source, Compton's Most Wanted, and Ice Cube, who costarred in the film with Cuba Gooding Jr., Morris Chestnut, and Laurence Fishburne. Yo-Yo made a brief cameo in the film as well.

The singles included fourteen-year-old Tevin Campbell's "Just Ask Me To," which reached #88 on the *Billboard* Hot 100 and #9 on the R&B chart. The soundtrack reached #12 on the *Billboard* 200 and #1 on the R&B chart.

JULY 23

Main Source release their debut album *Breaking Atoms* on Wild Pitch.

The three-man crew consisting of Toronto DJs K-Cut and Sir Scratch and legendary Queens, New York, producer and MC Large Professor, broke new ground with their first album, which pushed hip-hop music production to new heights.

Main Source self-produced this masterpiece, which spawned the classic hit songs, "Just Hangin' Out" and "Looking at the Front Door," which topped the Rap chart, as well as the singles "Peace Is Not the Word to Play" and "Watch Roger Do His Thing." The album spent thirty weeks on the R&B chart, peaking at #40.

CHUCK D:

Main Source reminds me of the Drifters in early R&B. They have had many MCs and DJs graduate through them. A launching pad with almost liquid A&R. Toronto to Queens directed. Nas, Mikey D, Large Professor, Kendo the Almost Famous—all have blessed the Main Source beats and shows.

Breaking Atoms is also noted for the first time the legendary Nas was ever heard on wax on the track "Live at the Barbeque," which also featured Akinyele and Joe Fatal.

JULY 30

Leaders of the New School release *A Future Without a Past...* on Elektra.

The Long Island hip-hop group of Charlie Brown, Dinco D, Busta Rhymes, and Cut Monitor Milo appeared together as guests on a few singles before releasing their debut.

The album spawned the singles including "Case of the P.T.A.," "Sobb Story," and "The International Zone Coaster," which all reached the top ten on the Rap chart.

The album, which peaked at #128 on the *Billboard* 200 and #53 on the R&B chart, served as the full-length debut of Busta Rhymes, who was just nineteen years old when the album was released.

AUGUST 6

P.M. Dawn release their classic debut album *Of the Heart, of the Soul and of the Cross: The Utopian Experience* on Gee Street.

Comprised of brothers Attrell and Jarrett Cordes, known professionally as Prince Be the Nocturnal and DJ Minutemix, P.M. Dawn were heavily influenced by the musical philosophy of the Native Tongues Posse, whose members included De La Soul, A Tribe Called Quest, the Jungle Brothers, and Monie Love, to name a few.

P.M. Dawn's bohemian hip-hop release became a worldwide sensation with fans and critics alike courtesy of hits like "A Watcher's Point of View (Don't 'Cha Think)," "Paper Doll," and the chart-topping, "Set Adrift on Memory Bliss," which sampled the 1983 Spandau Ballet hit "True." It also shared the distinction of being the first single in history by a rap group to go to the top of the *Billboard* Hot 100 since the introduction of the Nielsen SoundScan system.

With unusual samples and often psychedelic lyrics, the album reached #48 on the *Billboard* 200 and #29 on the R&B chart.

AUGUST 13

Cypress Hill release their self-titled debut on Columbia.

The California rap group's first album broke them in as the first Latino hip-hop stars and marked the most successful album of their career, selling more than two million copies.

Produced by DJ Muggs, the sixteen songs on the album, many with a pro-marijuana stance, sampled a number of classic artists from the '50s, '60s, and '70s including Jimi Hendrix, Muddy Waters, Curtis Mayfield, and Aretha Franklin. The album spent eighty-nine weeks on the *Billboard* 200, peaking at #31, and hit #4 on the R&B chart.

Cypress Hill yielded several singles, including "How I Could Just Kill a Man" and "The Phuncky Feel One," both of which topped the Rap chart.

SEPTEMBER 3

Naughty By Nature release their self-titled debut on Tommy Boy.

Queen Latifah discovered the New Jersey trio of Treach, Vinnie, and DJ Kay Gee and, through her management company, helped them land a deal at Tommy Boy. Treach, the group's lead vocalist, introduced a fast dancehall reggae delivery on this album reminiscent of KRS-One's style on Boogie Down's *Criminal Minded.*

Produced by Naughty By Nature and Little Louie Vega, the platinum-selling gritty debut featured the hit singles "Everything's Gonna Be Alright" (listed as "Ghetto Bastard" on certain explicit releases) and the top ten anthem that propelled them to stardom "O.P.P.," which reached #6 on the *Billboard* Hot 100 and #1 on the Rap chart. Guests on the album included Queen Latifah, Lakim Shabazz, Apache, and Aphrodity. The album reached #16 on the *Billboard* 200 and #10 on the R&B chart.

SEPTEMBER 17

MC Lyte releases *Act Like You Know* on First Priority Music.

Written with and produced by Wolf & Epic (Richard Wolf and Brett "Epic" Mazur), the third album from the pioneering Brooklyn rapper featured two hit singles: "Poor Georgie" and "When in Love," which reached #11 and #14 on the R&B chart respectively. In addition to Wolf & Epic, the album included production and cowriting credits from artists Audio Two, and The 45 King.

With more prominent R&B and melodic influences throughout, *Act Like You Know* was MC Lyte's most commercially accessible album to date, reaching #102 on the *Billboard* 200 and #14 on the R&B chart.

SEPTEMBER 24

A Tribe Called Quest release *The Low End Theory* on Jive.

Lauded primarily for its seamless fusion of jazz and hip-hop, the second album from the New York hip-hop group went on to become one of the most critically acclaimed landmark hip-hop albums of all time. Certified platinum in 1995, the album reached #45 on the *Billboard* 200 and #13 on the R&B chart.

The album spawned three singles: "Check the Rhime," "Jazz (We've Got)," and "Scenario," which reached #57 on the *Billboard* Hot 100. The album's "Verses from the Abstract" featured a famous bass line from legendary jazz double bassist Ron Carter.

1991

NAUGHTY BY NATURE

OCTOBER 1

Public Enemy release their fourth album *Apocalypse '91—The Enemy Strikes Black* on Def Jam.

The platinum-selling album, originally intended to be an EP called *Afraid of the Dark,* took on a life of its own. Debuting at #4 on the *Billboard* 200 and peaking at #1 on the R&B chart, the critically acclaimed album was packed with singles such as "Shut 'Em Down," "Nighttrain," and a remake of "Bring the Noise" with heavy metal band Anthrax and prompted hip-hop heads to call this set the "birth of hardcore rap." The album also produced the horn-driven smash hit single "Can't Truss It" which reached #50 on the *Billboard* Hot 100 and #9 on the R&B chart.

Executive produced by Hank Shocklee, the album's liner notes list the production team as the "Imperial Grand Ministers of Funk": Stuart Robertz, Cerwin "C-Dawg" Depper, and the JBL, which according to Bomb Squad producer Gary "G-Wiz" Rinaldo, were fictional names and added to give the impression it was produced by a crew, like the Bomb Squad. All of the production and beat-making was done exclusively by Wiz and Chuck D, with some minor assistance by Shocklee, all of which brought in a heavy drum influence meshed with melodic horn lines, while keeping PE's explosive sound.

Producer Pete Rock's remixes of singles like "Nighttrain" and "Shut 'Em Down" also ushered in the era of the hip-hop remix.

OCTOBER 15

Digital Underground release their second album *Sons of the P* on Tommy Boy.

The gold-selling but underrated album was one of the most innovative musically in hip-hop history, reaching #44 on the *Billboard* 200 and #23 on the R&B chart. It also produced two hit singles, "No Nose Job" and "Kiss You Back," which reached #40 on the *Billboard* Hot 100. The title track was coproduced by George Clinton and featured the P-Funk legend on the track as well.

OCTOBER 15

MC Solaar releases his debut album *Qui Sème Le Vent Récolte Le Tempo* on Musicrama.

The Senegal-born, France-based MC Solaar's globally acclaimed debut wowed with his clever, introspective poetic rhymes, coupled with such a controlled and cool delivery that some called him the French Rakim.

Produced by Jimmy Jay, the innovative album spawned several hit singles in France such as "Bouge de là (Part 1)," "Caroline," and the hypnotic title track.

Solaar would become a member of the Gang Starr Foundation, eventually collaborating with Guru on the first installment of his *Jazzmatazz* series in 1993.

OCTOBER 15

The UMC's release their debut album *Fruits of Nature* on Wild Pitch.

The Staten Island duo the UMC's was made up of Kool Kim (later known as NYOIL) and Haas G, who would go on to become a successful producer. The influences of De La Soul and the Native Tongues Posse, as well as Kid 'N Play, could be felt in their music and image. *Fruits of Nature* produced the hit singles "One to Grow On" and "Blue Cheese," which reached #2 and #1 on the Rap chart respectively.

The UMC's would release one more album called *Unleashed* in 1994 before going their separate ways.

OCTOBER 22

Black Sheep release their debut album *A Wolf in Sheep's Clothing* on Mercury.

Black Sheep, made up of Dres and Mr. Lawnge, were the latest artists in the Native Tongues Posse, which also included De La Soul, A Tribe Called Quest, the Jungle Brothers, Monie Love, and Queen Latifah. Unlike the other members, Black Sheep's material was more mischievous than socially conscious, hence the band's name.

The acclaimed gold-selling album spawned the smash hits "Strobelite Honey," "Similak Child," "Flavor of the Month," and the classic "The Choice Is Yours" which reached #1 on the Rap chart and spawned a groundbreaking music video that revolutionized the art form. The album reached #30 on the *Billboard* Hot 100 and #15 on the R&B chart.

OCTOBER 22

Del the Funky Homosapien releases his debut album *I Wish My Brother George Was Here* on Elektra.

With the help of Ice Cube, this West Coast eighteen-year-old rapper cracked the top fifty of the R&B/Hip-Hop Albums chart, and remained on the chart for thirteen weeks.

Titled to reference his idol George Clinton, the album yielded the hit single "Mistadobalina," which only reached #55 on the R&B/Hip-Hop chart but became a major hit throughout Europe.

OCTOBER 29

Ice Cube releases his second solo album *Death Certificate* on Priority.

The platinum-selling album, considered a masterpiece and one of Cube's finest by most, was produced by Sir Jinx, whose production on *Death Certificate* was heavily influenced by his previous producers, the Bomb Squad.

Filled with sharp insights, the album tackled an array of subjects such as racism, police brutality, venereal disease, sexual promiscuity, and gang violence. The Nation of Islam had a heavy influence on *Death Certificate* with then national representative Dr. Khalid Muhammad guesting on several tracks.

Death Certificate was a thematic album, told in story form, with side one called "The Death Side" and side two called "The Life Side." The three songs that close "The Death Side": "Man's Best Friend," "Alive on Arrival," and "Death" are some of the best album sequencing in recorded music history. The album also spawned the hit singles "True to the Game" and the chart topping "Steady Mobbin'." It certified platinum in two months, debuting at #2 on the *Billboard* 200 and #1 on the R&B chart.

OCTOBER 29

Organized Konfusion release their self-titled debut album on Elektra.

The groundbreaking lyrics of the Queens duo, Prince Po and Pharoahe Monch, covered a diverse set of topics that ranged from the lighthearted to the political and religious.

Mainly self-produced, the album featured the single "Walk into the Sun," which reached #15 on the Rap chart.

NOVEMBER 12

The Bronx's Tim Dog releases his debut album *Penicillin on Wax* on Ruffhouse.

Featuring production by TR Love, Bobby Crawford, Ced-Gee of the Ultramagnetic MC's, and Tim Dog and some appearances by Kool Keith, the album is mostly noted for the controversial "Fuck Compton" single, which many credited with sparking the eventual East Coast–West Coast hip-hop rivalry.

NOVEMBER 12

2Pac releases his debut solo album *2Pacalypse Now* on Interscope.

Previously a member of Digital Underground, 2Pac's debut is easily his most political work ever, as the songs on *2Pacalypse Now* tackled issues such as racism, police brutality, and teen pregnancy.

The gold-selling album produced the classic hit "Brenda's Got a Baby," featuring Dave Hollister. Other singles from the album included "Trapped" featuring Shock G of Digital Underground and "If My Homie Calls." It reached #64 on the *Billboard* 200 and #13 on the R&B charts.

Hip-hop artists such as 50 Cent, Eminem, the Game, Nas, and Talib Kweli have referred to this album as having a large influence on their early work.

CHUCK D:

Tupac didn't play and Pac wasn't afraid, simple as that. I know because I put Pac and Digital Underground on their first tour in 1990. Pac all throughout was trying to figure out how to bring bourgeoisie and the boulevard together in a rap song, and he is the closest to this day to ever do it. He was training from both areas and paying attention.

Many people don't give Pac the credit for the great voice he had. Too much emphasis is always on flow and lingo as opposed to Pac just had a great voice, projection, and diction, which often get overlooked. Pac's boldness and daringness was his political point of view. Whether it was talking about a mother, a woman who didn't have his support, or somebody that looked like they didn't have a future—this is why Pac is forever remembered.

DECEMBER 17

Biz Markie is successfully sued by singer-songwriter Gilbert O'Sullivan for copyright infringement.

Biz Markie, whose song "Alone Again" sampled Gilbert O'Sullivan's 1972 song "Alone Again (Naturally)" was sued for copyright infringement. The court's ruling, which declared that unlicensed sampling qualifies as copyright infringement, forever changed the precedents and standards for hip-hop sampling.

Biz Markie was ordered to pay $250,000 in damages and his label, Warner Bros., was ordered to discontinue all sales of the single. Biz Markie addresses the lawsuit on his subsequent 1993 album, titled *All Samples Cleared!*

DECEMBER 31

The soundtrack to the Paramount Pictures film *Juice* is released on the Bomb Squad's S.O.U.L. Records.

The Bomb Squad executive produced the gold-selling soundtrack to *Juice*, the hip-hop crime drama that costarred Tupac Shakur in his motion picture debut. It featured cameos from other hip-hop luminaries, such as EPMD, Treach of Naughty By Nature, Special Ed, and Fab Five Freddy.

The soundtrack featured EPMD, Cypress Hill, Salt-N-Pepa, and Aaron Hall, among others, and also spawned hits "Uptown Anthem" by Naughty By Nature; "What Could Be Better Bitch" by Son of Bazerk; "Juice (Know the Ledge)" by Eric B. & Rakim; and "Nuff Respect" by Big Daddy Kane. It reached #17 on the *Billboard* 200 and #3 on the R&B chart.

TUPAC SHAKUR

1992

FEBRUARY 4

Sir Mix-A-Lot releases his third album *Mack Daddy* on Def American.

Produced by Rick Rubin, Nate Foxx, Strange, and Sir Mix-A-Lot, *Mack Daddy* showcased the MC's aggressive, humorous rhymes coupled with strong rhythms.

Mack Daddy featured Sir Mix-A-Lot's biggest hit to date, "Baby Got Back," which ignited controversy but topped the charts for five weeks, selling more than two million copies and winning a Grammy. Fueled by the song's popularity, the album spent sixty-one weeks on the *Billboard* 200, peaking at #9.

MARCH 5

Das EFX release the hit single "They Want EFX" on East West.

The innovative self-produced hit from their platinum-selling debut album *Dead Serious* showcased the duo's playful rapid vocal delivery, which would add nonsense such as "–iggity" to words to increase syllables to their lines and mesh popular culture with hip-hop lingo.

Peaking at #25 on the *Billboard* Hot 100 and #29 on the Dance charts, the hit song has a profound effect on rap music at the time.

MARCH 17

Sister Souljah releases her album *360 Degrees of Power* on Epic.

Produced by the Bomb Squad, the onetime Public Enemy member's controversial album dealt with racism, politics, poverty, violence, and self-empowerment.

Ice Cube guested on the track "Killing Me Softly: Deadly Code of Silence," as did Chuck D on the cut "State of Accommodation: Why Aren't You Angry."

Reaching #72 on the R&B chart, the album was brought into the public fore when presidential hopeful Bill Clinton criticized her remarks about racism during the campaign.

SISTER SOULJAH

MARCH 24

A Tribe Called Quest release the single "Scenario" on Jive.

"Scenario," the third single from *The Low End Theory*, featured a memorable cameo from Busta Rhymes, then of the Leaders of the New School.

Peaking at #57 on the *Billboard* Hot 100 and topping the Rap chart, it would later be sampled by the Notorious B.I.G. and Afrika Bambaataa.

MARCH 24

Arrested Development release their debut album *3 Years, 5 Months, and 2 Days in the Life of...* on Chrysalis.

The earthy, Afrocentric, bohemian southern hip-hop sound of the group combined with socially conscious lyrics brought a whole new color to the hip-hop palette, causing Arrested Development to be named *Rolling Stone*'s band of the year.

The album, which sold four million copies, produced the smash hits: "Tennessee," "People Everyday," and "Mr. Wendal," all of which reached the top ten of the *Billboard* Hot 100. Peaking at #7 on the *Billboard* 200, the album won a Grammy for best rap album and the band for best new artist. Despite their promise, the band only recorded one more album, *Zingalamaduni*, before breaking up in 1996.

CHUCK D:
While gangsta rap was grabbing up its adherents, these guys first took Atlanta, where they came together, by storm—then spit their bohemian rap flavors full of hope all the way to a Grammy. That same energy, togetherness, and defiance in the face of negativity is just what we need today—so as a matter of fact, they're still putting it out to a worldwide audience.

APRIL 7

Das EFX release their debut album *Dead Serious* on East West.

Virginia State University duo Dray and Skoob were discovered in the early 1990s by EPMD, who were the executive producers of their debut.

Produced by the band along with their friends Chris Charity and Derek Lynch, the chart-topping *Dead Serious* featured the duo's unique fast, stuttering, chat-style vocal flow powered by beat-solid production.

The platinum-selling album contained the singles "Straight Out the Sewer," "Mic Checka," and the smash "They Want EFX."

APRIL 9

Dr. Dre and Snoop Doggy Dogg release the song "Deep Cover" on Epic.

"Deep Cover" was the theme song of the New Line Cinema crime drama of the same name, starring Laurence Fishburne and Jeff Goldblum, released the same year.

While the song wasn't a hit, it's historic because it was Dr. Dre's first solo release after leaving N.W.A as well as the first appearance of Snoop Doggy Dogg on a recording.

Dr. Dre produced the track, which was later featured in the 2004 Rockstar video game Grand Theft Auto: San Andreas.

APRIL 25

Kris Kross's "Jump" reaches #1 on the *Billboard* Hot 100.

"Jump" is the lead single from Kris Kross's platinum-selling debut album *Totally Krossed Out*, released in March. Released in February, the song topped the charts in April and then stayed at #1 for a total of eight weeks, a first for a rap song.

Chris "Mac Daddy" Kelly and Chris "Daddy Mac" Smith were only twelve and thirteen when they recorded "Jump." The song, written and produced by Jermaine Dupri, is the first mainstream hip-hop hit single from an Atlanta artist. Three months later, the hip-hop group Arrested Development became the second group from Atlanta to score a top ten with their hit single "Tennessee."

MAY 5

Gang Starr release their third album *Daily Operation* on EMI.

Daily Operation, the third studio album from the acclaimed hip-hop duo, sampled Aretha Franklin, Schoolly D, Eric B. & Rakim, and Charles Mingus, among others. Hits off the album include "Ex Girl to Next Girl" and "Take It Personal," both of which hit the top five on the Rap chart.

The streetwise, socially conscious album introduced listeners to members of the Gang Starr Foundation collective like Jeru the Damaja and Lil Dap. Reaching #65 on the *Billboard* 200 and #14 on the R&B chart, *Daily Operation* is considered to be one of the best hip-hop albums of the early '90s.

JUNE 9

Pete Rock & CL Smooth release their debut full-length album *Mecca and the Soul Brother* on Elektra.

The influential *Mecca and the Soul Brother*, mainly produced by the masterful Rock, spends eighty minutes covering diverse subject matter on spiritual, political, and criminal justice issues.

Reaching #43 on the *Billboard* 200 and #7 on the R&B chart, *Mecca and the Soul Brother* contained the hit singles "Lots of Lovin'," "Straighten It Out," and the classic "They Reminisce Over You (T.R.O.Y.)," an ode to dancer and friend Troy Dixon aka "Trouble T-Roy" of Heavy D & the Boyz, who was killed in an accidental fall while on tour in 1990 in Indiana. All of the singles reached the top ten on the Rap chart and the album would go on to be considered a classic.

JUNE 23

Eric B. & Rakim release their fourth and final album together as a group, *Don't Sweat the Technique*, on MCA.

Produced by the duo and Kerwin Young, the jazzier critically acclaimed album peaked at #22 on the *Billboard* 200 and #9 on the R&B chart. It contained the hits "Casualties of War," the title track, "What's on Your Mind" (featured on the soundtrack of the 1991 New Line Cinema film *House Party 2*), and "Know the Ledge," which was featured in the 1992 Paramount Pictures film *Juice.*

Tension about creating solo albums led to their breakup in 1992, making *Don't Sweat the Technique* their swan song.

JUNE 30

MC Ren of N.W.A releases his debut solo EP *Kizz My Black Azz* on Ruthless.

Ruthless and N.W.A founder Eazy-E was the executive producer of the album with knob-turning assistance by DJ Train, Bobby "Bobcat" Ervin, as well as MC Ren and the Torture Chamber.

Debuting at #12 on the *Billboard* 200 and #10 on the R&B chart, *Kizz My Black Azz* managed to miraculously attain platinum sales status with almost no radio airplay whatsoever. It contained the hit single "Final Frontier," which reached #80 on the R&B and #17 on the Rap charts.

PETE ROCK & CL SMOOTH

JULY 1992

EPMD release their fourth album *Business Never Personal* on Def Jam.

Produced by Charlie Marotta, Mr. Bozack, the group's DJ Scratch, as well as EPMD, the gold-selling album continued the duo's tradition of sampling Zapp records. One example of this is the album's lead single, as well as the group's biggest hit, "Crossover," which hit #42 on the *Billboard* 100 and #1 on the Rap chart.

Das EFX guested on the album cut "Cummin' at Cha" and Redman and K-Solo appeared on the hit single "Head Banger," which reached #11 on the Rap chart.

AUGUST 25

MC Serch releases his only solo album *Return of the Product* on Def Jam.

MC Serch, a member of the New York hip-hop trio 3rd Bass, released his only solo album to critical acclaim, which reached #103 on the *Billboard* 200 and #28 on the R&B chart.

The album spawned the hit single "Back to the Grill," which topped the Rap chart and featured an early cameo from Nas, whom MC Serch had recently discovered. The song also hit #71 on the *Billboard* Hot 100 and #33 on the R&B chart and featured appearances from Red Hot Lover Tone and Chubb Rock.

SEPTEMBER 8

Bushwick Bill releases his debut *Little Big Man* on Rap-A-Lot.

Little Big Man, the debut solo album from Bushwick Bill of the Geto Boys, chronicles the 1991 shooting incident in which he lost an eye. The loss was depicted on the cover of the Geto Boys' 1991 album *We Can't Be Stopped.*

Reaching #32 on the *Billboard* 200, the album contained the single "Ever So Clear," a hip-hop hit that cracked the top fifty on the R&B chart and topped the Rap chart.

SEPTEMBER 14

Ice Cube releases the single "True to the Game" on Priority.

"True to the Game" is the final single from Cube's third solo album, the Nation of Islam–inspired, platinum-selling *Death Certificate*, released the previous year.

Produced by Sir Jinx and Cube, the song's lyrics called out those who betray their roots for the mainstream, while brilliantly sampling the Gap Band's 1982 hit "Outstanding."

SEPTEMBER 15

Public Enemy release their fifth album *Greatest Misses* on Def Jam.

Def Jam wanted to release a greatest hits compilation, which PE frontman Chuck D thought seemed premature after only five years of recording.

The gold-selling *Greatest Misses* instead became a collection of new songs, unreleased material, and remixes of previous hits and album tracks courtesy of Chuck Chillout, Sir Jinx, Damon "Dollars" Kelly, Jeff Trotter, Greg Beasley, Shy Skillz, and Jam Master Jay.

Greatest Misses also featured a live UK television performance of Pete Rock's remix to "Shut 'Em Down," as well as new tracks, like the hit single "Hazy Shade of Criminal." The collection reached #13 on the *Billboard* 200 and #10 on the R&B chart.

SEPTEMBER 22

Diamond D releases his debut *Stunts, Blunts and Hip-Hop* on Mercury.

The debut release from the Bronx-born hip-hop producer featured early cameos from Fat Joe and Big L, who were, alongside Diamond D, all members of the New York–based Diggin' in the Crates Crew (D.I.T.C.). The album also featured coproduction from Q-Tip, the 45 King, and Jazzy Jay, among others.

The album, which reached #47 on the R&B chart, spawned three singles: "Best-Kept Secret," "Sally Got a One Track Mind," and "What U Heard."

SEPTEMBER 22

Da Lench Mob release their debut album *Guerillas in tha Mist* on East West.

Produced by Ice Cube, the unrepentantly political gold-selling album from the trio of J-Dee, Shorty, T-Bone, and Maulkie spawned two singles "Guerillas in tha Mist" and "Freedom Got an A.K.," which hit #7 on the Rap chart. It reached #24 on the *Billboard* 200 and #4 on the R&B chart.

SEPTEMBER 22

Showbiz & A.G. release their debut album *Runaway Slave* on Payday.

The critically acclaimed, innovative set from the Bronx D.I.T.C. duo was mainly produced by Showbiz, with Diamond D working on two cuts. Guests include Big L, Dres, Diamond D, Lord Finesse, and DeShawn, as well as interlude appearances by artists such as Fat Joe and Freddie Foxxx. Reaching #78 on the R&B chart, the raw gangsta album spawned two singles: "Bounce ta This" and "Fat Pockets," which reached #8 and #15 on the Rap chart respectively.

OCTOBER 6

Common Sense releases his debut album *Can I Borrow a Dollar?* on Relativity.

The Chi-Town rapper, who would later drop the "Sense" from his name, worked with producers the Beatnuts, No I.D., and Twilite Tone on his debut. Common's witty wordplay and intellectual conscientious approach would establish him as part of the new wave of conscious hip-hop that would eventually include Mos Def, Talib Kweli, Pharoahe Monch, and the Roots.

The well-received album spawned three singles: "Take It EZ," "Breaker 1/9," and "Soul by the Pound," all of which reached the top ten on the Rap chart.

OCTOBER 6

Redman releases his debut album *Whut? Thee Album* on Def Jam.

The gold-selling debut by the famed New Jersey MC featured production by EPMD, Pete Rock, Mr. Bozack, and Redman. Debuting at #49 on the *Billboard* 200 and reaching #5 on the R&B chart, the fan favorite generated the hit singles "Tonight's Da Night," "Blow Your Mind," featuring Hurricane G, and "Time 4 Sum Aksion," the latter two topping the Rap chart.

OCTOBER 8

Mad Cobra releases the single "Flex" on Columbia.

The lead single off the Jamaican dancehall DJ's major label debut, *Hard to Wet, Easy to Dry*, is an atypically soft, melodic R&B-influenced song from Mad Cobra, whose previous dancehall hits had been more up-tempo and rhythmic.

"Flex" became one of the biggest crossover hits of the year, reaching the top twenty in the *Billboard* Hot 100 and top ten on the R&B chart. Mad Cobra was also the first reggae artist to top the Rap Singles chart. Reggae veterans Sly and Robbie performed on the track, which was based on the Temptations' "Just My Imagination."

OCTOBER 20

Grand Puba releases his solo debut *Reel to Reel* on Elektra.

Reel to Reel is Grand Puba's first solo album after the rapper spent time in late '80s/early '90s groups like Masters of Ceremony and Brand Nubian. The album peaked at #28 on the *Billboard* 200, spending fourteen weeks on the chart, and was #14 on the R&B chart.

The album's lead single, "360 Degrees (What Goes Around)," topped the Rap Singles chart and reached #68 on the *Billboard* Hot 100. The album's second single, "Check It Out," featured an early guest vocal performance from Mary J. Blige.

NOVEMBER 10

UGK release their debut *Too Hard to Swallow* on Jive.

The debut album filled with memorable rhymes from the Texas hip-hop duo of Pimp C and Bun B and sampled artists like Bill Withers, Rufus, and the Isley Brothers, reached #37 on the R&B chart.

Too Hard to Swallow contains tracks from the group's successful debut EP, *The Southern Way*, released in the spring of 1992. A couple months before the release of their debut album, UGK released an EP of songs that had been rejected by Jive Records for their major label debut due to profanity and offensiveness. The EP is appropriately titled *Banned*.

NOVEMBER 17

Ice Cube releases his fourth album *The Predator* on Priority.

Fresh off the LA riots, after four police officers were acquitted of savagely beating African-American motorist Rodney King, the grim album addressed police brutality, racism, and the changing ideological tide of black America. The message resonated, debuting at the top of both the *Billboard* 200 and the R&B chart and going on to be certified double platinum.

Produced by DJ Pooh, Torcha Chamba, Sir Jinx, DJ Muggs of Cypress Hill, and Cube, the influential album contained the classic singles "Wicked," featuring Don Jagwarr; "It Was a Good Day," which reached #15 on the *Billboard* Hot 100; and "Check Yo Self," featuring Das EFX. The album also featured Cube's manifesto about the LA riots called "We Had to Tear This Mothafucka Up."

NOVEMBER 24

Wreckx-N-Effect release *Hard or Smooth* on MCA Records.

The second album from the New York hip-hop group was their most commercially successful, reaching #9 on the *Billboard* 200 and #6 on the R&B chart and selling more than a million copies in its first two months.

The platinum-selling party album featured production and increased involvement from Teddy Riley, the new jack swing pioneer who had appeared on the group's debut record. *Hard or Smooth* was propelled up the charts by the crossover hit "Rump Shaker," which topped the Rap Singles chart and reached #2 on the *Billboard* Hot 100.

NOVEMBER 24

Kool G Rap & DJ Polo release their third and final album together as a duo, *Live and Let Die*, on Cold Chillin'.

Produced by Sir Jinx, Trackmasters, and Kool G Rap, the album included appearances by fellow Juice Crew member Big Daddy Kane on the track "#1 with a Bullet" and Geto Boys' Scarface and Bushwick Bill as well as Ice Cube on "Two to the Head." The hardcore underground classic includes the hit singles "On the Run" and "Ill Street Blues," which helped it break into the *Billboard* 200 and reach #18 on the R&B chart.

NOVEMBER 24

The Pharcyde release their debut album *Bizarre Ride II the Pharcyde* on Delicious Vinyl.

The LA-based quartet's eccentric debut is critically acclaimed for having continued to push the boundaries of subject matter in rap music, much like their East Coast contemporaries in the Native Tongue Posse.

Group member and Delicious Vinyl house producer J-Swift produced the jazzy and inventive gold-selling album, which spawned the hits "Otha Fish" and the chart-topping "Passin' Me By," and reached #75 on the *Billboard* 200 and #23 on the R&B chart.

THE PHARCYDE

DECEMBER 15

Dr. Dre releases his debut solo album *The Chronic* on Suge Knight's new label, Death Row Records.

The Chronic's '70s funk samples, heavily laden with Moog synthesizers, and laid-back delivery helped to define the new West Coast G-funk sound and style that would come to dominate hip-hop album sales. The triple-platinum album featured appearances by Tha Dogg Pound, RBX, Lady of Rage, and made a star of Snoop Doggy Dogg.

Hit singles on the multi-platinum album included the Grammy Award–winning "Let Me Ride," "Dre Day," and the classic "Nuthin' But a G Thang." Considered one of the most influential hip-hop albums ever, *The Chronic* reached #3 on the *Billboard* 200 and topped the R&B chart.

CHUCK D:

I met Dre in 1987. As DJ and head of N.W.A and the Posse, he was the dude who made all the dope mixtapes for the swap meets out west. It was hard to find all these twelve-inch rap hits on cassette tapes. From that alone I knew the dude was gonna blow out. We played shows together and one day I handed Dre and Eazy-E our *Takes a Nation* record backstage at a Las Vegas concert. The next year *Straight Outta Compton* emerged and it was no doubt there was no looking back because the Doctor was a sonic sponge and more. This is all before 1990. Y'all know the rest of the story. What you don't know that the brother deep down has always been a nice guy.

1993

JANUARY 12

Heavy D & the Boyz release *Blue Funk* on Uptown.

The gold-selling fourth album from the likable New York group reached #40 on the *Billboard* 200 and #7 on the R&B chart.

Well produced by Tony Dofat, DJ Premier, Pete Rock, and Jesse West, the album featured guest appearances from Busta Rhymes, Gang Starr, and most notably, the Notorious B.I.G., whose appearance on the album-closing "A Buncha Niggas" was his debut recording for Uptown Records, where Puff Daddy was an A&R executive.

JANUARY 19

Oakland rapper Seagram releases his debut album *The Dark Roads* on Rap-A-Lot.

The Oaktown MC's first set, which included guest appearances from label mates Geto Boys and Ganksta N-I-P, reached #74 on the R&B chart.

The album produced the cult-favorite single "The Vill" as well as the album cut "Straight Mobbin'," which was the first hip-hop track to utilize the "-izzle" slang started by rappers like E-40 and later popularized by Snoop Dogg.

FEBRUARY 2

Brand Nubian release their sophomore album *In God We Trust* on Elektra.

With Grand Puba and DJ Alamo having left the group, Brand Nubian now consisted of original members Sadat X and Lord Jamar with DJ Sincere replacing Alamo. They produced the album along with Diamond D with contributions by Raphael and Sting International, which reached #12 on the *Billboard* 200 and #4 on the R&B chart.

The group's central theme continued to be the teachings of the Nation of God and Earth as evidenced on tracks like, "Meaning of the 5%," "Ain't No Mystery," "Allah & Justice," "Black Star Line," and the single "Allah U Akbar." *In God We Trust* also produced the classic hit singles "Love Me or Leave Me Alone" and the controversial "Punks Jump Up to Get Beat Down," which reached #77 on the *Billboard* Hot 100 and #2 on the Rap chart.

FEBRUARY 2

Young Black Teenagers release their second and final album *Dead Enz Kidz Doin' Lifetime Bidz* on MCA.

Produced by the Bomb Squad, with contributions from group member Kamron as well as the legendary Grandmaster Flash, the album spawned the hit single "Roll with the Flavor" and the classic "Tap the Bottle" produced by Public Enemy's Terminator X, which reached #55 on the *Billboard* Hot 100.

FEBRUARY 4

Lords of the Underground release the hit single "Funky Child" on Pendulum.

Produced by K-Def and the legendary Marley Marl, "Funky Child" was the second single from the New Jersey group's popular debut album *Here Come the Lords*, released the same year. The song reached #74 on the *Billboard* Hot 100, #52 on the R&B chart, and #2 on the Rap chart.

FEBRUARY 9

Digable Planets release their debut album *Reachin' (A New Refutation of Time and Space)* on Elektra.

Produced by group member Butterfly, the mellow gold-selling album is heavily sample laden with strong jazz and funk influences, as evidenced on the group's smash hit "Rebirth of Slick (Cool Like Dat)," which reached #15 on the *Billboard* Hot 100 and topped the Rap chart.

Peaking at #15 on the *Billboard* 200, *Reachin'* was peppered with Five-Percent theology, black consciousness, and new rhyme flows, giving it a unique and original sound that earned the group a Grammy for best new duo or group.

CHUCK D:
Digable Planets is a group that is far ahead of their time. The combination of MCs was right and made for the future. Yes, they won a Grammy in the '90s, but there is no reason why DP, with their skills, ability, choice of music, and their lineup appeal can't continue to make music until 2050. I long for that. Their group was purely millennial before the millennium even happened. Their music spits truth—to soul—to power.

FEBRUARY 16

Kam releases his debut album *Neva Again* on Street Knowledge.

The socially conscious debut album from Ice Cube's cousin was politically charged and influenced by the LA rapper's belief in the Nation of Islam. Ice Cube appeared on the track "Watts Riot."

Reaching #18 on the R&B chart, the album featured production by DJ Pooh, T-Bone, Mr. Woody, Chris Charity, and Stan Jones.

FEBRUARY 16

2Pac releases his second solo album *Strictly 4 My N.I.G.G.A.Z...* on Interscope.

Loaded with political and socially conscious content, the thoughtful album debuted at #24 on the *Billboard* 200 and has since been certified double platinum.

The album contained singles with deep introspective lyrics like "Keep Ya Head Up," featuring Dave Hollister, "Papa'z Song," "Holler If Ya Hear Me," and "I Get Around," all of which charted on the *Billboard* Hot 100, R&B, and Rap charts.

Guests on the set included Ice-T, Ice Cube, Deadly Threat, Live Squad, Treach of Naughty By Nature, Apache, Wycked, and Poppi, as well as Shock G and Money-B of Digital Underground.

THE BEATNUTS

FEBRUARY 23

Ice Cube releases the hit single "It Was a Good Day" on Priority.

"It Was a Good Day" is the gold-selling fourth single from Ice Cube's *The Predator*. The laid-back chart-topper was produced by DJ Pooh and reached #15 on the *Billboard* Hot 100.

FEBRUARY 23

Naughty By Nature release their third album *19 Naughty III* on Tommy Boy.

Reaching #3 on the *Billboard* Hot 100, the accessible, platinum-selling album featured guest appearances by Freddie Foxxx and Heavy D. It spawned the hits "Written on Ya Kitten," "It's On," and the R&B chart-topping "Hip Hop Hooray," the video which was directed by Spike Lee.

MARCH 12

Universal Pictures releases the hip-hop satirical film *CB4* in US theaters.

Written by Chris Rock and Nelson George, the film, loosely based on N.W.A, starred Chris Rock, Theresa Randle, Allen Payne, Chris Elliott, and Charlie Murphy, with a cameo by Flavor Flav.

The film, directed by Tamra Davis, also had cameo appearances by N.W.A founder Eazy-E and former member Ice Cube.

The soundtrack, released on MCA Records, featured songs by Public Enemy, KRS-One, P.M. Dawn, and MC Ren of N.W.A and reached #41 on the *Billboard* 200 and #13 on the R&B chart.

MARCH 23

Ice-T releases *Home Invasion* on Rhyme Syndicate.

Produced in the wake of the controversy surrounding his 1992 Body Count single "Cop Killer," Ice-T's fifth solo album was released on his own label. He parted ways with Sire after it had tried to censor and delay the release of the record due to lyrical content.

The album's famous cover art of a white listener surrounded by violence was designed by legendary hip-hop artist Dave Halili. *Home Invasion* spent eleven weeks on the *Billboard* 200, peaking at #14.

APRIL 6

The Beatnuts make their recording debut with the EP *Intoxicated Demons* on Relativity.

Self-produced by the three-man Latino crew of Psycho Les, Fashion, and JuJu, the album was lauded for their creative use of sampling, musical versatility, and raunchy sense of humor so often missing in modern hip-hop at that time.

Peaking at #50 on the R&B chart, the well-reviewed album featured the singles "Reign of the Tec" and "No Equal."

APRIL 15

95 South release their debut album *Quad City Knock* on Wrap.

The Miami bass duo from Jacksonville, Florida, was comprised of AB and Daddy Black. They had their career peak on *Quad City Knock*, which reached #71 on the *Billboard* 200.

Produced by C.C. Lemonhead and Jayski McGowan, the album sales were driven by the monster hit "Whoot! There It Is," which reached #11 on the *Billboard* Hot 100 and #7 on the R&B chart.

That same year, fellow Miami bass duo Tag Team put out the similar sounding "Whoomp! (There It Is)," on Life Records. This prompted a duel in 1993 on *The Arsenio Hall Show*, with 95 South winning the better song by call-in votes.

APRIL 23

***Who's the Man?* is released by New Line Cinema.**

The action-comedy featured *Yo! MTV Raps* hosts Doctor Dré and Ed Lover as bumbling police rookies. Appearances from a slew of hip-hop artists, including Kris Kross, Bushwick Bill, Busta Rhymes, Queen Latifah, Ice-T, and KRS-One, helped drive viewers to theaters.

The movie's soundtrack, featuring songs by the Notorious B.I.G., House of Pain, Mary J. Blige, and Pete Rock & CL Smooth, cracked the top forty of the *Billboard* 200, peaking at #32, and made it to #8 on the R&B chart.

MAY 4

Run-D.M.C. release their sixth album *Down with the King* on Profile.

Featuring production by the Bomb Squad, Pete Rock, Jermaine Dupri, Daniel Shulman, Q-Tip, and EPMD, who also appeared on the album, *Down with the King* peaked at #7 on the *Billboard* 200 and topped the R&B chart.

Showcasing their evolving style, this innovative album boasted guest spots by reggae star Mad Cobra and Rage Against the Machine guitarist Tom Morello. Singles include the gold-certified title track, which reached #21 on the *Billboard* Hot 100 and topped the Rap chart.

MAY 11

Onyx release their hit "Slam" on Def Jam.

"Slam," the second single from the group's platinum-selling debut album, *Bacdafucup*, was produced by Chyskillz and Jam Master Jay, who was responsible with getting the South Jamaica, Queens, group a deal with Def Jam.

The raucous song reached #4 on the *Billboard* Hot 100 and topped the Rap chart, as their first single "Throw Ya Gunz" had as well. A remix of the track with Brooklyn heavy metal band Biohazard was released shortly after. "Slam" was certified platinum three months after its release.

MAY 19

The Roots self-release their debut album *Organix.*

The Philly hip-hop band consisted at the time of drummer Ahmir "?uestlove" Thompson, lead vocalist Black Thought, bassist Leonard "Hub" Hubbard, keyboardist and future superstar producer Scott Storch, and MCs Malik B. and Kid Crumbs. Cut to sell on their European tour, their debut included fan favorites "Pass the Popcorn," "The Session (Longest Posse Cut in History, 12:43)," and "I'm Out Deah."

Organix eventually created a buzz for the Roots, who were courted by major labels before eventually signing with Geffen Records. It would later be rereleased in 1998 on Cargo Records.

MAY 26

Jive Records releases the soundtrack to the New Line Cinema film *Menace II Society*.

Directed by Albert and Allen Hughes, the gritty crime drama depicted life on the street in South Central Los Angeles. Among the artists included on the R&B chart–topping soundtrack were Boogie Down Productions, Brand Nubian, Da Lench Mob, Too $hort, Pete Rock & CL Smooth, Ant Banks, and UGK.

Reaching #11 on the *Billboard* 200, the platinum-selling soundtrack to the acclaimed movie spawned two hit singles: "Trigga Gots No Heart" by Spice 1 and "Streiht Up Menace" by MC Eiht, who also appears in the film.

MAY 27

MC Lyte releases the hit "Ruffneck" on Atlantic.

The gold-selling song became Lyte's first top forty single, peaking at #35 on the *Billboard* Hot 100, while also becoming her fourth of five singles to reach the #1 spot on the Rap chart.

Produced by Wreckx-N-Effect, the rugged lead song off Lyte's fourth hardcore album *Ain't No Other* was nominated for a Grammy Award.

JUNE 5

Reverend Calvin Butts steamrolls rap CDs and cassettes to protest their lyrics.

Reverend Butts, of the historical Abyssinian Baptist Church in Harlem, New York, rented a small steamroller for a demonstration to destroy rap CDs and cassettes he found offensive and lewd.

However, his demolition protest came to an abrupt end when, after only crushing a few cassettes, protesters stood in front of the rest of the recorded hip-hop material in a counterprotest.

JUNE 22

Yo-Yo releases her third album *You Better Ask Somebody* on East West.

Featuring production by QDIII, Laylaw, the Baker Boys, Tootie, Mr. Woody, Derrick McDowell, and Ice Cube, Yo-Yo's third album reached #21 on the R&B charts.

You Better Ask Somebody spawned the hit singles "West Side Story" and "The Bonnie and Clyde Theme," which featured Ice Cube and topped the Rap chart.

JULY 13

Milwaukee's Gumbo release their debut album, *Droppin' Soulful H20 On the Fiber,* on Chrysalis.

Gumbo were a part of Arrested Development's Life Music musical clique headed by AD leader Speech, who also produced Gumbo's debut set.

With a harder and sparer sound than AD, this intriguing debut produced cult favorites including "Soldier Boy," "No Need 2 Run Anymore," "The Boat," and the haunting "Basement Music," featuring singer Paulette Clark.

JULY 13

Ice Cube releases the hit single "Check Yo Self," on Priority.

From the album *The Predator*, "Check Yo Self" featured Das EFX and went straight to the top of the R&B and Rap charts, reaching #20 on the *Billboard* Hot 100. A remix was also released utilizing the beat from the classic 1982 Grandmaster Flash & the Furious Five classic hit "The Message."

The platinum-selling single, produced by DJ Muggs and Cube, would be remade in 2010 by Cube featuring Chuck D of Public Enemy.

JULY 20

Cypress Hill release their sophomore album *Black Sunday* on Ruffhouse.

Debuting at #1 on the *Billboard* 200, the multi-platinum album contained the group's crossover smash hit "Insane in the Brain," which garnered the group a huge cult following among rock audiences.

Produced by the group's DJ Muggs along with T-Ray, the accessible album produced a number of singles, including the hit "I Ain't Goin' Out Like That," which was nominated for a Grammy.

CHUCK D:
The fact that B-Real Sen Dog and DJ Muggs formed Cypress Hill as a Public Enemy in vocal reverse is evident. The earth was opened wide by the *High Times* shaman's beliefs, songs, and the connected salute to the Latino planet—previously undertapped. I was amazed nightly while touring on Smokin' Grooves with them in 1998. Fast-forward and I'm still amazed as Cypress travels the globe twenty-five-plus years just as PE does. And I get to perform with the great B-Real on a nightly basis as lead MC of Prophets of Rage. Still amazed. Go figure.

JULY 27

DMG releases his debut album *Rigormortiz* on Rap-A-Lot.

The hardcore debut by the Latino rapper was produced by Mike Dean, Big Chief, John Bido, N.O. Joe, and Scarface, who discovered the Minnesota native after meeting him at a concert where he was performing.

Reaching #40 on the R&B chart, it featured guest appearances from Mr. 3-2, 5th Ward Boyz, 2 Low, as well as Bushwick Bill, Big Mike, and Scarface of the Geto Boys.

JULY 27

Fat Joe da Gangsta releases his debut album *Represent* on Relativity.

Reaching #46 on the R&B chart, producers included members of Fat Joe's D.I.T.C. collective including Diamond D, Lord Finesse, and Showbiz.

Grand Puba of Brand Nubian, King Sun, and Kool G Rap all make guest appearances on the album. The single "Flow Joe" topped the Rap chart and reached #89 on the *Billboard* Hot 100.

AUGUST 17

Eightball & MJG release their debut *Comin' Out Hard* on Suave House.

The debut label-release from the Memphis hip-hop duo spent a total of fifty-nine weeks on the R&B chart, peaking at #40. The album was released by Tony Draper, who had founded the upstart Houston-based label Suave House Records three years earlier.

A landmark in southern rap, the pioneering record inspired an entire generation of Memphis and southern rappers including Yo Gotti, Don Trip, and Young Dolph.

SEPTEMBER 14

Poor Righteous Teachers release their third album *Black Business* on Profile.

Produced by Poor Righteous Teachers and Tony D, the thoughtful album cracked the *Billboard* 200 and reached #29 on the R&B chart.

Continuing PRT's philosophy of positive community involvement, black awareness, and Five-Percent teachings, it spawned the hit single "Nobody Move," which hit #98 on the R&B chart.

SEPTEMBER 14

The soundtrack to the movie *Judgment Night* is released on Epic.

Produced by Happy Walters, the genre-defying album, a collection of eleven collaborations between rock and hip-hop artists, reached #17 of the *Billboard* 200.

Some of the more high-profile collaborations on the album included Slayer and Ice-T ("Disorder"), Pearl Jam and Cypress Hill ("Real Thing"), and Living Colour and Run-D.M.C. ("Me, Myself & My Microphone").

The album spawned four singles: "Judgment Night" by Onyx and Biohazard, "Just Another Victim" by Helmet and House of Pain, "Another Body Murdered" by Faith No More and Boo-Yaa T.R.I.B.E., and "Fallin" by Teenage Fanclub and De La Soul.

OCTOBER 12

Salt-N-Pepa release their fourth album *Very Necessary* on Next Plateau.

Produced by Hurby "Luv Bug" Azor and Salt, the multi-platinum juggernaut from the all-female rap crew spent eighty-nine weeks on the *Billboard* 200, peaking at #4, and went to #6 on the R&B chart.

Sales were driven by the dance-oriented and sexy singles, including "Shoop," which reached #4 on the *Billboard* Hot 100, and "Whatta Man," which featured En Vogue and peaked at #3. "None of Your Business," #32 on the *Billboard* Hot 100, won the Grammy for best rap performance.

CHUCK D:
Salt-N-Pepa and Spinderella are absolute best that there is in show. Of any other individual or group, they can still mash out a performance in a crowd—to this very day. SNP build their whole thing alongside Run-D.M.C. They utilized Run-D.M.C.'s template to evolve later on. When they started getting into spitting from a liberated woman's point of view, it solidified an area men couldn't get close to coming across in. These women are still underrated and have never gotten the credit due because they have climbed twice as many mountains as the average rapper just dealing with motherhood and sexism. Not to mention being able to close out a stage full of males without showing anything and still exuding so much sexuality. They were far ahead of their time and probably the strongest examples of how women can team up and go much further than even males.

What is underrated about their album is their song tradeoffs and their distinct voices are still is better than any male has ever done it. They don't get enough credit for that. To me, all their records are greatest hits.

SALT-N-PEPA

OCTOBER 19

Erick Sermon of EPMD releases his debut solo album *No Pressure* on Def Jam.

Sermon's first solo set showcases his masterful production skills. Featuring guest appearances by Ice Cube, Kam, Keith Murray, Shadz of Lingo, Soup, Redman, and Joe Sinistr, the album reached #16 on the *Billboard* 200 and #2 on the R&B chart.

Like previous EPMD records, Sermon's solo offering featured plenty of funky Zapp samples like on one of the album's hit singles "Stay Real," which topped the Rap charts and cracked the *Billboard* Hot 100.

OCTOBER 19

Black Moon release their debut set *Enta Da Stage* on Nervous.

Reaching #33 on the R&B chart, the debut by the East Coast group featured the singles "Who Got da Props?" and "I Got Cha Opin," both of which cracked the *Billboard* Hot 100 and reached #60 and #55 on the R&B chart respectively.

Produced by the group's Buckshot with DJ Evil Dee and Mr. Walt of Da Beatminerz, the ferocious album included the debut of Smif-N-Wessun and appearances by Havoc of Mobb Deep and Dru-Ha, the cofounder of Duck Down Music.

OCTOBER 19

Eazy-E releases his second EP *It's On (Dr. Dre) 187um Killa* on Ruthless.

The N.W.A founder's third solo release, following his full-length album debut, *Eazy-Duz-It* (released in 1988) and his first EP *5150: Home 4 tha Sick* (released in 1992), reached #5 on the *Billboard* 200 and topped the R&B chart.

Produced by DJ Yella of N.W.A, Rhythm D, Cold 187um, Madness 4 Real, and Dr. Jam, the multi-platinum EP featured the smash hits "Real Muthaphuckkin G's," which reached #45 on the *Billboard* Hot 100, and "Any Last Werdz," featuring Kokane and Cold 187um, which reached #69 on the R&B and #5 on the Rap charts.

A response to Dr. Dre's *The Chronic, It's On (Dr. Dre) 187um Killa* would be Eazy-E's last album released before his untimely death in 1995, when he succumbed to the AIDS virus.

NOVEMBER 9

A Tribe Called Quest release their third album *Midnight Marauders* on Jive.

The platinum-selling set is considered one of the Tribe's finest works ever, reaching #8 on the *Billboard* 200 and #1 on the R&B chart. The smart, funky album's chart-topping favorites included "Oh My God," featuring Busta Rhymes, "Electric Relaxation," and the smash "Award Tour," which featured Trugoy the Dove of De La Soul and was their highest-charting single ever, reaching #47 on the *Billboard* Hot 100 and topping the Rap chart.

Self-produced with Skeff Anselm and Large Professor, the album's classic cover featured photos of more than seventy of the biggest names in hip-hop such as Kool DJ Red Alert, Ice-T, the late, great Heavy D, Jazzy Jay, Kool Moe Dee, the Rock Steady Crew, Too $hort, MC Lyte, Kid Capri, Grandmaster Flash, Dr. Dre, DJ Jazzy Joyce, Daddy-O of Stetsasonic, the Beastie Boys, Afrika Bambaataa, and Chuck D, as well as several others.

NOVEMBER 1993

Domino releases the single "Getto Jam" on Outburst.

The lead single on the Long Beach rapper's self-titled debut album, the gold-selling single, which sampled Sly & the Family Stone's "Sing a Simple Song," peaked at #7 on the *Billboard* Hot 100, #4 on the R&B chart, and topped the Rap chart.

NOVEMBER 9

Wu-Tang Clan release their debut album *Enter the Wu-Tang (36 Chambers)* on Loud.

The raw, menacing sound of the Staten Island nine-member crew—RZA, GZA, Ol' Dirty Bastard, Method Man, Raekwon the Chef, Ghostface Killah, U-God, Inspectah Deck, and Masta Killa—featured explicit and often humorous lyrics steeped in martial arts,

Five-Percent philosophy, and urban life over gritty minimalist beats.

Both critically acclaimed and commercially successful, the platinum-selling debut set, mainly produced by RZA, featured bona fide classics like "C.R.E.A.M.," "Protect Ya Neck," "Wu-Tang Clan Ain't Nuthing ta Fuck Wit," "Can It All Be So Simple," and "Method Man." Considered one of the most influential albums in hip-hop history, the album spent forty-three weeks on the *Billboard* 200, peaking at #41, and spent 140 weeks on the R&B chart, peaking at #8.

NOVEMBER 10

E-40 releases *Federal* on his own Sick Wid It label.

Produced by Studio Ton and featuring guest appearances from longtime collaborators like Mugzi, Kaveo, and E-40's cousin B-Legit, *Federal* established E-40 as one of the most influential Bay Area rappers. The gangsta album was deeply indebted to funk, sampling artists like Isaac Hayes and Cameo.

A year after its release E-40 signed with Jive Records, which rereleased the album and his catalog to date in 1995.

NOVEMBER 16

Das EFX release their sophomore album *Straight Up Sewaside* on East West.

Produced by the band as well as PMD, Solid Scheme, and Charlie Marotta, the gold-selling album reached #20 on the *Billboard* 200 and #6 on the R&B chart.

Employing a different style than their debut, the album contained the hit singles "Baknaffek" and "Freakit," which topped the charts and reached #6 on the Rap chart.

NOVEMBER 16

MC Ren releases his debut album *Shock of the Hour* on Ruthless.

Heavily influenced by speeches by Minister Louis Farrakhan of the Nation of Islam, the album by the former N.W.A member had a socially conscious and political theme throughout.

Produced by Rhythm D and DJ Train with N.W.A founder Eazy-E serving as the album's executive producer, the album topped the R&B chart and reached #22 on the *Billboard* 200. It spawned the singles "Fuck What Ya Heard," "Mayday on the Frontline," and "Same Ol' Shit," which cracked the *Billboard* Hot 100.

NOVEMBER 16

Queen Latifah releases her third album *Black Reign* on Motown.

Produced by Kay Gee of Naughty By Nature, Tony Dofat, Sidney "S.I.D." Reynolds, and Queen Latifah, the gold-selling set marked her move to Motown and reached #60 on the *Billboard* 200 and #15 on the R&B chart.

Black Reign contained the singles "Black Hand Side," "Weekend Love," featuring Tony Rebel, "Just Another Day," "Rough...," featuring Heavy D & the Boyz, Treach of Naughty By Nature, and KRS-One, and the anti-misogyny anthem "U.N.I.T.Y.," which hit the top ten on the R&B chart and won the Grammy for best rap solo performance.

NOVEMBER 23

Snoop Doggy Dogg releases his debut solo album *Doggystyle* on Death Row.

Debuting at #1 on the *Billboard* 200, the much-anticipated debut helped define West Coast rap. Buoyed by his star-making turn on Dr. Dre's *The Chronic*, Snoop's multi-platinum *Doggystyle* sold nearly a million copies in the US alone in the first week of its release and stayed on the chart for seventy-four weeks. The G-funk classic contained such smash hit singles as the Grammy-nominated gold record "Gin and Juice," featuring Daz Dillinger and David Ruffin Jr.; "Doggy Dogg World," which featured the Dramatics, Tha Dogg Pound, and Nanci Fletcher and reached #46 on the *Billboard* Hot 100; and "What's My Name?," which reached #9 on the *Billboard* Hot 100.

The album, produced entirely by Dr. Dre, also featured guest appearances by the Lady of Rage, Ricky Harris, Lil' Malik, Hug, Warren G, Nate Dogg, Jewell, Tony Green, RBX, and the D.O.C.

CHUCK D:

Dre changed the pace of the rap record game by slowing everything down to the speed of an electric worm. The perfect voice and style was Snoop Doggy Dogg, who was introduced via the *Deep Cover* "187" film track. Hit 'em hard then smoove 'em out. By the time of "Nuthin' But a G Thang," it was the surrounding tempo and Snoop could handle it with a little rap singing, plus influence beyond that. Still not afraid to take chances, the man is an *overstood* ambassador and brand.

DECEMBER 7

Ice Cube releases his fourth album *Lethal Injection* on Priority.

Influenced by the success of the new West Coast gangsta style, Ice Cube brought in producers QDIII, son of legendary producer Quincy Jones, and Madness 4 Real to bring a whole new sound to his music. Other producers on the album included Derrick McDowell, Laylaw, Brian G, 88 X Unit, as well as longtime producer Sir Jinx.

Debuting at #5 on the *Billboard* 200 and topping the R&B chart, the album was less provocative than previous releases. Guests include Dr. Khalid Muhammad, K-Dee, and George Clinton on the P-Funk inspired hit single "Bop Gun (One Nation)," which is based on the Funkadelic 1978 hit "One Nation Under a Groove." Other singles on the album included "Really Doe" and "You Know How We Do It." All three hit the top ten on the Rap chart.

SNOOP DOGGY DOGG

1994

JANUARY 31

Wu-Tang Clan release the hit single "C.R.E.A.M." on Loud.

"C.R.E.A.M." (an acronym for "Cash Rules Everything Around Me," the song's chorus) was from the Wu's debut album *Enter the Wu-Tang (36 Chambers)*. It reached #60 on the *Billboard* Hot 100, #32 on the R&B chart, making it one of their highest charting singles.

Produced by RZA, the classic track featured Method Man on the chorus with verses from Inspectah Deck and Raekwon, who told *This Day in Hip-Hop and Rap History*, that his verse on the classic gold-selling single was the best he had ever written.

FEBRUARY 1

Odd Squad release *Fadanuf Fa Erybody!!* on Rap-A-Lot.

The Houston hip-hop trio of Devin the Dude, Jugg Mugg, and Rob Quest, known today as the Coughee Brothaz, released just one album during their brief existence.

Featuring production from a slew of Southern hip-hop luminaries, including Mike Dean and N.O. Joe, the cult classic still sounds like a party.

FEBRUARY 1

The Fugees release their debut album *Blunted on Reality* on Ruffhouse.

Originally named Tranzlator Crew, the trio of Lauryn Hill, Pras, and Wyclef Jean, meshed hip-hop with reggae and pop, fueled by Five-Percent teachings and Rastafarian rhetoric. Powered by the soulful vocals and rhymes of Hill combined with the unique rhyme style of Wyclef Jean and Pras, the album spawned the hit "Nappy Heads," which reached #49 on the *Billboard* Hot 100 and fan favorites "Boof Baf" and "Vocab."

Blunted on Reality, which reached #62 on the *Billboard* 200, was produced by the Fugees along with Salaam Remi, Rashad Muhammad, Stephen Walker, Brand X, and Khalis Bayyan aka Ronald "Kool" Bell of Kool & the Gang.

FEBRUARY 9

France's MC Solaar releases his sophomore album *Prose Combat* on Cohiba.

Jimmy Jay produced the second set by the Senegalese MC, who was fresh off his appearance on Guru's *Jazzamataz* project. The gold-selling album filled with fluid rhymes topped the charts in twenty countries, reaching #5 on the World Album charts.

MARCH 1

Hammer releases his fifth album *The Funky Headhunter* on Giant.

The platinum-selling set, which reached #12 on the *Billboard* 200 and #2 on the R&B chart, featured production by Teddy Riley, the Whole 9, Stefan Adamek, the Hines Brothers, and G-Bomb.

More aggressive than his previous sets, *The Funky Headhunter* album featured Tha Dogg Pound on the track "Sleepin' on a Master Plan." Hit singles from the album included, "It's All Good," and the Riley-produced "Pumps and a Bump," whose controversial music video also included an appearance by legendary football star Deion "Prime Time" Sanders.

MARCH 8

Gang Starr release their fourth album *Hard to Earn* on Chrysalis.

Peaking at #25 on the *Billboard* 200 and #2 on the R&B chart, the self-produced album contained the classic singles "Code of the Streets," "Mass Appeal," and "DWYCK," featuring Nice & Smooth, all of which charted in the top forty on the Rap chart. Other guests on the hit album include Nas, MC Eiht, Jeru the Damaja, duo Group Home (Lil Dap and Melachi the Nutcracker), and Big Shug.

MARCH 22

Main Source release their second *Fuck What You Think* on Wild Pitch.

In the wake of the departure of Large Professor, DJ and producers Sir Scratch and K-Cut replaced him with MC Mikey D. They were joined on the album by Jadakiss and Sheek Louch as well as by Kool G. Rap's wife Shaqueen on the track "Set It Off," where the posse would be billed as the Dog Pack.

Fuck What You Think contained the single "What You Need," which reached #48 on the Rap chart. The group never produced another album.

APRIL 5

Virginia's Down South release the album *Lost in Brooklyn* on Big Beat.

The three-man crew of Soda Pop, Shawn J, and Myorr brought a southern, soulful approach to hip-hop on *Lost in Brooklyn*, which featured production by the Beatnuts, Stretch Armstrong, and T-Ray as well as the group's Shawn J. Playing on the urban-rural differences, the horn-heavy album was divided into a South side and a North side, and spawned the fan favorite "Southern Comfort." Shawn J would go on to be a successful producer working with Black Star, Da Bush Babees, and others.

APRIL 19

Nas releases his landmark debut album *Illmatic* on Columbia.

Nas's penchant for creative lyrical storytelling of his inner-city life, as well as confident and articulate flow, would make this a highly anticipated debut. It lived up to the hype, garnering universal acclaim. The legendary first set by the Queensbridge MC featured masterful production by Large Professor, Pete Rock, L.E.S., Q-Tip of A Tribe Called Quest, and DJ Premier.

Debuting at #12 on the *Billboard* 200 and peaking at #2 on the R&B chart, the platinum-selling set contained now-classic singles like "One Love," "It Ain't Hard to Tell," which hit the *Billboard* Hot 100, "Life's a Bitch" (featuring AZ), "Halftime," and "The World Is Yours." Other fan favorite cuts like "N.Y. State of Mind," "One Time 4 Your Mind," and "Represent" quickly propelled *Illmatic* and Nas to icon status.

CHUCK D:
Few folks know I lived in Queensbridge Projects up to the age of three years old. I say this because it has been a Hip-Hop Hive. Marley Marl, MC Shan, Roxanne Shanté, Cormega, et cetera. Nas was peeped by MC Serch of 3rd Bass and Faith Newman. From there Nas started his legend. Always deeper and warmly complex than most MCs. His *Illmatic* is Marvin Gaye's *What's Going On*—1994 for real. Nas takes conscious chances. He's jazz blues and word-soul all at once. It's good for the game to have such a high champion that takes this craft very seriously.

APRIL 19

Shyheim releases his debut album *AKA The Rugged Child* on Virgin.

A cousin of Wu-Tang Clan member Ghostface Killah, Shyheim was only fourteen years old when he released his debut, which peaked at #52 on the *Billboard* 200 and #7 on the R&B chart.

The RZA produced the track "Little Rascals," with all others being produced by RNS, including the hit single "On and On," which hit the *Billboard* Hot 100. Guests on *AKA The Rugged Child* included Rubbabandz, Pop Da Brown Hornet, Down Low Recka, June Luva, K-Tez, Quasi, and Prophet.

APRIL 26

Outkast release their debut album *Southernplayalisticadillacmuzik* on LaFace.

The bold and innovative set by the famed Atlanta duo, produced by the funky production team Organized Noize, was highly anticipated in the wake of the success of their first gold-selling, chart-topping single, "Player's Ball," which was released in November 1993.

The set's fresh and unique sound was influenced by multiple sources such as P-Funk, Prince, Sly & the Family Stone, and hip-hop from Houston's Rap-A-Lot label. Spending twenty-six weeks on the *Billboard* 200, peaking at #20, the platinum-selling debut

NAS

spawned the hit single title track as well as "Git Up, Git Out" and featured guest appearances by fellow ATL crew and posse partners Goodie Mob.

APRIL 28

Warren G releases the hit "Regulate" on Death Row.

The classic G-Funk single, featuring Nate Dogg on the unforgettable hook, was released as a single on Death Row from the soundtrack to the 1994 New Line Cinema basketball drama *Above the Rim*. Certified platinum, the single would be released again with Warren G's debut album *Regulate...G Funk Era* with Def Jam.

The Grammy-nominated rap chart topper, which reached #2 on the *Billboard* Hot 100 and #7 on the R&B chart, was nominated for both Grammy and MTV Movie awards.

MAY 10

LA's South Central Cartel release their sophomore album *'N Gatz We Truss* on Def Jam.

Peaking at #32 on the *Billboard* 200 and #4 on the R&B chart, the successful album spawned the hit single "Gang Stories," featuring Big Mike of the Geto Boys and Tre Duce and fan favorites "Servin' 'Em Heat," "Seventeen Switches," and "It's a S.C.C. Thang," featuring the Chi-Lites. Other guests on the album include 2Pac and Ice-T.

MAY 17

Tha Mexakinz release their debut album *Zig Zag* on Motown.

The debut of the duo from Long Beach, California, was produced by QDIII, Bird, Mo, Intellek, and group member Sinful, and spawned the singles "Extaseason" and "Phonkie Melodia."

MAY 24

Heavy D & the Boyz release their final album *Nuttin' But Love* on Uptown.

Produced by all-stars DJ Eddie F, Teddy Riley, Marley Marl, Erick Sermon, Kid Capri, Easy Mo Bee, the Trackmasters, and Pete Rock, the slick platinum-selling album reached #11 on the *Billboard* 200 and topped the R&B chart.

Singles from the album included "Nuttin' but Love," "Got Me Waiting," "Black Coffee," and "Sex wit You," all of which reached the charts.

MAY 24

Jeru the Damaja releases his debut album *The Sun Rises in the East* on PayDay.

With masterful production by Gang Starr's DJ Premier, the acclaimed debut of the East Coast rapper, which combined Five-Percent and Rasta doctrine with witty rhymes, reached #36 on the *Billboard* 200 and #5 on the R&B chart. *The Sun Rises in the East* produced the classic hits "Come Clean," which broke into the *Billboard* Hot 100, "D. Original," and "You Can't Stop the Prophet." Fellow Gang Starr Foundation member Afu-Ra guested on the track "Mental Stamina."

CHUCK D:
Jeru seemed like he came from another galaxy with his debut. Very deep Brooklyn. This was hip-hop trancelike. The whole aura seemed to scare anything non–jet black. Jeru is a world traveler and takes that BK to Africa vibe everywhere he goes. Jeru is a hip-hop god, and true ambassador.

MAY 27

69 Boyz release the single "Tootsee Roll" on Rip-It.

The platinum-selling lead single for the group's 1994 debut *199Quad*, produced and written by C.C. Lemonhead and Jayski, "Tootsee Roll" became a major crossover hit, reaching the top ten on the *Billboard* Hot 100 and the R&B/Hip-Hop chart.

MAY 31

The Beastie Boys release their fourth studio album *Ill Communication* on Grand Royal.

Reaching #1 on the *Billboard* 200 and #2 on the R&B chart, the multi-platinum album showcased the trio's signature blend of call-and-response rhymes, experimental instrumentals, pop cultural call outs, distortion, and funk.

Produced by the band with Mario Caldato Jr., the album spawned four singles: "Sabotage," released January 1994, with its Spike Jonze–directed '70s cop video; "Get It Together," which featured a cameo by Q-Tip on the album version; "Sure Shot"; and "Root Down." Biz Markie guested on "Do It."

JUNE 3

Samuel Goldwyn Company releases the rap mockumentary *Fear of a Black Hat* in US theaters.

Rusty Cundieff produced, directed, and starred in the film, whose title was a play on Public Enemy's 1990 album *Fear of a Black Planet.* The plot, which followed the fictional group Niggaz with Hats, was loosely based on N.W.A. The soundtrack, released by Avatar, was considered innovative for its ability to parody production styles of specific artists, such as LL Cool J and P.M. Dawn.

JUNE 7

Warren G releases his debut album *Regulate...G Funk Era* on Def Jam.

The multi-platinum first set by Dr. Dre's younger brother had a much smoother, laid-back, and melodic sound than most G-funk records of that era. This is most evident on the album's title track smash hit single with Nate Dogg, which sampled former Doobie Brother Michael McDonald's "I Keep Forgettin'."

Garnering two Grammy Award nominations and peaking at #2 on the *Billboard* 200, the hip-hop classic also featured the hits "Do You See" and the *Billboard* Hot 100 top ten–charting "This D.J.," featuring O.G.L.B. Other guests on the album included the Twinz, the Dove Shack, B-Tip, Ricky Harris, Mr. Malik, Jah Skills, Bo Roc, G. Child, Lady Levi, and Wayniac.

JUNE 14

Arrested Development release their second album *Zingalamaduni* on Chrysalis.

Named after the Swahili word for "beehive of culture," the group's sophomore effort employed a number of African musical elements. Peaking at #55 on the *Billboard* 200 and at #20 on the R&B chart, the Speech-produced album included the singles "Africa's Inside Me," "United Front," which reached #66 on the R&B chart, and "Ease My Mind," which reached #45 on the *Billboard* Hot 100.

JUNE 21

Bone Thugs-N-Harmony release their *Creepin on ah Come Up* EP on Ruthless.

Featuring production from the group's mentor Eazy-E, who also executive produced the album, the Cleveland group's harmonious, fast-paced rapping caused their debut to spend ninety-six weeks on the *Billboard* Top 200, peaking at #12 on the *Billboard* Hot 100 and at #2 on the R&B chart.

Creepin on ah Come Up spawned two hit singles: the smash "Thuggish Ruggish Bone," which hit #22 on the *Billboard* 200," and "Foe tha Love of $," which featured Eazy-E and reached #4 on the Rap chart.

JUNE 21

The Beatnuts release their full-length self-titled debut album on Relativity.

Produced by the band with V.I.C. and Lucien, the group's debut cracked the *Billboard* 200 and reached #28 on the R&B charts with the help of singles such as "Hit Me with That," and "Props Over Here." Grand Puba of Brand Nubian, Miss Jones, Lenny Underwood, and DJ Sinister all guested on the album.

The Latino trio's set is sometimes referred to as *Street Level* because those words appear on the album's cover, which was inspired by the Hank Mobley 1965 jazz album *The Turnaround!*

JUNE 28

Da Brat releases her debut *Funkdafied* on So So Def.

Jermaine Dupri produced the debut album from the Illinois-bred rapper, which featured appearances from Kris Kross, LaTocha Scott, and Y-Tee.

Reaching #11 on the *Billboard* 200 and topping the R&B/Hip-Hop chart, the album from the tough-talking MC yielded three consecutive top forty singles—"Funkdafied," "Fa All Y'all," and "Give It 2 You"—which helped make *Funkdafied* the first platinum-selling album from a female rapper.

JUNE 28

Big Mike releases his solo debut album *Somethin' Serious* on Rap-A-Lot.

Big Mike worked with a number of producers on this hard, funky album, including Mike Dean, N.O. Joe, and Pimp C, who also appeared on the track "Havin' Thangs." Other guests included Bun B, Tre'mendous, and Scarface of the Geto Boys, of which Big Mike was also a member.

Somethin' Serious spawned the hit single "World of Mine," which reached #45 on the Rap chart.

JUNE 28

House of Pain release their sophomore album *Same as It Ever Was* on Tommy Boy.

The gold-selling hardcore album from the Irish-American group, which reached #12 on the *Billboard* 200 chart, contained the singles "On Point" and "Who's the Man?" from the 1993 New Line Cinema comedy of the same name, both of which broke into the *Billboard* Hot 100. *Same as It Ever Was* featured production by DJ Muggs of Cypress Hill, Diamond D of the Diggin' in the Crates Crew, and the group's DJ Lethal.

JULY 19

Coolio releases his debut solo album *It Takes a Thief* on Tommy Boy.

Produced by Bryan Dobbs, Coolio's laid-back party jams featured thoughtful and often humorous rhymes about trying to get by in a hard world. Singles include "County Line," "I Remember," "Mama I'm in Love wit' a Gangsta," and the platinum-selling remake of the 1980 Lakeside funk classic "Fantastic Voyage," which reached #3 on the *Billboard* Hot 100 and #2 on the Rap chart. Its massive success helped the album reach #8 on the *Billboard* 200.

CHUCK D:
I've known Coolio from way back. One of the first Cali rappers I met. We performed with my man WC on Profile Records. When he hit on "Fantastic Voyage," it was already one of my favorite cuts from one of my favorite groups of all time, Lakeside. His whole album was actually reminiscent of the funk that came out of Ohio, in its way. Later on from there, after that album, Coolio and I acted in a film called *Burn Hollywood Burn*. We were the Brother Brothers. I also I found out Coolio shares the same birthday with me and Professor Griff, three years apart. Coolio is that real dude and a true solider in hip and opening it up to virtual hip-hop animation with a lot of years in.

JULY 19

MC Eiht releases his debut solo album *We Come Strapped* on Epic.

Produced by DJ Slip, the gold-selling solo debut from the former Compton's Most Wanted member contained the gangsta singles "All for the Money" and "Geez Make the Hood Go Round."

The spare set, which reached #5 on the *Billboard* 200 and topped the R&B chart, featured guest appearances by Redman, Spice 1, and CMW.

JULY 26

Craig Mack releases the hit single, "Flava in Ya Ear," on Bad Boy.

Produced by Easy Mo Bee, the chart-topping, platinum-selling smash is from Craig Mack's debut album *Project: Funk da World*, released the same year.

The Grammy-nominated track, which reached #9 on the *Billboard* Hot 100 and topped the Rap chart, was remixed with LL Cool J, Rampage, Busta Rhymes, and Biggie Smalls, popularizing the practice of getting a bunch of MCs on a song that is already hot.

Hype Williams directed the song's video, which featured cameos by Das EFX, Irv Gotti, and Mic Geronimo, who do not perform on the song.

AUGUST 2

Ill Al Skratch release their debut album *Creep wit' Me* on Mercury.

Produced by LoRider and the LG Experience, the New York duo's most commercially successful album reached #22 on the R&B chart. It had their biggest hit single, "I'll Take Her," which featured Brian McKnight and reached #62 on the *Billboard* Hot 100 and #16 on the R&B chart. *Creep wit' Me* also contained "Where My Homiez? (Come Around My Way)," which reached #34 on the R&B chart.

SEPTEMBER 13

Big Daddy Kane releases his sixth album *Daddy's Home* on MCA.

Produced by Big Daddy Kane with DJ Premier, Kool T, Crush, L.G., Easy Mo Bee, and Da Rock, the album, which reached #26 on the R&B charts, contained the singles "In the PJ's," featuring Scoob Lover and "Show & Prove," featuring Shyheim, Sauce Money, ODB, Scoob Lover, and then Big Daddy Kane protégé Jay Z.

SEPTEMBER 13

The Notorious B.I.G. releases his debut album *Ready to Die* on Bad Boy.

Ready to Die, the first album to be released on executive producer Sean "Puffy" Combs's Bad Boy imprint, was fueled by tight production and Biggie's above-and-beyond rhymes and storytelling skills. The multi-platinum album, which reached #15 on the *Billboard* 200 and #3 on the R&B chart, spawned three classic smash hit singles: the Grammy-nominated, platinum-selling "Big Poppa," the platinum-selling "One More Chance," and the gold-selling "Juicy."

The hardcore album's intro skit retraces Biggie's life since childhood through classic songs by Curtis Mayfield, the Sugar Hill Gang, Audio Two, Snoop Doggy Dogg, and Schoolly D. Producers included DJ Premier, Darnell Scott, Lord Finesse, Chucky Thompson, Easy Moe Bee, Poke, and Bluez Brothers, with Method Man of the Wu-Tang Clan as the only guest performer on the track "The What."

CHUCK D:
In the Brooklyn basement studio of the great Daddy-O of Stetsasonic, I first met Biggie Smalls. Dude hovered over the lab. Odad promised that I'd hear more from him. In 1995 Notorious B.I.G. the legend signed with Puff Daddy's Bad Boy. I was really impressed when I saw Puff and B.I.G. perform live as a duo in ATL. The confidence of working the crowds gave B.I.G. fuel for making the aura of those great rhymes come to life. Lost in perilous a period that still has me smdh.

OCTOBER 4

Paris releases his third album *Guerrilla Funk* on Priority.

The San Francisco native, known as the "Black Panther of hip-hop," released his pro-black revolutionary third album, which reached #20 on the R&B chart and cracked the *Billboard* 200.

Guests on *Guerrilla Funk* included Mystic and the Conscious Daughters and it produced the singles "It's Real" and the title track.

OCTOBER 11

Lords of the Underground release the hit single "Tic Toc" on Pendulum.

"Tic Toc," which was produced by the legendary Marley Marl, is from the group's sophomore album *Keepers of the Funk* released the same year.

Reaching #73 on the *Billboard* Hot 100 and #17 on the Rap chart, "Tic Toc" featured turntable work from the group's DJ Lord Jazz and samples Doug E. Fresh and Slick Rick's "La Di Da Di."

OCTOBER 11

Thug Life release their debut album *Thug Life: Vol. 1* on Out Da Gutta.

Thug Life, which included Big Syke, Big Kato, Stretch, the Rated R, Macadoshis, and 2Pac Shakur, as well as his older brother Mopreme Shakur, released their thoughtful debut on 2Pac's Out Da Gutta label.

Produced by Easy Mo Bee, Warren G, Nate Dogg, Johnny "J," Moe ZMD, and various members of the group, the gold-selling album contained the singles "How Long Will They Mourn Me?," "Pour Out a Little Liquor," "Shit Don't Stop," and the hit "Cradle to the Grave," which reached #91 on the R&B chart and #25 on the Rap chart. Guest performances include Prince Ital Joe, Spice 1, Richie Rich, Dramacydal, and Biggie Smalls.

OCTOBER 15

Death Row Records releases the soundtrack to the short film *Murder Was the Case* starring Snoop Doggy Dogg.

The eighteen-minute *Murder Was the Case*, directed by Dr. Dre and Fab Five Freddy, was mainly known for its multi-platinum soundtrack. Singles off the soundtrack included "U Better Recognize" by Sam Sneed, featuring Dr. Dre; "What Would U Do" by Tha Dogg Pound; "Natural Born Killaz" by Dr. Dre and Ice Cube; and "Murder Was the Case," the remix by Snoop of the song from his debut album.

Produced by DeVante Swing of Jodeci, Daz Dillinger of Tha Dogg Pound, Sam Sneed, Soopafly, DJ Quik, and Dr. Dre, the soundtrack went to the top of both the *Billboard* 200 and the Rap chart, and received a Grammy Award nomination.

OCTOBER 18

Digable Planets release their sophomore album *Blowout Comb* on EMI.

Peaking at #32 on the *Billboard* 200 and #13 on the R&B chart, the jazzy self-produced album featured guest appearances by Jeru the Damaja, Jazzy Joyce, and Guru of Gang Starr. Critically acclaimed, the more political album featured live musicians and spawned the hit singles "9th Wonder (Blackitolism)," which reached #8 on the Rap chart, and "Dial 7 (Axioms of Creamy Spies)," which hit the Rap and R&B charts.

OCTOBER 18

O.C. releases his debut album *Word...Life* on Wild Pitch.

O.C., a member of the Diggin' in the Crates Crew, had his debut set produced by fellow D.I.T.C. members Buckwild and Lord Finesse as well as by Prestige, DJ Ogee, and Organized Konfusion. It reached #32 on the R&B chart and contained the anti-gangster hit single "Time's Up."

OCTOBER 18

Scarface releases his third solo album *The Diary* on Rap-A-Lot.

Featuring production by Mike Dean, N.O. Joe, Uncle Eddie, as well as Scarface, the former Geto Boys member's platinum-selling album contained the hits "People Don't Believe," featuring Ice Cube and Devin the Dude and the gangsta ballad "I Seen a Man Die," which reached #74 and #34 on the *Billboard* Hot 100 respectively. Debuting at #2 on the *Billboard* 200, the ten-song album contained the classic "The Diary," with its lyrical imagery and creative storytelling, backed by Scarface's innovative flow, which catapulted him into hip-hop's elite club of respected MCs.

OCTOBER 25

Common releases his sophomore album *Resurrection* on Relativity.

Produced mainly by No I.D. with Ynot, the wordy *Resurrection* was divided into two sides, one side being "East Side of Stony" and the other "West Side of Stony," in reference to Stony Island Avenue in Chicago where Common was raised.

COMMON

Cracking the *Billboard* 200, the thoughtful hardcore album contained the title-track single and "I Used to Love H.E.R.," a track metaphorically using a failed relationship to symbolize what Common viewed as the downfall of hip-hop with the advent of gangsta rap. His father, Lonnie "Pops" Lynn, a onetime ABA player and poet, appears on the track "Pop's Rap."

OCTOBER 25

Fu-Schnickens release their sophomore album *Nervous Breakdown* on Jive.

Produced by Diamond D, Jim Nice, K-Cut, Lyvio G, and Rod "KP" Kirkpatrick, the innovative album from the Brooklyn trio, filled with high-speed cartoonish raps and backward rhymes, contained the hit singles "Sum Dum Monkey," "Breakdown," and the group's biggest hit "What's Up Doc? (Can We Rock?)," which featured basketball legend Shaquille O'Neal and reached #39 on the *Billboard* Hot 100 and #22 on the Rap chart.

Peaking at #81 on the *Billboard* 200 and #19 on the R&B chart, it was the group's last album of original material. Their greatest hits compilation would be released the following year.

OCTOBER 25

The Artifacts release their debut album *Between a Rock and a Hard Place* on Big Beat.

The Newark duo Tame One and El Da Sensei filled their debut with raps from their world of B-boys and graffiti. Cracking the *Billboard* 200 and reaching #17 on the R&B chart, the witty album featured production by Buckwild of the Diggin' in the Crates Crew and T-Ray of the Soul Assassins.

Featuring guest appearances by Busta Rhymes and Redman, the album spawned the hit singles "Wrong Side of da Tracks" and "C'mon Wit da Git Down."

NOVEMBER 1

Brand Nubian release their third album *Everything Is Everything* on Elektra.

Everything Is Everything marked the return of Grand Puba to the group, who was absent on the Nubian's sophomore set *In God We Trust.* Produced by Buckwild and the group's Lord Jamar, the album reached #54 on the *Billboard* 200 and #13 on the R&B chart.

Guests on *Everything Is Everything* included Laura Alfored, Serge, Snagglepuss, Starr, and Busta Rhymes and spawned the singles "Hold On" and "Word Is Bond," which topped the Dance charts.

NOVEMBER 1

Lords of the Underground release their sophomore album *Keepers of the Funk* on Pendulum.

Produced by K-Def, Marley Marl, Andre Booth, and the group, *Keepers of the Funk* contained the hit singles "Tic Toc," "Faith," and "What I'm After," all of which reached the Rap chart. Guests on *Keepers of the Funk* included funk legend George Clinton, Sah-B, and Supreme C.

NOVEMBER 8

Pete Rock & CL Smooth release their second, and last, album as a duo, *The Main Ingredient,* on Elektra.

Masterfully produced by Rock, the duo's final set utilized soul and jazz samples and instrumental interludes between the tracks, which set off CL Smooth's complex lyricism.

Reaching #51 on the *Billboard* 200 and #9 on the R&B chart, *The Main Ingredient* spawned the hit singles "Take You There," "I Got a Love," and "Searching," featuring Vinia Mojica.

NOVEMBER 8

Keith Murray releases his debut album *The Most Beautifullest Thing in This World* on Jive.

Murray's raw flow, clever wordplay, and verbal gymnastics are the highlight of his debut. The gold-selling album was mainly produced by EPMD's Erick Sermon, a fellow member of the Def Squad musical collective, along with additional production by Redman, KP, and Busta Rhymes.

Peaking at #34 on the *Billboard* Hot 100 and #5 on the R&B chart, *The Most Beautifullest Thing in This World* spawned the hit singles "Get Lifted" and the classic title track, both of which reached the top ten of the Dance and Rap charts. Guests on the set included Jamal, Hurricane G, and fellow Def Squad members Redman and Sermon.

NOVEMBER 15

K-Dee releases his only solo album *Ass, Gas or Cash (No One Rides for Free)* on Lench Mob.

K-Dee had been in the 1980s group C.I.A., along with Sir Jinx and Ice Cube, and was also a member of Cube's Lench Mob musical collective.

Produced by Lay Law, Vic V, D Mac, Madness 4 Real, Shaquille, 88 X Unit, and Ice Cube, the gangsta album featured a remake of the Time classic "Gigolos Get Lonely Too" featuring Time's Morris Day. Reaching #32 on the R&B charts, it spawned the hit singles "Hittin' Corners," "Thought I Saw a Pussy Cat" (featuring Bootsy Collins and Ice Cube), and "The Freshest M.C. in the World."

NOVEMBER 15

Method Man of the Wu-Tang Clan releases his debut solo album *Tical* on Def Jam.

Tical, the first Wu solo album after the group's debut, was highly anticipated and entered the *Billboard* 200 at #4 and spent forty-three weeks on the charts. Produced by the RZA, the dark and unpredictable platinum-selling album spawned the hits "Release Yo' Delf" which cracked the *Billboard* Hot 100 and featured Blue Raspberry and the classic "Bring the Pain," which hit #45 on the *Billboard* Hot 100.

Tical contained the single "All I Need," whose remix version retitled "I'll Be There For You/You're All I Need to Get By," won a Grammy Award for Method Man and Mary J. Blige, who joined him on the remix. Other guests included Raekwon, Inspectah Deck, Carlton Fisk, and Streetlife.

CHUCK D:
Voice is so important in rap. Of course, it is becoming a lesser priority as we move further into hip-hop's future. Method Man gets my vote on most compelling voice and style in the past twenty-five years. I could listen to him rhyme the newspaper. *Tical* was Def Jam's approach of being the major hip-hop's "major" label. By 1994, Def Jam merged over to Polygamy from Sony and solidified themselves as "The Yankees" of hip-hop labels. The open-ended loud record deal allowed individual Wu-Tang members to be free agent soloists. Method Man landed *Tical* and "Bring the Pain" banged the streets while "I'll be There For You/You're All I Need to Get By" bombed the world. Powerful shots by the Wu power center.

NOVEMBER 22

Redman releases his sophomore album *Dare Iz a Darkside* on Def Jam.

Debuting at #13 on the *Billboard* 200 and topping the R&B charts, the somewhat odd but humorous album by the legendary Newark, New Jersey, MC went gold.

Produced by Erick Sermon, Rockwilder, and Redman, the album spawned the singles "Rockafella" and "Can't Wait," which reached #10 and #11 on the Rap chart respectively. The track "Cosmic Slop," featuring Erick Sermon and Keith Murray, shares its name with a 1973 Funkadelic album. Hurricane G guested on the track "We Run N.Y."

1995

JANUARY 10

Smif-N-Wessun release their debut album *Dah Shinin'* on Duck Down.

The debut album by the Brooklyn duo of Tek and Steele also harkened the arrival of the supergroup the Boot Camp Clik, which included Smif-N-Wessun, Black Moon, Heltah Skeltah, and O.G.C. They all appeared on the posse cut, "Cession At Da Doghillee."

Well produced by Boot Camp Clik production squad Da Beatminerz, which included Black Moon's DJ Evil Dee, Baby Paul, Mr. Walt, and Rich Blak, the dark album contained the classic cuts "Stand Strong," "Let's Git It On," and "Sound Bwoy Bureill." Peaking at #59 on the *Billboard* 100 and #5 on the R&B chart, this classic set of New York City crime rap also spawned the underground hits "Bucktown," "Wrekonize," and "Wontime."

The firearms company Smith & Wesson filed a cease and desist order soon after the release of *Dah Shinin'* over the similarity of their name. To avoid a lawsuit, Smif-N-Wessun changed their name to the Cocoa Brovaz for their sophomore album but reverted back in 2005.

JANUARY 17

The Roots release their sophomore album *Do You Want More?!!!??!* on DGC.

The Philly group's first album on a major label was unusual for hip-hop because it was filled with live jams, as opposed to samples or prerecorded material.

Produced by Kelo, A.J. Shine, and the group's Questlove, Black Thought, and Rahzel, the critically acclaimed album contained the fan favorites "Proceed," "Silent Treatment," and "Distortion to Static" and reached #104 on the *Billboard* 200 and #22 on the R&B charts.

JANUARY 24

Nine releases the single "Whutcha Want?" on Profile.

"Whutcha Want?," the first single from the gravel-voiced Bronx MC's debut album, *Nine Livez*, reached #50 on the *Billboard* Hot 100 and #3 on the Rap chart. "Whutcha Want?" would be Nine's highest charting single with Rob Lewis, Portishead, the Brotherhood, and Dark Globe each contributing remixes to the hit track.

JANUARY 24

Too $hort releases his sixth album *Cocktails* on Jive.

Producers by Ant Banks with LA Dre, Shorty B, Spearhead X, B. Turner, the Dangerous Crew, and Too $hort, the platinum-selling album, filled with pimptastic lyrics and funky beats, reached #6 on the *Billboard* 200 and topped the R&B chart.

Guests on the Oakland legend's sixth full-length release included Old School Freddy B, Father Dom, MC Breed, Baby D, Malik and Jamal from Illegal, and 2Pac.

FEBRUARY 7

ODB of the Wu-Tang Clan releases the single "Brooklyn Zoo" on Elektra.

"Brooklyn Zoo," which refers to the rough street where ODB grew up as well as a rival rap crew, is the lead single from the rapper's 1995 gold-selling debut solo set *Return to the 36 Chambers*. Reaching #54 on the *Billboard* Hot 100 and #5 on the Rap chart, the single showcases ODB's distinctive rap-sung offbeat lyricism.

The Grammy Award–nominated album was mainly produced by RZA, with additional production and guest appearances by other Wu members, reaching #7 on the *Billboard* Hot 100 and #2 on the R&B charts.

FEBRUARY 7

Juvenile releases his debut album *Being Myself* on Warlock.

The debut set by the nineteen-year-old New Orleans rapper, produced by Leroy "Precise" Edwards, showcased the bounce craze. A remixed version of this album was released in 1999 and cracked the *Billboard* 200.

FEBRUARY 28

Tha Alkaholiks release their sophomore album *Coast II Coast* on Loud.

The West Coast party album, produced by Diamond D, Madlib, E-Swift, and Tha Liks, reached #50 on the *Billboard* 200 and #12 on the R&B chart. It spawned the hit singles "The Next Level" and "DAAAM!," which both charted on the Rap charts, and featured guest appearances by Q-Tip of A Tribe Called Quest, Xzibit, King Tee, Declaime, and Lootpack.

MARCH 14

2Pac releases his third studio album *Me Against the World* on Interscope.

Debuting at #1 on the *Billboard* 200 and the R&B chart, this confessional album was released while 2Pac was in prison. Working with numerous producers, the rapper created an honest, self-reflective album that many feel is his best.

The Grammy-nominated, multi-platinum album built on the sales of the lead single "Dear Mama," released in February, which topped the rap charts and reached #9 on the *Billboard* Hot 100. Other singles released were "So Many Tears" and "Temptations," both of which reached the top twenty on the Rap chart.

MARCH 14

E-40 releases his second studio album *In a Major Way* on Jive/Sick Wid It.

With work from a slew of producers, including Studio Ton, Mike Mosley, and Sam Bostic, and featuring great guests, such as B-Legit, Suga-T, 2Pac, and Celly Cel, the platinum-selling *In a Major Way* showcased E-40 at his most inspired. Reaching #13 on the *Billboard* 200 and #2 on the R&B chart, the Bay Area rapper's album spawned two hits "1-Luv" and "Sprinkle Me," which reached #4 and #5 on the Rap chart respectively, as well as the classic "Dusted 'n' Disgusted."

MARCH 26

Big L releases his debut album *Lifestylez ov da Poor & Dangerous* on Columbia.

Produced mainly by his D.I.T.C. Crew of Buckwild, Lord Finesse, and Showbiz, the debut from the Harlem street legend showcases his lyrical mastery. Cracking the *Billboard* 200 and reaching #22 on the R&B chart, this East Coast classic spawned fan favorites including "No Endz, No Skinz," "Street Struck," and "Da Graveyard," which featured both a young Cam'ron (credited as Killer Kam) and Jay Z.

MARCH 26

Eazy-E dies at the age of thirty.

The founding member of N.W.A, considered by many to be the godfather of gangsta rap, died from AIDS after being diagnosed with the disease just a month earlier.

Eazy-E wrote a message to his fans addressing his illness in the week before he died. "I have learned in the last week that this thing is real, and it doesn't discriminate," he wrote. "It affects everyone."

APRIL 11

The soundtrack for New Line Cinema's *Friday* is released on Priority.

Written by Ice Cube, who also costarred in the movie alongside Chris Tucker, *Friday* was a commercial success, earning almost $30 million and spawning two sequels: 2000's *Next Friday* and 2002's *Friday After Next*.

The soundtrack to *Friday* topped the *Billboard* 200 and the R&B chart and featured contributions from Dr. Dre, Ice Cube, Cypress Hill, 2 Live Crew, and Scarface.

APRIL 11

BMG Records releases the compilation *Pump Ya Fist: Hip-hop Inspired by the Black Panthers*.

The album was influenced by the Gramercy Pictures film *Panther* released the same year, which focused on the life of the Black Panther Party for Self-Defense's cofounder Huey P. Newton.

The compilation featured some of the top MCs in the game, such as Rakim, KRS-One, 2Pac, Fugees, Grand Puba, Jeru the Damaja, Yo-Yo, 5ive-O, Dred Scott, Ahmad, Speech of Arrested Development, Chuck D, and Kam.

APRIL 25

Mobb Deep release their hit sophomore album *The Infamous* on Loud.

Produced by the band as well as by The Abstract (aka Q-Tip), Matt Life, and Schott Free, *The Infamous* helped to define the New York hardcore sound and is still influential today.

Spending eighteen weeks on the *Billboard* 200, peaking at #15, and hitting #3 on the R&B chart, the hard street life album featured the hit singles "Shook Ones Pt. II," "Survival of the Fittest," and "Temperature's Rising." *The Infamous* featured guest appearances by Q-Tip, Big Noyd, Nas, as well as Raekwon and Ghostface Killah of the Wu-Tang Clan.

CHUCK D:

From Long Island, I heard of this duo from producer Kerwin Sleek Young who had done some things with them. The Dark East was ventured into by their mid-1990s music. Mobb Deep was hip-hop urban theater no question. Many followers got an outside peek in from their hardcore introductions.

MAY 2

Mercury Records releases the soundtrack to the 1995 Gramercy Pictures film *Panther*.

The soundtrack for the Black Panther biopic, directed by Mario Van Peebles, released the same year, peaked at #37 on the *Billboard* 200 and #5 on the R&B chart. It featured performances by many hip-hop artists, including, Biggie Smalls, Black Sheep, Busta Rhymes, Digable Planets, Salt-N-Pepa, Yo-Yo, and Da Lench Mob, among others.

The track "Freedom" was a collaboration of sixty R&B singers and rappers, including Yo-Yo, Aaliyah, Mary J. Blige, Queen Latifah, TLC, and Eshe and Laurneá of Arrested Development.

MAY 18

C. Delores Tucker attends Time Warner shareholders meeting to protest gangsta rap.

The lifelong Civil Rights activist and anti-rap crusader attended Time Warner's shareholders meeting to put pressure on the record label to sever ties with the company's subsidiary label, Interscope Records, which released and distributed records by West Coast gangsta rappers like Dr. Dre, Tupac, and Snoop Dogg.

As chairwoman of the National Congress of Black Women, Tucker signed a letter that was sent to Time Warner's board of directors encouraging them to cut ties with Interscope. Tucker's campaign was successful, and Time Warner sold its 50 percent share in Interscope Records back to the label in September 1995.

Tucker would end up in a prolonged legal battle with Death Row Records, the West Coast gangsta rap label owned by Interscope, for what they deemed contractual interference.

MAY 19

***The Simpsons* airs its "Homerpalooza" episode featuring Cypress Hill.**

The Simpsons' 152nd episode featured voice-overs from Cypress Hill, the first-ever rap act to appear on the cartoon. In later years, rappers 50 Cent, Sir Mix-A-Lot, Flavor Flav, Ludacris, and Pharrell Williams would all appear on the show.

MAY 23

Luniz releases the single "I Got 5 on It" on Noo Trybe.

The debut single from the Bay Area hip-hop duo was a major rap and crossover hit, reaching the top ten on both the *Billboard* Hot 100 and the R&B chart.

The infectious single off the group's first album, *Operation Stackola*, the platinum-selling song featured an early guest appearance from R&B singer Michael Marshall. The track's instrumentals have been sampled and used by artists including Jennifer Lopez, Puff Daddy, Big Sean, Meek Mill, and Big Freedia.

JUNE 4

Lost Boyz release their debut album *Legal Drug Money* on Uptown.

The gold-selling debut by the Queens quartet of Mr. Cheeks, Freaky Tah, DJ Spigg Nice, and Pretty Lou reached #6 on the *Billboard* 200 and #1 on the R&B chart. Working with producers such as Easy Mo Bee, Mr. Sexxx, and Pete Rock led to hit singles from the accessible album including "Renee," "Music Makes Me High," and "Get Up," all of which reached the top ten on the Rap chart.

JUNE 6

The Notorious B.I.G. releases the smash hit remix of "One More Chance," on Bad Boy.

The platinum-selling remix of the song from Biggie's *Ready to Die* released the previous year featured additional vocals by his wife Faith Evans and an uncredited Mary J. Blige. Produced by Trackmasters, it reached #2 on the *Billboard* Hot 100 and topped the R&B and Rap charts.

The video, directed by Hype Williams, featured cameos from eighteen hip-hop stars, including Heavy D, Luther Campbell, Da Brat, Kid Capri, Queen Latifah, and Jermaine Dupri.

JULY 11

Shaggy releases his third studio album *Boombastic* on Virgin.

Already huge in Europe, the Jamaican rapper's third album of party anthems served as his breakthrough in the United States. It spawned a number of hit singles, including "In the Summertime," which reached #3 on the *Billboard* Hot 100 and topped the R&B chart, and the platinum-selling title track, which peaked at #3 on the *Billboard* Hot 100.

The album was a commercial success, cracking the top forty of the *Billboard* 200 and winning the Grammy in 1996 for best reggae album.

JULY 25

Bone Thugs-N-Harmony release their second studio album *E. 1999 Eternal* on Ruthless.

The multi-platinum, Grammy-nominated album from the Cleveland group mixed rapid rap with street-corner crooning. Produced by DJ U-Neek, the somber album reached #1 on both the *Billboard* 200 and the R&B charts, and produced three hit singles: "1st of tha Month," "East 1999," and the chart-topping "Tha Crossroads," a Grammy-winning ode to Eazy-E, who mentored the group at Ruthless Records and had recently passed away from AIDS.

AUGUST 1

Chef Raekwon of the Wu-Tang Clan releases his debut solo album *Only Built 4 Cuban Linx...* on Loud.

The third solo release by a Wu member since the group's *Enter the Wu-Tang (36 Chambers)*, the platinum-selling album's theme was centered around organized crime and cocaine trafficking. Presented like a film, the album was directed by Wu-Tang leader the RZA and starred Raekwon and costarred fellow Wu banger Ghostface Killah. It also featured several samples from John Woo's 1989 Hong Kong thriller *The Killer*.

Filled with cinematic storytelling, the complex album featured four hit singles "Ice Cream," which reached #37 on the *Billboard* Hot 100, "Criminology," "Heaven & Hell," and "Rainy Dayz," with appearances from the other members of the Clan and Nas.

CHUCK D:
The Chef is an anchor in the Wu—heart and street soul. In fact, Ice-T said it best when he said they are like the first Superheroes of Hip-Hop—the damn *swarm effect*. The Chef was the third-time charm for the Wu solo releases. This was putting them into the rap stratosphere, and in truth Raekwon ain't really ever came down off that cloud, because as hood troubles continue ... there are a million tales to tell. The Chef still cooks 'em up and spits 'em out. Makes it all tick.

AUGUST 3

The East–West rivalry makes an appearance at the 1995 Source Awards in New York City.

The second annual awards show at Madison Square Garden was the first time the gradually building feud between East Coast and West Coast rap was broadcast nationwide. Lowlights included Suge Knight's speech criticizing Puff Daddy for appearing in all of his Bad Boy artists' music videos and Snoop Dogg being booed at the event by the New York crowd.

The Death Row Records and Bad Boy Entertainment feud grew sharply after the awards show. Both Tupac and Notorious B.I.G. would be killed within a little more than a year and a half after the show.

AUGUST 8

Coolio releases his single "Gangsta's Paradise" on Tommy Boy.

"Gangsta's Paradise," which featured the California rapper L.V., became a mega crossover hit, topping the charts and eventually becoming the bestselling single in any genre of 1995.

Produced by Doug Rasheed, the multi-platinum song, which famously sampled Stevie Wonder's 1976 "Pastime Paradise," appeared on Coolio's album of the same name and the soundtrack for the film *Dangerous Minds*. Topping the charts in sixteen countries, the song won Coolio a Grammy for best solo rap performance.

AUGUST 29

Junior M.A.F.I.A. release their debut studio album *Conspiracy* on Undeas.

Notorious B.I.G.'s Brooklyn group, which included Lil' Cease, Trife and Larceny of the Snakes, Lil' Kim, Nino Brown, Chico Del Vec, Kleptomaniac, Capone, and Bugsy, released their first album to much acclaim. Debuting at #8 on the *Billboard* 200, the gold-selling album sold 69,000 copies the first week and reached #2 on the R&B chart.

Sales were propelled by singles such as "Player's Anthem," which reached #13 on the *Billboard* Hot 100 and was certified gold; "I Need You Tonight," which featured Faith Evans on the album track and Aaliyah on the single version; and "Get Money," which peaked at #17 on the *Billboard* Hot 100 and was certified platinum.

SEPTEMBER 12

Kool G Rap releases his debut solo album *4, 5, 6* on Cold Chillin'.

Peaking at #24 on the *Billboard* 200 and topping the R&B charts, *4, 5, 6* was Kool G Rap's first release after disbanding with DJ Polo, as well as his final Cold Chillin' release.

Producers include, Dr. Butcher, T-Ray, Naughty Shorts, Buckwild, and Salaam Remi. *4, 5, 6* topped the Rap and R&B charts and produced the hit singles "Fast Life," featuring Nas, which reached #74 on the *Billboard* Hot 100, "It's a Shame," and the title track. Other guests on the album included MF Grimm and B-1.

OCTOBER 31

Master P's No Limit Records releases the compilation album *Down South Hustlers: Bouncin' and Swingin'*.

The funky compilation was hip-hop's first release as a double CD and featured Silkk the Shocker, C-Murder, UGK, and Eightball & MJG, among others.

Peaking at #139 on the *Billboard* 200 and #13 on the R&B chart, the album spawned the single "Playaz from Da South," by Silkk the Shocker and UGK.

OCTOBER 31

Tha Dogg Pound release their debut album *Dogg Food* on Death Row.

Produced by DJ Pooh, Dr. Dre, and Daz Dillinger among others, the chart-topping, multi-platinum G-funk album produced three singles, all of which reached the R&B chart: "Let's Play House," featuring Dr. Dre, Michel'le, Snoop Doggy Dogg, and Nate Dogg; "Respect"; and "New York, New York," featuring Snoop Doggy Dogg.

Other guests on the album included Prince Ital Joe, the Lady of Rage, as well as Jimmy Jam and Terry Lewis.

NOVEMBER 7

Erick Sermon releases his second solo album *Double or Nothing* on Def Jam.

Reaching #35 on the *Billboard* 200 and #6 on the R&B charts, the sought-after producer's album produced two singles, "Welcome" and "Bomdigi," which reached #12 and #9 on the Rap chart respectively. Guests on the album included Redman, Keith Murray, and Aaron Hall of Guy.

NOVEMBER 7

KRS-One releases his self-titled sophomore solo album on Jive.

Reaching #19 on the *Billboard* 200 and #2 on the R&B chart, the lyrically intense album spawned two hits, "Rappaz R. N. Dainja" and "MC's Act Like They Don't Know," which reached #9 on the Rap chart.

Producers on this set included DJ Premier, Diamond D, Showbiz, Norty Cotto, and Big French and guests included Das EFX, Rakim, Method Man, Lord Finesse, Jeru the Damaja, Mr. Magic (onetime lyrical rival MC Shan), Busta Rhymes, Mad Lion, Fat Joe, Channel Live, Dexter Thibou, and Rich Nice.

NOVEMBER 7

Goodie Mob release their debut album *Soul Food* on LaFace.

The pioneering Southern rap act, comprised of Big Gipp, T-Mo, Khujo, and future soul singer Cee-Lo Green were part of the Atlanta musical collective known as the Dungeon Family, which included Outkast and the production unit Organized Noize, who also produced *Soul Food*.

Goodie Mob, which was an acronym for "the Good Die Mostly Over Bullshit," put out a gold-selling album that resembled a southern version of the Wu-Tang Clan's 1993 debut *Enter the Wu-Tang (36 Chambers)*. Peaking at #45 on the *Billboard* 200 and #8 on the R&B chart, the critically acclaimed album spawned three hit singles: the title track, "Cell Therapy," and "Dirty South," which originated the expression used to describe the southern hip-hop sound. All three singles reached the top ten on the Rap chart.

Guests on the socially conscious *Soul Food* included Outkast, Joi, Cool Breeze, Sleepy Brown, Roni, and Witchdoctor.

CHUCK D:
I moved to ATL in the early 1990s and the scene was moving from more Miami bass–like sounds into the soul funk indigenous to the area's musical history. Rico Wade and his Dungeon Fam had an understanding of who they were and what regions of hip-hop the ATL had supported. The radio station HOT 97.5 emerging in the mid-1990s gave rise to the local scene, making the major urban stations expand their rap on their daily playlists. Prior to that, Atlanta limited rap to the weekends.

The Goodie Mob spoke volumes about the young Dirty South that few knew outside the A. The politics of the USA southeast were now transmitted worldwide via the sight, story, sound, and style of one of the best groups ever. Feel good music with a sharp point of view.

NOVEMBER 7

The Genius/GZA of the Wu-Tang Clan releases his sophomore album *Liquid Swords* on Geffen.

The gold-selling album, considered to be one of the best solo Wu-Tang albums, had an understated menace that heavily sampled dialogue from the martial arts film *Shogun Assassin*. Peaking at #9 on the *Billboard* 200 and #2 on the R&B chart, the album spawned the hit singles "Cold World," "Shadowboxin'," "I Gotcha Back," and the classic title track, all of which charted on the Rap chart.

Produced by the RZA with assistance by 4th Disciple, *Liquid Swords* featured guest appearances by fellow Wu-bangers such as Masta Killa, Inspectah Deck, Method Man, Killah Priest, Ghostface Killah, Raekwon, U-God, and ODB.

NOVEMBER 7

The Click release their sophomore album *Game Related* on Jive.

The California quartet of family members E-40, D-Shot, Suga-T, and B-Legit's second effort reached #21 on the *Billboard* 200 and #3 on the R&B chart. Producers on the gold-selling album included Tone Capone, Roger Troutman, and the Click's own E-40 and B-Legit.

The album produced two singles, "Hurricane," whose music video featured an appearance by Boots Riley of the Coup, and "Scandalous," which reached #4 and #18 on the Rap chart respectively.

NOVEMBER 14

The Pharcyde release their sophomore album *Labcabincalifornia* on Delicious Vinyl.

Produced by the band with Diamond D, M-Walk, and J Dilla, the introspective album reached #37 on the *Billboard* 200 and #17 R&B chart.

Hit singles from *Labcabincalifornia* included "Runnin'" and "Drop," whose groundbreaking music video was directed by Spike Jonze, both of which reached #5 on the Rap chart.

NOVEMBER 14

France's Alliance Ethnik release their debut album *Simple et Funky* on Delabel Records.

The five-member French group consisted of performers with roots in the Congo, Italy, Algeria, and France.

Produced by Bob Power, best known for his work with A Tribe Called Quest, the platinum-selling set produced three hit singles, the title track, "Honesty et Jalousie," and "Respect."

NOVEMBER 21

LL Cool J releases his sixth album *Mr. Smith* on Def Jam.

The multi-platinum set combined hardcore rap with love ballads and spawned hit singles including "Doin' It" (featuring LeShaun), "Loungin'" (featuring Terri & Monica), and "Hey Lover," (featuring Boyz II Men), all of which reached the top ten of *Billboard*'sHot 100, as well as the R&B and Rap charts. The song "I Shot Ya," featuring Keith Murray, produced a remix that included Fat Joe, Prodigy of Mobb Deep, and the earliest collaboration of a young Foxy Brown.

Mr. Smith featured production by the Trackmasters, Easy Mo Bee, Rashad Smith, Chyskillz, and Chad Elliott.

NOVEMBER 21

Kris Kross release the single "Tonite's tha Night" on Columbia.

The lead single off the group's third and final studio album, *Young, Rich & Dangerous,* topped the Rap chart, reached the top ten of the R&B chart, and peaked at #12 on the *Billboard* Hot 100.

Written and produced by Jermaine Dupri, the gold-selling single featured Trey Lorenz on vocals. A remix of the song featuring Redman was later released.

1996

JANUARY 30

Ruthless Records releases the posthumous album from Eazy-E, *Str8 off tha Streetz of Muthaphukkin Compton.*

Ten months after the death of Eazy-E, Ruthless released his second solo album, which went gold. Reaching #3 on the *Billboard* 200 and topping the R&B chart, the raunchy album featured production work by DJ Yella, Naughty By Nature, Bobby "Bobcat" Ervin, and Roger Troutman and guest appearances by MC Ren, Dresta, and B.G. Knocc Out.

The album spawned two singles, "Tha Muthaphukkin' Real" and "Just tah Let U Know," both of which just missed the top forty on the *Billboard* Hot 100 but reached #2 and #4 on the Rap chart respectively.

FEBRUARY 13

2Pac releases his fourth album and first for Death Row, *All Eyez on Me.*

Topping both the *Billboard* 200 and R&B chart, the double CD was 2Pac's celebration of Thug Life. The diamond-selling epic album spawned two number-one hit singles, the Grammy-nominated "California Love," featuring Dr. Dre and Roger Troutman of Zapp and "How Do You Want It?," featuring K-Ci & JoJo.

Other hit singles on this classic set included "2 of Amerikaz Most Wanted," (featuring Snoop Dogg), "All Bout U," and "I Ain't Mad at Cha." Guests on the album included Tha Dogg Pound, Danny Boy, Michel'le, Rappin' 4-Tay, Nate Dogg, Method Man, Redman, and P-Funk legend George Clinton.

FEBRUARY 13

The Fugees release their sophomore album *The Score* on Ruffhouse.

The trio of Wyclef Jean, Lauryn Hill, and Pras (formerly known as the Tranzlator Crew) broke crossover ground on this classic album which infused hip-hop, reggae, R&B, and pop, with strands of rock, spaghetti western, and classical themes thrown in for good measure.

The Score would win a Grammy Award for best rap album and the album's smash hit single, a cover of the Roberta Flack classic "Killing Me Softly with His Song," shortened here to "Killing Me Softly," took home another Grammy for best R&B performance by a duo or group.

Featuring production by the group along with Jerry Duplessis, Shawn King, Salaam Remi, Diamond D, and John Forté, the thoughtful multi-platinum album also produced the huge hits "Ready or Not," "Fu-Gee-La," "Cowboys," and a cover of Bob Marley's"No Woman, No Cry."

CHUCK D:
Flavor Flav was always a believer of the Fugees. I was a fan of whatever the Ruffhouse label put into the marketplace. Their first album showed great promise and was so diverse and gritty, I knew the group was meant to explode. I recall visiting the three members on their tour bus in Austin, Texas, during a 1996 South by Southwest convention. They appeared road torn and weary. I told them bright days were ahead from all their work. Little did I know the explosion with *The Score* was to happen right around the corner.

The demand for the Fugees internationally really impressed me because the worldwide Sony distribution couldn't handle the sensation initially. Their eclectic difference made them stand out big time. Wyclef, Lauryn, and Pras were hitting like hip-hop's Peter, Paul and Mary.

MARCH 19

Bahamadia releases her debut studio album *Kollage* on Chrysalis.

A protégée of Gang Starr's Guru, the Philadelphia native's jazzy debut reached #126 on the *Billboard* 200 and #13 on the R&B chart. Produced by Guru, DJ Premier, Da Beatminerz, N.O. Joe, and the Roots, the laid-back album spawned four singles, including "Oknowhowwedu," which reached the top twenty on the Rap chart.

MARCH 26

Busta Rhymes releases his debut solo album *The Coming* on Elektra.

This platinum-selling album was Busta's big solo coming out party after leaving Leaders of the New School. Reaching #6 on the *Billboard* 200 and #1 on the R&B chart, this inventive album filled with his complex cadences spawned the singles "Woo Hah!! Got You All in Check," which reached #8 on the *Billboard* Hot 100 (the video featured Ol' Dirty Bastard) and "It's a Party" featuring Zhané. Other guests on the album included Q-Tip, Redman, and Keith Murray.

APRIL 1

DJ Kool releases the live hit single "Let Me Clear My Throat" on American.

Recorded live at the hip-hop veteran's performance at the Bahama Bay Club in Philadelphia, "Let Me Clear My Throat" utilized samples from "Hollywood Swinging" by Kool & the Gang and "The 900 Number" by Mark the 45 King. It was a throwback to the 1970s style of hip-hop parties. The gold-selling song, which reached #30 on the *Billboard* Hot 100, also appeared on DJ Kool's album of the same name.

Funkmaster Flex and Mark the 45 King would produce remixes of "Let Me Clear My Throat," with the legendary Doug E. Fresh appearing on the "Old School Reunion Remix."

APRIL 9

Chino XL's debut album *Here to Save You All* is released on American.

Produced by B-Wiz, KutMasta Kurt, Bird, DJ Homicide, Eric Romero, and Dan Charnas, the critically acclaimed album from the Bronx native, which reached #56 on the R&B chart, featured guest appearances by Kool Keith of the legendary Ultramagnetic MC's and Ras Kass.

The lyrically dexterous album contained the underground cult classic "Riiiot" as well as the singles "Kreep," "Thousands," "Rise," and "No Complex."

MAY 7

Kool Keith of the Ultramagnetic MC's releases his first solo album *Dr. Octagon* on Bulk.

An alternative hip-hop classic was released under legendary Bronx MC's pseudonym Dr. Octagon. The album's experimental and eclectic sound with DJ QBert's scratching coupled with Keith's unique and alternative lyrical approach and subject matter made it a critical and fan favorite, especially on college radio.

Produced by Dan "the Automator" Nakamura of the future Handsome Boy Modeling School, with contributions by KutMasta Kurt and DJ QBert, the inventive album spawned the underground singles "Earth People," released the previous year, and "Blue Flowers."

JUNE 18

Heltah Skeltah release their debut album *Nocturnal* on Duck Down.

The debut of the Boot Camp Clik duo of Rock and Ruck (Sean Price) showcased their lyrical dynamism. Backed by production from Buckshot, Da Beatminerz, and E-Swift, among others, the East Coast classic reached #35 on the *Billboard* 200 and #5 on the R&B chart. The gangsta album spawned four singles, all of which reached the top twenty on the Rap chart, including "Lefaur Leflah Eshkoshka," which featured O.G.C.

JUNE 25

Jay Z releases his debut album *Reasonable Doubt* on Roc-A-Fella.

The platinum-selling album from the former street hustler featured no less than four hit singles: "Dead Presidents II"; "Can't Knock the Hustle," featuring Mary J. Blige; "Feelin' It," featuring Mecca; and "Ain't No Nigga," featuring Foxy Brown, which reached #50 on the *Billboard* Hot 100. Other guests on *Reasonable Doubt* included label mate Memphis Bleek, Big Jaz, Sauce Money, and the Notorious B.I.G. on a cut aptly titled "Brooklyn's Finest."

Produced by Big Jaz, DJ Premier, Sean Cane, Knobody, Ski, DJ Clark Kent, Irv Gotti, and Peter

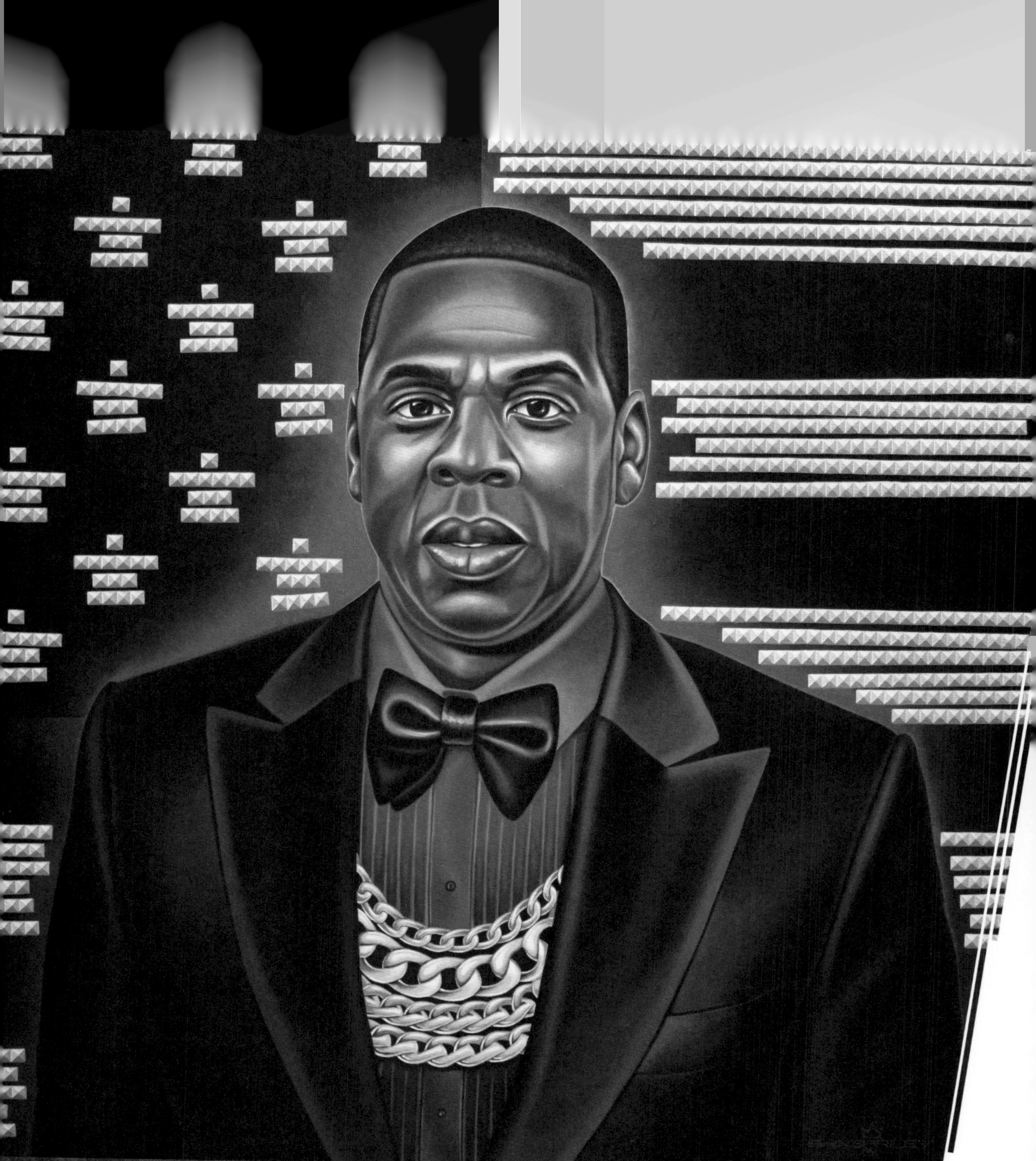

JAY Z

Panic, the album debuted at #23 on the *Billboard* 200 and reached #3 on the R&B chart. The rags-to-riches classic was released by Roc-A-Fella, an imprint started by Jay Z along with partners Kareem "Biggs" Burke and Damon Dash, through a distribution deal with Priority Records.

CHUCK D:
Jay Z brought a lyrical dexterity to the street reality of the Clinton-era 1990s. His "Three Card Molly" vocal delivery was so witty, with the brutal reality of the lyrics laced with clever rhymes that gave them an edge of comedy. The pop machinery knew what to do with hitting the masses with the streets, but Jay Z was independent from the jump—it was just that more folks were ready.

JULY 2

Nas releases *It Was Written* on Columbia.

Nas's second studio album, produced in large part by Trackmasters, featured a much more mainstream, accessible sound than his 1994 debut *Illmatic*. Debuting at #1 on the *Billboard* 200 and remaining there for four consecutive weeks, the album sold more than two million copies in its first three months, and has since become one of the bestselling albums of Nas's career.

The multi-platinum album spawned the singles "If I Ruled the World (Imagine That)," which reached #52 on the *Billboard* Hot 100 and "Street Dreams," which topped the Rap Singles chart. "Nas Is Coming" was a collaboration with Dr. Dre, which led to criticism during the height of the East Coast–West Coast feud.

The album samples Sam Cooke, the Ultramagnetic MC's, Al Green, and Sting, among others, and featured guest appearances by Foxy Brown, Mobb Deep, Dr. Dre, and Lauryn Hill.

JULY 15

Sadat X releases his debut solo album *Wild Cowboys* on Loud.

Reaching #83 on the *Billboard* 200 and #13 on the R&B chart, the jazzy, laid-back album spawned the hit singles "The Lump Lump" and "Hang 'Em High," featuring DV Alias Khrist. Also appearing are Shawn Black, Cool Chuck, Tec, Regina Hall, Money Boss Players, and fellow Brand Nubian Grand Puba.

The all-star production team included Pete Rock, DJ Alamo, DJ Ogee, Ali Malek, Ant Greene Father Time, Minnesota, Dante Ross, and Diamond D, Buckwild, and Showbiz of the Diggin' in the Crates Crew.

JULY 30

UGK release their third studio album *Ridin' Dirty* on Jive.

This classic of southern gangsta rap, produced by Pimp C with N.O. Joe, reached #15 on the *Billboard* 200 and #2 on the R&B chart, despite having no singles or musical videos released. The powerful, gritty album from the Texan duo includes the masterful album cuts "Murder," "Diamond & Wood," and "One Day," which helped make it UGK's bestselling album.

JULY 30

A Tribe Called Quest release their fourth album, *Beats, Rhymes and Life*, on Jive.

While darker than previous releases, the platinum-selling album reached the top of the *Billboard* 200 and R&B chart. Featuring production by Rashad Smith and the Ummah, a production collective consisting of Tribe's Q-Tip, Ali Shaheed Muhammad, and Jay Dee, the melancholy and laid-back album was nominated for two Grammy Awards and contained the fan favorites "1nce Again," featuring Tammy Lucas and "Stressed Out," featuring Faith Evans.

AUGUST 13

Facemob release their debut album *The Other Side of the Law* on Rap-A-Lot.

Facemob was put together by the legendary Scarface of the Geto Boys and consisted of Rap-A-Lot artists Devin the Dude, 350, Smit D, Chi-Ray, and DMG.

Written and produced mainly by Scarface, the album reached #51 on the *Billboard* 200 and #6 on the R&B chart.

AUGUST 27

Outkast release *ATLiens* on LaFace.

In the wake of the success of their debut, *Southernplayalisticadillacmuzik*, the Atlanta hip-hop duo's second album, which had a futuristic vibe, debuted at #2 on the *Billboard* 200 and topped the R&B chart and has since been certified multi-platinum.

Recorded in Atlanta primarily with their production team Organized Noize, the thoughtful but groovy album, which incorporated elements of soft funk, reggae, and gospel, spawned the singles "Elevators (Me & You)," which reached #5 on the R&B chart, "ATLiens," which reached #35 on the *Billboard* Hot 100, and "Jazzy Belle," which reached #52 on the Hot 100.

SEPTEMBER 7

Tupac Shakur is shot in Las Vegas, Nevada.

Shakur had just attended the Mike Tyson vs. Bruce Seldon heavyweight title fight at the MGM Grand. While riding in Death Row head Suge Knight's SUV, Shakur was shot in the pelvis, chest, hand, thigh, and lungs. After being placed on life support at the University Medical Center in Las Vegas, Nevada, Shakur would die from his wounds six days later on September 13, setting the whole hip-hop world in mourning.

SEPTEMBER 24

The Roots release their third studio album *Illadelph Halflife* on Geffen.

The thoughtful, genre-pushing album reached #21 on the *Billboard* 200 and #4 on the R&B chart. With twenty tracks, the innovative album spawned hit singles, including "What They Do," which reached #34 on the *Billboard* Hot 100, and "Clones," which reached #62 on the R&B chart and the Rap top five, and employs interludes from Quincy Jones's "Summer in the City."

OCTOBER 1

Ras Kass releases his debut album *Soul on Ice* on Priority.

Named after the 1968 book by the Black Panther Party's Eldridge Cleaver, Kass's debut set was a hip-hop manifesto of the black struggle in the 1990s and its relation to the turbulent 1960s.

Ras Kass, who at the time was a member of the supergroup Golden State Warriors along with Xzibit and Saafir, produced *Soul on Ice* along with Battlecat, Bird, Voodu, and others. Coolio was the only guest on the album, appearing on the track "Drama."

The critically acclaimed album, which cracked the *Billboard* 200, contained the hit singles, "Miami Life," "Anything Goes," and the powerful title track. The controversial album cut "Nature of the Threat," despite not being released as a single, drew lots of attention because of its political content.

OCTOBER 15

Poor Righteous Teachers release their fourth album *The New World Order* on Profile.

Production for the group's final album was handled by members Father Shaheed and Culture Freedom as well as DJ Clark Kent and KRS-One, who also joins PRT on the single he produced on the set called "Conscious Style." Other guests on the thoughtful album, which reached #57 on the R&B chart, included the Fugees, Brother J of X Clan, Miss Jones, Nine, and reggae singer Junior Reid.

OCTOBER 15

Xzibit releases his debut studio album *At the Speed of Life* on RCA.

The West Coast rapper's hardcore debut, which reached #74 on the *Billboard* 200 and #22 on the R&B chart, included production from Diamond D, E-Swift, DJ Muggs, and Saafir.

The album spawned three singles, including lead breakout single "Paparazzi," which became a major hit in Europe and reached #9 on the Rap chart. Xzibit's second single, "The Foundation," a song addressed to his infant son that included his cries, reached #16 on the Rap chart.

OCTOBER 22

Chuck D releases his debut solo album *Autobiography of Mistachuck* on Mercury.

The groove-oriented album from the Public Enemy frontman, which cracked the *Billboard* 200, focuses on hip-hop's infighting and materialism. Guests on *Autobiography of Mistachuck* included Da Brat, Abnormal, B-Wyze, Dow Jonz, Kendu, Melquan, and the legendary Isaac Hayes. The track "Horizontal Heroin" reunites Chuck and Professor Griff on record for the first time since 1988.

OCTOBER 22

Westside Connection releases *Bow Down* on Priority.

The West Coast supergroup, comprised of Ice Cube, Mack 10, and WC, released the gangsta classic *Bow Down*, which debuted at #2 on the *Billboard* 200. Less than a year after release, the album was certified platinum.

Featuring several diss tracks directed at Cypress Hill, *Bow Down* yielded two singles, "Bow Down" and "Gangstas Make the World Go Round," both of which became top ten hits on the Rap chart.

OCTOBER 29

Ghostface Killah, of the Wu-Tang Clan, releases his debut solo album *Ironman* on Razor Sharp.

With almost a year since the last Wu solo release, *Liquid Swords* by the GZA, Ghostface Killah's solo debut, was one of the most anticipated albums of the year.

As with all other Wu solo projects at the time, the chart-topping, platinum-selling album was produced almost entirely by the RZA, except for the track "Fish," which was produced by Wu affiliate True Master.

The Blaxploitation-inspired album spawned the hits, "All That I Got Is You," featuring Mary J. Blige and a Jackson 5 sample, and fan favorite "Daytona 500," featuring Raekwon, Cappadonna, and Force M.D.'s.

Wu members Raekwon and Cappadonna are given artist cocredits as they appear on twelve of the album's seventeen tracks. Other guests on the album included the legendary Delfonics, Scotty Wotty, Jamie Sommers, as well as Wu affiliates Popa Wu and Masta Killa and Clan members Method Man, U-God, Inspectah Deck, and the RZA.

NOVEMBER 5

Tela releases his debut album *Piece of Mind* on Suave House.

Part of the Suave House crew, which included the duo 8Ball & MJG, Tela produced his well-received debut with Jazze Pha, T-Mix, and Slice Tee, which peaked at #70 on the *Billboard* 200 and #17 on the R&B chart.

This southern hustler classic produced the hit single "Sho Nuff," which reached #58 on the *Billboard* Hot 100 and included guests Crime Boss, legendary go-go godfather Chuck Brown, Fedz, NOLA, and Thorough of South Circle.

NOVEMBER 5

Death Row release the first posthumous albums by Tupac Shakur, *The Don Killuminati: The 7 Day Theory*.

The multi-platinum album, which debuted at #1 on the US charts, is credited to Makaveli, an ode to the Italian fifteenth-century philosopher and politician Niccolò Machiavelli.

The album, originally meant as a sort of a mixtape, promo-only project, was released two months after 2Pac's tragic murder. Hit singles released are "To Live & Die in L.A.," "Toss It Up," which reached #34 on the *Billboard* Hot 100, and "Hail Mary," which reached #12 on the R&B chart and #8 on the Rap chart.

Producers on the album included QDIII, Darryl "Big D" Harper, and Tommy "D" Daugherty, among others and guests included K-Ci & JoJo, Young Noble, Val Young, Aaron Hall, Danny Boy, Virginya Slim, E.D.I. Mean, Yaki Kadafi, Prince Ital Joe, the Outlawz, and Kastro.

NOVEMBER 12

Lil' Kim releases her debut album *Hard Core* on Undeas.

The multi-platinum album by Biggie Smalls protégée and Junior M.A.F.I.A. member debuted at #11 on the *Billboard* 200 and #3 on the R&B chart. The raunchy set featured production by Stevie J, Andreao "Fanatic" Heard, Ski, Carlos Broady, Jermaine Dupri, and Sean "Puffy" Combs, who appeared on the smash hit singles "Not Tonight" and "No Time." "No Time" reached #8 on the *Billboard* Hot 100 and topped the Rap chart for nine weeks. Another huge hit off the album was "Crush on You," featuring a posthumous appearance by her mentor the Notorious B.I.G. and Lil' Cease of Junior M.A.F.I.A. Album favorites include "Dreams," "Queen B," and "Big Momma Thang," featuring Jay Z and Lil' Cease.

CHUCK D:

Lil' Kim could straight rhyme. Her voice got deeper than dude MCs when inspired. Her direction obviously had confidence from the MC who helped discover her—Biggie Notorious B.I.G. Smalls. With male MCs talking their smack, Lil' Kim not only balanced her Junior M.A.F.I.A. group but the whole rap game. But with her counterpart, Foxy Brown, a woman's point of view was heard at that time. Aggressive—even beyond what was going on from the dudes.

NOVEMBER 12

Snoop Doggy Dogg releases his sophomore album *Tha Doggfather* on Death Row.

The multi-platinum release, which debuted at #1 on the *Billboard* 200 and the R&B chart, was Snoop's last release for Death Row and would feature production by DJ Pooh, Sam Sneed, L.T. Hutton, Daz Dillinger, Soopafly, and Arkim & Flair among others.

Tha Doggfather also contained the gold-selling single "Snoop's Upside Ya Head," featuring Charlie Wilson and samples from the Gap Band classic, "Doggfather," featuring Charlie Wilson and a cover of the Biz Markie classic "Vapors," featuring Charlie Wilson and the Teena Marie. Other guests on *Tha Doggfather* included Tray Dee, Tha Dogg Pound, Warren G, Nate Dogg, Kurupt tha Kingpin, LBC Crew, Too $hort, and 2Pac Shakur.

NOVEMBER 12

MC Lyte releases the single "Cold Rock a Party" on East West.

Produced by Rashad Smith, the debut gold-selling single for MC Lyte's fifth album, *Bad As I Wanna B*, reached #11 on the *Billboard* Hot 100 and #5 on the R&B chart.

The single version of the song, different from the studio album version, was remixed by Puff Daddy and featured an appearance from Missy Elliott.

NOVEMBER 16

DJ Shadow releases his debut studio album *Entroducing...* on Mo' Wax.

Composed almost entirely of sampled content, the sonically adventurous instrumental debut from the California music producer was originally a success in England, where he had a following. The critically acclaimed, surreal album gradually gained traction in the United States, hitting #37 on the *Billboard* chart and making a number of best of the year lists.

NOVEMBER 19

Foxy Brown releases her debut album *Ill Na Na* on Def Jam.

After guesting on a number of hit singles, the Brooklyn-born rapper's long-awaited set quickly went platinum. Mainly produced by Trackmasters with additional work by Teddy Riley, Divine Allah, Rich Nice, George Pearson, and Charly Charles, the debut featured the hit singles, "Get Me Home," featuring BLACKstreet and reaching #42 on the *Billboard* Hot 100, "Big Bad Mama," featuring Dru Hill, which reached #53 on the *Billboard* Hot 100, and "I'll Be," featuring Jay Z, which reached #5 on the R&B chart. "I'll Be" was a reworking of the 1985 hit "I'll Be Good" by René & Angela. Other guests on *Ill Na Na* included Method Man, Kid Capri, and Havoc of Mobb Deep.

NOVEMBER 19

Mobb Deep release their third album *Hell on Earth* on Loud.

Produced by Mobb Deep, the gritty gold-selling album topped the R&B charts and reached #6 on the *Billboard* 200, featured the hit singles "Drop a Gem on 'Em," "Front Lines (Hell on Earth)," which reached #13 on the Rap chart, and the haunting "G.O.D. Pt. III," which reached #8 on the Dance charts and #18 on the Rap chart.

The haunting album also featured guest appearances from Big Noyd, Method Man, Raekwon, Nas, Ty Nitty, and Twin Gambino.

NOVEMBER 26

Dr. Dre releases the compilation *Dr. Dre Presents the Aftermath* on Aftermath.

Dre's first release after leaving Death Row Records was named after his new label, Aftermath. Reaching #6 on the *Billboard* 200 and #3 on the R&B chart, the album shifted away from the gangsta G-funk template.

Dr. Dre produced the platinum-selling set, which spawned the hit singles "East Coast/West Coast Killas," featuring KRS-One, Nas, B-Real, and RBX and "Been There Done That." Other guests included King Tee, Jheryl Lockhart, Sid McCoy, RC, D-Ruff, Hands-On, Mel-Man, Nowl, Kim Summerson, Sharief, Whoz Who, Nicole Johnson, Maurice Wilcher, Stu-B-Doo, Flossy P, Mike Lynn, and Cassandra McCowan.

DECEMBER 10

Redman releases his third album *Muddy Waters* on Def Jam.

Executive produced by Erick Sermon, the gold-seller from the Brick City–native topped the R&B charts and reached #12 on the *Billboard* 200. The funky album, which showcased Redman's lyrical dexterity and comedic chops, spawned the singles "It's Like That (My Big Brother)" with K-Solo, "Whateva Man" featuring Erick Sermon, and "Pick It Up." Method Man guested on "Do What Ya Feel."

1997

JANUARY 28

Camp Lo release their debut studio album *Uptown Saturday Night* on Profile.

The Bronx duo Sonny Cheeba and Geechi Suede released their critically acclaimed debut, which skillfully mixed hip-hop, funk, and jazz with the rapper's funky flow. Mainly produced by Ski and Trugoy the Dove, the catchy album reached #27 on the *Billboard* 200 and #5 on the R&B chart. The sales were propelled by the lead single "Luchini AKA This Is It," which peaked at #50 on the *Billboard* Hot 100 and #5 on the Rap chart.

FEBRUARY 5

Saukrates releases the EP *Brick House* on Capitol Hill.

Toronto MC and producer Saukrates released his underground classic, which featured guest appearances by Common, No I.D., Masta Ace, and O.C. and produced the single "Father Time."

FEBRUARY 11

Jive Records releases the soundtrack to the New Line Cinema film *Dangerous Ground*.

The soundtrack featured songs from Jay Z, Spice 1, and Too $hort, to name a few, as well as Ice Cube on the single "The World Is Mine." The soundtrack also featured an all-female posse cut with MC Lyte, Bahamadia, Nonchalant, and Yo-Yo called "Keep on Pushin'."

MARCH 9

Notorious B.I.G. is shot in a drive-by shooting in Los Angeles.

The twenty-four-year-old Brooklyn rapper was shot four times after attending a party hosted by *Vibe* magazine earlier in the evening. He died hours later.

Nine days after his death, a public memorial service for the beloved rapper was held in Manhattan. Among the attendees of Biggie's funeral were Queen Latifah, Flavor Flav, Puff Daddy, Run-D.M.C., DJ Kool Herc, Busta Rhymes, Lil' Kim, and his former wife Faith Evans. Faith Evans sang at the funeral and Puff Daddy delivered a eulogy. After Notorious B.I.G.'s funeral, thousands lined the streets throughout Brooklyn and Manhattan as the funeral procession led his body through his hometown neighborhood of Bedford-Stuyvesant, Brooklyn.

Despite years of investigation and speculation, the legendary rapper's death remains unsolved.

MARCH 11

Scarface releases his fourth studio album *The Untouchable* on Rap-A-lot.

Debuting at #1 on the *Billboard* 200 and topping the R&B chart, the hardcore gangsta album featured production by the artist as well as N.O. Joe, Mike Dean, Tone Capone, and Dr. Dre, who also appeared with Ice Cube and Too $hort on the track "Game Over." The platinum-seller contained the gold-selling "Smile," featuring 2Pac, which reached #12 on the *Billboard* Hot 100.

MARCH 25

Bad Boy posthumously releases the sophomore album by the Notorious B.I.G., *Life After Death*.

Released as scheduled two weeks after his murder in Los Angeles, *Life After Death*, the ambitious multi-platinum double disc entered on top of the *Billboard* 200, staying there for 4 weeks.

The landmark album spawned hit singles, including the platinum-selling "Hypnotize" and "Mo' Money, Mo' Problems," both of which debuted at #1 on the *Billboard* Hot 100, as well as "Notorious Thugs," "Going Back to Cali," and "Nasty Boy."

Produced by the RZA, DJ Premier, Kay Gee of Naughty By Nature, Easy Mo Bee, and Puff Daddy, among others, the Grammy-nominated mafioso classic featured guest spots from Kelly Price, R. Kelly, Carl Thomas, the Lox, Lil' Kim, 112, D.M.C., Faith Evans, and Bone Thugs-N-Harmony.

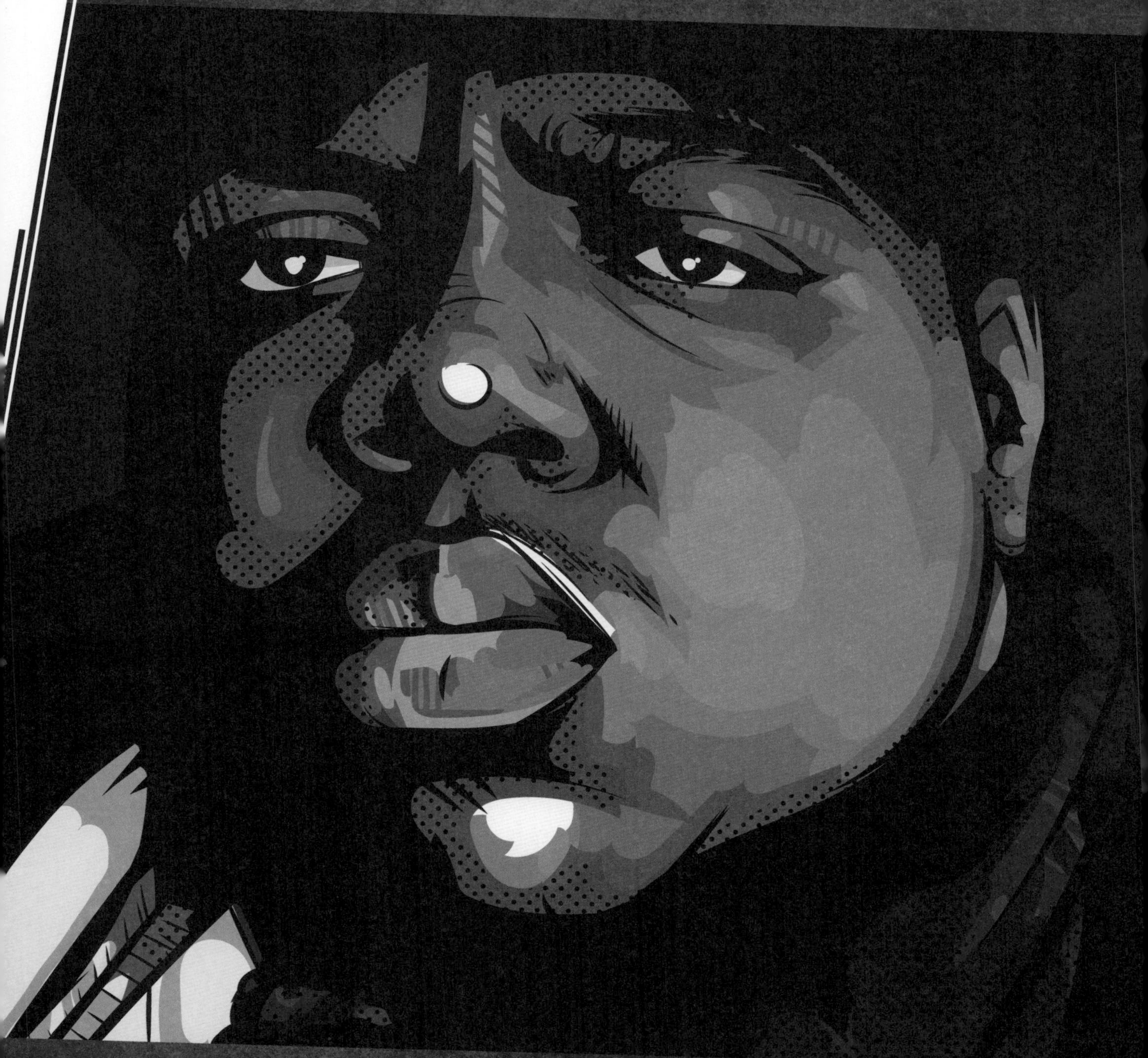

THE NOTORIOUS B.I.G.

CHUCK D:
With the shakeup behind the murders, beefs, and tensions between coasts, this album was a painful reminder of how talent that is snuffed out too soon, and over too little, was and is one of the number-one problems in the industry. Yet this project brought many artists together and helped lay some balm over the loss for his mourning audience.

APRIL 3

Minister Louis Farrakhan, head of the Nation of Islam, holds a Hip-Hop Summit in Chicago.

Organized to address the ongoing coastal feuds in hip-hop, the summit is attended by various hip-hop stars including Snoop Dogg, Ice Cube, Common, Fat Joe, Doug E. Fresh, and Kam.

APRIL 15

The Artifacts release their sophomore album *That's Them* on Big Beat.

The three-man crew of El Da Sensei, Tame One, and DJ Chaos, was produced by Showbiz, Shawn J. Period, Da Beatminerz, and Lord Finesse, who along with Lord Jamar of Brand Nubian appeared on the track "Collaboration of Mics." Peaking at #25 on the R&B chart, it was the final album from the Newark crew.

MAY 20

KRS-One releases his third solo album *I Got Next* on Jive.

Peaking at #3 on the *Billboard* 200 and #2 on the R&B chart, the gold-selling album was the Blastmaster's biggest selling album to date. Featuring production by Puff Daddy, Showbiz, DJ Muggs of Cypress Hill, Stevie J, Jesse West, KRS himself, and others, the hard-hitting album featured guest appearances by Angie Martinez of Hot 97 FM, Redman, Keva, G. Simone, Anthony Mills, Thor-El, Lamont Fields, and Mic Vandalz.

I Got Next spawned the hit singles "Heartbeat," "Can't Stop, Won't Stop," and the classic "Step Into a World (Rapture's Delight)," which sampled the classic hip-hop breakbeat of "The Champ" by the Mohawks and an interpolation of Blondie's 1981 ode to hip-hop "Rapture," which reached #70 on the *Billboard* Hot 100.

MAY 20

No Limit releases the soundtrack to the No Limit film *I'm Bout It*.

Produced by Master P, Beats By the Pound, Brotha Lynch Hung, and E-A-Ski among others, the hardcore gangsta rap soundtrack reached #4 on the *Billboard* 200 and topped the R&B charts, a first for No Limit. Singles included "If I Could Change" by Master P and Steady Mobb'n, which reached #5 on the Rap chart, and "Pushin' Inside You" by Sons of Funk, which hit the *Billboard* Hot 100.

JUNE 3

Wu-Tang Clan release their second studio album *Wu-Tang Forever* on RCA.

Debuting at #1 on the *Billboard* 200, the multi-platinum adventurous double album featured twenty-seven songs, many of which exceeded the five-minute mark. For example, the album's lead single, "Triumph," was a nearly six-minute song with nine verses rapped by various group members that did not feature a chorus. The sprawling 112-minute length allowed the members room to shine, including Inspectah Deck on "Triumph" and Ghostface Killah on "Impossible." Yet RZA's tight production kept it from losing focus.

In 2013, Drake would pay tribute to the landmark album in a song called "Wu-Tang Forever," which sampled the original album track "It's Yourz."

JUNE 17

Capone-N-Noreaga release their debut album *The War Report* on Penalty.

The Queens duo of Capone and N.O.R.E.'s lyrical street smarts are spotlighted in this hardcore underground classic featuring production by Buckwild, Marley Marl, Clark Kent, Lord Finesse, the Hitmen, among others. Tragedy Khadafi both produced tracks and guested on the East Coast album, along with Busta Rhymes, Havoc, and Mobb Deep.

Reaching #4 on the R&B chart and #21 on the *Billboard* 200, the gritty set contained the hits "Illegal Life," "L.A. L.A.," T.O.N.Y," and "Closer," all of which reached the top forty on the Rap chart.

JUNE 24

The Beatnuts release their third album *Stone Crazy* on Relativity.

The Beatnuts self-produced this jazzy breakthrough set, the first after the departure of group member Fashion, which cracked the *Billboard* 200 and reached #38 on the R&B chart. *Stone Crazy* contained the hit singles "Do You Believe" and "Off the Books," featuring Big Pun and Cuban Link, which reached #27 and #12 on the Rap chart respectively.

JUNE 24

Wyclef Jean releases his debut solo album *The Carnival* on Columbia.

The double-platinum eclectic set from the Fugee member featured a potpourri of hip-hop-influenced musical styles with guest appearances by the Neville Brothers, Celia Cruz, and band members Pras and Lauryn Hill.

Reaching #16 on the *Billboard* 200 and #4 on the R&B chart, the innovative set contained the hits "We Trying to Stay Alive"; "Anything Can Happen"; a cover of the Cuban classic "Guantanamera"; and the Grammy-nominated "Gone Till November," which reached #7 on the *Billboard* Hot 100.

JULY 1

Puff Daddy releases his debut studio album *No Way Out* on Bad Boy.

Produced by Puff Daddy along with the production group the Hitmen, the multi-platinum album topped the *Billboard* 200 and the R&B chart. While it featured some upbeat tunes, the album reflected Puff Daddy's feeling of loss after the murder of the Notorious B.I.G.

Featuring all-star guests including Busta Rhymes, the Notorious B.I.G., Lil' Kim, Ma$e, Jay Z, Foxy Brown, and Ginuwine, the compelling juggernaut produced five hit singles, including "Can't Nobody Hold Me Down," which spent six weeks on the *Billboard* Hot 100 as well as topping the R&B and Rap charts; "I'll Be Missing You," a Grammy Award–winning tribute to the Notorious B.I.G. that is one of the bestselling singles of all time; "It's All About the Benjamins," which topped the R&B and Rap charts; the platinum-selling "Been Around the World"; and the gold-selling "Victory."

JULY 11

Timbaland and Magoo release the single "Up Jumps da Boogie" on Atlantic.

The debut single from the Virginia hip-hop duo, featuring Missy Elliott and Aaliyah, served as the lead single on the platinum-selling *Welcome to Our World*, the group's first studio album.

The gold-selling party anthem topped the Rap chart, hit #4 on the R&B chart, and peaked at #12 on the *Billboard* Hot 100.

JULY 15

Bad Boy releases the hit "Mo Money Mo Problems" by the Notorious B.I.G.

The Grammy Award–nominated chart-topper from Biggie's posthumously released sophomore album *Life After Death* featured Puff Daddy, Ma$e, and Kelly Price.

Produced by Stevie J, the hit song's #1 spot on the *Billboard* Hot 100 was ironically preceded by the Biggie tribute hit "I'll Be Missing You" by Puff Daddy, featuring Faith Evans and 112.

JULY 15

Missy Elliott releases her debut album *Supa Dupa Fly* on Elektra.

Produced by Timbaland, the critically acclaimed debut landed at #3 on the *Billboard* 200, topped the R&B chart, and was certified platinum in September 1997, only three months after its release.

The adventurous and forward-thinking *Supa Dupa Fly*, featuring guest appearances from Ginuwine, Busta Rhymes, Aaliyah, Lil' Kim, and Queen Latifah, among others, spawned four singles: the gold-selling "Sock It 2 Me," featuring Da Brat; "Beep Me 911"; "Hit Em wit da Hee"; and the Grammy-nominated "The Rain (Supa Dupa Fly)," which sampled Ann Peebles's 1973 hit "I Can't Stand the Rain."

CHUCK D:
This album stretches the perimeters of what an MC can do. Missy Elliott checked the perimeters of visual and audio art—even past Busta Rhymes, her label mate. Her wit and her humor are necessary, and even to this day evidenced in her Super Bowl performance with Katy Perry. Her partner and coproducer, Timbaland, simply changed the game to his rhythms and is thus the Fela Kuti of hip-hop.

JULY 22

Company Flow release their full-length album, *Funcrusher Plus,* on Rawkus.

In 1996, the Brooklyn three-man crew of El-P, Mr. Len, and Big Juss released their debut EP *Funcrusher* on their own imprint Official but rereleased the landmark on the indie underground hip-hop label a year later.

The arty, self-produced album featured seven of the eight songs off its predecessor, including the singles "8 Steps to Perfection" and "Population Control," as well as the new single "Blind." The vinyl and cassette editions of the set contained the bonus album cut "Corners '94."

Two tracks from the off-kilter album, "The Fire in Which You Burn" and "Lune TNS," were featured on the popular 1997 Rawkus compilation *Soundbombing*.

JULY 29

Bone Thugs-N-Harmony release their fourth album *The Art of War* on Ruthless.

Produced by DJ U-Neek, the multi-platinum double album discs were called "World War 1" and "World War 2." Topping both the *Billboard* 200 and the R&B chart, the Cleveland group's fourth set dealt mainly with what they perceived as copycats riding the coattails of their chart success.

The Art of War, which featured a guest appearance by 2Pac on "Thug Luv," contained the platinum-selling single "Look into My Eyes," which topped the R&B chart, and the gold-selling "If I Could Teach the World," which reached #3 on the Rap chart.

AUGUST 5

Atmosphere releases their debut album *Overcast!* on Rhymesayers.

The debut album from the pioneering Minneapolis hip-hop outfit of Slug, Ant, and Spawn brought the groups its first bout of national attention, thanks in large part to the group's single "Scapegoat" becoming a college radio hit.

As the first landmark release from the Twin Cities' local Rhymesayers Entertainment label, *Overcast!* would end up influencing a generation of Twin Cities rappers.

SEPTEMBER 2

Master P releases his sixth album *Ghetto D* on his own No Limit.

The multi-platinum breakthrough that topped the *Billboard* 200 and R&B chart was the biggest selling album of Master P's career to date.

The gangsta *Ghetto D* produced the blockbuster hits "I Miss My Homies," which featured Fiend, Mystikal, Silkk the Shocker, Sons of Funk, Mo B Dick, Pimp C, Mercedes, and O'Dell and reached #2 on the Rap chart; "Bourbons & Lacs," featuring Lil Gotti, Mo B. Dick, and Silkk the Shocker; and the anthem "Make 'Em Say Uhh!," which featured Mia X, Fiend, Silkk the Shocker, and Mystikal, topped the Rap chart, and reached #9 on the *Billboard* Hot 100.

SEPTEMBER 16

Busta Rhymes releases his sophomore solo album *When Disaster Strikes...* on Flipmode.

The platinum-selling second solo set by the former member of Leaders of the New School, which continued the apocalypse theme of his debut, earned Busta a Grammy Award nomination. With production by DJ Scratch, the Ummah, Rockwilder, Easy Mo Bee, and Diddy, among others, the innovative album spawned the hits "Turn It Up (Remix) (Fire It Up)," which went gold; the multi-platinum "Dangerous"; and the anthem "Put Your Hands Where My Eyes Could See," which went platinum as well.

Topping the R&B chart and peaking at #3 on the *Billboard* 200, Busta's sometime manic set included guest appearances by Erykah Badu, Jamal, Ma$e, Lord Have Mercy, Rampage, Anthony Hamilton & the Chosen Generation, and Busta's Flipmode Squad.

BUSTA RHYMES

SEPTEMBER 30

Common releases his third studio album *One Day It'll All Make Sense* on Relativity.

Mainly produced by No I.D., the critically acclaimed, thoughtful album reached #12 on the R&B chart and #62 on the *Billboard* 200. The album, filled with Common's meditations and observations, spawned the single "Retrospect for Life," featuring Lauryn Hill; "Reminding Me (of Sef)," which featured Chantay Savage and reached #9 on the Rap chart; and "All Night Long," which featured Erykah Badu and was produced by the Roots. Other guests on the album include Cee-Lo Green on "G.O.D.," De La Soul on "Gettin' Down at the Amphitheater," and Canibus on "Making a Name for Ourselves."

OCTOBER 5

Jason Nevins releases his remix of Run-D.M.C.'s "It's Like That" on Profile.

Fourteen years after Run-D.M.C. first released the 1983 single, the remix from dance music producer Jason Nevins transformed a somewhat obscure track into a massive global hit. Officially released under the name Run-D.M.C. vs. Jason Nevins, the single sold approximately five million copies worldwide.

OCTOBER 14

Ma$e releases the hit single "Feel So Good" on Bad Boy.

The platinum-selling, chart-topping single was released off Ma$e's debut album *Harlem World*. Produced by Sean "Puffy" Combs and D-Dot, the track sampled the Kool & the Gang classic hit "Hollywood Swingin'" and featured a guest appearance by Kelly Price. The bestselling song of Ma$e's career reached #5 on the *Billboard* Hot 100 and #1 on the Rap chart.

OCTOBER 14

Gravediggaz release their second studio album *The Pick, the Sickle, and the Shovel* on Gee Street.

The horrorcore supergroup of Prince Paul, Frukwan, Poetic, and RZA under their alter egos released a socially conscious, intelligent set backed by inventive production. Mainly produced by Wu members True Master, 4th Disciple, and Darkim Be Allah, the dark album reached #20 on the *Billboard* 200 and #7 on the R&B chart.

OCTOBER 21

Salt-N-Pepa release their fifth album *Brand New* on Red Ant.

The gold-selling album, produced by Pepa, DJ Spinderella, and Esmail, was their last together as a group.

Released shortly before Red Ant Records filed for bankruptcy, the album reached #38 on the *Billboard* 200 and #16 on the R&B chart, and featured the hits "R U Ready" and "Gitty Up," which reached #50 on the *Billboard* Hot 100.

OCTOBER 21

Rap supergroup The Firm release their only album, *The Firm: The Album,* on Aftermath.

Consisting of Nas, Foxy Brown, AZ, and Nature, who eventually replace Cormega, the anticipated album debuted at #1 on the *Billboard* 200, and topped the R&B chart as well.

Produced by Dr. Dre and Trackmasters, the gangsta album featured the smash hit singles "Firm Biz," featuring Dawn Robinson of En Vogue and Lucy Pearl, and "Phone Tap," featuring Dr. Dre. Other guests on *The Album* included Pretty Boy, Canibus, and Half A Mill.

OCTOBER 28

Ma$e releases his debut album *Harlem World* on Bad Boy.

Ma$e, who made a splash appearing on Puff Daddy's multi-platinum *No Way Out* and the Notorious B.I.G.'s *Life After Death*, now carried the torch as Bad Boy's new resident superstar after the murder of B.I.G. in Los Angeles.

The critically acclaimed, Grammy-nominated debut featured production by the Neptunes, Dame Grease,

Mo-Suave-A, Jermaine Dupri, as well as by Puff Daddy's Hitmen production crew. Debuting at #1 on the *Billboard* 200 and R&B chart, the album contained the huge hits "Feels So Good," "Lookin' at Me," and "What You Want," all of which reached the top ten on the *Billboard* Hot 100, R&B, and Rap charts.

Guests on *Harlem World* included the L.O.X., DMX, Black Rob, Kelis, the Madd Rapper, Lil' Kim, 8Ball & MJG, Billy Lawrence, 112, Monifah, Jay Z, Lil' Cease, Busta Rhymes, Total, Kelly Price, as well as Puff Daddy.

CHUCK D:
I heard Mason Betha was the pop formula idea for P. Diddy's Bad Boy label. He said he got the idea from Erick Sermon's style. The style of *"rap gloss over the music while never getting in its way"* was brilliant and harder than one would think. Especially rocking over vicious dance loops and tracks you can't have a vocalist stab the beat dead. Ma$e never ever got in the way, and his rhymes proved to be a subtle instrument, while the videos rocketed the songs.

NOVEMBER 4

Jay Z releases his second studio album *In My Lifetime, Vol. 1* on Roc-A-Fella.

Debuting at #3 on the *Billboard* 200, the platinum-selling album featured production from Damon Dash, the Hitmen, Teddy Riley, DJ Premier, Buckwild, as well as Poke and Tone.

The album, which showcased Jay Z's incredible flow and stories of ghetto celebrity, featured guest appearances from BLACKstreet, Lil' Kim, Puff Daddy, Foxy Brown, Babyface, Sauce Money, Kelly Price, and Too $hort.

Singles from the album included "Who You Wit," which was featured in the soundtrack for the film *Sprung*; "(Always Be My) Sunshine"; "The City Is Mine"; and "Wishing on a Star," which featured Gwen Dickey of the R&B group Rose Royce. All of the singles reached the top twenty on the Rap chart.

NOVEMBER 4

Rakim releases his debut solo album *The 18th Letter* on Universal.

Debuting at #4 on the *Billboard* 200, the highly anticipated gold-selling debut from the veteran MC included production from DJ Premier, Father Shaheed of the Poor Righteous Teachers, Clark Kent, and Pete Rock.

The powerful, critically acclaimed debut featured the singles "It's Been a Long Time" and "Guess Who's Back."

NOVEMBER 4

Mystikal releases his second studio album *Unpredictable* on No Limit.

Peaking at #3 on the *Billboard* 200 and topping the R&B chart, the platinum-selling album, produced mainly by Beats by the Pound, showcases the Dirty South rapper's rough and fast style. It contained the hit single "Ain't No Limit," with Master P and Silkk the Shocker, which reached #23 on the R&B chart.

NOVEMBER 11

Nadanuf release their only album *Worldwide* on Reprise.

Cincinnati female rap duo of Skwert and Phor-One-One released their debut promoted hits "6 A.M. (We Be Rollin')," featuring Melieck Britt, which reached #55 on the R&B chart, and their remake of the 1980 Kurtis Blow classic "The Breaks," with the legendary MC joining the girls. The fun album was produced by Howie Tee, H&H Productions, Soul G, Michael Little, Def Jef, and Aaron "Babyboy" Griffin, who discovered the group.

NOVEMBER 25

Will Smith releases his debut solo studio album *Big Willie Style* on Columbia.

While starring in the summer blockbuster *Men in Black*, Will Smith also was recording his multi-platinum party-rap debut, which topped the R&B

chart and reached #8 on the *Billboard* 200, spending ninety-nine weeks on the chart. The crowd-pleasing album, built on his humorous style, featured slick production and select guest appearances, including Lisa "Left Eye" Lopes from TLC, Camp Lo, and Cameo, and writing from Nas on "Chasing Forever" and "Yes Yes Y'all."

Hit singles included the theme song to his movie, the Grammy-winning "Men in Black"; "Just Cruisin," which was produced by Trackmasters Poke and Tone and reached #56 on the *Billboard* Hot 100; the Grammy-winning multi-platinum "Gettin' Jiggy wit It"; "Just the Two of Us," which sampled the Bill Withers's song and reached #20 on the *Billboard* Hot 100; and "Miami," which reached #17 on the *Billboard* Hot 100.

NOVEMBER 25

Priority Records releases the compilation *In tha Beginning... There Was Rap.*

Peaking at #15 on the *Billboard* 200 and #4 on the R&B chart, the gold-selling compilation featured contemporary artists covering classic hip-hop songs from legendary MCs and groups. Some of the pairings included the Wu-Tang Clan's cover of Run-D.M.C.'s "Sucker M.C.'s (Krush-Groove 1)"; Def Squad covering the Sugar Hill Gang's "Rapper's Delight"; P. Diddy doing LL Cool J's "Big Ole Butt"; Master P's take on Ice-T's "6 in the Mornin'"; and Cypress Hill doing the Boogie Down Productions classic "I'm Still #1."

DECEMBER 9

LL Cool J releases his single "4, 3, 2, 1" on Def Jam.

Reaching the top ten on the Rap chart, the song featured guest appearances by DMX, Method Man, Redman, and Canibus. The latter's verse on the song instigated a longstanding feud between LL Cool J and the New York rapper. This resulted in several diss tracks the rappers directed at one another, including Canibus's "Second Round K.O.," and LL Cool J's "Ripper Strikes Back."

DECEMBER 9

Lord Tariq and Peter Gunz release their single "Deja Vu (Uptown Baby)" on Columbia.

The lead single to the Bronx duo's only studio album, *Make It Reign,* was a Top Ten crossover hit and was certified platinum four months after its release. The song illegally sampled "Black Cow" by Steely Dan, who took legal action and were awarded 100 percent of all publishing rights and 90 percent of the royalties for the song in order to clear the sample.

DECEMBER 16

Queen Pen releases her debut album *My Melody* on Lil' Man.

Queen Pen, a Teddy Riley protégée, had made a splash in the industry the previous year appearing on BLACKstreet's classic smash-hit "No Diggity," which also featured Dr. Dre.

Produced by Riley as well as Knobody, William "Skylz" Stewart, and Kaseem "Mixture" Coleman, *My Melody* contained the hit singles "Man Behind the Music," "All My Love," and "Party Ain't a Party," featuring Mr. Cheeks, Nutta Butta, and Markell Riley, all of which reached the top twenty on the Rap chart. Other guests on the album included Ronald Isley of the Isley Brothers, Phil Collins, and Meshell Ndegeocello on the controversial cut "Girlfriend."

1998

JANUARY 13

The L.O.X. release their debut *Money, Power & Respect* on Bad Boy.

The lyrically dexterous debut album from the Yonkers hip-hop trio of Jadakiss, Sheek Louch, and Styles P topped the R&B chart and reached #3 on the *Billboard* 200. Sales were spurred by two successful singles: "If You Think I'm Jiggy," which reached #30 on the *Billboard* Hot 100, and the gold-selling "Money, Power & Respect," which featured Lil' Kim and DMX and topped the Rap chart and reached #18 on the *Billboard* Hot 100.

Puff Daddy served as executive producer on the album, with notable New York producers like Swizz Beats, Dame Grease, and Younglord all contributing production.

JANUARY 27

Sylk-E. Fyne releases the single "Romeo and Juliet" on RCA.

"Romeo and Juliet," the Los Angeles rapper's lead single from her debut 1998 album *Raw Sylk*, featured singer William "Chill" Warner, who also cowrote the song. Peaking at #6 on the *Billboard* Hot 100 and topping the Rap chart, the gold-selling single was the high point of Sylk-E. Fyne's career.

FEBRUARY 17

Silkk the Shocker releases his second studio album *Charge It 2 da Game* on No Limit Records.

Produced mainly by Beats by the Pound, the platinum-selling gangsta album from Master P's brother debuted at #3 on the *Billboard* 200 and topped the R&B chart. There were numerous guest appearances from his No Limit band mates, including Master P on "Just Be Straight with Me," which also featured Destiny's Child and reached the top forty on the R&B and Rap charts. A second charting single, "It Ain't My Fault," which featured Mystikal, reached #15 on the *Billboard* Hot 100 and topped the Rap chart.

MARCH 17

C-Murder releases his debut *Life or Death* on No Limit Records.

Like much of the No Limit output in 1998, C-Murder's platinum-selling debut, produced by Beats by the Pound, focused on gangsta life and featured appearances by a number of his label mates, including his brothers Master P and Silkk the Shocker, as well as Mystikal and UGK. Peaking at #3 on the *Billboard* 200 and #1 on the R&B chart, the album stands out for C-Murder's original style and wordplay.

MARCH 24

Cappadonna releases his solo debut *The Pillage* on Razor Sharp Records.

Produced by the RZA, along with True Master and GoldFingaz, 4th Disciple, and Mathematics, the Cappadonna's gold-selling debut featured guest appearances from other Wu members as well. Reaching #3 on the *Billboard* 200 and topping the R&B chart, the set includes classic album cuts like the title track, "Splish Splash," and "Dart Throwing."

MARCH 31

Gang Starr release their fifth album *Moment of Truth* on Noo Trybe.

Debuting at #1 on the R&B chart and reaching #6 on the *Billboard* 200, the long-awaited follow-up to *Hard to Earn* was the group's most successful to date. The gold-selling, jazzy twenty-track set, self-produced by the band, featured the single "You Know My Steez," which cracked the *Billboard* Hot 100.

APRIL 28

Big Pun releases his debut album *Capital Punishment* on Terror Squad.

Big Pun's debut is the only studio album the Bronx rapper released during his lifetime. With guests that included Busta Rhymes, Funkmaster Flex, Fat Joe,

Wyclef, and Black Thought, the accessible album showcases the MC's virtuosity on the mic.

Pun's lyrical rhymes are evident on the hit singles, which included the platinum-selling "I'm Not a Player," which topped the R&B charts; the follow-up remix hit single "Still Not a Player," featuring Joe, which reached #24 on the *Billboard* Hot 100; and "You Came Up," featuring fellow New Yorker Noreaga, which hit both the R&B and Rap charts.

Nominated for a Grammy in 1999 for best rap album, *Capital Punishment* topped the R&B charts, reached #5 on the *Billboard* 200, and was certified platinum, the first solo Latino rapper to earn that distinction.

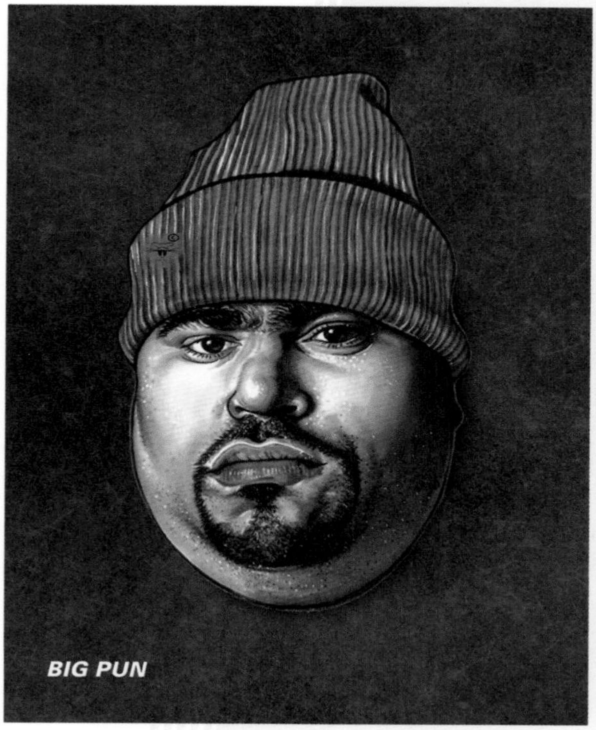

BIG PUN

APRIL 28

Public Enemy release the soundtrack to the film *He Got Game* on Def Jam Recordings.

The Touchstone Pictures basketball film *He Got Game*, directed by Spike Lee, starred Denzel Washington and Miami Heat player Ray Allen. Public Enemy became the first hip-hop group to score an entire major motion picture when they provided the musical backdrop for this b-ball drama, which reached #26 on the *Billboard* 200 and #10 on the R&B chart. KRS-One and Masta Killa from the Wu-Tang Clan guested on this set, which would be their last for the Def Jam label.

Public Enemy had a hit with the innovative title track, a reworking on the Buffalo Springfield 1960s classic "For What It's Worth" with a guest spot from Springfield leader Stephen Stills.

MAY 12

Jay Z releases the soundtrack to Roc-A-Fella Film, *Streets Is Watching*, on Roc-A-Fella Records.

The soundtrack to the documentary about Jay Z's life, which was more of a collection of continuous music videos in story form, was shown before his performances during the 1999 Hard Knock Life Tour.

Peaking at #3 on the R&B chart and #27 on the *Billboard* 200, the soundtrack featured production by DJ Clue?, Irv Gotti, M.O.P., Big Jaz, Mahogany, Ty Fyffe, Tone Capone, among others. *Streets Is Watching* spawned the hit singles "Love for Free," which featured Rell and cracked the *Billboard* Hot 100 and "It's Alright," which featured Memphis Bleek and reached #9 on the Rap chart. Other guests on the soundtrack included DMX, Noreaga, Ja Rule, Usual Suspects, Diamonds in da Rough, Sauce Money, Wais, and Christión, a Roc-A-Fella R&B duo.

MAY 19

DMX releases his debut album *It's Dark and Hell Is Hot* on Ruff Ryders Entertainment.

The hard-hitting multi-platinum debut by the MC from Yonkers, New York, would feature production by Swizz Beatz, P.K., Dame Grease, and Irv Gotti.

Debuting at #1 on the *Billboard* 200 and the R&B chart, the menacing album propelled by DMX's sermon preaching–style flow featured the hit singles "How's It Goin' Down" featuring Faith Evans and "Stop Being Greedy" as well as the classics "Get at Me Dog," featuring Sheek Louch of the L.O.X., which reached #6 on the Rap chart, and "Ruff Ryders' Anthem," produced by the then-unknown Swizz Beatz, which cracked the *Billboard* Hot 100.

CHUCK D:

Dark Man Unknown is not an act. Earl Simmons got my respect visiting the Hard Knock Life Tour in 1999 with Jay Z, the Roc Crew, and Redman and Method Man. I give Jay credit for being the ringmaster of it all, yet coming on after the blaze DMX left the stage. All dude had was a chain around his neck and a bucket of water. He gave 200 percent effort and skill in all those performances. His songs and videos exemplify this as well. His 3-4 album flurry hasn't been matched on that high level yet. Energy and passion on every bar. Naysayers usually stay out of his way.

JUNE 2

Onyx release the lead single "React" on Def Jam.

The lead single off Onyx's third album *Shut 'Em Down*, which reached #10 on the *Billboard* 200, was produced by Bud'da and featured a sample from the Slick Rick song "Mona Lisa." While it reached #44 on the Rap chart, what made the song notable was the appearance of 50 Cent in his first major label debut.

JUNE 9

Pras releases the single "Ghetto Supastar (That Is What You Are)" on Interscope Records.

The track by the former Fugee, featuring Mýa and Ol' Dirty Bastard of the Wu-Tang Clan, was produced by Wyclef Jean and his songwriting partner Jerry "Wonda" Duplessis.

"Ghetto Supastar" interpolates the 1983 Kenny Rogers–Dolly Parton hit "Islands in the Stream," written by the Bee Gees. The platinum-selling Grammy-nominated hit, which reached #15 on the *Billboard* Hot 100, was originally from the soundtrack of the 20th Century Fox film *Bulworth* and would later appear on Pras's debut of the same name.

JUNE 30

The Black Eyed Peas release their debut album *Behind the Front* on Interscope Records.

The Black Eyed Peas, made up of will.i.am, apl.de.ap, and Taboo, released a debut set that harked back to the days of early hip-hop with a modern approach, echoing the styles of the Cold Crush Brothers, the Treacherous Three, and the Sugar Hill Gang. The album contained the hit "Joints & Jam," an indirect ode to the Funky 4 + 1. The song, which featured vocals by Ingrid Dupre, was also featured in the 20th Century Fox film *Bulworth*. Other singles from their debut included "Head Bobs," "Fallin' Up," and "Karma."

Some of the songs from *Behind the Front* were demos for an album entitled *Grass Roots* recorded by an early incarnation of the band called A.T.B.A.N. Klann, that was to be released a year earlier on Ruthless Records before Eazy-E's death.

JULY 1

Puff Daddy releases his single "Come with Me" on Epic Records.

Released on the 1998 soundtrack for *Godzilla*, the rock-rap song updated the classic Led Zeppelin song

"Kashmir" and featured Zeppelin guitarist Jimmy Page. Rage Against the Machine guitarist Tom Morello also played guitar and bass on the track. The song reached #4 on the *Billboard* Hot 100 and was certified platinum.

JULY 7

Noreaga, of Capone-N-Noreaga, releases his debut solo album *N.O.R.E.* on Penalty Recordings.

The platinum-selling *N.O.R.E.*, which stands for Niggers on the Run Eating, featured an array of producers including Dame Grease, the Neptunes, Marley Marl, L.E.S., Poke, and Swizz Beatz, among others.

Peaking at #3 on the *Billboard* 200 and topping the R&B chart, the album featured guests such as Busta Rhymes, Spliff Star, Nas, Chico DeBarge, Kid Capri, Mussolini, Kool G. Rap, and Carl Thomas. It would spawn the smash hit singles "Superthug," a Neptunes-produced song that reached the top of the Rap chart and #36 on the *Billboard* Hot 100, "Banned From T.V.," featuring Cam'ron, Nature, Jadakiss and Styles P of the L.O.X., and Big Pun.

JULY 14

Beastie Boys release their fifth studio album *Hello Nasty* on Capitol Records.

With the addition of Mix Master Mike to their crew, the Beastie Boys release their multi-platinum set after a four-year hiatus, which topped the *Billboard* 200 list. Produced by the band with Mario Caldato Jr., the sonically adventurous, electronic funk album spawned the Grammy-winning "Intergalactic," which hit #28 on the *Billboard* Hot 100; "Body Movin'," which was remixed by Fatboy Slim; and the limerick-filled "The Negotiation Limerick File."

AUGUST 25

Lauryn Hill releases her debut *The Miseducation of Lauryn Hill* on Columbia Records.

The blockbuster album from the former Fugee was an instant classic, debuting at #1 on the *Billboard* 200 to rave reviews that lauded the album's sonic adventurousness and incorporation of genres ranging from reggae to hip-hop to neo-soul.

Carlos Santana, Mary J. Blige, and D'Angelo all appear as featured artists on the multi-platinum album, which spawned three singles: the Grammy Award–winning "Doo Wop (That Thing)," which debuted at #1 on the *Billboard* Hot 100; "Ex-Factor," which reached #7 on the R&B chart; and the Grammy-nominated, gold-selling "Everything Is Everything," which featured the first appearance by a teenage John Legend playing piano.

AUGUST 25

Xzibit releases his second studio album *40 Dayz & 40 Nightz* on RCA.

A follow-up to his critically acclaimed 1996 album *At the Speed of Life*, Xzibit's second set samples a range of artists including Quincy Jones, the Ohio Players, Raekwon, and Roy Ayers. But it's the MC's lyrical dexterity that makes this album shine.

Reaching #14 on the R&B chart and #58 on the *Billboard* 200, the album's Jesse West–produced single "What U See Is What U Get" became the rapper's most successful single to date, cracking the top fifty on the *Billboard* Hot 100 and #3 on the Rap chart. The album also featured the classic cuts "Los Angeles Time," "3 Card Molly," and "Pussy Pop."

SEPTEMBER 29

Outkast release their third studio album *Aquemini* on LaFace Records.

Largely produced on their own in Atlanta, Outkast used a great amount of live instrumentation on the blockbuster, which sold more than two million copies in its first year. Debuting at #2 on the *Billboard* 200, the experimental platinum-selling album, which was executive produced by Babyface, also featured Raekwon, George Clinton, Cee-Lo, and Erykah Badu as featured artists.

The eclectic album's lead single "Rosa Parks" reached #19 on the R&B charts, but in 1999 the song resulted in a lawsuit from Rosa Parks herself, who claimed the group wrongly misappropriated her name. The lawsuit was settled out of court in 2005.

SEPTEMBER 29

Jay Z releases *Vol. 2...Hard Knock Life* on Roc-A-Fella Records.

Released a year after 1998's *In My Lifetime, Vol. 1* the multi-platinum album debuted at the top of the *Billboard* 200 and featured appearances from Memphis Bleek, DMX, Too $hort, Ja Rule, the L.O.X., and Foxy Brown, among others.

Producers Timbaland, Irv Gotti, and Jermaine Dupri all helped shape the more mainstream, pop-oriented sound on the album, which spawned four singles, including the major hits "Can I Get A...," which reached #19 on the *Billboard* Hot 100, and the Grammy-nominated, platinum-selling "Hard Knock Life (Ghetto Anthem)," which audaciously sampled a song from the Broadway show *Annie*.

In 1999, *Vol. 2...Hard Knock Life* won the Grammy for best rap album. Jay Z did not attend the awards ceremony as a way of protesting the awards show's continued disregard for hip-hop and rap music.

SEPTEMBER 29

Black Star release *Mos Def & Talib Kweli Are Black Star* on Rawkus Records.

The collaborative album was the only studio release from rappers Mos Def and Talib Kweli under the name Black Star, which is a reference to a shipping line to Africa founded by Marcus Garvey in 1919.

Politically conscious and intellectually curious, the album incorporates a wide range of artistic influences, including jazz and Toni Morrison literature. Peaking at #13 on the R&B chart and #53 on the *Billboard* 200, the critically acclaimed album's lead single "Definition," which reached #3 on the Rap chart, addressed violence in hip-hop and was dedicated to Tupac and Biggie.

SEPTEMBER 29

A Tribe Called Quest release their fifth studio album *The Love Movement* on Jive Records.

Built around the theme of love, the jazzy, gold-selling set reached #3 on the *Billboard* 200 and R&B chart. Mainly produced by the Ummah, the laid-back album featured the song "Find a Way," which reached #18 on the Rap chart, "Like It Like That," and "Steppin' It Up," featuring Busta Rhymes and Redman.

OCTOBER 6

Cypress Hill release their fourth album, aptly titled *Cypress Hill IV*, on Ruffhouse Records.

Produced as usual by DJ Muggs, the gold-selling album, which reached #11 on both the *Billboard* 200 and R&B charts, spawned the hit single "Dr. Greenthumb" about a marijuana grower. Guest appearances on *Cypress Hill IV* included MC Eiht, Baron Ricks, and Chace Infinite.

OCTOBER 13

The posthumous 2Pac hit "Changes" is released on Interscope/Amaru/Death Row.

Recorded in 1992 while the late rapper was still with Interscope, the hit song, produced by Deon Evans, sampled the classic Bruce Hornsby and the Range hit of the 1980s "The Way It Is," with the chorus sung by Talent. The Grammy-nominated song tackles issues such as racism, police brutality, violence, poverty, and the war on drugs with some lyrics taken from another of his tracks, "I Wonder If Heaven Got a Ghetto."

OCTOBER 27

Ice Cube releases the hit single "Pushin' Weight" on Priority.

"Pushin' Weight," which featured Cube protégé Mr. Short Khop, was from the Los Angeles, California, rapper's platinum-selling album *War & Peace Vol.1 (The War Disc)*. Topping the Rap chart, the gold-selling hit single was produced by N.O. Joe as well as Ice Cube.

NOVEMBER 3

Juvenile releases his third album *400 Degreez* on Cash Money.

The breakthrough multi-platinum album from the New Orleans rapper was the highest-selling album on Bryan and Ronald Williams's Cash Money Records. Produced by Mannie Fresh, the Dirty South album featured many artists from the Cash Money roster, including Big Tymers, Lil Wayne, Mannie Fresh, and Turk.

With his structured rhymes, Juvenile scored his first top ten *Billboard* Hot 100 hit with "Back That Azz Up," known in its censored radio edit as "Back That Thang Up." The album's second single, "Ha," charted at #19 on the *Billboard* Hot 100. Two remixes of the song were included on *400 Degreez*, one with members of Juvenile's fellow Hot Boys collaborators Lil Wayne, Turk, and B.G., and one with Jay Z.

NOVEMBER 3

Mo Thugs releases his single "Ghetto Cowboy" on Relativity.

The lead single off *Chapter II: Family Reunion* from Mo Thugs, a Cleveland hip-hop group comprised of members of Bone Thugs-N-Harmony, Krayzie Bone and Layzie Bone, along with Thug Queen and Powder P.

The gold-selling track became the highest, and only, charting single of Mo Thugs' recording career, peaking at #15 on the *Billboard* Hot 100 and topping the Rap chart.

NOVEMBER 4

Artisan Entertainment Pictures' *Belly* is released in US theaters.

The crime drama, directed and coproduced by renowned hip-hop video director Hype Williams, starred DMX, Method Man, T-Boz of TLC, and Nas, who cowrote the film with Williams. Dancehall reggae stars Sean Paul and Mr. Vegas also had cameo roles in the film.

The soundtrack, with production by Poke and Tone, Sean Combs, Swizz Beatz, among others, was more successful than the film. The album peaked at #5 on the *Billboard* 200 and #2 on the R&B chart on the strength of the tracks, including "Grand Finale" by DMX, Method Man, Nas, and Ja Rule, which reached #18 on the Rap chart.

NOVEMBER 10

Pete Rock releases his debut solo album *Soul Survivor* on Loud.

Famed producer and former member of the duo Pete Rock & CL Smooth pulls in all of his famous friends to guest on his solo debut, including Method Man, Raekwon, Prodigy, Ghostface Killah, Large Professor, Kool G. Rap, Cappadonna, Common, Big Pun, Noreaga, and Tragedy Khadafi. Reaching #9 on the R&B chart and cracking the top forty on the *Billboard* 200, the well-produced album spawned two singles that hit the R&B and Rap charts: "Tru Master," which featured verses by Inspectah Deck and Kurupt, and "Take Your Time," which sampled Michael Jackson's "Billy Jean."

NOVEMBER 10

Method Man releases his second studio Album *Tical 2000:Judgement Day* on Def Jam.

With a slew of talented producers, including RZA, Inspectah Deck, Erick Sermon, and Trackmasters, the ambitious, twenty-eight-track album built around a doomsday scenario showcases Method Man at his finest. Debuting at #2 on the *Billboard* 200 and #1 on the R&B charts, this opus featured numerous skits, as well as the hit singles "Break Ups 2 Make Ups," featuring D'Angelo, which reached #29 on the R&B chart, and "Judgement Day," which reached #42 on the R&B chart.

NOVEMBER 24

RZA, as Bobby Digital, releases the album *Bobby Digital in Stereo* on Gee Street Records.

Exploring the adventures of RZA's fun-loving alter ego, the gold-selling experimental album was almost entirely produced by the RZA with contributions from King Tech and Inspectah Deck as well.

The keyboard-heavy album reached #3 on the R&B charts, and #16 on the *Billboard* 200. Guests on the album included fellow Wu-Tang members Method Man, Masta Killa, Ghostface Killah, ODB, and U-God, as well as Ras Kass, Doc Doom, Timbo King, Tekitha, and the Force MD's.

DECEMBER 1

Cool Breeze releases the single "Watch for the Hook" on Interscope.

The Atlanta rapper, a member of the Dungeon Family collective, whose debut album, *East Point's Greatest Hit* spawned one bestselling single. Produced by Organized Noize, "Watch for the Hook," which featured Dungeon Family members Outkast, Goodie Mob, and Witchdoctor, topped the Rap chart for three weeks.

DECEMBER 1

Jurassic 5 release their self-titled debut album on Pan.

The six-man crew, made up of former members of the rap crews Unity Committee and Rebels of Rhythm, consisted of Chali 2na, Akil, Marc 7, Zaakir, DJ Nu-Mark, and Cut Chemist, with the latter two producing the set. The underground classic featured cuts from their 1997 EP, simply titled *EP*, released the previous year on Rumble Records.

The twenty-minute album is filled with top-notch rapping combined with fresh and eclectic samples from a wide-ranging group of artists like Henry Mancini, Led Zeppelin, Mahavishnu Orchestra, John Williams, Ike Turner & the Kings of Rhythm, Quincy Jones, Michael White's Magic Music Company, Ramsey Lewis, and LL Cool J.

DECEMBER 15

Busta Rhymes releases his third solo album *E.L.E. (Extinction Level Event): The Final World Front* on Flipmode.

Like his previous solo sets, *E.L.E.* followed in the apocalyptic theme of Rhymes's two previous efforts, *The Coming* and *When Disaster Strikes*. And like those albums, it sold like crazy, debuting at #12 on the *Billboard* 200 and staying on the chart for thirty-two weeks.

The platinum-selling, boundary-pushing *E.L.E.*, which was nominated for three Grammy Awards, was filled with sharp rhymes and odd samples, contained the hit singles "Gimme Some More," which reached the top forty on both the *Billboard* Hot 100 and R&B chart, and "What's It Gonna Be?!," featuring Janet Jackson, which reached #3 on the *Billboard* Hot 100. Producers include Diamond D, Swizz Beatz, Nottz, Rockwilder, DJ Scratch, Deric "D-Dot" Angelettie, among others.

CHUCK D:

Well, the story's been told repeatedly by now: 510 Franklin Street was the Bomb Squad HQ in the 1980s. Eric "Vietnam" Sadler was a musician who had the downstairs studio. Darrell Higgins was his friend. Brian Higgins was his brother. Trevor Smith was his friend. We wanted to tell the neighborhood acts that they should have a stand-out identity coming from Long Island. These guys hung around. PE got the Def Jam deal after having a neighborhood audition for the DJ Johnny Juice–led Kings of Pressure.

We made "Rebel Without a Pause" as a demo and these young guys were climbing up the walls. I kept looking at Trevor going nuts. Later the name Leaders of the New School was suggested to them. Buster Rhymes was a popular collegiate football running back at the time. I thought, what a great name for an MC. I don't remember how receptive the guys were about name changes—few were—but the name Leaders of the New School was from a bar in "Don't Believe the Hype," and Hank Shocklee came up with Charlie Brown for Brian.

LONS signed on to Elektra. Exhibiting explosive energy, as tutored. From there Busta Rhymes because that name helped legitimize him—more MC than footballer, with many songs, albums, shows, and tours running up to this conglomerating moment. And other than history like Ice Cube, he ain't never looked back once he got the blueprint.

DECEMBER 15

Mystikal releases his fourth album *Ghetto Fabulous* on No Limit.

Produced by in-house production squad Beats by the Pound, *Ghetto Fabulous* was his last for the New Orleans–based No Limit label. Peaking at #5 on the *Billboard* 200 and topping the R&B chart, the platinum-selling album would include classic cuts as the title track, and "That's the Nigga."

Guests on *Ghetto Fabulous* included label mates Mia X, Fiend, Silkk the Shocker, Snoop Dogg, C-Murder, Mac, and imprint founder Master P, as well as Charlie Wilson of the Gap Band, Naughty By Nature, Busta Rhymes, and others.

1999

JANUARY 19

Silkk the Shocker releases his third studio album *Made Man* on No Limit.

The platinum-selling set from the New Orleans rapper, produced by Master P and Beats by the Pound, featured appearances from Jay Z, Mystikal, Snoop Dogg, and Mýa.

Made Man was a bona fide crossover success, topping the *Billboard* 200 and R&B chart, and selling a million copies in its first three months. Silkk the Shocker scored two #1 singles on the Rap chart with "Somebody Like Me" and "It Ain't My Fault Pt. 2," featuring Mystikal, which was a remix of his 1998 top twenty pop hit "It Ain't My Fault."

JANUARY 26

Foxy Brown releases her second album *Chyna Doll* on Def Jam.

Debuting at #1 on the *Billboard* 200 and the R&B chart, the platinum-selling album, was executive produced by Foxy along with a number of producers, including Irv Gotti, Swizz Beatz, and Fyffe.

Full of raunchy rhymes and slick beats, the album contained the single "Hot Spot," cowritten by Jay Z, which cracked the *Billboard* Hot 100, and "I Can't," which featured Total and reached #61 on the R&B chart.

FEBRUARY 9

JT Money releases his single "Who Dat" on Priority.

The gold-selling lead single from the Miami rapper's debut album, *Pimpin' on Wax*, featuring a guest verse from the rapper Solé, was produced by Tricky Stewart. The song became JT Money's sole solo hit, topping the Rap chart and reaching the top five on the *Billboard* Hot 100.

FEBRUARY 23

The Roots release their fourth album *Things Fall Apart* on Geffen.

The platinum-selling, Grammy-nominated album's title comes from the book of the same name by Nigerian author Chinua Achebe. It was issued with five different album covers depicting images of the Civil Rights movement, war, sadness, destruction, and death.

Recorded in Electric Lady Studios in New York City and produced by the Grand Wizzards, Scott Storch, and J Dilla, *Things Fall Apart* spawned the hits "The Next Movement," featuring DJ Jazzy Jeff and Jazzyfatnastees; "Adrenaline!," featuring Dice Raw and Beanie Sigel; and "You Got Me" featuring Erykah Badu and written by Jill Scott, who originally recorded the chorus hook for the song. The touching single earned the group, and Badu, a Grammy Award for best rap performance by a duo or group.

Other guests on *Things Fall Apart* included Mos Def, Common, Eve, Ursula Rucker, Philly pioneer Lady B, D'Angelo, James Poyser, and Marie Daulne.

FEBRUARY 23

Prince Paul releases his second album *A Prince Among Thieves* on Warner Bros.

The Long Island rapper's second set is an ambitious, thirty-five-song concept album that traces the story of two aspiring rappers navigating the music business.

Hailed as the first-ever hip-hopera, it featured voice cameos from Chris Rock, Kool Keith, Big Daddy Kane, RZA, Biz Markie, and Chubb Rock, among others. Hitting the *Billboard* 200 and reaching #46 on the R&B/Hip-Hop chart, the brilliant album also sampled a diverse range of unexpected work, such as Beethoven's Fifth Symphony and the theme from *Popeye*. The single "More Than U Know," which featured De La Soul and a sample of Liberace playing "Chopsticks" peaked at #45 on the Rap chart.

FEBRUARY 23

Eminem releases his major label debut *The Slim Shady LP* on Interscope.

The Detroit rapper's breakthrough album was produced by Eminem, the Bass Brothers, and his mentor Dr. Dre.

Showcasing his unique lyrical style, the multi-platinum album, which debuted at #2 on the *Billboard* 200, spawned several singles, including his first top forty hit "My Name Is," as well as "Just Don't Give a Fuck" and "Guilty Conscience."

In 2000, Eminem won three Grammys for the album, including rap album of the year. He also won best rap solo performance for "My Name Is," which reached #36 on the *Billboard* Hot 100, and best rap performance by a duo or group for his song "Guilty Conscience," performed with Dr. Dre, which reached #56 on the R&B chart.

FEBRUARY 24

Lauryn Hill wins the Grammy for album of the year.

With Hill's award, *The Miseducation of Lauryn Hill* became the first-ever hip-hop album to win the Grammy for album of the year. Lauryn Hill earned a record-breaking total of ten Grammy nominations, five of which she won. At the time, Hill's five Grammy wins set a record for the most Grammys ever to win in one year for a female artist.

Performing her song "To Zion" with Carlos Santana during the broadcast, Hill also won Grammys for best new artist, best female R&B vocal performance, best R&B song, and best R&B album.

MARCH 30

dead prez release their single "Hip Hop" on Columbia.

The song from the politically conscious duo of stic.man and M-1 was the group's second-ever single, and their first to chart. It was released a year before the group's debut studio album, *Let's Get Free.*

A cult hit on college radio, "Hip Hop" was remixed by Kanye West under the title "It's Bigger Than Hip Hop" and used by Dave Chappelle as the intro to his wildly popular show on Comedy Central.

MARCH 30

B.G. releases his single "Bling Bling" on Cash Money.

The teenage New Orleans rapper's debut single from his platinum-selling *Chopper City* featured Cash Money label mates Big Tymers and Hot Boys and beats by Mannie Fresh.

B.G.'s sole top forty pop hit, peaking at #36 on the *Billboard* Hot 100 and #14 on the R&B/Hip-Hop chart, featured a seventeen-year-old Lil Wayne and introduced the term "bling bling" to American popular culture.

APRIL 6

Nas releases his third album *I Am...* on Columbia.

Keeping with the style of his previous two albums, the cover depicts Nas's face as an Egyptian God.The multi-platinum set featured an array of producers including Timbaland, Trackmasters, L.E.S., DJ Premier, Dame Grease, and several others. The album, which debuted at #1 on the *Billboard* 200, spawned the hit singles "Nas Is Like," which reached #3 on the Rap chart, and "Hate Me Now," featuring Puff Daddy, which reached #8 on the Rap chart. The album also contains the 2Pac Shakur–Biggie Smalls tribute called "We Will Survive." Other guests on *I Am...* include DMX, Scarface, and Aaliyah.

"Hate Me Now" featured a controversial music video directed by Hype Williams depicting Nas and Puffy being crucified on crosses like Jesus Christ.

APRIL 20

Rap superstar Ma$e announces his retirement from the music industry.

In an interview with Funkmaster Flex on New York's Hot 97 FM, Ma$e announced he was retiring due to religious reasons, two weeks before the release of his sophomore album *Double Up* on Bad Boy Records.

He joined the ministry but returned to the industry five years later with the album *Welcome Back* on Bad Boy.

APRIL 20

MF Doom releases his debut solo album *Operation: Doomsday* on Fondle 'Em.

The underground cult classic is the first from the British rapper after his hip-hop trio KMD disbanded in the mid '90 s. The nineteen-song album, which included several skits from the 1967 cartoon *Fantastic Four*, showcases Doom's raw and dexterous lyrics and delivery.

MAY 1999

Sporty Thievz release their single "No Pigeons" on Ruffhouse.

The gold-selling single from the short-lived Yonkers hip-hop trio of King Kirk, Big Dubez, and Marlon Bryant Brando is a response to TLC's 1999 chart-topping hit "No Scrubs."

Topping the Rap chart and reaching #12 on the *Billboard* 100, Sporty Thievz built on its popularity by rereleasing their 1998 debut album *Street Cinema* with the "No Pigeons" tacked on to the end of the album.

MAY 11

Snoop Dogg releases *No Limit Top Dogg* on No Limit.

Produced mainly by Master P, Dr. Dre, and KLC, the platinum-selling album debuted at #2 on the *Billboard* 200 and topped the R&B/Hip-Hop chart. The funky gangsta set included the singles "G Bedtime Stories," which was produced by Meech Wells; "Bitch Please," which reached #26 on the R&B/Hip-Hop chart and featured Xzibit and Nate Dogg; and "Down for My N's," featuring C-Murder and Magic, which peaked at #29 on the R&B chart. Other guests on the album included Sticky Fingaz, Silkk the Shocker, Mia X, Mystikal, and Goldie Loc.

MAY 25

Slick Rick releases his fourth album *The Art of Storytelling* on Def Jam.

In his first release since 1994, the British-born legendary MC's gold-selling set is his highest charting album ever, topping the R&B/Hip-Hop charts and reaching #8 on the *Billboard* 200.

Produced by Jazze Pha, Dame Grease, DJ Clark Kent, and Trackmasters among others, Rick's stellar rhymes and smooth flow would shine on singles like the Kid Capri–produced "Unify," featuring Snoop Dogg, the crime-spree "Kill Niggaz," "We Turn It On," featuring longtime collaborator Doug E. Fresh, and the hit "Street Talkin'" featuring Big Boi from Outkast, which reached #22 on the Rap chart. Other guests on *The Art of Storytelling* included Nas, Canibus, Raekwon of the Wu-Tang Clan, Peter Gunz, Q-Tip, Redman, Kid Capri, and Ed Lover.

JUNE 1

Ja Rule releases his debut album *Venni Vetti Vecci* on Murder Inc.

The multi-platinum selling album's name, a Latin phrase translated as "I came, I saw, I conquered" was the first full-length release on Irv Gotti's Murder Inc. imprint. Featuring production by Gotti, Erick Sermon, Tyrone Fyffe, Tai, DL, and Lil Rob, the debut set by the gravelly-voiced Queens, New York, native spawned the hit "Holla, Holla," which reached #2 on the Rap chart.

Reaching #2 on the *Billboard* 200, *Venni Vetti Vecci* included guest appearances by Jay Z, Ronald Isley, Case, DMX, Nemesis, Memphis Bleek, Black Child, and Tah Murdah.

JUNE 22

Missy Elliott releases *Da Real World* on East West.

Like her debut, Missy Elliott's second studio album was produced by Timbaland. Despite not featuring any crossover hit singles, Elliott's platinum-selling album sold more than one million copies in its first seven months.

The album's singles are "She's a Bitch," which reached #30 on the R&B chart, "All n My Grill," which featured Big Boi on the radio edit and reached #16 on the R&B charts, and the hit remix of "Hot Boyz," with Nas, Eve, and Q-Tip that spent sixteen weeks on the top of the Rap chart. *Da Real World* also includes appearances from Lil' Kim, Redman, Eminem, Juvenile, and an eighteen-year-old Beyoncé.

JUNE 29

GZA/Genius releases his third album *Beneath the Surface* on MCA.

GZA's Wu-produced album showcased his lyrical prowess. Topping the R&B chart and reaching #9 on the *Billboard* 200, the atmospheric album had some classic cuts, including the title track, which featured Killah Priest, Res, and Santigold; "Breaker Breaker," with its walkie-talkie chorus; and the RZA-produced "1112," which featured Masta Killa, Killah Priest, and Njeri Earth.

JULY 27

The Hot Boys release their second studio album *Guerrilla Warfare* on Cash Money.

Following the success of their Mannie Fresh–produced debut *Get It How U Live!*, the New Orleans hardcore teen quartet of B.G., Juvenile, Young Turk, and Lil Wayne's second release was highly anticipated. Their album debuted at #5 on the *Billboard* 200 and topped the R&B chart, in part due to the strong singles "We on Fire," which reached #5 on the Rap chart, and "I Need a Hot Girl," which reached #23 on the R&B chart.

AUGUST 3

Memphis Bleek releases his debut solo album *Coming of Age* on Roc-A-Fella.

Named after a Jay Z track on which Bleek appeared, the Brooklyn MC's debut release featured production by Swizz Beatz, Irv Gotti, Patrick Viala, Buckwild, Mr. Fingers, Dark Half, J-Runnah, Omen, Bernard "Big Demi" Parker, and the Burn Unit.

Peaking at #7 on the *Billboard* 200, the gold-selling street set spawned the hit singles "Murda 4 Life," featuring Ja Rule; "Memphis Bleek Is...," which reached #93 on the R&B chart; and "What You Think of That," featuring Jay Z. *Coming of Age* also featured guest appearances by label mates Beanie Sigel, Noreaga, and Da Ranjahs.

AUGUST 4

Q-Tip releases the single "Vivrant Thing" on Arista.

The New York rapper's solo debut after A Tribe Called Quest broke up in 1998 is this lead single off his gold-selling album *Amplified.*

The song peaked at #26 on the *Billboard* Hot 100, and #7 on the R&B chart. A remix to "Vivrant Thing" featuring Missy Elliott and Busta Rhymes was later released.

AUGUST 24

Ol' Dirty Bastard of the Wu-Tang Clan releases the single "Got Your Money" on Elektra.

The track was produced by the Neptunes and was off ODB's hit sophomore set *Nigga Please*. Peaking at #33 on the *Billboard* Hot 100, #19 on the R&B chart, and #6 on the Rap chart, "Got Your Money" featured R&B singer Kelis, whose debut album *Kaleidoscope* came out the same year.

SEPTEMBER 14

Eve releases *Let There Be Eve...Ruff Ryders' First Lady* on Ruff Ryders.

Entering the *Billboard* 200 and R&B charts at #1, the multi-platinum album from the Philadelphia street MC featured Missy Elliott, Beanie Sigel, Faith Evans, and Ruff Ryders label mates DMX and the L.O.X.

Produced mainly by Swizz Beatz and written by Eve, the hard-hitting album's three singles, "Gotta Man," about domestic violence, "Love Is Blind," and "Let's Talk About" with Drag-On, all hit the R&B chart.

SEPTEMBER 28

Method Man and Redman release *Blackout!* on Def Jam.

The first full-length album collaboration between the two East Coast rappers went platinum within months. Debuting at #3 on the *Billboard* 200, the creative album packed with tight and inventive rhymes spawned three singles: "Tear It Off," "Y.O.U.," and "Da Rockwilder," all of which became top twenty hits on the Rap chart. LL Cool J, Ja Rule, and Ghostface Killah all make appearances on the album, which included work from Redman as well as producers Erick Sermon, RZA, and Mathematics.

Ten years later, the duo released a sequel to the album titled *The Blackout! 2.*

CHUCK D:

The Cheech and Chong of hip-hop and rap music have been an unpredictable and incredible fit to the genre. Nobody saw this combination coming, but these brothers were two of my fav MCs who merge in the 1990s that did it in multimedia like no other. They have done it on records; excelled by far in films, and performances since the late '90s. And whenever they get together, antics will happen. Personally, I can hear these two guys rhyming the dictionary and I would be a fan.

OCTOBER 12

Warren G releases *I Want It All* on Restless.

After releasing his first two records on Def Jam, *I Want It All* was the West Coast rapper's first album with the independent California label Restless Records. Warren G's third studio album is a star-studded affair featuring Jermaine Dupri, Snoop Dogg, Eve, Memphis Bleek, Slick Rick, and Nate Dogg.

Peaking at #21 on the *Billboard* 200 and reaching the top five in the R&B chart, the platinum-selling album's lead single "I Want It All" sold more than half a million copies alone and reached #23 on the *Billboard* Hot 100.

On *I Want It All*, Warren G focused more intently on his production, leaving much of the album's vocals to the featured guest artists. The album featured a laid-back, jazz-rock take on the producer's trademark G-funk.

OCTOBER 12

Solé releases the single "4, 5, 6" on DreamWorks.

The Kansas City rapper's lead single from her debut album *Skin Deep* featured JT Money and Kandi Burruss. Selling more than half a million copies in the first three months after its release,"4, 5, 6" was the second-highest-selling rap single of 2000, trailing only Missy Elliott's "Hot Boyz." The song was the rapper's only charting pop hit, reaching the top twenty-five on the *Billboard* Hot 100.

OCTOBER 12

Mos Def releases his solo debut album *Black on Both Sides* on Rawkus.

Building on the success of *Mos Def & Talib Kweli Are Black Star*, the Brooklyn MC released his gold-selling debut to critical acclaim. Mos Def worked with a variety of producers, including DJ Premier, Diamond D, and 88-Keys, to create an album that is known for its intricate wordplay and socially conscious lyrics. With few guests outside of Busta Rhymes, Q-Tip, Vinia Mojica, and his Black Star partner Talib Kweli, the album topped the Rap chart and reached #3 on the R&B chart. The only single, "Ms. Fat Booty," reached #20 on the Rap chart.

OCTOBER 19

Handsome Boy Modeling School release their debut album *So...How's Your Girl?* on Tommy Boy.

The duo, made up of Prince Paul and Dan the Automator, produced the inventive album and brought in an eclectic list of guests on their critically acclaimed album, including Del the Funky Homosapien, Sean Lennon, Biz Markie, Trugoy the Dove of De La Soul, DJ Shadow, Mike D of the Beastie Boys, Sadat X, and comedian Father Guido Sarducci.

OCTOBER 19

Pharoahe Monch releases his solo debut *Internal Affairs* on Priority.

The pioneering Queens rapper, who began his career as one half of the underground hip-hop duo Organized Konfusion, released a high-profile debut that featured appearances from Talib Kweli, Busta Rhymes, Canibus, and Redman.

The hard, lyrically taut album reached #41 on the *Billboard* 200 and #6 on the R&B charts, yielding two singles, "The Light," which reached #30 on the Rap chart, and the club hit "Simon Says," which cracked the *Billboard* Hot 100 and reached #3 on the Rap chart.

When "Simon Says" became a hit, Monch was successfully sued for using an uncleared sample from the *Godzilla* theme in the song. The rapper was then forced to remove his album from stores, hampering the commercial success it deserved.

DR. DRE

THE ROOTS

NOVEMBER 2

The Roots release the live album, *The Roots Come Alive*, on MCA.

Referencing the title of the 1976 multi-platinum selling *Frampton Comes Alive*, this concert album captured the essence of the band's performances in Zurich and New York City, as well as some other cities.

Reaching #12 on the R&B chart and #50 on the *Billboard* 200, *The Roots Come Alive* featured guest performances by Common, Jaguar Wright, longtime Roots collaborator Dice Raw and Jill Scott, who is featured on the live performance of "You Got Me." Other band classics included "Step into the Realm," "Proceed," and "The Next Movement."

NOVEMBER 2

Lil Wayne releases his debut album *Tha Block Is Hot* on Cash Money.

A former member of the Hot Boys, the teenage New Orleans MC released his rough but smart debut surrounded by his Cash Money label mates and produced by Mannie Fresh. Debuting at #3 on the *Billboard* 200, the double platinum set showcases Wayne's curse-free rhymes (at the request of his mother). The debut title track reached #24 on the R&B chart and #27 on the Rap chart.

NOVEMBER 16

Dr. Dre releases his sophomore solo album *2001* on Aftermath.

Dr. Dre produced the sonically inventive, multi-platinum album with assistance from Mel-Man, Scott Storch, and Lord Finesse.

Debuting at #2 on the *Billboard* 200 and topping the R&B chart for the decade, the album contained the smash hits "Still D.R.E.," featuring Snoop Dogg, which cracked the *Billboard* Hot 100; "the Grammy-winning "Forgot About Dre," featuring Eminem; "The Next Episode," featuring Snoop Dogg, Kurupt, and Nate Dogg, which reached #23 on the *Billboard* Hot 100; and "Xxplosive," featuring Hittman, Devin the Dude, Nate Dogg, and Kurupt, which was not released as a single but still reached #51 on the R&B charts.

Other guests on *2001* included Xzibit, Mary J. Blige, Rell, Knoc-Turn'al, Tray Dee, Traci Nelson, Ms. Roq, Eddie Griffin, Jake Steed, Defari, Six-Two, Charis Henry, Time Bomb, King T, and Dr. Dre's old N.W.A cohort MC Ren.

NOVEMBER 23

Nas releases his fourth album *Nastradamus* on Columbia.

The album's title, and front cover shot of Nas dressed as a monk, was a reference to the sixteenth-century prophet Nostradamus.

The platinum-selling set by the Queens, New York, MC had originally been slated as a double-disc project but the concept was scrapped due to bootlegging. Debuting at #7 on the *Billboard* 200, it produced the title track single, which reached #4 on the Rap chart, and the hit "You Owe Me," featuring Ginuwine, which reached #13 on the R&B chart. Featuring production by Dame Grease, Timbaland, DJ Premier, L.E.S., Rich Nice, and Havoc of Mobb Deep, it also featured guest appearances by Ronald Isley of the Isley Brothers, Nashawn, Mobb Deep, and Nas's musical posse Bravehearts.

NOVEMBER 30

Rakim releases his second solo album *The Master* on Universal.

Reaching #7 on the R&B chart and #72 on the *Billboard* 200, *The Master* showcases the MC's smooth flow and inventive internal rhymes. Featuring production by DJ Clark Kent, Punch, Ron "Amen-Ra" Lawrence of the Hitmen, TR Love, Naughty Shorts, Big Jaz, Mark the 45 King, Nick Wiz, and Rakim as well, the critically acclaimed album spawned the hit DJ Premier–produced "When I B on tha Mic," which reached #20 on the Rap chart. Guests on the album included Rahzel, Nneka Morton, and Connie McKendrick.

DECEMBER 21

DMX releases *...And Then There Was X* on Def Jam.

After releasing two highly successful albums, the Yonkers rapper's third full-length release served as his pop breakthrough, selling more than five million copies by early 2001.

...And Then There Was X was DMX's third straight album to top the *Billboard* 200 chart and featured several hit singles, including "What's My Name" and "Party Up (Up in Here)." The latter became the highest-charting single of DMX's career. The album's third single, "What These Bitches Want," which featured Sisqó, also became a top fifty pop hit. The song's radio edit was titled "What You Want." DMX was nominated for two Grammys for best rap album and best rap solo performance for "Party Up (Up in Here)."

DECEMBER 28

Jay Z releases his fourth album *Vol.3...Life and Times of S. Carter* on Roc-A-Fella.

Debuting at #1 on the *Billboard* 200, the multi-platinum set featured Jay Z's unique flow over some of the hottest producers of the day like DJ Premier, Swizz Beatz, Timbaland, DJ Clue, Irv Gotti, and several others.

The street-oriented album would produce five smash hit singles, "Jigga My Nigga," which reached #28 on the *Billboard* Hot 100; "Do It Again (Put Ya Hands Up)," featuring Beanie Sigel and Amil, which reached #9 on the Rap chart; "Big Pimpin'," featuring UGK and reaching #18 on the *Billboard* Hot 100; and "Things That You Do," featuring Mariah Carey. Juvenile, Dr. Dre, Serena Altschul, and label mate Memphis Bleek also guested on the album.

2000

JANUARY 4

The Jungle Brothers release their fifth album *V.I.P.* on Gee Street.

V.I.P., produced by Alex Gifford of the Propellerheads and the duo, had a more dance vibe than a traditional hip-hop sound. The party album contained the track "Down with the Jbeez," featuring the Black Eyed Peas.

JANUARY 26

De La Soul release the single "All Good?" on Tommy Boy.

"All Good?" featured legendary R&B vocalist Chaka Khan and was from the group's fifth album *Art Official Intelligence: Mosaic Thump* released in August. Cracking the *Billboard* Hot 100, the self-produced song reached #41 on the R&B/Hip-Hop chart.

FEBRUARY 8

Ghostface Killah releases *Supreme Clientele* on Epic Records.

Supreme Clientele, the second studio album from the founding Wu-Tang Clan rapper, considered one of his best, featured a slew of appearances from other Wu members, including RZA, Raekwon, Method Man, and GZA.

Produced mainly by Ghostface and RZA, the critically acclaimed, gold-selling album debuted #7 on the *Billboard* 200 and #2 on the R&B/Hip-Hop chart. The rapper's lyrical dexterity was showcased on the hits "Apollo Kids" and "Cherchez La Ghost," reaching #32 and #3 on the Rap chart respectively.

FEBRUARY 8

dead prez release their debut album *Let's Get Free* on Loud.

dead prez, a duo comprised of stic.man and M-1, continued the legacy of socially conscious, political and Afrocentric hip-hop started by their predecessors like Public Enemy, Boogie Down Productions, X Clan, and Poor Righteous Teachers.

Produced by the band along with Hedrush, Kanye West, and Lord Jamar of Brand Nubian, the critically acclaimed album spawned the singles "It's Bigger Than Hip-Hop" and "Hip-Hop," both of which reached the top fifty on the Rap chart, and the underground cult hit "I'm an African."

FEBRUARY 8

Drama releases his debut album *Causin' Drama* on Atlantic.

Reaching #37 on the *Billboard* 200 and #6 on the R&B/Hip-Hop chart, the Alabama MC's debut was produced by himself and Shawty Redd. The Dirty South gold-selling album contained the hit singles "Double Time (Drama's Cadence)" and "Left, Right, Left," which reached #2 on the Rap chart.

MARCH 7

Black Rob releases *Life Story* on Bad Boy.

The platinum-selling debut by the Harlem rapper, which featured a number of his Bad Boy Entertainment label mates, sold more than a million copies by August 2000. Peaking at #3 on the *Billboard* 200 and topping the R&B/Hip-Hop chart, the album featured guest appearances from Cee-Lo Green, Puff Daddy, Ma$e, Jennifer Lopez, the L.O.X., and Lil' Kim.

The street life album yielded the only crossover hit of Black Rob's career with the lead single "Whoa!," which cracked the top fifty of the *Billboard* Hot 100 and was a top ten hit on both the R&B/Hip-Hop and Rap charts.

MARCH 28

504 Boyz release the single "Wobble Wobble" on No Limit Records.

"Wobble Wobble," the lead single off the band's inaugural studio debut *Goodfellas*, was produced by Carlos Stephens, the in-house producer for Master P's No Limit Records.

The third-highest-selling rap single of the year reached the top twenty of the *Billboard* Hot 100 and provided the New Orleans hip-hop group with the only crossover hit of their career.

MARCH 28

Common releases his fourth album *Like Water for Chocolate* on MCA Records.

Recorded at Jimi Hendrix's famed Greenwich Village Electric Lady Studios in New York City, the critically acclaimed spiritual album featured the segregation-era photograph of a "colored-only" water fountain taken by Gordon Parks titled *1956 Alabama*.

Reaching #16 on *Billboard* 200 and #5 on the R&B/Hip-Hop chart, the gold-selling album included guest appearances by Vinia Mojica, Roy Hargrove, Femi Kuti, Rahzel and Black Thought of the Roots, Bilal, Jill Scott, Mos Def, MC Lyte, Slum Village, Macy Gray, Cee-Lo Green, and Common's father Lonnie "Pops" Lynn. The hit single "The Light" reached #12 on the R&B/Hip-Hop chart and #13 on the Rap chart.

The thoughtful and uplifting album also marked the official formation of the Soulquarians musical collective consisting of Questlove of the Roots, singer D'Angelo, producer MC Jay Dee, keyboardist Pino Palladino, and bassist James Poyser. It would later include Raphael Saadiq of Tony!Toni!Toné! and Lucy Pearl fame.

APRIL 11

Da Brat releases her third studio album *Unrestricted* on So Def.

The chart-topping platinum set released on Jermaine Dupri's label reached #5 on the *Billboard* 200 and #1 on the R&B/Hip-Hop chart. He also produced a number of the tracks, along with Aaron Pittman, Kanye West, Timbaland, Bryan-Michael Cox, and Carl So-Lowe.

The hit single "What'chu Like," featuring a hook by Tyrese, reached #36 on the *Billboard* 100. Other guests on the polished set included Lil Jon, Mystikal, Kelly Price, and Twista.

MAY 23

Eminem releases his third album *The Marshall Mathers LP* on Shady/Aftermath Records.

Produced by the rapper with Dr. Dre, Mel-Man, the 45 King, and the Bass Brothers, the unsettling and personal album topped the *Billboard* 200 and R&B/Hip-Hop chart. The multi-platinum album sold more than twenty-two million units worldwide, won the Grammy Award for rap album and was nominated for album of the year. The diamond-selling often macabre set included the smash hits "The Real Slim Shady," "The Way I Am," and the classic "Stan," featuring Dido, which Eminem would go on to perform at the 2000 Grammy Awards with Elton John on piano and vocals.

The Marshall Mathers LP also featured classic album cuts like "Kim," "Who Knew," and "Bitch Please II," featuring Snoop Dogg, Nate Dogg, Xzibit, and Dr. Dre.

CHUCK D:
The USA and the Western world is fueled on race. Em knew this coming out of Detroit. His comments about his self-background and privileges have been as integral as 21C Lives Matter protests. He honed into the dynamic by being himself. He knew all of the time by default he would receive the Elvis of Rap attachment. He works hard on expanding the discussion on percussion. As a rap god, Marshall Mathers matters.

MAY 30

Big L releases the single "Flamboyant" on Rawkus.

The posthumous hit from the esteemed New York rapper, released more than a year after his murder, ended up becoming the biggest hit of his career, topping the Rap chart and reaching the top forty on the *Billboard* Hot 100.

The Mike Heron–produced classic's title referenced Flamboyant Entertainment, the indie rap label Big L had founded in 1998.

DA BRAT

JUNE 6

Lil' Zane releases the single "Callin' Me" on Priority.

The lead single from the East Coast rapper's debut album *Young World: The Future*, featuring 112, became a crossover pop hit that peaked at #21 on the *Billboard* Hot 100, #2 on the R&B/Hip-Hop chart, and topped the Rap chart.

JUNE 6

LaFace Records releases the soundtrack to the Paramount Pictures film *Shaft*.

The film, a sequel to the classic 1971 MGM film starring Richard Roundtree, was directed by John Singleton and starred Samuel L. Jackson as the nephew to the original John Shaft.

Peaking at #22 on the *Billboard* 200 and #3 on the R&B/Hip-Hop chart, the soundtrack featured R&B stars including R. Kelly, Alicia Keys, Angie Stone, and Isaac Hayes, who remakes his 1971 Grammy Award–winning theme song, as well as hip-hop artists like Mystikal, Too $hort, Beanie Sigel, UGK, and the earliest appearance by T.I. on "2 Glock 9's."

JUNE 20

Busta Rhymes releases his fourth solo album *Anarchy* on Flipmode.

Debuting at #4 on the *Billboard* 200, the platinum-selling *Anarchy* featured production by DJ Scratch of EPMD fame, Nottz, Just Blaze, Scott Storch, Large Professor, Rockwilder, P. Killer Trackz, DJ Shok, Swizz Beatz, and Jay Dee.

Guests on the sometimes manic but inventive album included Ghostface Killah and Raekwon of the Wu-Tang Clan, Lenny Kravitz, Jay Z, M.O.P., DMX, and Busta's Flipmode Squad. It spawned the hit singles "Get Out" and "Fire," which reached #35 and #67 on the R&B/Hip-Hop chart respectively.

JUNE 27

Lil' Kim releases her sophomore album *The Notorious K.I.M.* on Atlantic.

Debuting at #4 on the *Billboard* 200, the platinum-selling set featured the hit single "How Many Licks," featuring Sisqó of Dru Hill as well as "Hold On," featuring Mary J. Blige, and "No Matter What They Say," which reached #36 and #15 on the R&B/Hip-Hop chart respectively.

Other guests on the raunchy *The Notorious K.I.M.* included Cee-Lo Green, Redman, Mario Winans, Lil' Shanice, Carl Thomas, Lil' Cease, Junior M.A.F.I.A., and Puff Daddy, who along with Kanye West, Rockwilder, Deric "D-Dot" Angelettie and others, produced the album.

JUNE 27

Nelly releases his debut album *Country Grammar* on Universal.

The St. Louis rapper's hook-filled debut was titled to reflect Nelly's Midwest laid-back vocal and lyrical style. Produced by City Spud, Basement Beats, Steve "Blast" Wills, and Jason "Jay E" Epperson, the diamond-selling album topped the *Billboard* 200 for five weeks and contained the smash hit singles, "Ride wit Me," featuring City Spud, which reached #3 on the *Billboard* Hot 100; "E.I.," which reached #16 on the *Billboard* Hot 100; "Batter Up," featuring Murphy Lee and Ali; as well as the classic title track, which reached #7 on the *Billboard* Hot 100.

Other guests on *Country Grammar* include comedian Cedric the Entertainer, Lil Wayne, the Teamsters, and the rest of Nelly's musical posse St. Lunatics, whose name was an homage to St. Louis.

AUGUST 8

Lil' Bow Wow releases the single "Bounce with Me" on So So Def.

The debut single from Lil' Bow Wow, who was just thirteen at its release, was written by Jermaine Dupri and featured the R&B group Xscape.

The lead single on his first album *Beware of Dog* released the next month, was a crossover hit, reaching the top twenty of the *Billboard* Hot 100, topping both the Rap and R&B/Hip-Hop charts.

AUGUST 8

Shaggy releases *Hot Shot* on MCA.

The reggae star's fifth album, which featured his most pop-friendly, commercially accessible melodies to date, was the most successful album of the Jamaican rapper's career. The album yielded two smash singles: "It Wasn't Me," which featured the singer Rikrok, and "Angel," both of which topped the *Billboard* Hot 100 chart. The multi-platinum album topped the *Billboard* 200 and spent a total of eighty-four weeks on the chart.

SEPTEMBER 9

M.O.P. release the single "Ante Up (Robbing-Hoodz Theory)" on Loud.

Reaching #19 on the Rap chart, the breakthrough song from the New York duo's album *Warriorz*, released the following month, would later be rereleased with a remix that included Busta Rhymes, Teflon, and Remy Ma.

Produced by DR Period, the song was a minor hit in the United States, but the remix became a top ten pop hit in the United Kingdom and throughout Western Europe.

SEPTEMBER 12

LL Cool J releases his eighth album *G.O.A.T.* on Def Jam.

With a title that was an acronym for "Greatest of All Time," the platinum-selling album sales lived up to the name, reaching #1 on the *Billboard* 200 and the R&B/Hip-Hop chart.

The classic set included guest appearances by Prodigy of Mobb Deep, DMX, Method Man, Redman, as well as R&B singers Carl Thomas, Kelly Price, and Case and featured the hit single "Imagine That" with LeShaun, which reached #16 on the Rap chart.

SEPTEMBER 12

Too $hort releases *You Nasty* on Jive.

Produced by Ant Banks, Erick Sermon, and Jazze Pha, the Godfather of Pimpin's album included guest appearances by Kokane, Chyna Whyte, the Nation Riders, Captain Save 'Em, as well as E-40.

Peaking at #12 on the *Billboard* 200 and #4 on the R&B/Hip-Hop chart, the raunchy album produced two hit singles, "2 Bitches" and "You Nasty."

SEPTEMBER 26

Mystikal releases *Let's Get Ready* on Jive.

Mystikal's fourth studio album, his first since parting ways with No Limit, would end up becoming the most successful of his career. Debuting at #1 on the *Billboard* 200, the funky album's sales were spurred by two hit singles: "Shake Ya Ass" and "Danger (Been So Long)," both of which became top twenty hits on the *Billboard* Hot 100.

Produced by the Neptunes, the Medicine Men, KLC, and Earthtone III, among others, the New Orleans masterful MC's multi-platinum album included appearances from Pharrell Williams, Petey Pablo, Nivea, Da Brat, and Outkast.

OCTOBER 3

Scarface releases his sixth album *Last of a Dying Breed* on Rap-A-Lot.

The critically acclaimed set debuted at #7 on the *Billboard* 200, and featured production by Scarface, Mike Dean, N.O. Joe, Mr. Lee, Swift, Tone Capone, and Erick Sermon. With singles that included "It Ain't Part II," which reached #77 on the R&B/Hip-Hop chart, the introspective and focused album led to him being signed to Def Jam for his next release.

SCARFACE

OCTOBER 3

Jedi Mind Tricks release their second album *Violent by Design* on Superegular.

The underground classic by the trio of Vinnie Paz, Stoupe the Enemy of Mankind, and Jus Allah recorded the album in Stoupe's bedroom in his parents' house and released it on their own label. With a bevy of guest appearances and a violent bent, the well-received set spawned the single "Heavenly Divine," which is considered their trademark song.

OCTOBER 17

Ludacris releases his sophomore album *Back for the First Time* on Def Jam.

The multi-platinum smash hit album's title is reference to the many tracks that were taken from his debut album *Incognegro*, which Ludacris released on his own Disturbing tha Peace Records. As his imprint was now distributed by Def Jam, this release also marked his major label debut.

Cementing the Atlanta-based MC's place in hip-hop superstardom, the Dirty South album, which reached #4 on the *Billboard* 200, featured production by Organized Noize, Jermaine Dupri, the Neptunes, Timbaland, and Mr. Bangladesh, among others. It spawned the huge hit singles "What's Your Fantasy," featuring Shawnna, and "Southern Hospitality," featuring Pharrell, which reached #21 and #23 on the *Billboard* Hot 100 respectively. Other guests on *Back for the First Time* included Trina, Foxy Brown, Pastor Troy, I-20, Fate Wilson, UGK, and 4-Ize.

OCTOBER 17

Deltron 3030 release their self-titled debut album on 75 Ark.

Deltron 3030, a hip-hop supergroup consisting of MC Del the Funky Homosapien, producer Dan the Automator, and DJ Kid Koala, pushed the boundaries of hip-hop with this release, using sci-fi imagery to tackle social issues and at the same time marrying humor and quirky imagination in the mix.

CHUCK D:

Luda is someone I'll always recall as the infamous Chris Luva Luva from Atlanta's Hot 97.5 radio in the '90s. He broke in a lot of records and simply knew who was doing the right and wrong thing in hip-hop by doing radio. Before 1996, Atlanta only played hip-hop on the weekends and Hot played and supported hip-hop as well as rap scene artists from the region. Luda, and program director Chaka Zulu, cemented their NY–LA industry relationship with a shot at making the South boom big along with what was happening with Outkast. Chris Luva was already a Def Jam artist, so Ludacris was born—becoming the hip-hop South's first superstar soloist. He quietly has never stopped his fast-and-furious pace. And one of the rap game's best voices, I may add.

Cracking the *Billboard* 200 and the R&B/Hip-Hop chart, the cult classic featured guests that include legendary producer and DJ Prince Paul, Peanut Butter Wolf, and MC Paul Barman among others.

OCTOBER 17

Reflection Eternal release their debut album *Train of Thought* on Rawkus.

The duo of Talib Kweli and producer Hi-Tek collaborated on this thoughtful and noteworthy debut, which featured contributions from Les Nubians, De La Soul, Dave Chappelle, Kool G. Rap, and Black Star. Reaching #17 on the *Billboard* 200 and #5 on the R&B/Hip-Hop chart, the critically acclaimed set included the singles "Move Somethin'" and "The Blast," which reached #1 and #2 on the Rap chart respectively.

OCTOBER 31

Outkast release *Stankonia* on LaFace.

Outkast's third album became the group's mainstream pop breakthrough, debuting at #2 on the *Billboard* 200. The multi-platinum album featured longtime

Outkast collaborators like Cee-Lo Green, Sleepy Brown, Erykah Badu, and Atlanta rapper Killer Mike, making his recording debut on the album track "Snappin & Trappin'."

Produced by Earthtone III and Organized Noize, the bold and experimental album spawned three singles: "B.O.B.," "Ms. Jackson," which topped the *Billboard* Hot 100, and "So Fresh, So Clean." Critically acclaimed, Outkast's work on *Stankonia* earned the duo five Grammy nominations, winning two for best rap album and best rap performance by a duo or group for "Ms. Jackson."

OCTOBER 31

Jay Z releases his fifth studio album *The Dynasty: Roc La Familia* on Roc-A-Fella.

Debuting at #1 on the *Billboard* 200, the critically acclaimed set showcased a number of Roc-A-Fella artists, such as Memphis Bleek and Beanie Sigel, and up-and-coming producers, like future superstars Kanye West and the Neptunes. Pharrell Williams of the Neptunes appears on the single they produced, "I Just Wanna Love You (Give It 2 Me)," which topped the R&B/Hip-Hop chart. Other singles from the multi-platinum album included "Change the Game," with Memphis Bleek and Beanie Sigel, and "Guilty Until Proven Innocent," with R. Kelly, both reaching the top forty on the R&B/Hip-Hop chart.

NOVEMBER 7

Outlawz release their sophomore album *Ride wit Us or Collide wit Us* on Outlawz Recordz.

Outlawz, founded in 1995 by 2Pac, featured members with stage names that represented controversial historical figures, including Kastro, E.D.I. Mean, Hussein Fatal, and Kadafi.

Produced by Mike Dean, Quimmy Quim, Femi Ojetunde, Mr. Lee and the group's E.D.I. Mean, guests on the album included Coolio, Val Young, Spice 1, TQ, as well as late Black Panther Party member and freedom fighter Geronimo Pratt. The West Coast thug rap album reached #95 on the *Billboard* 200.

NOVEMBER 21

Wu-Tang Clan release their third studio album *The W* on Loud.

The W, the second-highest-charting album of the group's career, peaked in the top five of the *Billboard* 200 and topped the R&B/Hip-Hop chart.

With lean production by RZA and other Wu members, the innovative, platinum-selling set featured guest appearances from Busta Rhymes, Snoop Dogg, Nas, Redman, and Isaac Hayes.

The album spawned the singles "Protect Ya Neck (The Jump Off)," which reached #52 on the R&B/Hip-Hop chart; "Gravel Pit," which reached #20 on the Rap chart; and "Careful (Click, Click)."

NOVEMBER 28

Rawkus releases the compilation *Lyricist Lounge 2.*

Reaching #33 on the *Billboard* 200 and #7 on the R&B/Hip-Hop chart, the album featured tracks by Erick Sermon, Beanie Sigel, Q-Tip, Mos Def, Dilated Peoples, Royce da 5'9", Redman, dead prez, M.O.P., Kool G. Rap, Saukrates, Ghostface Killah, Macy Gray, the Big L, as well as the Notorious B.I.G., to name a few.

Producers manning the board for the cuts on the inclusive compilation included Hi-Tek, J Dilla, Nottz, Scott Storch, the Alchemist, Rockwilder, DJ Mighty Mi, Madlib, DJ Roddy Rod, Erick Sermon, DJ Premier, and Guru of Gang Starr.

Lyricist Lounge 2 contained the hits "Get Up" by the Cocoa Brovaz, "Ms. Fat Booty 2" by Mos Def and Ghostface Killah, as well as "Oh No" by Mos Def, Pharoahe Monch, and Nate Dogg, which reached #9, #15, and #1 on the Rap chart respectively.

DECEMBER 12

Xzibit releases his third album *Restless* on Loud.

Executive produced by Dr. Dre, the platinum-selling set featured production from a slew of all-stars, including DJ Quik, Eminem, Sir Jinx, Battlecat, Rick Rock, Soopafly, Erick Sermon, Rockwilder, Mel-Man, Nottz, Scott Storch, and Thayod Ausar.

Debuting at #14 on the *Billboard* 200, the highly anticipated album featured the hit singles "X," which featured Snoop Dogg, "Get Your Walk On," and "Front 2 Back," as well as guest appearances by Nate Dogg, Defari, King T, Butch Cassidy, Suga Free, Goldie Loc, KRS-One, Erick Sermon, J-Ro, Tash, Eminem, and Dr. Dre.

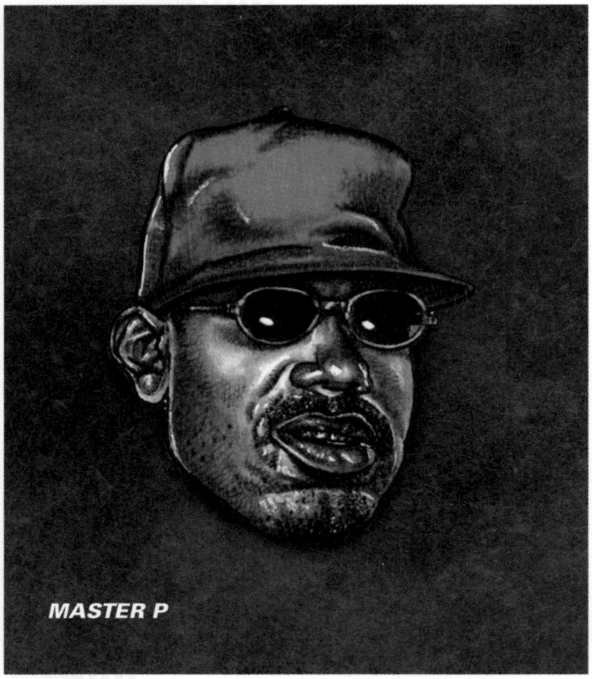
MASTER P

DECEMBER 19

Snoop Dogg releases his fifth album *Tha Last Meal* on No Limit.

Snoop's multi-platinum fifth album would be the last for Master P's No Limit label. Peaking at #4 on the *Billboard* 200 and topping the R&B/Hip-Hop chart, the laid-back set featured production by Dr. Dre, Scott Storch, Meech Wells, Mike Elizondo, Jelly Roll, Soopafly, Carlos Stephens, Studio Ton, and Battlecat.

The languid bass-heavy set featured guest appearances by MC Ren, Ice Cube, Lil 1/2 Dead, the Lady of Rage, Magic, Eve, Suga Free, and Mac Minister, and contained the smash hits "Lay Low" (which featured Nate Dog, Butch Cassidy, Tha Eastsidaz, and Master P and reached #8 on the R&B/Hip-Hop chart) and the Timbaland-produced "Snoop Dogg (What's My Name Pt. 2)," which reached #9 on the Rap chart.

2001

FEBRUARY 21

Eminem and Elton John perform "Stan" at the 43rd Grammy Awards.

Due to what some perceived as homophobic lyrics in Eminem's music, the Gay & Lesbian Alliance Against Defamation protested the performance the day of the Awards, outside the Staples Center in Los Angeles, California. In response, Eminem invited the openly gay Elton John to perform with him, singing the Dido chorus on his song "Stan."

FEBRUARY 27

City High release the single "What Would You Do?" on Interscope.

The lead single for the New Jersey group's debut album, *City High* became a top ten crossover pop hit, topped the Rap chart, and was nominated for a Grammy for best R&B performance by a duo or group with vocals in 2002.

MARCH 15

Eve releases the single "Let Me Blow Ya Mind" on Ruff Ryders.

Coproduced by Dr. Dre and Scott Storch, the second single off Eve's album *Scorpion* would become one of the biggest hits of 2001, peaking at #2 on the *Billboard* Hot 100 and charting in more than a dozen countries.

With Gwen Stefani on vocals, the song won the first-ever Grammy in the best rap/sung performance category and the MTV Video Music Award for best female video.

MARCH 27

Amaru Entertainment releases the posthumous 2Pac album, *Until the End of Time.*

Debuting at #1 on the *Billboard* 200, the multi-platinum double disc featured Death Row recordings from 1996, a number of them remixes by producers that included Trackmasters, Ant Banks, and Cold 187um.

The highlight of the collection is the multi-platinum title track, which featured R.L. Huggar of the R&B group Next and sampled the Mr. Mister 1985 chart-topper "Broken Wings," and reached #52 on the *Billboard* Hot 100.

APRIL 13

Run-D.M.C. release their seventh and final album *Crown Royal* on Arista.

Reaching #37 on the *Billboard* 200 and #22 on the R&B/Hip-Hop chart, the classic album featured rap-rock collaborations with artists such as Sugar Ray, Fred Durst of Limp Bizkit, Kid Rock, Stephan Jenkins of Third Eye Blind, and Everlast. Other guests on *Crown Royal* included Method Man, Jermaine Dupri, Nas, Prodigy, and Fat Joe.

APRIL 24

O.C. releases his third solo album on JCOR.

O.C., a member of the Diggin' in the Crates Crew, had fellow D.I.T.C. members Lord Finesse and Buckwild handle much of the production on *Bon Appetit*, with previous collaborator Ahmed handling some beat-making duties as well. Reaching #84 on the R&B/Hip-Hop chart, the album contained the single "Bonafide," featuring Jay Z, which was released two years prior to the album's launch. Other guests on *Bon Appetit* included A.G., UNI, TL, A-Bless, and the Ghetto Dwellas.

APRIL 26

Missy Elliott releases her third album *Miss E... So Addictive* on Elektra.

Reaching #40 on the *Billboard* 200, the Virginia rapper's third album sold more than a million copies in the first three months after its release.

Mainly coproduced with Timbaland, Elliott's platinum album featured the lead single "Get Ur Freak On," Elliott's second top ten *Billboard* Hot 100, as well as "Lick Shots," "One Minute Man," which reached #15 on the *Billboard* Hot 100, "Take Away, " which featured vocals from Ginuwine and reached #13 on the R&B/Hip-Hop chart, and "4 My People." Ludacris, Method Man, Redman, Busta Rhymes, Jay Z, and Eve all make guest appearances on the album.

In 2001, Elliott won the Grammy for best rap solo performance for "Get Ur Freak On" and in 2002, she won the Grammy for best female rap solo performance for the album track "Scream a.k.a. Itchin'."

MAY 8

Carmen: A Hip Hopera premieres on MTV.

The film, starring Mekhi Phifer and Beyoncé Knowles in the title roles, is a modern day remake of the nineteenth-century Georges Bizet opera of the same name. *Carmen* was directed by Robert Townsend and featured appearances by Wyclef Jean, Rah Digga, Lil' Bow Wow, Mos Def, and was narrated by Da Brat.

MOS DEF

MAY 14

Jagged Edge releases the single "Where the Party At" on So So Def Recordings.

Featuring a prominent guest appearance from Nelly, the song became a major crossover hit during the summer of 2001, peaking at #3 on the *Billboard* Hot 100, topping the R&B/Hip-Hop charts, and continuing Jagged Edge's streak of three consecutive #1 Rap hits, following 2000's "Let's Get Married" and "Promise." "Where the Party At" was nominated for a Grammy in 2002 for best rap/sung collaboration.

MAY 15

Cannibal Ox release their debut album _The Cold Vein_ on Definitive Jux.

The Harlem duo of Vast Aire and Vordul Mega's critically acclaimed debut featured lush production work from Company Flow's El-P. Their flow paints a dark but vivid portrait of New York life and is now considered an underground classic.

MAY 29

Interscope releases the soundtrack to the MGM film _What's the Worst That Could Happen?_

The film, directed by Sam Weisman and starring Martin Lawrence and Danny DeVito, had a soundtrack that featured various hip-hop artists like Snoop Dogg, Benzino, Queen Latifah, Craig Mack, as well as the hit single "Music" by Erick Sermon featuring a newly discovered vocal track by Marvin Gaye and reached #2 on the R&B/Hip-Hop chart.

JUNE 5

D12 release the single "Purple Pills" on Interscope.

Best known in its radio-friendly censored version, "Purple Hills," the Eminem-produced song served as the Detroit group's second single on their debut album *Devil's Night*. The song, which was a #1 hit on the Rap chart and top twenty hit on the *Billboard* Hot 100, also became a major hit throughout Western Europe.

JUNE 5

St. Lunatics release their debut studio album *Free City* on Universal.

In the wake of the success of Nelly's *Country Grammar*, there was a lot of anticipation for the debut of the St. Louis group, comprised of Nelly, Ali, Murphy Lee, Kyjuan, and City Spud.

Debuting at #3 on the *Billboard* 200 and topping the R&B/Hip-Hop chart, the platinum-selling party album featured a few guest appearances, most notably Brian McKnight on "Groovin' Tonight." Produced by Jay E, Wally, and the group's City Spud, the album contained the hit "Midwest Swing," which reached #88 on the *Billboard* Hot 100.

JUNE 26

T.I. releases his debut single "I'm Serious" on Arista.

Produced by the Neptunes, the debut track from the Atlanta rapper featured dancehall reggae king Beenie Man. His album of the same name would be released four months later.

JUNE 26

Beanie Sigel releases his second studio album *The Reason* on Roc-A-Fella.

Debuting at #5 on the *Billboard* 200 and topping the R&B/Hip-Hop chart, the second set from the streetwise Philadelphia rapper featured a slew of high-profile guests, including Jay Z, Freeway, and Young Chris on "Think It's a Game" and Scarface on the thoughtful "Mom Praying." Produced primarily by Just Blaze, the bestselling set also featured work from Kanye West, Rick Rock, 88-Keys, No I.D., Big Demi, and Sha-Self. The single "Beanie (Mack Bitch)" reached #52 on the R&B/Hip-Hop chart and #11 on the Rap chart.

JULY 3

Lil' Romeo releases his self-titled debut album on No Limit.

Lil' Romeo, the eleven-year-old son of No Limit founder Master P, who also produced part of the album, was joined on his first set by his uncle Silkk the Shocker as well as Lil' Zane, Afficial, 6 Piece, and Little D. After debuting at #6 on the *Billboard* 200, the gold-selling album went on to produce the hits "The Girlies" and "My Baby," which sampled the Jackson 5's "I Want You Back," topped the R&B/Hip-Hop chart, and reached #3 on the *Billboard* Hot 100.

JULY 10

P. Diddy & the Bad Boy Family release the album *The Saga Continues...* on Bad Boy.

Topping the R&B/Hip-Hop charts and reaching #2 on the *Billboard* 200, the platinum-selling album marked the transition of Sean Combs from Puff Daddy, his most popular moniker to date, to P. Diddy.

The album spawned the hit single "I Need A Girl (To Bella)," featuring Loon, Lo & Jack, and Mario Winans, and label anthem "Bad Boys for Life," which reached #5 on the Rap chart. Other guests on *The Saga Continues...* included Black Rob, Mark Curry, Faith Evans, G. Dep, Carl Thomas, as well as several other artists.

CHUCK D:
Remember the MTV TV show *Making of the Band?* In one episode, P. Diddy said that to get his Bad Boy Record attention, da band had to walk across NYC to Brooklyn to get him some Junior's cheesecake. Well Puff was that kind of worker himself. He did all of that. I admired his drive before he was a known commodity. He would task his acts as he would himself. After the B.I.G. tragedy, he would have to task himself to save his company and he sure did.

JULY 22

Cormega releases his debut studio album *The Realness* on Landspeed.

The debut from the former member of The Firm featured work from a number of producers, including Havoc and the Alchemist, but also Ayatollah, Sha

P. DIDDY

FABOLOUS

Money XL, and Godfather Don. Reaching #24 on the R&B/Hip-Hop chart, the Queensbridge thug's poetic set includes guest appearances by Prodigy on "Thun & Kicko," Tragedy Khadafi on "They Forced My Hand," and Mobb Deep on the hidden track "Killaz Theme II."

AUGUST 7

Jadakiss releases his debut solo album *Kiss tha Game Goodbye* on Ruff Ryders.

Debuting at #5 on the *Billboard* 200, the debut of the L.O.X. member was highly anticipated. Guests on the gold-selling set included Nas, Nate Dogg, Pharrell, Carl Thomas, Ann Nesby (formerly of Sounds of Blackness), and DMX.

Swizz Beatz, Timbaland, DJ Premier, Just Blaze, Eric McCaine, Mahogany, the Neptunes, the Alchemist, Wayne-O, Fiend, Mas, Rated R, Icepick, Grimy, P.K., and Sheek Louch handled production duties on the album. It produced three singles, including "We Gonna Make It," which featured Styles P of the L.O.X. and hit #53 on the R&B/Hip-Hop chart.

AUGUST 12

Mr. Cheeks releases the single "Lights, Camera, Action!" on Universal.

The lead single from the New York rapper's debut solo album *John P. Kelly* featured skilled production from Bink! The song became a top twenty crossover hit, peaking at #14 on the *Billboard* Hot 100 and topping the Rap and R&B/Hip-Hop charts. The following year, a remix of the song featuring P. Diddy, Petey Pablo, and Missy Elliott appeared on the soundtrack to *XXX*.

AUGUST 26

Petey Pablo releases the single "Raise Up" on Jive.

Timbaland produced this Dirty South anthem, the lead single off the North Carolina rapper's debut album *Diary of a Sinner: 1st Entry*. The gold-selling song became a top thirty hit on the *Billboard* Hot 100, a top ten hit on the R&B/Hip-Hop charts, and a #1 Rap single.

SEPTEMBER 11

Jay Z releases his sixth album *The Blueprint* on Roc-A-Fella.

Despite its untimely release on the day of the terrorist attacks, *The Blueprint* sold over 420,000 copies in its first week, eventually going multi-platinum.

Produced by all-stars such as Just Blaze, Bink!, Timbaland, Trackmasters, and Eminem and critically acclaimed for its lyrical dexterity, the set featured three smash-hits "Jigga," "Girls, Girls, Girls," and "Izzo (H.O.V.A.)" produced by then-aspiring beat-maker Kanye West. All three reached the top ten on the Rap chart. The only guest on "The Blueprint" was Eminem on the killer track "Renegade."

SEPTEMBER 11

Professor Griff releases his fifth solo album *And the Word Became Flesh* on the Right Stuff.

Public Enemy's X Minista's album was produced by Griff, Kerwin "Sleek" Young, and Chuck D, who performs on the song "Hypocrites." Umar Bin Hassan, of the Last Poets, also joined Griff on the track "European on Me." Other songs included "T.H.I.N.K.," "Sudden Death," "Imagination," and "It Ain't Right."

SEPTEMBER 11

Fabolous releases his debut studio album *Ghetto Fabolous* on Desert Storm.

With an all-star production and guest team that included the Neptunes, Rockwilder, Timbaland, Ja Rule, Jagged Edge, and Lil' Mo, it's no wonder the debut from the Brooklyn rapper reached #3 on the *Billboard* 200 and #2 on the R&B/Hip-Hop chart.

The Rick Rock–produced debut single "Can't Deny It," which featured Nate Dogg, helped fuel interest, reaching #25 on the *Billboard* Hot 100, as the second single "Young'n (Holla Back)," which peaked at #33 on the *Billboard* Hot 100.

SEPTEMBER 18

Coo Coo Cal releases his sophomore album *Disturbed* on Tommy Boy.

The Milwaukee rapper's second album, which just barely missed going platinum, was produced by Bigg Hank, Bink!, Rated X, DJ Cipha Sounds, and Kay Gee of Naughty By Nature. Peaking at #45 on the *Billboard* 200, guests on *Disturbed* included Koffee Brown, Twista, Mocha, Mr. Do It To Death, Midwikid, and Nothing Typical. It contained the hit single "My Projects," which topped the Rap chart and reached #22 on the R&B/Hip-Hop chart.

OCTOBER 2

Ja Rule releases his third album *Pain Is Love* on Murder Inc.

Produced mainly by Irv Gotti with help from Missy Elliott, Lil Rob, and Ty Fyffe, the multi-platinum, chart-topping set was made for the radio. Debuting at #1 on the *Billboard* 200, the Grammy-nominated album spawned three huge hits "Livin' It Up," featuring Case, which reached the top ten on the *Billboard* Hot 100, the R&B/Hip-Hop and Rap charts, "Always on Time," featuring Ashanti, and the "I'm Real (Murder Remix)," featuring Jennifer Lopez, both of which topped the *Billboard* Hot 100.

Other guests on *Pain Is Love* included Missy Elliott, Tweet, Caddillac Tah, Charli Baltimore, Black Child, Boo & Gotti, Jodie Mack & 0-1, and 2Pac Shakur.

CHUCK D:
A voice is important as a MC. I always thought that Ja Rule's voice was gold and made those rap and B tracks happen, with him able to duet with almost anybody on that tip. The radio and clubs were automatic to the Murder Inc. sound because that's how feet were hitting that floor.

OCTOBER 2

will.i.am of the Black Eyed Peas releases his debut album *Lost Change* on Atlantic.

The sophisticated album, a part of the UK label BBE's Beat Generation series, is also the soundtrack to a Levi's Silvertab sponsored short film of the same name directed by Albert Watson. Produced by will.i.am with Printz Board, Michael Angelo Batio, and Dylan "3D" Dresdow, the critically acclaimed album was supported by two singles, "I Am" and "Lay Me Down."

OCTOBER 16

Masta Ace releases *Disposable Arts* on JCOR.

Technically Ace's first solo album, since his three previous releases were credited to his group Masta Ace Incorporated, this critically acclaimed concept album was produced by the member of Marley Marl's Juice Crew along with a slew of other beat-makers including Ayatollah, DJ Rob, Paul Nice, and Rodney Hunter.

Cracking the R&B/Hip-Hop chart, *Disposable Arts* included guest appearances by Greg Nice, of Nice & Smooth, Rah Digga, of the Flipmode Squad, Leschea, J-Ro, King Tee, Punchline, Wordsworth, Jane Doe, Apocalypse, Tonedeff, Jean Grae, Mr. Lee Gee, Sas, Young Zee, and Strick.

OCTOBER 23

DMX releases his fourth studio album *The Great Depression* on Ruff Ryders.

DMX's fourth in a row to debut at the top of the *Billboard* 200, the platinum-selling album was produced by the rapper, along with Just Blaze, Swizz Beatz, Kidd Kold, P.K., Dame Grease, and Black Key. The introspective set featured the singles "We Right Here," which reached #8 on the Rap chart, the Grammy-nominated "Who We Be," which reached #60 on the *Billboard* Hot 100, and the ode to his grandmother "I Miss You," which featured Faith Evans and reached #37 on the R&B/Hip-Hop chart.

NOVEMBER 6

Aftermath releases the soundtrack to the Lionsgate comedy film *The Wash.*

The Wash, a sort of quasi remake of the 1977 classic comedy *Car Wash* was directed by DJ Pooh and starred Dr. Dre and Snoop Dogg, with cameo appearances by Eminem, Ludacris, and Xzibit.

Peaking at #1 on the *Billboard* 200, the gold-selling soundtrack featured an array of hip-hop and R&B stars such as Bubba Sparxxx, Soopafly, Bilal, Truth Hurts, Shaunta, and D12. It contained the hit singles "Bad Intentions" by Dr. Dre, featuring Knoc-turn'al and peaking at #1 on the *Billboard* Hot 100, and the title track also by Dr. Dre, featuring Snoop Dogg.

NOVEMBER 13

Swollen Members release their sophomore album *Bad Dreams* on Battleaxe.

The Vancouver hip-hop group's inspired set featured production from the Alchemist, Evidence, DJ Kemo, Concise, Joey Chavez, Roger Swan, Seanski and the group's Rob the Viking.

Platinum-selling in Canada, it spawned the singles "Take It Back," featuring DJ Revolution, "Bring It Home," and "Fuel Injected," both featuring Moka Only. Other guests on *Bad Dreams* included Son Doobie of Funkdoobiest, Chali 2na of Jurassic 5, Rattlesnake Jones, Chris Guy, Planet Asia, Buc Fifty, Saukrates, and DJ Babu.

NOVEMBER 13

UGK releases its fourth album *Dirty Money* on Jive.

The Texas group's first studio release since 1996's *Ridin' Dirty* was highly anticipated, peaking at #19 on the *Billboard* 200 and #2 on the R&B/Hip-Hop charts. Produced mainly by N.O. Joe and Pimp C, the explicit album featured guest appearances by Juicy J, Too $hort, Devin the Dude, and Jermaine Dupri.

Reaching #15 on the *Billboard* 200, the album spawned a number of singles including "Pimpin' Ain't No Illusion," which became a top ten Rap hit.

NOVEMBER 27

Ludacris releases his third album *Word of Mouf* on Disturbing tha Peace.

Reaching #3 on the *Billboard* 200 and topping the R&B/Hip-Hop chart, the multi-platinum album established the Atlanta-based rapper as a major superstar in the industry. His clever wordplay, original laid-back flow, and slightly offbeat delivery would spark smash hits off *Word of Mouf*, such as the Grammy-nominated "Rollout (My Business)," "Area Codes" (featuring Nate Dogg), "Saturday (Oooh, Oooh)" (featuring Sleepy Brown), and "Move," which featured Mystikal and I-20 and reached #10 on the *Billboard* Hot 100.

Produced by Jazze Pha, Swizz Beatz, Timbaland, Jook, Paul King, Organized Noize, KLC, and Bangladesh, the Grammy-nominated album featured appearances by Jermaine Dupri, Twista, Jagged Edge, Three 6 Mafia, Fate Wilson, Keon Bryce, 4-Ize, and Chimere.

DECEMBER 4

De La Soul release their sixth album *Bionix* on Tommy Boy.

The second installment in the group's three-disc series, A.O.I. (Art Official Intelligence), after *Mosaic Thump* was released the previous year, was their last on their career-long label, as Tommy Boy would fold shortly after the album's release. The third disc, which was to be mainly focused on the group's DJ Mase, was never released.

Produced mainly by Dave West, the groovy and smart *Bionix* produced the hit single "Baby Phat," an ode to extra voluptuous women featuring Devin the Dude and Yummy Bingham. Other guests on the second A.O.I. installment included Slick Rick, Cee-Lo Green, B-Real of Cypress Hill, Canadian R&B crooner Glenn Lewis, Shell Council, Philly Black, and the J Dilla.

DECEMBER 11

Jonell and Method Man release the single "Round and Round" on Def Jam.

Originally released on the producer Hi-Tek's 2001 album *Hi-Teknology*, the song became a hit when it was released as a remix with Method Man on the soundtrack to Method Man and Redman's stoner comedy film *How High*. The only charting single of Jonell's career was #1 on the Rap chart and reached #62 on the *Billboard* Hot 100.

METHOD MAN

DECEMBER 11

Mobb Deep release their fifth album *Infamy* on Loud.

Produced by Scott Storch, the Alchemist, Ez Elpee, and Havoc of Mobb Deep, the gold-selling set featured the singles "Get Away," "Pray for Me," featuring Lil' Mo, "The Learning (Burn)," featuring Big Noyd and Vita, and "Hey Luv (Anything)," featuring 112. Topping the R&B/Hip-Hop chart and reaching #22 on the *Billboard* 200, the accessible but rugged album featured Ron Isley of the legendary Isley Brothers on the track "There I Go Again/So Long."

DECEMBER 18

Nas releases his fifth studio album *Stillmatic* on Columbia.

Peaking at #5 on the *Billboard* 200, the album was certified platinum one month after its release. The thoughtful album spawned three singles: "Rule," which featured Amerie and reached #67 on the R&B/Hip-Hop chart, "Got Ur Self A...," and "One Mic," which reached #10 on the Rap chart.

Critically acclaimed, the album included "Ether," a diss track directed at Jay Z that served as Nas's response to Jay Z's diss track "Takeover," which Jay Z had released three months earlier. "Ether" became one of the most renowned diss tracks in hip-hop history, with various rappers sampling the song for their own respective diss tracks in the ensuing decade.

2002

FEBRUARY 5

Fat Joe releases the single "What's Luv?" on Atlantic.

Featuring Ashanti, with Ja Rule appearing on the song's remix and album version, the catchy song peaked at #2 on the *Billboard* Hot 100 and topped the Rap chart. Produced by Irv Gotti, the song was the second single from Fat Joe's album *Jealous Ones Still Envy*.

When "What's Luv?" reached #2 on the *Billboard* Hot 100, Ashanti was responsible for the top two songs in the country, with her single "Foolish" at #1.

FEBRUARY 26

Nappy Roots release their debut album *Watermelon, Chicken & Gritz* on Atlantic.

The southern sextet of Skinny DeVille, B. Stille, Ron Clutch, Fish Scales, R. Prophet, and Big V released two independent collections before making their major label debut on Atlantic.

Mainly produced by James "Groove" Chambers, the platinum-selling album reached #3 on the R&B/Hip-Hop charts. The down-home set spawned the hit singles "Awnaw," which featured Jazze Pha and reached #18 on the R&B/Hip-Hop chart, the Grammy-nominated "Po' Folks," which featured Anthony Hamilton and was produced by Trackboyz, and "Headz Up," which cracked the R&B/Hip-Hop chart.

APRIL 2

Cam'ron releases the smash hit "Oh Boy," on Roc-A-Fella.

The Grammy-nominated chart-topper featured Juelz Santana, who along with Cam'ron were members of the Diplomats. Produced by Just Blaze, the lead single off his platinum-selling album *Come Home with Me* topped both the R&B/Hip-Hop and Rap charts, where it spent five weeks, and dominated summer radio.

APRIL 16

Nelly releases the single "Hot in Herre" on Universal.

Produced by the Neptunes, "Hot in Herre" is the second breakthrough single on *Nellyville*, topping the *Billboard* Hot 100 for seven weeks during the summer of 2002. Featuring samples from Neil Young, Nancy Sinatra, and Chuck Brown, the song earned Nelly a win for the first-ever Grammy for best male rap solo performance.

APRIL 26

50 Cent releases his debut album *Guess Who's Back?* on Full Clip.

Following the underground hits on Trackmasters Records, "How to Rob" and "Ghetto Qu'ran (Forgive Me)," 50 was set to release his debut album *Power of the Dollar* on the label before being dropped. Three years later 50 would assemble *Guess Who's Back?* in Toronto as a mixtape.

Reaching #28 on the *Billboard* 200 and #13 on the R&B/Hip-Hop chart, the well-reviewed debut featured production by DJ Clark Kent, Sha Money XL, Terence Dudley, Chop D.I.E.S.E.L., Red Spyda, Fantom of the Beat, and Trackmasters and guests such as Nas, Nature, Bravehearts, Bun B, and his musical crew G Unit.

Eminem's manager Paul Rosenberg would play a role in the impressive debut of the Detroit superstar by winning the bidding war to sign 50 Cent to his label.

APRIL 30

Naughty By Nature release the single "Feels Good (Don't Worry Bout a Thing)" on TVT.

The lead single from the group's sixth album *IIcons* featured vocal harmonies from the group 3LW, the song became a dance hit and cracked the *Billboard* Hot 100, reaching #53, and topping the Rap chart.

FAT JOE

EMINEM

MAY 21

Eminem releases his fourth album *The Eminem Show* on Shady/Aftermath.

The Grammy-winning, diamond-selling set debuted at #1 on the *Billboard* 200, staying there for five weeks. Mainly self-produced along with Jeff Bass, the personal, smart, and often political album produced a number of singles, including the chart-topping, gold-selling "Without Me," the introspective "Cleaning Out My Closet," which reached #4 on the *Billboard* Hot 100, "Sing for the Moment," which sampled the Aerosmith song "Dream On" and reached #14 on the *Billboard* Hot 100. One album cut that charted is "Till I Collapse," which featured Nate Dogg and has been used in pop culture so often that digital downloads of the song have topped two million.

MAY 21

Afu-Ra releases his sophomore album *Life Force Radio* on Koch.

Cracking the *Billboard* 200 and reaching #29 on the R&B/Hip-Hop chart, the Gang Starr Foundation member's second album featured production by DJ Premier, Easy Mo Bee, Ayatollah, True Master, the Arabian Knight, and Kenny Muhammad, among others.

The Rastafarian's critically acclaimed set included appearances by Big Daddy Kane, Guru of Gang Starr and R&B songstress Teena Marie as well as the RZA of the Wu-Tang Clan in the guise of his alter ego Bobby Digital, and spawned the single "Crossfire," which reached #56 on the R&B/Hip-Hop chart.

JUNE 15

Paul Wall and Chamillionaire release *Get Ya Mind Correct* on Paid in Full.

The debut collaborative album from the Houston rappers was an indie success story, reaching #67 on the R&B/Hip-Hop chart. Produced by Drathoven, Lee, Bluenote, Pretty Todd, Deep Fried Camp, and Bruce Takara, the album would become a major landmark for early twenty-first century Houston rap, helping further establish the city as one of the biggest centers for southern rap.

JUNE 25

Nelly releases his second studio album *Nellyville* on Universal.

The second set from the St. Louis rapper debuted atop the *Billboard* 200, selling more than six million copies within a year.

Featuring production from the Neptunes, Just Blaze, Ryan Bowser, as well as Jay E, Nelly's longtime St. Louis producer, the blockbuster album yielded five crossover singles on the *Billboard* Hot 100, including the top five hits "Hot in Herre," and "Dilemma," featuring Kelly Rowland, both of which won Grammy Awards and topped the *Billboard* Hot 100 for seven and ten weeks respectively. Other guests on the album include Cedric the Entertainer, Justin Timberlake, Beanie Sigel, Memphis Bleek, and Nelly's St. Louis rap group St. Lunatics.

CHUCK D:
With this album, Nelly continued to show his musical talent, while continuing to give us an insight into St. Louis, Missouri, rap music and hip-hop culture. The production throughout the album is great and Nelly showcases his voice control by mixing traditional rap flow with singing.

JULY 23

Public Enemy release the album *Revolverlution* on Koch.

The group made history when, for the first time in recorded music history, fans were able to participate in the production of the album. Through an online contest, winners were able to remix such classics like "Public Enemy No. 1," "Shut 'Em Down," "B-Side Wins Again," and "By the Time I Get to Arizona," via an Internet technology.

Reaching #16 on the R&B/Hip-Hop chart, the innovative album featured new singles like "Gotta Give the Peeps What They Need" and the controversial "Son of a Bush," as well as some live versions of PE classics like "Fight the Power" and "Welcome to the Terrordome."

AUGUST 6

Scarface releases his seventh studio album *The Fix* on Def Jam.

Debuting at #4 on the *Billboard* 200 and topping the R&B/Hip-Hop chart, the Houston rapper's seventh studio album featured guests such as Faith Evans and Nas.

Featuring production from Kanye West, Nottz, Tony Pizarro, and the Neptunes, Scarface's first release with Def Jam yielded the popular Single "My Block," which reached #46 on the R&B/Hip-Hop charts, and the Kanye West–produced "Guess Who's Back" featuring Jay Z and Beanie Sigel, which reached #28 on the R&B and #5 on the Rap charts.

AUGUST 20

Clipse release their debut studio album *Lord Willin'* on Arista.

The Virginia Beach hip-hop duo Malice and Pusha T's gold-selling debut highlighted their hustler past and featured appearances from Jermaine Dupri, Fabolous, Jadakiss, and Styles P.

Produced by mentors the Neptunes, the album spawned the summer smash "Grindin'," which reached #30 on the *Billboard* Hot 100 and #8 on the Rap chart; "When the Last Time," which topped the R&B/Hip-Hop and Rap charts; "Ma, I Don't Love Her," featuring Faith Evans; and "Cot Damn," which featured Ab-Liva and Rosco P. Coldchain.

AUGUST 27

Eve releases her third studio album *Eve-Olution* on Ruff Ryders.

Eve's fluid rhymes helped drive the gold-selling album to the top of the R&B/Hip-Hop charts, reaching #6 on the *Billboard* 200. A range of producers worked on the album, including Dr. Dre, Swizz Beatz, Irv Gotti, and Bink!

The rapper teams up with Alicia Keys on the album's lead single "Gangsta Lovin'," which reached #2 on the *Billboard* Hot 100, the R&B/Hip-Hop, and the Rap charts. Other guests on the album include Anthony Hamilton, Snoop Dogg, Nate Dogg, Jadakiss, Styles P, Truth Hurts, and Mashonda.

OCTOBER 1

Xzibit releases his fourth studio album *Man vs. Machine* on Loud Records.

Debuting at #3 on the *Billboard* 200, the gold-selling set, which was executive produced by Dr. Dre, featured an all-star guest list that included Dr. Dre, Snoop Dogg, Eminem, and M.O.P. The Mr. Porter–produced lead single, "Multiply," featuring Nate Dogg, reached #23 on the Rap chart, with three singles, "My Name," "Symphony in X Major," and "Choke Me Spank Me (Pull My Hair)" all reaching the R&B/Hip-Hop chart.

OCTOBER 15

LL Cool J releases his ninth album *10* on Def Jam.

Topping the R&B chart and reaching #2 on the *Billboard* 200, the gold-selling album was technically his tenth full-length release, including 1996's *All World: Greatest Hits* package.

Working with producers including the Neptunes, Ron Lawrence, Chop & Big Joe, and Poke & Tone, the album would spawn three smash hits, "Luv U Better," which reached top five on the *Billboard* 100 and R&B/Hip-Hop and Rap charts; "Amazin'," featuring Kandice Love; and "Paradise," featuring Amerie, which would reach #10 on the Rap chart.

OCTOBER 29

Lil Jon & the East Side Boyz release their fourth studio album *Kings of Crunk* on TVT.

Reaching #2 on the R&B/Hip-Hop charts and #14 on the *Billboard* 200, the platinum-selling party album was a breakthrough moment for crunk and is considered an Atlanta classic.

Kings of Crunk included their signature single "Get Low," featuring the Ying Yang Twins, which peaked at #2 on the *Billboard* Hot 100 and topped the Rap chart. Several remixes of "Get Low" were released, with various versions featuring Busta Rhymes, Beenie Man, Pitbull, Elephant Man, and Nelly. The album also featured appearances from Fat Joe, Pitbull, E-40, Petey Pablo, Jadakiss, Styles P, Trick Daddy, Bun B, and Oobie.

OCTOBER 30

Jam Master Jay is shot and killed.

The pioneering and immensely influential DJ for Run-D.M.C. was killed at the age of thirty-seven in a shooting in Queens. His murder remains unsolved.

NOVEMBER 8

The Universal Pictures film *8 Mile* is released in US theaters.

Eminem made his acting debut in this semiautobiographical film, which was directed by Curtis Hanson and costarred Kim Basinger and Mekhi Phifer. The critically acclaimed film opened at #1.

Eminem's song "Lose Yourself" from the soundtrack won an Oscar for best original song, the first hip-hop song to win an Academy Award, and reached #1 on the *Billboard* Hot 100. The multi-platinum soundtrack debuted at #1 on the *Billboard* 200 and also featured songs from Rakim, Nas, Jay Z, Gang Starr, Obie Trice, Macy Gray, among others.

NOVEMBER 12

Jay Z releases his seventh album *The Blueprint 2: The Gift & The Curse* on Roc-A-Fella.

A sequel of sorts to the Brooklyn-born rapper's critically acclaimed 2001 release *The Blueprint*, the platinum-selling album featured production by Kanye West, Just Blaze, Heavy D, Timbaland, No I.D., the Neptunes, and several others.

Singles from this blockbuster set included the Grammy-nominated "Excuse Me Miss," featuring Pharrell, which reached #8 on the *Billboard* Hot 100 and "'03 Bonnie & Clyde," which sampled 2Pac's song "Me and My Girlfriend" and featured Jay Z's future wife Beyoncé. "'03 Bonnie & Clyde" reached #4 on the *Billboard* Hot 100.

Other guests on the ambitious album included Rakim, Truth Hurts, Dr. Dre, Sean Paul, Michael W. Smith, Big Boi of Outkast, Twista, Killer Mike, Memphis Bleek, Rell, Freeway, Young Gunz, Beanie Sigel, Omillio Sparks, Peedi Peedi, Young Chris, Scarface, M.O.P., Marc Dorsey, Lenny Kravitz, Kanye West, Faith Evans, and the Notorious B.I.G.

NOVEMBER 12

Missy Elliott releases her fourth studio album *Under Construction* on Elektra.

Missy Elliott teamed up once again with longtime producer Timbaland for this multi-platinum, Grammy-nominated set. Debuting at #3 on the *Billboard* 200, the inspired collection spawned three singles: the Grammy-winning "Work It," which reached #2 on the *Billboard* Hot 100, "Gossip Folks," which featured Ludacris and reached #8 on the *Billboard* Hot 100, and "Back in the Day," which featured Jay Z and Tweet. Featured on many best of the year charts, the album included guest appearances from Beyoncé, Method Man, and TLC.

NOVEMBER 12

Sean Paul releases his second studio album *Dutty Rock* on Atlantic.

Reaching the top ten on the *Billboard* 200, the Jamaican dancehall artist's multi-platinum album spawned a number of crossover hits, including the chart-topping "Get Busy," which reached #13 on the *Billboard* Hot 100, "Like Glue," which reached #7 on the *Billboard* Hot 100, "Gimme the Light," and "Baby Boy," which featured Beyoncé and spent nine weeks at #1 on the *Billboard* Hot 100. It was not included in the album's original 2002 release, but was added to the album's edited rerelease in 2003. A variety of producers worked on the album, including Sly and Robbie, the Neptunes, and Steven "Lenky" Marsden. The infectious album also featured guest appearances by Busta Rhymes, Rahzel of the Roots, and Tony Touch.

NOVEMBER 26

2Pac releases fourth posthumous album *Better Dayz* on Interscope.

Debuting at #5 on the *Billboard* 200, the multi-platinum two-disc set featured material recorded for Death Row between 1994 and 1996.

Two singles were released "Still Ballin'," which reached #31 on the R&B/Hip-Hop chart, and "Thugz Mansion," which reached #19 on the *Billboard* Hot 100. Two versions of "Thugz Mansion" are included on the album, an acoustic version featuring Nas and a hip-hop version featuring Anthony Hamilton.

NOVEMBER 26

The Roots release their fifth studio album *Phrenology* on MCA.

As it reached #28 on the *Billboard* 200, many would consider *Phrenology* the Philly band's big commercial breakthrough. The electric album would contain the hits "Break You Off," featuring Musiq Soulchild, which broke the *Billboard* Hot 100 and the classic soulful pop-rock gem "The Seed (2.0)," featuring Cody ChessnuTT, which was an international hit.

Praised for its musical diversity, the gold-selling set featured guest appearances by Alicia Keys, Jill Scott, Talib Kweli, Nelly Furtado, Ursula Rucker, Amiri Baraka, and Mos Def.

DECEMBER 10

Common releases his fifth album *Electric Circus* on MCA.

The album cover, influenced by the 1967 Beatles classic *Sgt. Pepper's Lonely Hearts Club Band* featured images of Jimi Hendrix, Erykah Badu, Jill Scott, Minister Louis Farrakhan, Black Thought, Big Daddy Kane, Prince, Chris Webber, the Last Poets, Assata Shakur, Richard Pryor, among others.

The experimental album, which reached #47 on the *Billboard* 200 and #9 on the R&B/Hip-Hop chart, contained the hit single "Come Close," featuring Mary J. Blige, hitting #18 on the Rap chart. Other guests that appeared on the album included Prince, Erykah Badu, Vinia Mojica, Cee-Lo Green, Bilal, Sonny Sandoval, Jill Scott, Pharrell, Omar, and Laetitia Sadler.

Influenced by a 1968 Rolling Stones TV special, *Electric Circus* featured production by Questlove, the Neptunes, Pino Palladino, James Poyser, Jeff Lee Johnson, Karriem Riggins, and J Dilla.

CHUCK D:
Common really stepped out of his comfort zone on this one. He blended so many genres of music and it works so perfectly with his voice. Common has always had this great ability to blend his voice with the actual instruments, sounds, et cetera, that make up each of his records and on *Electric Circus* he did just that.

DECEMBER 13

Nas releases his sixth album *God's Son* on Columbia.

Covering an array of topics including death, self-empowerment, children, spirituality, and violence, the deeply personal album resonated with fans and critics alike, peaking at #12 on the *Billboard* 200 and topping the R&B/Hip-Hop charts.

Produced by the Alchemist, Salaam Remi, Ron Browz, Agile, Chucky Thompson, Eminem, and Nas himself, the set included the singles "Made You Look," which reached #9 on the Rap chart, "Get Down," and "I Can," which reached #7 on the R&B/Hip-Hop chart. Guest appearances on the album included Kelis, Alicia Keys, Lake, Jully Black, Claudette Ortiz, Bravehearts, J. Phoenix, and a posthumous appearance by 2Pac.

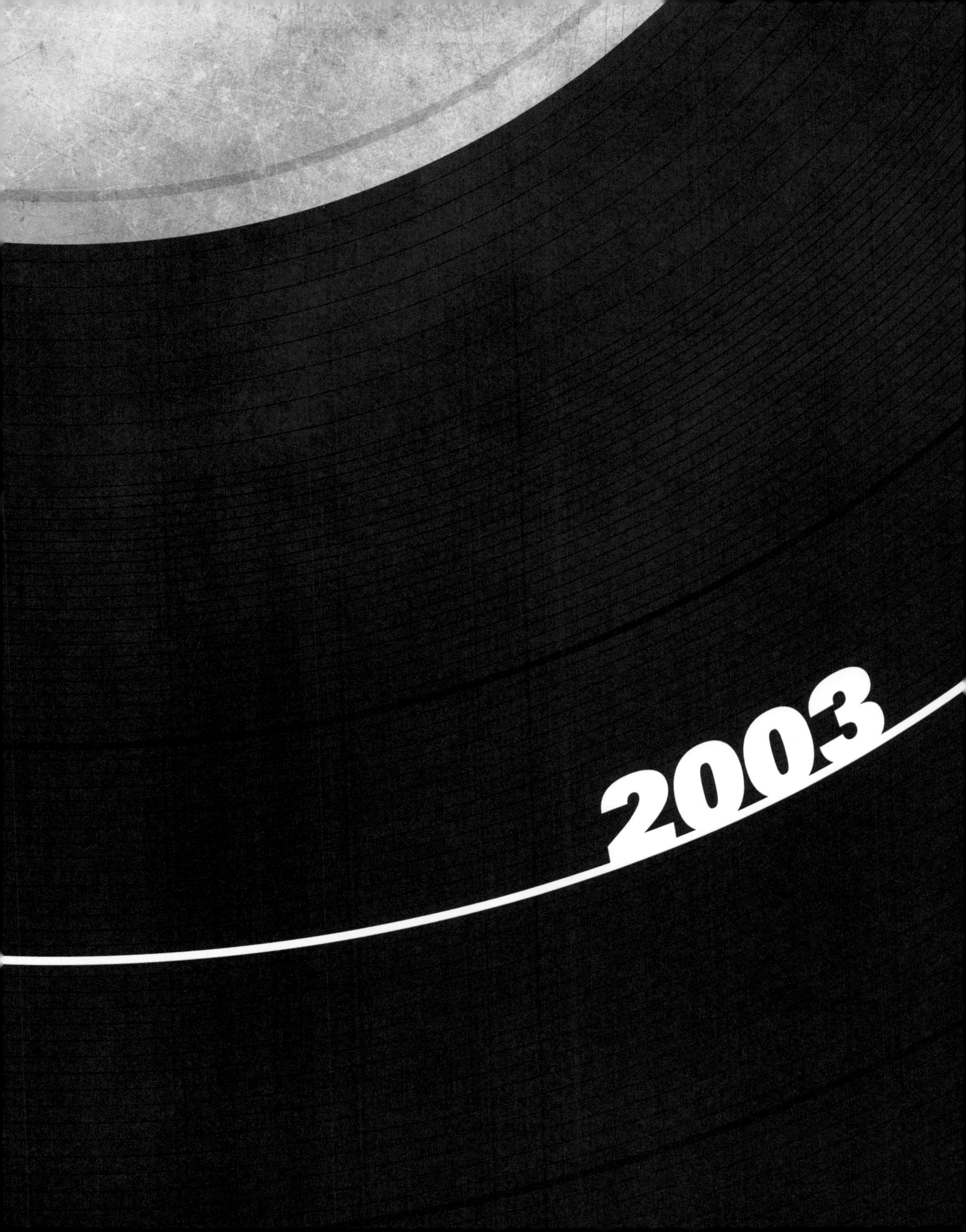
2003

50 CENT

FEBRUARY 6

50 Cent releases his sophomore album *Get Rich or Die Tryin'* in a joint release by Shady/Aftermath.

Debuting atop the *Billboard* 200, the Grammy-nominated, multi-platinum-selling smash showcased 50 Cent's hypnotic singsong flow, accentuated with both New York and southern drawls, and propelled him to be one of the biggest rap and pop stars in the world.

"In da Club," the chart-topping platinum lead single produced by Dr. Dre and Mike Elizondo would, within two months, become the most listened to song in radio history. It also topped the charts in Australia, Switzerland, Germany, Greece, the Netherlands, Ireland, Belgium, Norway, Sweden, Denmark, Austria, and Finland.

Featuring all-star production by Eminem, Rockwilder, Megahertz, and Mr. Porter, among others, *Get Rich or Die Tryin'* also spawned the #1 hits "21 Questions," featuring Nate Dogg, and "P.I.M.P.," featuring Snoop Dogg, Lloyd Banks, and Young Buck. It also contained the hit singles "Patiently Waiting," "If I Can't," and the bluesy reggae-esque "Many Men (Wish Death)."

CHUCK D:

I heard about 50 from working with Sony, with Jam Master Jay. Columbia was a label that gave many other rappers their first look and releases à la DMX. When he evolved with his first breakthrough record, *Wanksta*, I said to myself, "Here's a cat that enjoys going against the grain." It struck me as immediately impressive, and I didn't yet know his story. Here was a cat who was gonna say and probably do anything to win, and not be politically correct on anything. His style—taking a little of Mase of Bad Boy gloss over on mean tracks—told me that he was a scientist at it. So the best A&Rs at times are MCs like Eminem, who know what realities a rapper may have come through, rather than just merely going off on a recording or performance standpoint. 50 Cent brought surety to another era.

FEBRUARY 25

Freeway releases his debut studio release *Philadelphia Freeway* on Roc-A-Fella/Def Jam.

The highly anticipated debut from the Philadelphia rapper reached #5 on the *Billboard* 200 and #3 on the R&B/Hip-Hop chart. Featuring stellar work by producers that included Just Blaze, Bink!, and Kanye West, the critically acclaimed set spawned the charting singles "What We Do," which featured Beanie Sigel and Jay Z, and "Flipside," which featured Peedi Crakk. Other guests on the album included Nelly, Snoop Dogg, Faith Evans, Nate Dogg, and Mariah Carey.

MARCH 4

Lil' Kim releases her third studio album *La Bella Mafia* on Atlantic.

Debuting at #5 on the *Billboard* 200, this platinum-selling set featured two Grammy-nominated singles. The first is "Magic Stick" featuring 50 Cent, which reached #2 on the *Billboard* Hot 100. Produced by Carlos "Fantom of the Beat" Evans, the song sold over two million copies. The second was the Kanye West–produced "Came Back for You."

Another hit from the confident, sexy album is "The Jump Off," produced by Timbaland and featuring Mr. Cheeks, which reached the top ten on the R&B/Hip-Hop and Rap charts.

MARCH 25

The Diplomats release their debut album *Diplomatic Immunity* on Roc-A-Fella.

Harlem's the Diplomats, aka Dipset, consisted of Cam'ron, Hell Rell, Jim Jones, Freekey Zekey, and Juelz Santana. Their gold-selling two-disc set, which debuted at #8 on the *Billboard* 200, featured production by Kanye West, Just Blaze, Heatmakerz, and E Bass among others.

The album spawned the hit singles, "Built This City" and "Dipset Anthem," both of which reached the R&B/Hip-Hop chart. Guests on the set included Master P, Un Kasa, Freeway, DMX, Monique Chandler, Shaniqua Williams, and Toya.

APRIL 29

Bone Crusher releases his debut album *AttenCHUN!* on So So Def/Arista.

Produced by Jermaine Dupri, the Atlanta rapper's debut contained the monster hit "Never Scared," which featured Killer Mike and T.I., reaching #26 on the *Billboard* Hot 100. The album was certified gold after nineteen weeks on the *Billboard* 200, peaking at #11, and topped the R&B/Hip-Hop chart.

JUNE 10

Joe Budden releases his self-titled debut album on Def Jam.

Mainly produced by Whiteboyz Noize as well as by Just Blaze and Lofey, the gold-selling album debuted at #8 on the *Billboard* 200.

The witty set spawned the hit singles, "Pump It Up," which reached #38 on the *Billboard* Hot 100 and #16 on the R&B/Hip-Hop chart, and "Fire (Yes Yes Y'all)" featuring Busta Rhymes, which reached #48 on the R&B/Hip-Hop chart. Other guests on the set included 112 and Lil' Mo.

JUNE 24

Gang Starr release their sixth and final album, *The Ownerz,* on Virgin/EMI.

After a four-year break, Guru and DJ Premier return with a tough and talent-filled set that peaked at #18 on the *Billboard* 200 and #5 on the R&B/Hip-Hop chart. Guests on this critically acclaimed, self-produced album include Snoop Dogg, Fat Joe, M.O.P., NYG'z, H. Stax, Big Shug, and Freddie Foxxx. Charting singles include "Nice Girl, Wrong Place," featuring Boy Big, and the fan favorite "Rite Where U Stand," featuring Jadakiss.

JUNE 29

Nelly, P. Diddy, and Murphy Lee release their collaborative single "Shake Ya Tailfeather" on Universal.

Featured on the soundtrack to *Bad Boys II* and eventually released on Murphy Lee's debut album *Murphy's Law,* "Shake Ya Tailfeather" became a #1 *Billboard* Hot 100 hit in September 2003, remaining on the top of the charts for four consecutive weeks. The song won the Grammy for best rap performance by a duo or group and ended up being the only #1 hit of Murphy Lee's career.

JULY 15

Chingy releases his debut studio album *Jackpot* on Disturbing tha Peace.

The St. Louis–based rapper released his debut on his mentor Ludacris's Disturbing Tha Peace imprint. Produced mainly by the Trak Starz, the multi-platinum album debuted at #2 on the *Billboard* 200 and featured the hit lead single "Right Thurr," which reached #2 on the *Billboard* Hot 100. Chingy matched the success of "Right Thurr" with his follow-up singles, "Holidae In," which featured Ludacris and Snoop Dogg, and "One Call Away," which featured J-Weav, both of which reached the top five of the *Billboard* Hot 100.

JULY 21

Dizzee Rascal releases his debut *Boy in da Corner* on XL in the UK.

Released in the United States in 2004 by Matador Records, the critically acclaimed album served as a prime example of grime, a UK dark subgenre that originated in London's East End.

Winning the prestigious Mercury Prize in the UK, the thoughtful album spawned three hit singles in the United Kingdom: "I Luv U," "Fix Up, Look Sharp," and "Jus' a Rascal."

AUGUST 19

The Neptunes release *The Neptunes Present... Clones* on Arista.

This gold-selling compilation album from the production team of Pharrell Williams and Chad Hugo remains the only studio album released under the Neptunes name. Featuring a star-studded array of guests, including Busta Rhymes, Snoop Dogg,

2003

Ludacris, Jay Z, Nelly, Pusha T, Kelis, Nas, Ol' Dirty Bastard, and Jadakiss, also helped the set top both the *Billboard* 200 and the R&B/Hip-Hop chart.

Self-produced, the album's biggest hit, "Frontin'," which featured Jay Z, was Pharrell's debut solo single as the primary artist and became a top five hit on the *Billboard* Hot 100.

SEPTEMBER 23

Outkast release *Speakerboxxx/The Love Below* on LaFace.

Outkast's fifth studio album, which sold more than eleven million copies in the first three years after its release, would establish the group as one of the most successful, influential artists of the decade.

Released as a double album, with *Speakerboxxx* being fronted by Big Boi and *The Love Below* by André 3000, the diamond-selling album featured appearances from Norah Jones, Kelis, Jay Z, Lil Jon & the East Side Boyz, as well as longtime collaborators Cee-Lo Green, Sleepy Brown, and Killer Mike.

Topping the *Billboard* 200, the ambitious set spawned two #1 pop singles the Grammy-nominated "Hey Ya!," which spent nine weeks at #1 on the *Billboard* Hot 100, and "The Way You Move," which replaced it at the top of the charts. "Roses," the album's third single, was also a top five *Billboard* Hot 100 hit.

Outkast won three Grammys in 2004, including the Grammy for album of the year and best rap album.

CHUCK D:

By far their most commercially successful record, Big Boi and André 3000 delivered the goods via separate projects that came together to form a whole. Outkast is great because the two artists complement each other well. Even though *Speakerboxxx/The Love Below* are technically two separate albums, the genius of them is that you can view them as a full Outkast album or a Big Boi album and an André 3000 album.

OCTOBER 7

Ludacris releases *Chicken-n-Beer* on Disturbing Tha Peace.

The multi-platinum, lyrically dexterous set debuted at #1 on the *Billboard* 200. The album produced five smash hits: "Diamond in the Back," "P-Poppin'," "Splash Waterfalls," "Stand Up" (featuring Shawnna), and "Blow It Out," which was a jab at Fox conservative pundit Bill O'Reilly, who had made derogatory comments about the superstar rapper.

Pulling in all kinds of talent, the album featured production from Kanye West, DJ Nasty & LVM, Ron Browz, Mo B. Dick, the Neptunes, T-Storm, Erick Sermon, Icedrake, DJ Paul, Juicy J, Black Key, and Jook and guest spots by Chingy, I-20, Tity Boi (later known as 2 Chainz), Snoop Dogg, 8Ball & MJG, Carl Thomas, Lil' Flip, and Lil' Fate.

OCTOBER 21

Loon released his self-titled debut album on Bad Boy.

The Harlem native's debut set included production by Sean "Puffy" Combs, Scott Storch, Mario Winans, Poke & Tone, Akon, Anthony "Scoe" Walker, and Buckwild, among others. The album spawned the smash hit "Down For Me," which featured Mario Winans and peaked at #19 on the Rap chart.

Hitting #6 on the *Billboard* 200 and #2 on the R&B/Hip-Hop chart, guests on the romantic album included Kelis, Aaron Hall, Carl Thomas, Claudette Ortiz, Tammy, Trina, Missy Elliott, and Joe Hooker.

NOVEMBER 12

Cam'ron and Damon Dash appear on *The O'Reilly Factor*.

Roc-A-Fella CEO Damon Dash and MC Cam'ron went on Fox's *The O'Reilly Factor* to debate the social and artistic merits of hip-hop with an inner-city Philadelphia elementary school principal and host Bill O'Reilly. Levelheaded in the face of O'Reilly's increased frustration, Cam'ron uttered his infamous "You maaadd!"

NOVEMBER 14

Jay Z releases his *The Black Album* on Roc-A-Fella.

Promoted as his retirement album, the multi-platinum set debuted at #1 on the *Billboard* 200, fulfilling Jay Z's desire to go out on top, at least temporarily.

The original plan was to work with a different producer on each song, so the album featured songs with Kanye West, Just Blaze, Aqua, 3H, DJ Quik, the Neptunes, Rick Rubin, Timbaland, 9th Wonder, the Buchannans, and Eminem, who was also featured on the track "Moment of Clarity."

The blockbuster would spawn a number of hits, including the Grammy-winning, platinum-selling "99 Problems," Timbaland-produced "Dirt Off Your Shoulder," "Encore," "What More Can I Say," which opens with a quote from the movie *Gladiator*, and "Change Clothes," featuring Pharrell, which reached #10 on the *Billboard* Hot 100.

NOVEMBER 14

G Unit release their debut label *Beg for Mercy* on Interscope.

50 Cent's group G Unit, which included Lloyd Banks, Young Buck, and Tony Yayo, released their debut on the same day as *The Black Album*, yet still debuted at #3 on the *Billboard* 200.

Produced by a number of superstars, including Dr. Dre, Eminem, DJ Khalil, Mr. Porter, and No I.D., the brash, multi-platinum album spawned several top twenty *Billboard* Hot 100 hits, including "Stunt 101," which reached #13, and "Wanna Get to Know You," featuring Joe, which reached #15.

NOVEMBER 14

Paramount Pictures releases the documentary *Tupac: Resurrection*.

Directed by Lauren Lazin, the documentary about the slain rapper and actor is narrated by Tupac himself. The film was nominated for best documentary feature at the 77th Academy Awards. The accompanying platinum-selling soundtrack, released on Amaru Entertainment, contained nine Tupac songs that appeared in the film and featured production work by Eminem, among others.

DECEMBER 16

Raekwon of the Wu-Tang Clan releases his third solo album *The Lex Diamond Story* on his label Ice H20.

Reaching #18 on the R&B/Hip-Hop chart, this is Raekwon's first solo album to not credit him as "Chef" Raekwon. The gangsta album featured guest appearances by fellow Wu-Tang members Ghostface Killah, Inspectah Deck, Method Man, Masta Killa, and Cappadonna, as well as partners in rhyme like Fat Joe, Havoc of Mobb Deep, and Capone of CNN. Not working with RZA meant there were new producers on this album, including DJ Khalil, Emile, and EZ Elpee.

DECEMBER 16

Memphis Bleek releases his third album *M.A.D.E.* on Get Low/Roc-A-Fella.

Reaching #35 on the *Billboard* 200, the Brooklyn rapper's ferocious set featured work from producers including Just Blaze, Scott Storch, and Kanye West. Charting singles on the gold-selling album included "Round Here," which featured Trick Daddy and T.I. and "Everything's a Go," featuring Jay Z. Other guests on the album include Nate Dogg, M.O.P., Beanie Sigel, and Freeway.

DECEMBER 23

Juvenile releases his sixth album *Juve the Great* on Cash Money.

Reaching #28 on the *Billboard* 200, the platinum set was produced by Mannie Fresh, Sha Money XL, Ad Future, Slice T, and Griz with Cash Money heads and brothers Bryan "Baby" Williams and Ronald "Slim" Williams acting as executive producers.

The album spawned the chart-topping single "Slow Motion," featuring Soulja Slim, who was tragically shot to death a month before the album's release.

2004

JANUARY 27

Usher releases the single "Yeah!" on Arista.

The lead single from Usher's album *Confessions*, "Yeah!" was the most popular song of 2004, spending a total of twelve weeks at #1 on the *Billboard* Hot 100, more than any other single.

The smash hit prominently featured Lil Jon, who produced the track, and Ludacris, incorporating elements of R&B, crunk, and southern rap. It won the Grammy for best rap/sung collaboration.

FEBRUARY 10

J-Kwon releases the single "Tipsy" on Arista.

Produced by the St. Louis production duo Trackboyz "Tipsy" became St. Louis rapper J-Kwon's biggest career hit, peaking at #2 on the *Billboard* Hot 100 and topping the Rap chart.

A remix to the song, titled "Still Tipsy," was released featuring Chingy and Murphy Lee.

FEBRUARY 10

Kanye West releases his debut album *The College Dropout* on Roc-A-Fella.

Produced entirely by West, a house producer/beatmaker at Roc-A-Fella, the multi-platinum, smash hit won the Grammy Award for best rap album, one of ten he was nominated for that year.

Debuting at #2 on the *Billboard* 200, the critically acclaimed, self-reflective set produced no less than five smash hits: "Through the Wire," a surprise hit about a 2002 automobile accident that left West hospitalized with his jaw wired shut; "All Falls Down," featuring Syleena Johnson, a commentary on materialism; the chart-topping "Slow Jamz," featuring Jamie Foxx and Twista; the gold-selling, Grammy-winning "Jesus Walks"; and "The New Workout Plan." Other guests on *College Dropout* included Jay Z, Mos Def, Talib Kweli, the Boys Choir of Harlem, Ludacris, J. Ivy, GLC, and Consequence.

CHUCK D:

What can be said about Mr. Ye that ain't been said? He has almost become his own religion. His groundbreaking production work exponentially carried the past into the future. His rhyme styles evolved to impress me as time went on, as well as his freedom seeking for the arts. One time, walking the crowd early in his career, we bypassed in a large hall. He was shook to see me out there, even as I was surprised—but we kept it moving. I actually like Kanye when he rants and self-raves. The entertainment biz has room for a few to do that. Why not the man who boldly suggested GW Bush don't dig black folk?

MARCH 9

Twista releases the single "Overnight Celebrity" on Atlantic.

Produced by Kanye West, the second single off Twista's *Kamikaze* provided the Chicago rapper with his second-ever top ten *Billboard* Hot 100 hit and his second consecutive #1 Rap single.

The song's official remix featured Cam'ron and Bumpy Johnson, and another unofficial remix that featured Cam'ron, 50 Cent, and DJ Clue? was also released.

MARCH 16

Cassidy releases his debut album *Split Personality* on Full Surface.

Debuting at #2 on the *Billboard* 200 and topping the R&B chart, the gold-selling album from the promising rapper was broken up into three parts, his pop side, his underground side, and third focusing on his early roots.

Singles included the Swizz Beatz–produced hits "Gets No Better," featuring Mashonda and "Hotel," featuring R. Kelly, which reached #4 on the *Billboard* Hot 100.

Featuring production by Neo da Matrix, Nottz, Rockwilder, among others, the commercially successful album featured guests that included Snoop Dogg, Jazze Pha, Jadakiss, Styles P of the L.O.X., and Trina.

I
FEEL
LIKE

MARCH 23

Madvillain releases his debut *Madvillainy* on Stones Throw.

The duo of rapper MF Doom and producer Madlib recorded their debut on a sparse $13,000 budget. A modest seller that peaked at #179 on the *Billboard* 200, the self-produced, eclectic set was widely acclaimed, making many critics' "best of" lists.

The talented duo are reported to have worked on a follow-up to the album for many years, but *Madvillainy* remains the duo's sole proper studio release outside of a collection of remixes of the original album.

MARCH 23

Murs and 9th Wonder release their first collaboration album *Murs 3:16: The 9th Edition* on Definitive Jux.

The first of five collaborations together, the album's title was a reference to Murs's birthday in March and 9th Wonder, who produced the set. This is the second solo album for the Little Brother member, who released his acclaimed debut *The End of the Beginning* in 2003.

Peaking at #87 on the R&B/Hip-Hop chart, the thoughtful gangsta album contained the singles "Bad Man" and "H-U-S-T-L-E," whose remix featured E-40, Chingo Bling, and WWE wrestling superstar John Cena. Former Little Brother member Phonte would guest on the track "The Animal."

APRIL 15

Lloyd Banks releases the single "On Fire" on Interscope.

After releasing his debut album as a member of G Unit the previous year, "On Fire" was the Queens rapper's breakthrough solo hit, reaching #8 of the *Billboard* Hot 100.

Produced by Eminem and Kwamé, the gold-selling lead single to 50 Cent's protégé's debut album *The Hunger for More*, contained 50's uncredited vocals in the song's chorus.

APRIL 20

Ghostface releases his fourth studio album *The Pretty Toney Album* on Def Jam.

The only release from Ghostface (no "Killah"), the critically acclaimed set featured some high-profile guests, including Jadakiss, Musiq Soulchild, and Missy Elliott, who appeared on the club-friendly "Tush." Reaching #6 on the *Billboard* 200 and #4 on the R&B/Hip-Hop chart, the album featured production from Ghostface as well as RZA, No I.D., Digga, and K-Def, among others.

APRIL 27

Jay Z releases the single "99 Problems" on Roc-A-Fella.

Produced by the legendary Rick Rubin, best known for his work with Run-D.M.C. and LL Cool J, this was his first hip-hop production since leaving Def Jam. Among the several samples he used for the Grammy-winning track was Billy Squier's "The Big Beat," a hip-hop breakbeat staple. The song's hook was from the 1993 Ice-T track of the same name featuring Brother Marquis of the 2 Live Crew.

MAY 11

8Ball & MG release their sixth album *Living Legends* on Bad Boy South.

The move to Bad Boy helped this southern duo's album top the R&B/Hip-Hop chart and peak at #3 on the *Billboard* 200. Featuring a slew of producers, including Bangladesh, Lil Jon, and Cool & Dre, the gold-selling set included a number of hits such as the club classic "You Don't Want Drama," featuring Diddy (#30 on the R&B chart) and "Look at the Grillz," featuring T.I. and Twista.

JUNE 8

Terror Squad release the single "Lean Back" on Universal.

From Terror Squad's Big Pun-less second album *True Story*, the club hit from the Bronx collective featured vocals from Fat Joe and Remy Ma. Topping both the *Billboard* Hot 100 and R&B/Hip-Hop chart for weeks, the hypnotic classic was produced by Scott Storch. The following year, an official remix featuring Lil Jon, Eminem, and Ma$e was released.

JUNE 15

The Beastie Boys release their sixth studio album *To the 5 Boroughs* on Capitol.

Debuting at the top of the *Billboard* 200, the platinum-selling hip-hop album from the New York trio is their first release in six years. Self-produced, the streamlined set contained a number of now-classic album cuts, including the Grammy-nominated "Ch-Check It Out" and their love note to their hometown "An Open Letter to NYC."

JUNE 29

Lil Wayne releases his fourth studio album *Tha Carter* on Cash Money.

Produced primarily by Mannie Fresh, the multi-platinum album is the first in the Tha Carter series and featured appearances from Cash Money label mates Birdman and longtime collaborator Reel.

Peaking at #5 on the *Billboard* 200, the southern rapper's set spawned three singles, including the *Billboard* Hot 100 hit "Go D.J.," which at #14 was the rapper's highest-charting pop single of his career at that point.

JULY 13

The Roots release the album *The Tipping Point* on Geffen.

Questlove produced the album with contributions from former member Scott Storch. The versatile and diverse set shows the Roots experimenting more with time signatures, sounds, and subject matter.

Debuting at #4 on the *Billboard* 200, the well-reviewed album spawned the hit single "Don't Say Nuthin'" and featured guest appearances by Devin the Dude, Jean Grae, Mack Dub, Martin Luther, Wadud Ahmad, Latif, Dom, Aaron Livingston, and longtime collaborator Dice Raw.

Titled after the Malcolm Gladwell book of the same name, the album's cover is a photograph of a young Malcolm X, then known as Malcolm Little, with a stylish hat tipped to the side in reference to the album's title. Limited editions of the album featured the group's Black Thought in the exact same pose.

CHUCK D:

Questlove and Black Thought are the Kenny Gamble and Leon Huff of hip-hop—Philly millennium style. Their roots (big pun intended) are woven beyond the '80s, into the '40s and '50s even. They have straddled a few worlds and have simply claimed MFSB, Booker T., and the Band all in one shot. Their consistency is recognized as they make history overnight on *The Tonight Show.* They are married deeply to the genre and their work is unparalleled. Amazing and so necessary. Questlove's interviews are a performance in itself.

AUGUST 3

Masta Ace releases his third studio album *A Long Hot Summer* on M3 Macmil Music.

The concept album from the veteran MC follows the story of an underground rapper through the course of his summer. The critically acclaimed set by the former Juice Crew member cracked the R&B/Hip-Hop chart. One highlight is the 9th Wonder–produced "Good Ol' Love," which featured background vocals by Mr. Lee G & Leschea.

SEPTEMBER 13

Nelly releases two albums simultaneously, *Suit* and *Sweat,* on Universal.

Nelly decided to release two separate albums, each with a different theme. *Suit,* which he described as the more grown-up and romantic, topped the *Billboard*

QUESTLOVE

200 and R&B/Hip-Hop and Rap charts. The Grammy-nominated multi-platinum set featured work from a slew of producers, including the Neptunes, Jazze Pha, and Bridges. Singles include "My Place," featuring Jaheim, which reached #4 on both the *Billboard* Hot 100 and R&B/Hip-Hop chart and the country-tinged "Over and Over" with Tim McGraw that reached #3 on the *Billboard* Hot 100.

The second is the up-tempo party *Sweat*, which debuted at #2 on the *Billboard* 200, making Nelly the first artist to have both the first and second spot on the chart. Hits from this disc include the gold-selling "Tilt Ya Head Back" with Christina Aguilera.

OCTOBER 3

VH1 hosts its first Hip Hop Honors at the Hammerstein Ballroom in New York.

The network's first-ever annual Hip Hop Honors, hosted by MC Lyte and Vivica A. Fox, paid tribute to a wide range of hip-hop luminaries that included Tupac, Run-D.M.C., DJ Hollywood, DJ Kool Herc, KRS-One, Public Enemy, the Rock Steady Crew, the Sugarhill Gang, and, as the show called it, "the graffiti movement."

With presenters including P. Diddy, Ice-T, Foxy Brown, Debbie Harry, and Wyclef Jean, the show featured performances from Fat Joe and the Terror Squad, Common, the Beastie Boys, Public Enemy, Nas, the Sugarhill Gang, Doug E. Fresh, Grandmaster Flash, and MC Hammer.

OCTOBER 5

De La Soul release their seventh album *The Grind Date* on AOI.

Featuring production by group member Posdnuos, Jake One, Madlib, Supa Dave West, 9th Wonder, and J Dilla, the underrated and creative set spawned the singles "Shoomp," featuring Sean Paul and "Much More," featuring Yummy Bingham as a double A-side. Other guests on *The Grind Date* included DJ Premier, Ghostface Killah, Common, MF Doom, Carl Thomas, and director Spike Lee.

OCTOBER 27

Ja Rule releases the single "New York," on The Inc.

Featuring Fat Joe and Jadakiss, the hit single from Ja Rule's album *R.U.L.E. was produced by Cool & Dre. Ja Rule's verse* is a diss on rapper 50 Cent.

Peaking at #27 on the *Billboard* Hot 100, the song's chorus was an interpolation of the classic album cut "100 Guns" by Boogie Down Productions from their 1990 album *Edutainment.*

NOVEMBER 5

Jay Z releases his concert film *Fade to Black* on Paramount Classics.

Chronicling Jay Z's supposed final concert at Madison Square Garden on November 25, 2003, before his short-lived retirement, the concert film featured appearances from a who's who in hip-hop, including Mary J. Blige, Memphis Bleek, P. Diddy, R. Kelly, Beyoncé, R. Kelly, Timbaland, Common, Pharrell Williams, Usher, Kanye West, Q-Tip, and Ghostface Killah.

The concert film's set list featured hits from throughout Jay Z's career, including "Big Pimpin'," "Song Cry," "What More Can I Say," "Hard Knock Life (Ghetto Anthem)," and "Can't Knock the Hustle."

NOVEMBER 12

Eminem releases his fifth studio album *Encore* on Interscope.

Topping the *Billboard* 200 and R&B/Hip-Hop chart, the multi-platinum album expands upon several recurring themes in his music, including Eminem's relationship with his ex-wife and daughter. Production was split between Eminem and Dr. Dre, with contributions by Mike Elizondo, Luis Resto, and Mark Batson.

Featuring appearances from 50 Cent, Nate Dogg, D12, Obie Trice, and Dr. Dre, the introspective, plainspoken album spawned five singles: "Just Lose It," which reached #6 on the *Billboard* Hot100, the Grammy-nominated "Encore," the gold-selling "Like Toy Soldiers," "Mockingbird," which reached #11 on the *Billboard* Hot 100, and "Ass Like That."

NOVEMBER 13

Ol' Dirty Bastard dies at the age of thirty-five.

The founding member of Wu-Tang Clan died suddenly in a recording studio in Manhattan. An autopsy later confirmed that the rapper died from a heart attack induced by a drug overdose. At the time of his death, the rapper was working on what would become his posthumously released solo album *Osirus*.

NOVEMBER 16

Lil Jon & the East Side Boyz release *Crunk Juice* on BME.

Lil Jon was the main producer on this final studio album with the Eastside Boyz, which was packed with crunk party tunes. The multi-platinum set yielded one top five crossover hit on the *Billboard* Hot 100 with "Lovers & Friends," which featured Usher and Ludacris. The B-side "Real Nigga Roll Call," featuring Ice Cube, is thought to be a world record holder for the most curse words in one song.

Other artists to appear on this star-packed album included Lil Scrappy, Nate Dogg, Snoop Dogg, R. Kelly, Jadakiss, Nas, T.I., and Pharrell, with skits by Chris Rock.

The album was also released with a bonus disc that featured remixes with artists like Pitbull, Vivica A. Fox, Fat Joe, Trick Daddy, Daddy Yankee, and Eminem.

NOVEMBER 16

Snoop Dogg releases *R&G (Rhythm & Gangsta): The Masterpiece* on Geffen.

Snoop Dogg's seventh album continued his mid-career renaissance, debuting at #6 on the *Billboard* 200. The Neptunes-produced lead single "Drop It Like It's Hot," which featured Pharrell, would earn Snoop his first-ever #1 on the *Billboard* Hot 100, as well as two Grammy nominations. Other singles included the gold-selling "Signs," which featured Charlie Wilson and Justin Timberlake, and "Let's Get Blown," which reached #12 on the Rap chart.

With a range of producers, including Lil Jon, the Alchemist, and Mr. Porter, the platinum album featured guest appearances by Bootsy Collins, 50 Cent, Lil Jon, and Nelly.

NOVEMBER 30

T.I. releases his third studio album *Urban Legend* on Atlantic.

Peaking at #7 on the *Billboard* 200, *Urban Legend* began T.I.'s streak of seven straight #1 R&B/Hip-Hop albums.

The platinum-selling album spawned T.I.'s first-ever top ten *Billboard* Hot 100 with the lead single, the Swizz Beatz–produced "Bring Em Out," as well as the hits "U Don't Know Me," which reached #4 on the Rap chart and the gold-selling "ASAP."

Urban Legend featured production from DJ Toomp, the Neptunes, Lil Jon, Jazze Pha, and Scott Storch, among others and a host of guest artists that included Lil' Kim, Mannie Fresh, Lil Wayne, Nelly, B.G., and Pharrell.

CHUCK D:

T.I. is an incredible MC who can rhyme about any subject brought his way. The great thing about *Urban Legend* is that T.I.'s flow, wordplay, and understanding how to use his voice over each produced track is on full display.

DECEMBER 7

Cam'ron releases his fourth studio album *Purple Haze* on Def Jam.

Debuting at #20 on the *Billboard* 200, Cam'ron's last album with Def Jam featured production from Kanye West, the Heatmakerz, the Legendary Traxster, and Pop & Versatile. Juelz Santana and Jim Jones all appear on the gold-selling set, with Kanye West guesting along with Syleena Johnson on the single "Down and Out," which reached #20 on the Rap chart.

T.I.

DECEMBER 7

Ludacris releases his fourth studio album *The Red Light District* on Disturbing tha Peace.

Debuting at #1 on top of the *Billboard* 200, Rap, and R&B/Hip-Hop charts, the multi-platinum album produced the smash hit singles "Pimpin' All Over the World," featuring Bobby Valentino (#2 on the Rap chart), "Get Back" (#13 on the *Billboard* 100), and "Number One Spot," which sampled Quincy Jones's classic "Soul Bossa Nova." Jones also appeared in the song's Austin Powers–themed video.

Filled with humor and wit, the smash set included guest appearances from Nate Dogg, DMX, DJ Quik, Kimmi J, Small World, Dolla Boy, Nas, Doug E. Fresh, Trick Daddy, Sleepy Brown, and Sum 41 and production by DJ Green Lantern, DJ Toomp, Organized Noize, LT Moe, Salaam Remi, and Timbaland.

DECEMBER 14

Xzibit releases his fifth album *Weapons of Mass Destruction* on Columbia.

Debuting at #43 on the *Billboard* 200, the gold-selling album from MTV's popular *Pimp My Ride* host spawned the Timbaland-produced hit "Hey Now (Mean Muggin)," which featured Keri Hilson and cracked the *Billboard* Hot 100.

With production by Hi-Tek, Rick Rock, Danja, DJ Khalil, Mr. Porter, Thayod Ausar, Battlecat, and longtime Ice Cube collaborator Sir Jinx, the album showcased guest appearances by Truth Hurts, Busta Rhymes, Krondon, Mitchy Slick, Tone, Strong Arm Steady, Suga Free, and Butch Cassidy.

2005

JANUARY 3

Island/Def Jam purchases the independent Roc-A-Fella Records.

Damon Dash, Kareem "Biggs" Burke, and Jay Z sold Roc-A-Fella to Def Jam, which announced Jay Z would be named president of the label.

JANUARY 18

The Game releases his debut studio album *The Documentary* on G Unit/Aftermath.

Discovered by Dr. Dre, The Game joined 50 Cent's G Unit musical clique. Dre did some production work on the multi-platinum selling set, which also featured production by Kanye West, Scott Storch, Just Blaze, Timbaland, Mike Elizondo, Buckwild, Cool & Dre, and several others including Eminem, who appeared on the track "We Ain't."

Debuting at #1 on the *Billboard* 200 as well as the R&B/Hip-Hop and Rap charts, the well-produced set contains the smash hit singles "Put You on the Game," "Dreams," "Higher," "Hate It or Love It," "Westside Story," and the gold-selling "How We Do," three of which featured 50 Cent.

CHUCK D:

As with Eminem doing inner homework on 50 Cent—50 thus did his homework on The Game. Of course bringing one's aura into the orbit of other ones can create friction and clash. The Game comes from a thin line school of reality and fantasy that can go either way. Game is a student and a good songwriter, as well as somebody who can present themselves as a star even without the smash records. Sometimes a smash act wins over an audience—The Game brings a backdrop of history with him and is quick to remind all.

Other guests on *The Documentary* included Busta Rhymes, Faith Evans, Mary J. Blige, Marsha Ambrosius, Dion, fellow G Unit member Tony Yayo, and Nate Dogg.

FEBRUARY 22

Cormega releases his fourth album *The Testament* on his own Legal Hustle Records.

The Testament was originally to be released as the Queens MC's Def Jam debut album in 1998 but was eventually shelved, only to be released seven years later on his own imprint.

Featuring guest appearances by Mobb Deep, Hussein Fatal, Niko, and Tiffany, the thoughtful gangsta set featured production from Sha Money XL, Nashiem Myrick, and Cormega as well and produced the cult hit "One Love."

MARCH 3

50 Cent releases his album *The Massacre* on Shady/Aftermath.

The highly anticipated follow-up to 50's big breakthrough *Get Rich or Die Tryin'* did not disappoint. Debuting at #1 on the *Billboard* 200, the multi-platinum set produced no less than four smash hits, the chart-topping, Grammy-nominated "Candy Shop," the Grammy-nominated gold-selling "Disco Inferno," which reached #3 on the *Billboard* 200, the platinum-selling "Just A Lil' Bit," and "Outta Control (Remix)," which featured Mobb Deep and reached #6 on the *Billboard* Hot 100.

Produced by Dr. Dre, Scott Storch, Sha Money XL, Hi-Tek, Buckwild, and Mike Elizondo, among others, the album contained The G Unit remix of the monster hit "Hate It or Love It" from The Game's debut album *The Documentary.* The remix featured Lloyd Banks, Tony Yayo, and Young Buck. Other guests on the Grammy-nominated album included Eminem, Olivia, and Jamie Foxx.

2005

THE GAME

GUCCI MANE

APRIL 13

Gucci Mane releases the single "Icy" on Tommy Boy.

The debut single from the Atlanta rapper served as the lead single from his first studio album *Trap House*. Produced by noted Atlanta producer Zaytoven, the song featured Young Jeezy and Boo. Reaching #46 on the R&B/Hip-Hop chart and #23 on the Rap chart, the spare single led to a feud with Young Jeezy over rights.

APRIL 19

Mike Jones releases the album *Who Is Mike Jones?* on Jive.

Peaking at #3 on the *Billboard* 200 and topping the R&B/Hip-Hop and Rap charts, the debut studio album from the likable Houston rapper spawned two singles: "Still Tippin'," featuring Paul Wall, which hit #14 on the Rap charts and "Back Then," which hit #22 on the *Billboard* Hot 100.

Produced by Michael Watts and Salih Williams, the platinum-selling set also featured appearances from Bun B, and Slim Thug.

MAY 9

Gorillaz releases the single "Feel Good Inc." on Virgin.

The hit single from the virtual British band led by Damon Albarn featured De La Soul, with their highest ever appearance on the *Billboard* Hot 100 of #14. "Feel Good Inc." became an international hit throughout Europe and Australia and was nominated for two Grammys, including record of the year, winning best pop collaboration.

MAY 24

Common releases his sixth album *Be* on GOOD.

Produced primarily by Kanye West, who is also featured on the album and released it under his imprint, the critically acclaimed gold-selling set debuted at #2 on the *Billboard* 200.

The focused set kicked off with the Grammy-nominated lead single "The Corner," a gritty track that featured spoken word lyrics by the Last Poets, and followed with "Go!," which featured Kanye and John Mayer and reached #21 on the Rap chart, and the Grammy-nominated "Testify." The album was also nominated for a Grammy for best rap album.

JUNE 28

Ying Yang Twins releases their fourth studio album *United State of Atlanta* on TVT.

Debuted at #2 on the *Billboard* 200, the platinum-selling album featured guest appearances from Adam Levine, Anthony Hamilton, Pitbull, Busta Rhymes, and Missy Elliott. Executive produced by Mr. Collipark and Bryan Leach, the party album yielded two top forty *Billboard* Hot 100 hits in the snap song "Wait (The Whisper Song)," which reached #15 and "Badd," which was #6 on the Rap chart.

JULY 12

Bow Wow releases his fourth studio album *Wanted* on Columbia.

Featuring production from Bow Wow's longtime producer Jermaine Dupri, as well as No I.D., Bryan-Michael Cox, and LRoc, the album yielded three top forty singles on the *Billboard* Hot 100, including "Let Me Hold You" and "Like You," both of which cracked the top five. Debuting at #3 on the *Billboard* 200 and topping the Rap chart, the platinum-selling album from the now-adult Bow Wow featured appearances by Ciara, Snoop Dogg, Omarion, J-Kwon, and Jermaine Dupri.

JULY 12

Grand Hustle Records releases the soundtrack to the Paramount film *Hustle & Flow*.

The film, starring Terrence Howard and Ludacris, was directed by Craig Brewer and produced by John Singleton.

Reaching #30 on the *Billboard* 200, the soundtrack was a who's who in Dirty South hip-hop with 8Ball & MJG, Juvenile, Trina, T.I., and Lil Scrappy. E-40 represented for the West Coast.

The soundtrack's centerpiece, however, is the hit song "It's Hard Out Here for a Pimp" by Three 6 Mafia, which won an Academy Award for best original song.

CHUCK D:

I've spent a lot of time in Memphis and *overstood* the film. The mid-South is the birthplace of Black USA music period. It only made sense that rap and hip-hop would be a natural there, as well as downriver in New Orleans. I, along with Daddy-O from Stetsasonic, were always about rap regions getting their due. Eight Ball, MJG and Three 6 Mafia were obvious choices. Few heads know that when Three 6 Mafia won the Academy Award for best original song, it was thirty-three years after Memphis legend Isaac Hayes won his in 1972 for *Shaft*.

JULY 26

Young Jeezy releases his third album *Let's Get It: Thug Motivation 101* on CTE/Def Jam.

Jeezy's first album for a major label, the platinum-selling set included the hit songs "Go Crazy," featuring Jay Z, which reached #22 on the R&B/Hip-Hop and Rap charts; "Soul Survivor," featuring Akon, which reached #4 on the *Billboard* 100; "And Then What," which reached #13 on the Rap chart; and "My Hood," which reached #19 on the Rap chart.

With producers that included Akon, Don Cannon, Shawty Redd, Mannie Fresh, and Jazze Pha, the acclaimed southern MC's album debuted at #2 on the *Billboard* 200 and featured guests such as Mannie Fresh, Trick Daddy, Young Buck, and Bun B.

AUGUST 30

Kanye West releases his second studio album *Late Registration* on Def Jam.

With more in-depth, richly arranged production than his debut album *The College Dropout*—in part due to West's collaboration with producer Jon Brion—the album reached #1 on the *Billboard* 200, thus beginning West's six-albums-and-counting streak of consecutive #1 hits.

Featuring guest appearances from Brandy, The Game, Common, Adam Levine, Jay Z, Nas, and Jamie Foxx, the multi-platinum album spawned five singles: the Grammy-winning "Diamonds from Sierra Leone," the chart-topping, platinum-selling "Gold Digger," the gold-selling "Heard 'Em Say," "Touch the Sky," featuring the debut performance of Lupe Fiasco, and "Drive Slow," featuring Paul Wall and GLC. With "Gold Digger," West earned his first #1 on the *Billboard* Hot 100, where it spent nine weeks.

For the critically acclaimed set, West earned eight Grammy nominations, including a nomination for album of the year and record of the year, and won three, best rap solo performance, best rap song, and best rap album.

SEPTEMBER 2

Kanye West utters his infamous "George Bush doesn't care about black people" during A Concert for Hurricane Relief.

During the NBC's simulcast of the hour-long televised benefit concert to raise funds for the victims of Hurricane Katrina, West made his controversial remark while hosting with actor Mike Myers. Said in response to the reported slow response by the Federal Emergency Management Agency and other government response resources to largely African-American areas that were hit by the hurricane, the comment caught Myers off guard, as well as actor-comedian Chris Tucker, to whom producers would order cameras panned to after West's comments.

SEPTEMBER 6

AZ releases his fifth album *A.W.O.L.* on Quiet Money.

The skillful Brooklyn MC released this street set on his own label, which spawned the single "The Come Up," produced by DJ Premier.

Other producers on *A.W.O.L.* included Heatmakerz, Emile, Buckwild, Vinny Idol, DJ Absolut, Frade, Moss, Tone Manson, Fizzy Womack, Baby Paul, J-Hen, and Jimi Kendrix. Reaching #10 on the Rap chart, the lyrically complex tracks included guest appearances by Ghostface Killah and Raekwon of the Wu-Tang Clan, CL Smooth, Half A Mill, and Begetz as well as reggae great Bounty Killer.

SEPTEMBER 13

Paul Wall releases his second studio album *The Peoples Champ* on Atlantic.

Debuting at #1 on the *Billboard* 200, the platinum-selling album from the Houston rapper spawned four singles: "Drive Slow," with Kanye West and GLC; the Texas-loving "They Don't Know," featuring Mike Jones; the gold-selling "Sittin' Sidewayz," featuring Big Pokey; and "Girl," which reached #35 on the *Billboard* Hot 100. Other guests on the album featured appearances from T.I., Three 6 Mafia, Trey Songz, and Bun B.

OCTOBER 27

Jay Z and Nas squash their longstanding beef at a concert in New Jersey.

Performing as part of Power 105.1's Powerhouse concert at the Continental Airlines Arena in New Jersey, Jay Z and Nas ended their beef by performing together during Jay Z's headlining set. Jay Z invited Nas out to perform "Dead Presidents" before the two stood together for several minutes on stage. Nas performed a short fifteen-minute set after the duo's collaboration. The concert ended with an ensemble performance of "Encore" by Jay Z, Nas, Kanye West, and P. Diddy.

During his performance, Jay Z told the crowd that he was motivated to make up with Nas by P. Diddy's recent reuniting with the L.O.X. The following year, Nas signed with Def Jam, Jay Z's longtime label.

NOVEMBER 1

Public Enemy release their ninth studio album *New Whirl Odor* on Slam Jamz Records.

New Whirl Odor featured production by longtime Public Enemy contributor Johnny "Juice" Rosado, PE's X Minista Professor Griff, C-Doc (the Warhammer), Abnormal, and Moby who collaborated with the group on the antiwar single "MKLVFKWR," which also appeared on *Unity: The Official Athens 2004 Olympic Games Album.*

New Whirl Odor contains the fan favorites "Bring That Beat Back," "Superman's Black in the Building," and "66.6 Strikes Again," which was a sort of continuation of a track from the group's magnum opus *Fear of a Black Planet* called "Incident at 66.6FM."

NOVEMBER 8

D4L release debut album *Down for Life* on Atlantic.

The debut album from the Atlanta-based rap group is the only studio album the group ever released. *Down for Life* became a touchstone album for the crunk subgenre of southern rap known as snap, a sound oriented around a dance beat and light, tinny percussion.

The lead single "Laffy Taffy," became a #1 hit on the *Billboard* Hot 100, with the follow-up "Betcha Can't Do It Like Me," cracking the top thirty on the R&B/Hip-Hop and Rap charts. At the time of its release, "Laffy Taffy" set the record of 175,000 downloads for most digital purchases of a single track in one week since songs began being sold online.

NOVEMBER 9

Paramount Pictures semiautobiographical film of 50 Cent's life, *Get Rich or Die Tryin'*, opens in US theaters.

The film, which was 50 Cent's acting debut, costarred Terrence Howard and Bill Duke and was directed by Jim Sheridan. Debuting at #2 on the *Billboard* 200, the platinum-selling soundtrack featured G Unit artists including Lloyd Banks, Mobb Deep, and Young Buck.

DECEMBER 6

Lil Wayne releases his fifth studio album *Tha Carter II* on Young Money.

Debuting at #2 on the *Billboard* 200 and topping the R&B/Hip-Hop and Rap charts, the platinum album by the popular Big Easy rapper was a favorite of fans and critics alike. Lyrically dexterous, it spawned the Doe Boyz–produced hit "Fireman," which reached #10 on the Rap chart, "Hustler Musik," which reached #16 on the Rap chart, and "Shooter," featuring Robin Thicke. Executive produced by Birdman and Ronald "Slim" Williams, *Tha Carter II* included guest appearances from Kurupt of Tha Dogg Pound, Birdman, Curren$y, and Nikki.

CHUCK D:

Here is an artist who takes swagger and the grip his music has on its demographic and runs it all the way to the bank. Having started so young in the game, who knows what time will offer from his future repertoire?

2006

JANUARY 4

Queen Latifah becomes the first hip-hop artist to be given a star on the Hollywood Walk of Fame.

The legendary New Jersey native has released seven albums, appeared in over thirty films and television shows, and has won Grammy, Golden Globe, Screen Actors Guild, and NAACP Image awards, as well as being nominated for an Academy and Emmy award.

JANUARY 6

The Beastie Boys release their fan-filmed concert movie *Awesome; I Fuckin' Shot That*.

The group handed out fifty cameras to audience members at their Madison Square Garden concert on October 9, 2004, who in turn shot the performance from their very own angle, view, and perspective. The crowd-sourced movie featured cameos from Doug E. Fresh and D.M.C.

JANUARY 12

Chamillionaire releases the single "Ridin'" on Universal.

Featuring Krayzie Bone, the single off of Chamillionaire's debut album *The Sound of Revenge* was the biggest hit of his career. It spent three weeks at #1 on the *Billboard* Hot 100 in June 2006.

Produced by Play-N-Skillz, "Ridin'" earned two Grammy nominations for the Texas rapper, including best rap song and best rap performance by a duo or group, which he won.

A number of official remixes to the song featuring artists such as Papoose, Akon, UGK, and The Game, were eventually released.

JANUARY 17

Dem Franchize Boyz release the single "Lean Wit It, Rock Wit It" on EMI.

A major crossover hit, the southern snap song for the Atlanta group reached #7 on the *Billboard* Hot 100 and topped the Rap chart. Produced by Maurice "Parlae" Gleaton, "Lean Wit It, Rock Wit It" would be the only top ten single that the Atlanta group would earn during their career.

JANUARY 24

Tha Alkaholiks release their fifth album *Firewater* on Waxploitation.

The LA-based trio of DJ and producer E-Swift, MCs Tash and J-Ro announced that they would retire as a group after the release of *Firewater* but would all continue to pursue solo careers. The party album featured the accessible "The Flute Song" and the Danger Mouse–produced "Chaos."

FEBRUARY 7

J Dilla releases the instrumental album *Donuts* on Stones Throw Records.

The legendary producer and MC from Detroit was diagnosed with a rare blood disease and the album took its name from the rare donut treat that Dilla allowed himself in the last stages of his life.

He worked on the classic instrumental set while in the hospital and at home while on dialysis. The unique ambient and versatile sound on *Donuts* propelled it to legendary status among true hip-hop heads. Many MCs including Ghostface Killah, Skyzoo, Big Sean, Talib Kweli, and Drake have used instrumentals off the set.

J Dilla would pass away from the disease three days after its release.

MARCH 7

Public Enemy release *Rebirth of a Nation* on Paris's Guerrilla Funk.

Written and produced by legendary Bay Area MC, Paris gets a special feature credit alongside Public Enemy on the album cover. The album, whose title is a play on the 1915 white supremacist film *The Birth of a Nation*, also featured PE's Professor Griff, MC Ren (formerly of N.W.A), former PE member Sister Souljah, dead prez, Kam, Immortal Technique, and the Conscious Daughters. Among some of the songs were

2006

"Hell No We Ain't Alright," "Plastic Nation," "Watch the Door," "They Call Me Flava," "Hard Rhymin'," and "Can't Hold Us Back."

MARCH 28

T.I. releases his fourth studio album *King* on Atlantic.

Debuting at #1 on the *Billboard* 200 and certified platinum within a month, the album was released to coincide with T.I.'s feature film debut in *ATL*. The critically acclaimed set spawned four singles: DJ Toomp–produced "What You Know," T.I.'s first top five hit on the *Billboard* Hot 100, "Why You Wanna," "Live in the Sky," and "Top Back."

Pharrell, Common, Young Buck, B.G., Young Jeezy, UGK, and Jamie Foxx all appear on the album. The Grammy-nominated album included production efforts from Mannie Fresh, Swizz Beatz, the Neptunes, Just Blaze, and Travis Barker.

GHOSTFACE KILLAH

MARCH 28

Ghostface Killah releases his fifth solo album *Fishscale* on Def Jam.

Named after uncut cocaine, Ghostface Killah's critically acclaimed album has a strong recurring theme of organized crime and the drug trade. Featuring stellar production from Just Blaze, MF Doom, J Dilla, and Pete Rock, among others, the riveting street-story album spawned two singles "Back Like That" featuring Ne-Yo, which reached #14 on the R&B/Hip-Hop chart, and "Be Easy," which cracked the R&B/Hip-Hop chart as well.

Debuting at #4 on the *Billboard* 200 and reaching #2 on the Rap chart, the tremendous album featured all remaining members of the Wu-Tang Clan.

APRIL 24

Kanye West releases the live album *Late Orchestration* on Mercury.

Recorded at the famed Abbey Road Studios in London the previous year, before an audience of three hundred specially invited guests, West was backed by an all-female seventeen-piece string orchestra performing all the songs from his sophomore album *Late Registration*, released in 2005. John Legend and Lupe Fiasco were featured guests during the performance.

MAY 16

Cam'ron releases his fifth studio album *Killa Season* on Diplomat.

Serving as executive producer, Cam'ron's eclectic set debuted at #2 on the *Billboard* 200 and reached the top of the R&B/Hip-Hop and Rap charts. The release coincided with a self-directed movie of the same name that went straight to DVD. With producers that included the Heatmakerz and the Alchemist, the

New York rapper's set included Jay Z diss track "You Gotta Love It" and "Touch It or Not" with Lil Wayne. Other guests on the album include Juelz Santana, Mo Money, Hell Rell, 40 Cal, J.R. Writer, and Jim Jones.

MAY 22

Lil Wayne releases the *Dedication 2* mixtape on 101 Distribution.

The second collaboration between Lil Wayne and DJ Drama, who produced the rapper's *The Dedication* mixtape the previous year, the critically acclaimed mixtape featured appearances from T.I., Juelz Santana, Remy Ma, Curren$y, and Pharrell. While only distributed digitally, the twenty-four-cut set reached #69 on the R&B/Hip-Hop chart.

JUNE 13

Busta Rhymes releases his seventh album *The Big Bang* on Flipmode in collaboration with Aftermath.

Busta's first album to debut at #1 on the *Billboard* 200, it spawned the hit singles "Touch It," which reached #16 on the *Billboard* Hot 100, "Don't Get Carried Away," featuring Nas, "New York Shit," featuring Swizz Beatz, "In the Ghetto," featuring Rick James, and "I Love My Chick," featuring Kelis and will.i.am.

With production by DJ Green Lantern, Swizz Beatz, Erick Sermon, DJ Scratch, Mr. Porter, Timbaland, J Dilla, and Dr. Dre, the gold-selling set featured guests including Missy Elliott, Stevie Wonder, Marsha Ambrosius, and Raekwon of the Wu-Tang Clan.

JUNE 13

Yung Joc releases the single "It's Goin' Down" on Atlantic.

"It's Goin' Down," the lead single off the Atlantic rapper's debut album *New Joc City*, was nominated for a Grammy for best rap song in 2007.

Produced by Nitti, the song peaked at #3 on the *Billboard* Hot 100, and the song was the highest-charting single of Yung Joc's career.

JULY 4

Young Dro releases the single "Shoulder Lean" on Grand Hustle.

Featuring T.I. on the hook, "Shoulder Lean" served as the debut single on the Atlanta rapper's debut album *Best Thang Smokin'*. The multi-platinum song would serve as the only charting top ten hit on the *Billboard* Hot 100 of Young Dro's career.

JULY 11

Pimp C releases his sophomore album *Pimpalation* on Rap-A-Lot.

The critically acclaimed set from the Texan MC garnered gold sales and cemented Pimp C as a star of the South in the Dirty, Dirty.

Featuring production by Jazze Pha, Mr. Lee, Beatmaster Clay D., among others, *Pimpalation* reached #3 on the *Billboard* 200 and top of the R&B/Hip-Hop chart. The club-heavy set contained the hit singles, "Pourin' Up," "I'm Free" (which featured a sample from Tom Petty's "Free Fallin'"), and "Knockin' Doorz Down."

JULY 25

Pharrell Williams releases his debut solo album *In My Mind* on his own Star Trak label.

One half of the Neptunes production team and N.E.R.D. member self-produced "In My Mind." Debuting at #3 on the *Billboard* 200, the album spawned the hit singles "Can I Have It Like That?" (featuring Gwen Stefani), "Angel," "Number One" (featuring Kanye West), and "That Girl," which featured Snoop Dogg and Charlie Wilson of the legendary Gap Band.

Other guests on the Grammy-nominated set included Jay Z, Lauren London, Nelly, Pusha T, Slim Thug, and Jamie Cullum. A remake of the album entitled *Out of My Mind*, would be a collaboration effort with Williams, Questlove, and James Poyser.

CHUCK D:

Virginia has always been a great rap state to get a total survey on the nation of its North its South its East and they shake their heads to the Midwest and West and Pharrell exemplifies somebody who has paid attention. The Neptunes, which is also Pharrell and his partner Chad Hugo, have paid attention to Virginia's greats before them like Timbaland and have created sounds that rappers and singers alike can enjoy. There is no reason to even guess why the Neptunes have been the tracks for the stars. They've done their homework and it comes out into the work that rocks all the homes.

AUGUST 1

DMX releases his sixth album *Year of the Dog... Again* on Ruff Ryders.

Featuring production by Swizz Beatz, Teflon, Sean Garett, Eddie Timmons, Dame Grease, Shok, and Elite, the consistent album spawned the Scott Storch–produced "Lord Give Me a Sign" and "We in Here," which reached #8 on the Rap chart.

Debuting at #2 on the *Billboard* 200 and #1 on the Rap chart, *Year of The Dog...Again* also featured guest appearances by Busta Rhymes, Kashmir, Bazaar Royale, Styles P, Jadakiss of the L.O.X., Big Stan, Janyce, and Jinx.

AUGUST 8

Rick Ross releases his debut album *Port of Miami* on Slip-n-Slide.

Debuting at #1 on the *Billboard* 200 and the R&B/Hip-Hop chart, the platinum-selling album is an ode to Ross's history in the drug trade in Miami. With stellar work by a slew of producers, including Akon, Cool & Dre, the Runners, DJ Khaled, and Jazze Pha, *Port of Miami* spawned two street anthems "Hustlin'," which reached #54 on the *Billboard* Hot 100 and "Push It," which reached #9 on the Rap chart.

AUGUST 22

Outkast release the soundtrack to their movie *Idlewild* on LaFace.

Produced mainly by Organized Noize and André 3000, the platinum-selling soundtrack to the Outkast movie reached #2 on the *Billboard* 200 and topped the R&B/Hip-Hop and Rap charts. As the movie is set in the Prohibition era, the soundtrack is colored by the swing and blues of the time, such as "Mighty 'O'" which featured a sample of Cab Calloway's "Minnie the Moocher" and reached #77 on the *Billboard* Hot 100 and "Call the Law" featuring Janelle Monáe. Other highlights are "Morris Brown," featuring Sleepy Brown and Scar and the Morris Brown College Marching Wolverines, which cracked the *Billboard* Hot 100.

SEPTEMBER 19

Lupe Fiasco releases his debut album *Food & Liquor* on Atlantic.

The debut set from the Chicago rapper was both critically acclaimed and commercially successful, reaching #8 on the *Billboard* 200 and topping the Rap chart. The smart and compelling disc included production from Kanye West, Soundtrakk, with Jay Z receiving credit as an executive producer.

Fiasco was nominated for four Grammys for the record, including best rap album, and winning one Grammy for best urban/alternative performance for his single "Daydreamin'," which featured Jill Scott. Other tracks on the album included the skateboard anthem "Kick, Push," the Neptunes-produced "I Gotcha," and the esteemed "Hurt Me Soul."

SEPTEMBER 26

Ludacris releases his fifth studio album *Release Therapy* on Def Jam.

The Grammy-winning set by the veteran MC debuted at #1 on the *Billboard* 200, his third in a row. The chart-topping lead single "Money Maker" (based on the 1961 song "Shake Your Money Maker" by Chicago bluesman Elmore James) was produced by the Neptunes and featured Pharrell. It won the Grammy Award for best rap song.

Other singles on the platinum-selling set include the Polow da Don–produced "Runaway Love," featuring Mary J. Blige and "Grew Up a Screw Up," which featured Young Jeezy.

SEPTEMBER 26

Akon releases the single "Smack That" on Universal.

Peaking at #2 on the *Billboard* Hot 100, "Smack That" was the lead single on Akon's breakthrough second album *Konvicted*. Produced and featuring Eminem, it is the most successful single of Akon's career to date, selling more than three million copies and earning a Grammy for best rap/sung collaboration.

OCTOBER 3

Sadat X releases his third solo album *Black October* on Female Fun Music.

The Brand Nubian member had a potential prison sentence hanging over his head when he wrote and recorded this self-reflective album. He worked with producers that included Da Beatminerz, Ayatollah, DJ Spinna, J-Zone, Marco Polo, DJ Pawl, the Asmatik, Spencer Doran, longtime Brand Nubian DJ Diamond D, and Greg Nice, of Nice & Smooth, who also guested on the track "My Mind." Other guests on *Black October* include Sadat's musical clique Boss Money Gangstas and fellow Brand Nubians Grand Puba and Lord Jamar.

OCTOBER 21

Jim Jones releases the single "We Fly High" on Diplomat.

Peaking at #5 on the *Billboard* Hot 100 and topping the Rap chart, the platinum-selling lead single from the New York rapper's third album, *Hustler's P.O.M.E.*, became the highest-charting single of his career.

Produced by Zukhan Bey, the official remix of the song featured T.I., Young Dro, Birdman, P. Diddy, and Juelz Santana.

Jay Z released a response to the song called "Brooklyn High," which was viewed by many as a diss track. Jones responded shortly thereafter with a remix of the song with Juelz Santana known as "We Fly High (Beef Mix)."

OCTOBER 31

Flavor Flav releases his self-titled debut solo album on his own Draytown label.

Reaching #80 on the R&B/Hip-Hop chart, the long-awaited album, almost seven years in the making, contains the single "Hot 1," released in 1999. Other titles on the fun and funky set included "Flavor Man," "Col-Leepin'," "Hotter Than Ice," "Platinum," and "The Jookz."

With producers that included Craig Valentino Williams, Andrew Williams, Clinton Sands, Tracy Pierce, and Charles Hester, the album also featured a guest appearance by Smooth B of Nice & Smooth.

NOVEMBER 21

Jay Z releases his ninth studio album *Kingdom Come* on Roc-A-Fella.

The multi-platinum *Kingdom Come*, which debuted at #1 on the *Billboard* 200, was considered Jay Z's comeback album after he claimed he was retiring from studio recordings after 2003's *The Black Album*.

The Grammy-nominated set contained the hit singles, "Hollywood," featuring Jay Z's future wife Beyoncé and "Lost One," featuring Chrisette Michele. The Just Blaze–produced "Show Me What You Got," reached #8 on the *Billboard* Hot 100 and sampled Public Enemy's "Show 'Em What You Got."

Production duties were handled by Syience, Dr. Dre, the Neptunes, DJ Khalil, Ne-Yo, Swizz Beatz, B-Money, Kanye West, and Chris Martin of Coldplay.

NOVEMBER 28

Clipse release their second studio album *Hell Hath No Fury* on Jive.

Produced, like their first album, by the Neptunes, the Virginia duo's second set included two singles: "Mr. Me Too," with Pharrell Williams, and "Wamp Wamp (What It Do)" both of which hit the R&B/Hip-Hop chart.

Reaching #14 on the *Billboard* 200, the lean and critically acclaimed album was released after the group's prolonged legal struggle with their label Jive over the group's contract and the release of their second album.

DECEMBER 5

Shady Records releases the compilation *Eminem Presents: The Re-Up*.

Debuting at #2 on the *Billboard* 200, the platinum-selling collection of various artists signed to Eminem's Shady imprint featured production by the Alchemist, Dr. Dre, Disco D, Akon, Dawaun Parker, Luis Resto, Rikinatti, Parker Focus, and Witt & Pep.

The album produced two hit singles, "You Don't Know Me," featuring Eminem, 50 Cent, Lloyd Banks, and Ca$his, which reached #12 on the Billboard 100, and "Jimmy Crack Corn," featuring Eminem, 50 Cent, and Ca$his. *The Re-Up* also featured a remix to a previous Eminem single "Shake That," featuring Nate Dogg, Obie Trice, and Bobby Creekwater and for "Smack That," featuring Akon, Stat Quo, and Bobby Creekwater.

DECEMBER 9

ESPN airs the Muhammad Ali documentary *Ali Rap*.

Joseph Maar directed this fascinating documentary that explores the legendary three-time World Heavyweight Champ's influence on rap culture. Hosted by Public Enemy's Chuck D, *Ali Rap* also featured footage and interviews with other hip-hop luminaries such as Fab Five Freddy, Doug E. Fresh, MC Lyte, Ludacris, Jermaine Dupri, and Rakim.

DECEMBER 12

Young Jeezy releases his second studio album *The Inspiration* on Def Jam.

Debuting atop the *Billboard* 200, the first #1 of Jeezy's career, the well-received set spawned the DJ Toomp–produced "I Luv it," which reached #7 on the Rap chart, "Go Getta," which featured R. Kelly and peaked at #18 on the *Billboard* Hot 100, and "Dreamin'," which featured Keyshia Cole and was produced by the Runners.

DECEMBER 19

Nas releases his eighth studio album *Hip Hop Is Dead* on Def Jam.

Debuting at #1 on the *Billboard* 200, Nas's fourth chart-topper, *Hip Hop Is Dead,* is Nas's first release on Def Jam. The platinum-selling, Grammy-nominated set spawned a number of hit singles, including the will.i.am-produced "Can't Forget About You," which featured Chrisette Michele on vocals, and the controversial title track, which featured will.i.am. Both singles reached the forties on the *Billboard* Hot 100.

Other guests on the critically acclaimed album include The Game, Snoop Dogg, Jay Z, and Kanye West, who also produced along with Scott Storch, Dr. Dre, L.E.S., and Chris Webber, among others.

DECEMBER 25

James Brown dies of congestive heart failure in Atlanta, Georgia.

James Brown, whose career began in the late 1950s and continued until his death, influenced performers in soul, gospel, rock, blues, jazz, pop, and especially hip-hop. He died on Christmas Day at the age of seventy-three.

Driven through the streets of Harlem in a white horse-drawn carriage, his body then lay in state on December 28 at the Apollo Theater in Harlem in a white Promethean casket.

His public funeral took place at the James Brown Arena in his hometown of Augusta, Georgia. His protégé Reverend Al Sharpton presided over the service, which was attended by thousands of fans and family members. Brown's band the Soul Generals performed, as did MC Hammer. Michael Jackson told the sold-out crowd that James Brown was the reason he became a performer.

2007

JANUARY 23

Mims releases the single "This Is Why I'm Hot" on Capitol.

Mims's debut single became a breakthrough hit, reaching #1 on the *Billboard* Hot 100 and the Rap chart, the high point of his career to date. Produced by Blackout Movement, the catchy, platinum-selling song served as the lead single off the New York rapper's full-length debut *Music Is My Savior.*

JANUARY 30

X Clan release their third album, *Return from Mecca,* on Suburban Noize.

After the death of two of their founding members and a long hiatus, the socially conscious group returned with a powerful album, which produced the single "Weapon X" and featured guest appearances from KRS-One, Chali 2na from Jurassic 5, Kottonmouth Kings, RBX, Abstract Rude, Jacoby Shaddix of Papa Roach, Damian Marley, Tech N9ne, Tri State, Daddy X, YZ, Hannah Barbera, Jah Orah, and Christian Scott.

FEBRUARY 4

Timbaland releases his second studio album *Shock Value* on Mosley.

Timbaland's platinum-selling set, mainly self-produced, featured an impressive roster of artists including Nelly Furtado, Justin Timberlake, Dr. Dre, Missy Elliott, and 50 Cent.

Reaching #5 on the *Billboard* 200, *Shock Value* featured three top five–charting singles on the *Billboard* Hot 100: the chart-topping, Grammy-nominated "Give It to Me," featuring Nelly Furtado and Justin Timberlake, "The Way I Are," featuring Keri Hilson and D.O.E., and "Apologize," featuring OneRepublic.

MARCH 12

Grandmaster Flash & the Furious Five are inducted into the Rock & Roll Hall of Fame.

With their induction, the pioneering New York hip-hop group became the first hip-hop act to be inducted into the Rock & Roll Hall of Fame. Inducted alongside Patti Smith, the Ronettes, R.E.M., and Van Halen, Jay Z introduced the group during the awards ceremony in New York, where they performed a medley of hits that included "White Lines" and "The Message."

CHUCK D:

A timely and long overdue situation where the foundations of a genre get appreciated while the artists are—not just still with us—but in their own way still very relevant to rap music's movement. They stayed true to the game and this showed as they remain as iconic pioneers throughout the industry.

MARCH 13

Rich Boy releases his self-titled debut album on Interscope.

The debut set from the Alabama MC propelled to #3 on the *Billboard* 200 off the success for his platinum-selling lead single "Throw Some D's," which was produced with and featured Polow da Don. Some other producers on the set included Lil Jon, Needlz, Mr. DJ, Donnie Scantz, Willy Will, and Rich Boy himself.

A remix of "Throw Some D's" is also on the album and featured Nelly, André 3000 of Outkast, Jim Jones, Murphy Lee, and The Game.

MARCH 27

Young Buck releases his second studio album *Buck the World* on Interscope.

Featuring a slew of all-star guests and producers, including Dr. Dre, 50 Cent, Snoop Dogg, Lil Jon, Young Jeezy, and Bun B, the hard-hitting set from the G Unit rapper hit #3 on the *Billboard* 200. Singles from the well-reviewed album include the Jazze Pha–produced "I Know You Want Me," "Get Buck," and "U Ain't Goin Nowhere," featuring LaToiya Williams, all of which made the R&B/Hip-Hop chart.

MAY 2

Soulja Boy releases his debut single, "Crank That (Soulja Boy)," on Interscope.

Topping the *Billboard* Hot 100 for seven weeks, the Grammy-nominated hit was the first song to sell three million digital copies. "Crank That," which launched a Soulja Boy dance craze, was from the Mississippi rapper's debut album *souljajboytellem.com.*

MAY 8

Bone Thugs-N-Harmony release their seventh album *Strength & Loyalty* on Interscope.

Debuting at #2 on the *Billboard* 200, the first album in five years by the Cleveland group was executively produced by Swizz Beatz and also featured production by DJ Toomp, Jermaine Dupri, will.i.am, Mally Mall, Pretty Boy, Ty Fyffe, Street Radio, DJ Scratch, Neo da Matrix, and LRoc.

Featured guests on the gold-selling set included gospel singer Yolanda Adams, Felicia, The Game, Autumn Rowe, and Fleetwood Mac, who were credited as featured guests for the usage of a sample of the track "The Chain" from their 1977 multi-platinum classic album *Rumours* as well as Mariah Carey and Bow Wow, who joined the group on the album single "Lil' Love." Akon produced and appeared on the lead, platinum-selling single "I Tried," which reached #6 on the *Billboard* Hot 100.

MAY 11

Shop Boyz release their debut single "Party Like a Rockstar" on Universal.

The Atlanta hip-hop group's lead single off their first album *Rockstar Mentality* uses the riff from Ozzy Osborne's 1980 song "Crazy Train." Reaching #2 on the *Billboard* Hot 100 and topping the Rap chart, the song was nominated for a Grammy for best rap performance by a duo or group and was the biggest selling ringtone of 2007. An official remix to the song was released that featured Lil Wayne, Chamillionaire, and Jim Jones.

MAY 28

Hurricane Chris releases his debut single "A Bay Bay," on J Records.

"A Bay Bay," produced by Phunk Dawg, was from the Shreveport, Louisiana, rapper's debut album *51/50 Rachet* released the same year. Reaching #7 on the *Billboard* Hot 100 and #3 on the Rap chart, a remix was later released featuring Birdman, Lil Boosie, The Game, E-40, Jadakiss, and Angie Locc.

JUNE 5

T-Pain releases his second studio album *Epiphany* on his Nappy Boy label.

The second self-produced set from the Florida rapper is the first release on his new label. Debuting at #1 on the *Billboard* 200, the gold-selling set featured the hit singles "Buy U a Drank (Shawty Snappin')" which featured Yung Joc and topped both the *Billboard* Hot 100 and R&B/Hip-Hop chart, and the platinum-selling "Bartender," which featured Akon.

JUNE 5

Belly releases his debut album *The Revolution* on CP.

The Juno and Much Music Award–winning set garnered Canadian gold sales and established Belly as a Canadian hip-hop star.

Featuring production by Beat Merchant, Daheala, Whosane, Barcardy, Goggs, *The Revolution* would contain the singles "I'm the Man," featuring Kurupt, "Don't Be Shy," featuring Nina Sky as well as the big hits "Ridin'," featuring Mario Winans and "Pressure," featuring Ginuwine. Other guests on the album included Scarface, Massari, Fabolous, Dru, and Monique.

JUNE 12

Plies releases his debut single "Shawty" on Atlantic.

"Shawty," featuring T-Pain, is the lead single on the Florida rapper's debut album *The Real Testament.*

A Top Ten crossover hit, reaching #9 on the Billboard Hot 100, the song sampled "Fantasy" by Earth, Wind & Fire.

JUNE 12

Fabolous releases his fourth album *From Nothin' to Somethin'* on Desert Storm.

The gold-selling release went to #2 on the *Billboard* 200, spawning the hit singles "Baby Don't Go," which featured T-Pain and reached #4 on the Rap chart; the Timbaland-produced "Make Me Better," which featured Ne-Yo and topped the Rap chart for fourteen weeks; and "Diamonds," which featured Young Jeezy.

With a slew of all-star producers, including Just Blaze, Neo da Matrix, Jermaine Dupri, the album also showcased a number of guests including Akon, Lil' Mo, Lloyd, Junior Reid, Swizz Beatz, Rihanna, Pusha T, Red Café, Jay Z, Uncle Murda, Paul Cain, Joe Budden, Freck Billionaire, and Ransom.

JUNE 19

Huey releases his debut album *Notebook Paper* on Jive.

The St. Louis MC's debut, which featured production by Jazze Pha, Mannie Fresh, and the Bakery Productions, among others, also spawned the smash hits, "When I Hustle," featuring Lloyd, "Tell Me Why (G-5)," featuring MeMpHiTz and the dance craze chart topper "Pop, Lock & Drop It," which reached #6 on the *Billboard* Hot 100 and #2 on the Rap chart.

Notebook Paper also featured the "Pop, Lock & Drop It" remix with Bow Wow and T-Pain.

JULY 3

T.I. releases his fifth studio album, *T.I. vs T.I.P.* on Atlantic.

The Grammy-nominated, platinum-selling set debuted at the top of the *Billboard* 200, as well as the R&B/Hip-Hop and Rap charts. The concept of the album is the difference between the artist's gangster and business personality. Singles on the set included the gold-selling, Grammy-nominated "Big Poppin' (Do It)," the Wyclef Jean–produced "You Know What It Is," and "Hurt," which featured Busta Rhymes. T.I. worked with a number of producers, including Just Blaze, Mannie Fresh, Lil' C, the Runners, and Eminem, who also guested on "Touchdown." Other guests on the album included Nelly and Jay Z.

JULY 24

Camp Lo release their third album *Black Hollywood* on Good Hands.

The Bronx duo's first two albums were named after the early 1970s Sidney Poitier–Bill Cosby comedy classics *Uptown Saturday Night* and its sequel *Let's Do It Again*, respectively. *Black Hollywood* was originally going to be called *A Piece of the Action*, the third film in the Poitier-Cosby trilogy. Produced by longtime Camp Lo collaborator Ski Beatz, who also appeared on the track "82 Afros" with Jungle Brown appearing on "Suga Willie's Revenge."

JULY 24

Freekey Zekey releases his debut album *Book of Ezekiel* on Diplomat.

The longtime Diplomats member's debut contains the singles "Daddy Back," featuring fellow Diplomats Cam'ron and Juelz Santana, "Hater What You Looking At" and "Like This," featuring Sen.

Peaking at #23 on the R&B/Hip-Hop chart, the well-received album included guest appearances by Lil Wayne, Jha Jha, Ash, Tobb, and Diplomats' Jim Jones, Hell Rell, and J.R. Writer.

JULY 28

The Rock the Bells Tour pulls into New York City.

The hip-hop star-studded tour began in 2004 in California, as a mainly West Coast hip-hop festival. In 2007, it held its first NYC edition on Randall's Island.

On the main stage, fans were treated to performances by Wu-Tang Clan, Cypress Hill, the Roots, Nas, EPMD, Jedi Mind Tricks, the Coup, Pharoahe Monch,

MF Doom, Mos Def, Talib Kweli, Blackalicious, Hieroglyphics, Immortal Technique, Rage Against the Machine, and Public Enemy.

Performing on the other stage were Brother Ali, Lucky I Am, Felt (Slug and Murs), Living Legends, Blueprint, Sage Francis, Hangar 18, Cage, Grouch & Eligh, and Mr. Lif.

After the Saturday show sold out quickly at the box office, a second show was added for the next day on July 29, featuring a similar lineup minus the Roots and the Coup, who were replaced by UGK and the Boot Camp Clik.

CHUCK D:

Rock the Bells was a full experience. Public Enemy was one of the first acts to really take on massive music festivals worldwide as they reemerged in the 1990s, mainly in Europe. Rock the Bells had the idea of taking a twenty-plus genre and giving it the proper space—fan and performer wise. The big cities were met with great enthusiasm, as expected. The smaller cities and venue had expectations before its time.

AUGUST 7

UGK release their fifth studio album *Underground Kingz* on Jive.

Debuting at #1 on the *Billboard* 200 and the R&B/Hip-Hop chart, the duo's fifth and final studio album was released several months before the group's founding member Pimp C died of a drug overdose in December.

Featuring appearances from Charlie Wilson, Too $hort, Rick Ross, Talib Kweli, Big Daddy Kane, and Dizzee Rascal, the critically acclaimed album's second single, "International Players Anthem (I Choose You)," featured Outkast, and reached #10 on the Rap chart and #12 R&B/Hip-Hop chart, the highest of their career, as well as earning a Grammy for best rap performance by a duo or group.

UGK

AUGUST 28

Yung Joc releases his second studio album *Hustlenomics* on Bad Boy South.

Executive produced by Diddy, the strong set by the Southern rapper reached #3 on the *Billboard* 200 and topped both the R&B and Rap charts. Sales were aided by the catchy single "Coffee Shop" and cracked the *Billboard* Hot 100 chart, and "Bottle Poppin'," both of which featured Gorilla Zoe. Other guests on the set included The Game, Jim Jones, Young Dro, Snoop Dogg, Rick Ross, and Bun B.

SEPTEMBER 11

50 Cent releases his third studio album *Curtis* on Shady/Aftermath.

Debuting at #2 on the *Billboard* 200, *Curtis* was titled after the artist's given name. Featuring production by Dr. Dre, Jake One, Eminem, Timbaland, Ty Fyffe, Danja, Don Cannon, among others, the hard-hitting set featured the singles, "Ayo Technology," which featured Justin Timberlake and reached #10 on the Rap chart; the gold-selling "I Get Money," which reached #20 on the *Billboard* Hot 100; and "I'll Still Kill," which featured Akon and cracked the *Billboard* Hot 100.

Other guests on *Curtis* included Mary J. Blige, Robin Thicke, Eminem, Dr. Dre, Nicole Scherzinger of the Pussycat Dolls as well as Tony Yayo and Young Buck of 50's G Unit.

SEPTEMBER 11

Kanye West releases his third album *Graduation* on Roc-A-Fella.

Continuing West's education theme of his two previous efforts, *The College Dropout* and *Late Registration*, the Grammy Award–winning *Graduation* although hip-hop at its core, merged snippets of electronica, rock, lounge music, prog rock, reggae, dub, pop and synth pop. Debuting at #1 on the *Billboard* 200, the multi-platinum set won West a Grammy for best album, his third.

Beloved by both critics and fans alike, the innovative set spawned the Grammy-winning, multi-platinum single "Good Life," featuring T-Pain, "Flashing Lights," featuring Dwele, "Homecoming," featuring Chris Martin of Coldplay, the platinum-selling "Can't Tell Me Nothing," and the chart-topping "Stronger."

West self-produced the tracks along with Mike Dean, DJ Toomp, Nottz, Warryn Campbell, among others and featured guests that included Mos Def, DJ Premier, Lil Wayne, Jay Z, Ne-Yo, John Legend, and Connie Mitchell of Sneaky Sound System.

West's album dropped on the same day 50 Cent's *Curtis*, sparking a wager on which would sell more, which West won.

SEPTEMBER 18

Chamillionaire releases his second studio album *Ultimate Victory* on Universal.

Debuting at #8 on the *Billboard* 200, the second set from Houston's mixtape king is unique in that it doesn't contain any profanity.

Featuring a variety of producers including Kane Beatz, J.R. Rotem, the Runners, Happy Perez, the Beat Bullies, the lyrically dexterous set included the single "Hip Hop Police" which featured the legendary Slick Rick as a guest and samples his rap classic "Children's Story."

OCTOBER 9

Flo Rida releases his debut single "Low" on Atlantic.

The multi-platinum lead single off the Florida rapper's debut album, *Mail on Sunday*, spent ten weeks atop the *Billboard* Hot 100 and set the record at the time for digital downloads.

NOVEMBER 6

Jay Z releases his tenth studio album *American Gangster* on Roc-A-Fella.

A concept album inspired by the Universal Pictures biopic of drug kingpin Frank Lucas of the same name, *American Gangster* is not the soundtrack. (The film's actual soundtrack featured period pieces by John Lee Hooker, the Staple Singers, Bobby Womack, Sam & Dave, Public Enemy, and a score by Hank Shocklee of the Bomb Squad.) Featuring production by Jermaine Dupri, Diddy and the Hitmen, the Neptunes, DJ Toomp, Just Blaze, No I.D., Bigg, among others, Jay Z's platinum-selling album debuted at #1 on the *Billboard* 200 and topped the R&B/Hip-Hop and Rap charts as well.

The critically acclaimed album spawned the hit singles, "Roc Boys (And the Winner Is...)," which reached #8 on the Rap chart, as well as "I Know" and "Blue Magic," both featuring Pharrell Williams. Other guests on the set included Lil Wayne, Beanie Sigel, Bilal, and Nas.

DECEMBER 18

Lupe Fiasco releases his second studio album *The Cool* on Atlantic.

Released during the rapper's critical height, the album peaked at #14 on the *Billboard* 200 and topped the Rap chart. The gold-selling lead single, "Superstar," which featured Matthew Santos, became the rapper's first-ever top ten on the *Billboard* Hot 100. Other guest appearances included Snoop Dogg and Gemini.

Executive produced by Lupe and Charles "Chilly" Patton, the gold-selling set earned four Grammy nominations in 2008, including for best rap album.

2008

FEBRUARY 11

M.I.A. releases the single "Paper Planes" on Interscope.

"Paper Planes" served as M.I.A.'s breakthrough pop single, peaking at #4 on the *Billboard* Hot 100. Produced by Diplo and Switch, the song, which sampled the Clash's 1982 song "Straight to Hell," was an international hit, reaching the top forty in more than a half-dozen countries.

Nominated for record of the year at the 2009 Grammys, the song off her second studio album *Kala* is certified multi-platinum. M.I.A. later released a series of remixes to the song, one of which featured Bun B and Rich Boy.

FEBRUARY 19

KRS-One releases his tenth solo album *Adventures in Emceein* on Echo-Vista.

The album from the legendary rapper featured appearances by Rakim, MC Lyte, Chuck D of Public Enemy, Non-Stop, S-Five, and Just Blaze. The well-received set contained the hit single "The Real Hip-Hop," featuring Nas, which reached #19 on the Rap chart.

MARCH 11

Rick Ross releases his sophomore album *Trilla* on Slip-n-Slide.

Debuting at #1 on the Billboard 200, the gold-selling album from the Miami rapper spawned the J.R. Rotem–produced, platinum-selling "The Boss," which featured T-Pain and reached #17 on the *Billboard* Hot 100; "Speedin'," which featured R. Kelly and was produced by the Runners; and "Here I Am," which featured Nelly and Avery Storm and reached #5 on the Rap chart.

Other guests on *Trilla* included Jay Z, Flo Rida, Lil Wayne, Young Jeezy, Trick Daddy, Trey Songz, Mannie Fresh, Triple C's Brisco, Rodney, and J Rock.

APRIL 4

Jay Z and Beyoncé Knowles marry in a private ceremony in New York City.

The secretive wedding between the superstar duo was attended by a few of Jay Z and Beyoncé's close family members and friends. Guests included Kanye West; Diddy; Chris Martin; Beyoncé's sister, singer Solange; and her former Destiny's Child cohorts, Michelle Williams and Kelly Rowland.

APRIL 29

The Roots release their eighth studio album *Rising Down* on Def Jam.

The politically and socially conscious album's title was inspired by the 2004 William T. Vollman seven-volume literary work, *Rising Up and Rising Down: Some Thoughts On Violence, Freedom, and Urgent Means*. Self-produced with Tahir Jamal, James Poyser, Richard Nichols, and Khari Mateen, the critically acclaimed album, darker than its predecessors, debuted at #6 on the *Billboard* 200 and atop the Rap chart.

The variety of guests on *Rising Down* included Mos Def, DJ Jazzy Jeff, Wadud Ahmad, Chrisette Michele, Talib Kweli, Mercedes Martinez, Kelli Scarr, Shane Clark, Patrick Stump of Fall Out Boy, Wale, P.O.R.N., Saigon, Kevin Hanson, Peedi Peedi, Styles P of the L.O.X., and longtime collaborators Malik B, Truck North, and Dice Raw.

MAY 23

Slick Rick is pardoned by New York governor David Paterson.

The British rapper received a full pardon from the governor after serving six years in prison for an attempted murder conviction in 1991. Paterson cited Slick Rick's flawless disciplinary record during his incarceration and his ten years of parole following his 1997 release.

Governor David Paterson's pardon greatly reduced the risk that the rapper, who was born in England, would be deported by the United States government as a convicted felon.

LIL WAYNE

JUNE 10

Lil Wayne releases his sixth album *Tha Carter III* on Cash Money.

Tha Carter III, which won a Grammy Award for rap album of the year, produced no less than six monster hits, "Mrs. Officer," featuring Bobby V, which reached #3 on the Rap chart; the multi-platinum "Lollipop," featuring Static Major, which topped the *Billboard* Hot 100 for five weeks; the Grammy-nominated "Mrs. Carter," featuring Jay Z; the Grammy-nominated, multi-platinum "Got Money," featuring T-Pain; "You Ain't Got Nuthin'," featuring Juelz Santana; and the Grammy-winning "A Milli," which topped the R&B/Hip-Hop and Rap charts.

Debuting at #1 on the *Billboard* 200 and topping the R&B/Hip-Hop and Rap charts, the multi-platinum, critically acclaimed album included guest appearances by Babyface, Brisco, Busta Rhymes, Betty Wright, D. Smith, and Robin Thicke, who also produced alongside Maestro, DJ Infamous, Drew Correa, Bangladesh, Play-N-Skillz, Kanye West, Swizz Beatz, Cool & Dre, Deezle, David Banner, Jim Jonsin, StreetRunner, the Alchemist, and Rodnae.

JUNE 24

Ice Cube releases the hit single "Do Ya Thang" on his label Lench Mob via iTunes.

"Do Ya Thang," produced by Dre Dogg of Palumbo Beats, is the second single from Ice Cube's chart-topping album *Raw Footage*, which debuted at #5 on the *Billboard* Hot 100. The video for "Do Ya Thang" was released on July 1 and has millions of views on YouTube.

JULY 15

Nas releases his ninth studio album on Def Jam.

Nas had originally wanted the album to contain the controversial title *Nigger*, but the label refused to let him use that name so it went untitled. Debuting at #1 on the *Billboard* 200, which at the time was the New York rapper's fourth #1, the gold-selling album featured production from Mark Ronson, Stargate, Jay Electronica, DJ Toomp, and Cool & Dre, among others.

The socially conscious album's lead single is "Hero," featuring Keri Hilson, which cracked the *Billboard* Hot 100. Other guests include Busta Rhymes, Chris Brown, The Game, and the Last Poets.

AUGUST 26

The Game releases his third studio album *LAX* on Geffen.

Debuting at #2 on the *Billboard* 200 and topping the R&B/Hip-Hop and Rap charts, The Game's third album included production from Kanye West, Scott Storch, DJ Quik, Cool & Dre, Irv Gotti, and Trackmasters.

The album's most successful single was "My Life," which featured Lil Wayne and reached #21 on the *Billboard* Hot 100 and #4 on the Rap chart. Ludacris, Ice Cube, Bilal, Raekwon, Ne-Yo, Common, Keyshia Cole, and Nas also appeared as featured artists on the album.

SEPTEMBER 2

Young Jeezy releases his third album *The Recession* on Def Jam.

Debuting at #1 on the *Billboard* 200, the gold-selling album from the Atlanta rapper featured stellar production by Don Cannon, Drumma Boy, and Kanye West, among others.

The Grammy-nominated, multi-platinum lead single "Put It On" featuring Kanye West and produced by Drumma Boy reached #1 on the Rap chart and peaked at #12 on the *Billboard* 200. The album's biggest surprise, however, was Young Jeezy's collaboration with one time rival Nas on the smash hit, "My President," about Barack Obama, which reached #13 on the Rap chart.

SEPTEMBER 29

T.I. releases his sixth studio album *Paper Trail* on Atlantic.

With this multi-platinum release, T.I. earned his third straight #1 album on the *Billboard* 200. T.I. wrote and recorded the bulk of the album while under house arrest as he awaited trial for federal gun charges.

Earning T.I. four Grammy nominations in 2009, the album spawned eight singles, including two that were #1 on the *Billboard* Hot 100: "Whatever You Like" and "Live Your Life," which featured Rihanna and "Dead and Gone," which featured Justin Timberlake and was nominated for two Grammy awards. Other guests on the album included B.o.B., Ludacris, Usher, Jay Z, Kanye West, Lil Wayne, and John Legend. Drumma Boy, Kanye West, DJ Toomp, Just Blaze, Swizz Beatz, and Jim Jonsin all contributed production.

NOVEMBER 4

Q-Tip releases his second studio album *The Renaissance* on Universal.

Q-Tip's second set since the disbanding of A Tribe Called Quest featured an impressive array of guests, including Norah Jones, D'Angelo, and Raphael Saadiq. The album samples '70s R&B from groups like the Jackson 5 and Black Ivory.

2008

Q-TIP

Debuting at #11 on the *Billboard* 200, Q-Tip's first studio album in nine years was nominated for a Grammy for best rap album.

NOVEMBER 24

Kanye West releases his fourth studio album *808s & Heartbreak* on Def Jam.

With its minimalist electronic production and heavy reliance on vocal processing, Kanye West's fourth set represented a stark departure from his previous work. The album's title is a reference to the Roland TR-808 drum machine, which featured prominently in the album's stark sound.

West's third straight #1 album on the *Billboard* 200, *808s & Heartbreak* spawned four singles: "Love Lockdown" and "Heartless" (both of which reached the top five on the *Billboard* Hot 100), as well as "Amazing" and "Paranoid." "Love Lockdown" sold over 200,000 digital downloads in the first four days of its release, propelling the hit single to #3 on the *Billboard* Hot 100 chart. Kid Cudi, Young Jeezy, Lil Wayne, and Mr Hudson all appear on the album.

The album would eventually be considered one of the most influential pop-rap albums of the decade for its musical adventurousness and emotional vulnerability.

NOVEMBER 27

Soulja Boy Tellem releases the single "Kiss Me Thru the Phone" on Interscope.

Peaking at #3 on the *Billboard* Hot 100 and topping the Rap chart, the second single from *iSouljaBoyTellem* featured the R&B singer Sammie and was produced by Jim Jonsin.

"Kiss Me Thru the Phone" sold close to six million digital copies in 2009, making it the eighth bestselling digital single of the year.

DECEMBER 9

Common releases his eighth album, *Universal Mind Control*, on Geffen Records.

The Grammy-nominated, "electronic"-inspired set contained the singles "Announcement" and the title track, both featuring Pharrell. Reaching #12 on the *Billboard* 200 and topping the Rap chart, the innovative disc included appearances by Kanye West, Cee-Lo Green, Martina Topley-Bird, Chester French, Muhsinah, and Omoye Assata Lynn and featured production by the Neptunes and Outkast's Mr. DJ.

DECEMBER 24

Ludacris releases his sixth studio album *Theater of the Mind* on Disturbing tha Peace.

Reaching #5 on the *Billboard* 200 and topping the Rap chart, the gold-selling album has an all-star production cast, including DJ Premier, DJ Toomp, Clinton Sparks & Kamau Georges, 9th Wonder, the Runners, Darkchild, Don Cannon, Sean Garrett, Scott Storch, Swizz Beatz, StreetRunner, Wyldfyer, and Trackmasters.

Theater of the Mind contained the hit singles "Last of a Dying Breed," featuring Lil Wayne; "Nasty Girl," featuring Plies; "One More Drink," featuring T-Pain, which reached #24 on the *Billboard* Hot 100; and "What Them Girls Like" featuring Chris Brown and Sean Garrett, which reached #6 on the Rap chart.

Other guests on the theatrical set included Rick Ross, The Game, Willy Northpole, Playaz Circle, Ving Rhames, Chris Rock, Jamie Foxx, Jay Z, Nas, Common, and Spike Lee.

2009

JANUARY 16

The Fox Searchlight Films release *Notorious,* a biopic about the late Notorious B.I.G., opened in US theaters.

Notorious was directed by George Tillman Jr. and starred Jamal Woolard as the late Biggie Smalls and Angela Bassett as his mother Voletta. The soundtrack, which reached the top of the R&B and Rap charts, featured a number of songs from Biggie, as well as two new songs, "Brooklyn Go Hard," by Jay Z and "Letter to B.I.G," by Jadakiss and Faith Evans.

JANUARY 18

Obama's inaugural celebration concert takes place at the National Mall in Washington, DC.

Performers at the We Are One concert included Beyoncé, will.i.am, Usher, and Mary J. Blige. Queen Latifah also appeared at the concert and gave a reading during the show.

At the show, Usher performed "Higher Ground" with Stevie Wonder and will.i.am performed Bob Marley's "One Love" with Herbie Hancock and Sheryl Crow.

FEBRUARY 24

K'naan releases his sophomore studio album *Troubadour* on A&M.

Reaching #32 on the *Billboard* 200 and #12 on the Rap chart, the Toronto MC's album spawned the hit singles "I Come Prepared," featuring Damian Marley, "ABC's," featuring Chubb Rock, and "If Rap Gets Jealous," featuring Kirk Hammett of Metallica. Other guests on the Somali-Canadian rapper's second set included Mos Def, Charli 2Na of Jurassic 5, and Adam Levine of Maroon 5.

The single "Wavin' Flag," which cracked the *Billboard* Hot 100, was chosen by Coca-Cola as the official 2010 theme for the FIFA World Cup of Soccer in South Africa and was rerecorded as a fund-raiser for earthquake relief in Haiti.

MARCH 31

The Black Eyed Peas release the single "Boom Boom Pow" on Interscope.

The multi-platinum rap single, off the group's multi-platinum, Grammy-winning *The E.N.D,* was *Billboard*'s #1 song of the year, topping the Rap chart as well. Influenced by "Planet Rock," the propulsive song has been remixed a number of times, including a Boys Noize version that featured 50 Cent, a Megamix version that featured Gucci Mane, and additional ones that featured Flo Rida and Busta Rhymes. The Black Eyed Peas performed the song during their 2011 Super Bowl half time show, the first hip-hop group to headline.

APRIL 4

Run-D.M.C. Is Inducted into the Rock & Roll Hall of Fame.

Inducted by Eminem, Run-D.M.C. became the second-ever hip-hop act to be inducted into the Rock & Roll Hall of Fame. Joseph Simmons and Darryl McDaniels, the surviving members of Run-D.M.C., accepted the award at the ceremony. Simmons and McDaniels, who swore to never perform again after Jam Master Jay died in 2002, declined to perform at the ceremony.

APRIL 7

Jadakiss releases his third solo album *The Last Kiss* on D-Block.

Debuting at #3 on *Billboard* 200 and topping the R&B/Hip-Hop chart, the popular set spawned the hit singles "What If," featuring Nas; "By My Side," which featured Ne-Yo and reached #16 on the Rap chart; "Can't Stop Me," featuring Ayanna Irish; "Who's Real," featuring Swizz Beatz and OJ da Juiceman; "Death Wish," featuring Lil Wayne; and "Letter to B.I.G.," featuring Faith Evans, which also appeared in the Biggie Smalls biopic *Notorious*.

Other guest appearances included Young Jeezy, Mary J. Blige, Jadakiss's former L.O.X. cohorts Sheek Louch and Styles P, as well as Raekwon and Ghostface Killah of the Wu-Tang Clan. Producers included Swizz Beatz, the Neptunes, Baby Grand, and the Alchemist, among others.

APRIL 21

Rick Ross releases his third album *Deeper Than Rap* on Maybach.

The third set from the Miami MC featured production by DJ Toomp, Drumma Boy, Bink!, J.U.S.T.I.C.E. League, the Inkredibles, Tricky Stewart, Bigg D, and the Runners.

Debuting at #1 on the *Billboard* 200 chart, the smash set contained the hits "All I Really Want," featuring The-Dream; "Mafia Music"; "Magnificent," which featured John Legend and reached #5 on the Rap chart; and "Maybach Music 2," which featured T-Pain, Kanye West, and Lil Wayne and cracked the *Billboard* Hot 100. Other guests on *Deeper Than Rap* included Ne-Yo, Gunplay, Magazeen, Foxy Brown, Avery Storm, Robin Thicke, Nas, and Kevin Cossom.

CHUCK D:

I heard all these things about Rick Ross aka Rick Rose. At first I wondering what was up, because I didn't see the story of the real Rick Ross and I wondered what did this rap guy have to offer this particular story. I met RR while doing a performance in Lagos, Nigeria, for MTV Base. I tried to catch up with him the whole time and couldn't. Finally, I saw him upon leaving and saw him writing lyrics on the other side of first class. I introduced myself and he knew who I was. We had the greatest of talks. He told me about his life and I listened and left knowing he let me into his world. I think he has a fantastic MC voice and style of spitting. And I think Ricky Ross will eventually teach a lot of people to look up instead of down.

MAY 5

Sadat X releases his fifth solo album *Brand New Bein'* on Loud.

The well-received set by the Brand Nubian was produced by JW and DJ JS-One of the Rock Steady Crew. Guests on the album included KRS-One, CL Smooth, Buckshot of Black Moon, Craig G, Jak-D, C-Rayz Walz, Poison Pen, Rahzel, Twan, and fellow Brand Nubians Lord Jamar and Grand Puba. Fan favorites include "Blow Up Da Spot" and "Lyrics?".

MAY 19

Eminem releases his sixth album *Relapse* on Interscope.

Eminem's first release in five years, the critically acclaimed, multi-platinum album was produced with Dr. Dre. Eminem's fourth consecutive #1 on the *Billboard* 200 was nominated for three Grammys, winning for best rap album and for best rap performance by a duo or group for the single "Crack a Bottle," which featured Dr. Dre and 50 Cent and topped the *Billboard* Hot 100.

The dark and lyrically complex set spawned a number of singles, including "We Made You," which reached #9 on the *Billboard* Hot 100; the serial killer story "3 a.m."; and the Grammy-nominated "Beautiful," which reached #17 on the *Billboard* Hot 100.

MAY 26

Snowgoons release their third album *A Fist in the Thought* on Babygrande.

German hip-hop producers Snowgoons, made up of DJ Waxwork, Illegal, and Det, worked with Lord Lhus and The Savage Brothers for their classic underground set. Other guests on the album included Reef the Lost Cauze, Planet X, King Syze of Army of the Pharaohs, and Sean Price.

JUNE 9

DJ Quik and Kurupt release their debut album *BlaQKout* on Fontana.

The Dogg Pound member and producer collaborated on this well-received set, which reached #61 on the *Billboard* 200 and #6 on the Rap chart. Highlights of the album include "Whacha Wan Do" featuring Problem and Yo-Yo, "Ohhh!," and "Do You Know."

JUNE 9

Mos Def releases his fourth solo album *The Ecstatic* on Downtown.

Featuring production by the Neptunes, Mr. Flash, Madlib, Oh No, Preservation, J Dilla, as well as Mos Def himself, the critically acclaimed set earned him a Grammy Award for best rap album of the year.

The socially conscious set included appearances by Slick Rick, Talib Kweli, and Anne Muldrow and spawned the samba-tinged hit single "Casa Bey."

The album cover for *The Ecstatic* is based on Charles Burnett's 1977 film *Killer of Sheep* and take its title from Victor LaValle's 2002 book of the same name.

JUNE 29

Young Money Entertainment announces signing Toronto actor and MC Drake to its label.

After a huge bidding war involving several labels, Drake went with the Lil Wayne imprint after the latter was introduced to the Canadian's music via Jas Prince, son of Rap-A-Lot Records founder J. Prince, with the two eventually touring together.

Drake then became part of Lil Wayne's musical clique Young Money while not yet having signed with the label, which was also home to artists such as Nicki Minaj and Tyga.

Drake, who had previously been part of the cast on the long-running Canadian teen drama *Degrassi: The Next Generation*, had already achieved chart success with three mixtapes.

SEPTEMBER 8

Jay Z releases his eleventh album *The Blueprint 3* on Roc Nation.

The chart-topping, platinum-selling third album of the Blueprint series, contained five hit singles, the Grammy-winning, multi-platinum "Empire State of Mind," featuring Alicia Keys, which topped the R&B/Hip-Hop and Rap charts; the Grammy-nominated "D.O.A. (Death of Auto-Tune)," which reached #15 on the Rap chart; "Young Forever," featuring Mr Hudson; the Grammy-nominated "On to the Next One," featuring Swizz Beatz; and the Grammy-winning "Run This Town," which featured Rihanna and Kanye West and topped the Rap chart.

Other guests on this platinum-selling set included Luke Steele, Pharrell Williams, Young Jeezy, Kid Cudi, Drake, and J. Cole.

This was Jay Z's eleventh time debuting atop the *Billboard* 200, which broke the record held by Elvis Presley. The critically acclaimed set included production from the Neptunes, No I.D., Timbaland, Jerome Harmon, Jeff Bhasker, Al Shux, Janet Sewell-Ulepic, Angela Hunte, the Inkredibles, Swizz Beatz, and Kanye West.

SEPTEMBER 8

Raekwon releases his fourth solo album *Only Built 4 Cuban Linx...Pt. II* on EMI.

The sequel to the Wu-Tang Clan members 1995 classic featured guest appearances by Beanie Sigel, Styles P, Jadakiss of the L.O.X., Lyfe Jennings, Slick Rick, Bun B, Busta Rhymes, The Game, Wu affiliates, Blue Raspberry, Matsa Killa, Cappadonna, Tash Mahogany, Popa Wu, and Stone Mecca as well as Wu-Tang Clansmen Ghostface Killah, Method Man, and Inspectah Deck.

The RZA, who produced the 1995 classic, handled production on the 2009 sequel along with Travis Barker, Scram Jones, BT, Dr. Dre, Mark Batson, Mathematics, True Master, Allah Justice, Icewater Productions, Erick Sermon, the Alchemist, Necro, Marley Marl, Pete Rock, and the J Dilla.

The chart-topping album, which reached #4 on the *Billboard* 200 and #2 on the Rap and R&B/Hip-Hop charts, contained the hit single "New Wu," featuring Ghostface Killah and Method Man.

SEPTEMBER 13

Kanye West interrupts Taylor Swift at MTV's VMAs.

Taylor Swift edged out Beyoncé for best female video for "You Belong with Me." West stormed the stage during Swift's acceptance speech, grabbing the microphone and declaring that Beyoncé deserved the award. West publicly apologized to Swift on Twitter the following year.

KID CUDI

SEPTEMBER 15

Drake releases his first EP *So Far Gone* on Universal.

The EP marked the first official label release from the Toronto rapper and was comprised of songs from Drake's *So Far Gone* mixtape, which he had released earlier in the year and featured production by Boi-1da, DJ Khalil, 40, and Needlz.

Debuting at #6 on the *Billboard* 200, the gold-selling EP spawned three top forty charting singles on the *Billboard* Hot 100: "Best I Ever Had," Drake's breakthrough hit which peaked at #2; "Successful," which featured Trey Songz and Lil Wayne; and "I'm Goin' In," which featured Lil Wayne and Young Jeezy.

CHUCK D:

I've been watching rap music out of Canada from the beginning with Michie Mee, Maestro Fresh-Wes, Kardinal Offishall, and Choclair and such. But although I felt it coming, I never felt it coming as hard as Drake brought it—and I didn't think it was going to come from a television fan base either. He is the first example since Tupac of a rapper that can do it all and be quite a chameleon at popular songs. A superstar in the mode of a Kanye West, and knows it—which is important.

SEPTEMBER 15

Kid Cudi releases his debut album *Man on the Moon: The End of Day* on Universal.

The gold-selling debut release from the Cleveland rapper is a concept album narrated by Common, with appearances by MGMT, Kanye West, Ratatat, and King Chip.

Peaking at #4 on the *Billboard* 200, *Man on the Moon: The End of Day* spawned three platinum-selling singles: the Grammy-nominated "Make Her Say," "Pursuit of Happiness," and the Grammy-nominated "Day 'n' Nite," which served as Kid Cudi's breakthrough hit and peaked at #3 on the *Billboard* Hot 100. Jon Brion, Kid Cudi, No I.D., Ratatat, Dot da Genius, and Jeff Bhasker all contributed production to the album.

OCTOBER 20

Fashawn releases his debut studio album *Boy Meets World* on One Records.

The critically acclaimed debut by the California rapper was produced by Exile. Considered an underground classic, the thoughtful set featured guest appearances by Mistah F.A.B., Evidence, and Aloe Blacc.

DECEMBER 8

Gucci Mane releases the single "Lemonade" on Warner Bros.

The third official single on Gucci Mane's stellar studio album *The State vs. Radric Davis* reached #8 on the Rap chart. The remix of the song featured Nicki Minaj, Fabolous, and Trey Songz.

The instrumental to the song, produced by Bangladesh, has been used by a variety of rappers for freestyles including Big Sean, Curren$y, Bun B, and Action Bronson.

DECEMBER 21

Lil Wayne's Young Money label releases the imprint's first compilation album, *We Are Young Money*.

The set featured appearances by new Young Money signees like Drake, Nicki Minaj, Tyga, and Jae Millz to name a few. The compilation also featured appearances by Lloyd, Gucci Mane, and Birdman. Producers on the compilation included, Tha Bizness, Cool & Dre, David Banners, and Willy Will.

Peaking at #9 on the *Billboard* 200, the gold-selling set produced the hits "Every Girl," which reached #2 on the Rap and R&B charts, "Roger That," which topped the Rap charts, and "BedRock," which peaked at #2 on the *Billboard* Hot 100 and topped the rap chart. A variety of alternate versions of "BedRock" were released, all of which feature slightly different verses and configurations of Young Money artists.

DECEMBER 22

Jay Electronica releases the song "Exhibit C" on Decon Records, via iTunes.

"Exhibit C," which was produced by Just Blaze, contained lyrics about Jay's time living homeless on the streets of New York City while pursuing his dream to land a recording contract. Hitting the R&B charts, the single led Jay to be signed to Jay Z's Roc Nation label.

2010

JANUARY 23

Jay Z, Rihanna, and Bono and the Edge of U2 release the single "Stranded (Haiti Mon Amour)" on MTV Records.

The song featured on the live album *Hope for Haiti Now*, which would come out the following week. Proceeds from the sale of the set went to the relief fund for victims of the disastrous January 12 earthquake that left 316,000 dead and some three million people severely affected.

Reaching #16 on the *Billboard* Hot 100, "Stranded (Haiti Mon Amour)" was produced by Swizz Beatz and featured a live and a studio version.

FEBRUARY 2

Lil Wayne releases his seventh album *Rebirth* on Young Money.

Rebirth is Wayne's foray into rock and punk, which wasn't universally well received. Debuting at #2 on the *Billboard* 200, *Rebirth* was originally titled *Rebirth of Auto-Tune* in response to Jay Z's recent hit song "Death of Auto-Tune" and because of Wayne's heavy usage of the vocal effect on the album.

With production by Cool & Dre, DJ Infamous, J.U.S.T.I.C.E League, among others, the gold-selling set spawned the hit single "Prom Queen," which featured Shannell and reached #15 on the *Billboard* Hot 100 and "Drop the World," which featured Eminem and reached #18 on the *Billboard* Hot 100.

FEBRUARY 9

Canibus releases his ninth album *Melatonin Magik* on War Lab.

The well-received album, heavily influenced by the hit film *The Matrix*, featured guest appearances by K-Solo, Bronze Nazareth, Copywrite, Born X Son, Willie Dynamite, Maintain, Blaq Poet, Skarlet Rose, Presto, Jaecyn Bayne, Son One, Chopp Devize, Journalist, the Goddess Psalm One, D12, DZK, Warbux, and Public Enemy's Professor Griff, who appears on almost half the tracks on *Melatonin Magik*. Fan favorite tracks include "Dead by Design," "Kriminal Kindness," and "Post Traumatic Warlab Stress," which featured DZK and Warbux.

FEBRUARY 23

Ludacris release the single "My Chick Bad" on Def Jam.

Peaking at #11 on the *Billboard* Hot 100 and #2 on the R&B/Hip-Hop and Rap charts, the Grammy-nominated single was the second from Ludacris's *Battle of the Sexes*. Featuring Nicki Minaj, who cowrote the track, the song is certified multi-platinum.

MARCH 30

Diddy-Dirty Money releases "Hello Good Morning," on Bad Boy.

Produced by Danja and Sr. Shakur, the gold-selling hit, which featured T.I., is from Diddy's fifth solo album, *Last Train to Paris*, released the same year.

Reaching #13 on the R&B chart, the song spawned several remixes featuring Rick Ross, Nicki Minaj, Tinie Tempah, Tinchy Stryder, and Skepta.

MARCH 31

Earl Sweatshirt self-releases his debut mixtape *Earl*.

The debut mixtape from the Los Angeles Odd Future member featured production from Branden BeatBoy, Left Brain, and Tyler, the Creator but was predominantly produced by Tyler, the Creator.

The critically acclaimed but lyrically violent set included appearances by Vince Staples, Hodgy Beats, as well as Odd Future members Tyler, the Creator, Syd tha Kid, and Taco Bennett.

APRIL 12

Cali Swag District digitally release the single "Teach Me How to Dougie," on Capitol.

The platinum-selling, #1 R&B/Hip-Hop hit from the Inglewood, California, group's debut album *The Kickback* references a dance craze, which originated in Dallas, Texas. The song is an ode to hip-hop legend Doug E. Fresh, that the dance tries to emulate.

APRIL 13

Nicki Minaj releases the single "Massive Attack" on Young Money.

The hit song featured R&B crooner Sean Garrett, who along with Alex da Kid also produced the track. The single was supposed to be on Minaj's upcoming debut album *Pink Friday* but did not make the final cut when the Trinidadian-American artist's first album came out seven months later. The futuristic hip-hop track, with a reggae vibe, reached #27 on the R&B/Hip-Hop chart and cracked the *Billboard* Hot 100.

APRIL 14

Wiz Khalifa releases the mixtape *Kush & Orange Juice*.

When initially offered as a free download, the critically acclaimed but relaxed set caused the mixtape title to be the #1 trending topic on Twitter that day.

APRIL 20

Cypress Hill release their eighth studio album *Rise Up* on Priority.

Five years in the making, *Rise Up* was their most political release to date as well as their first set not produced by the group's DJ Muggs. Cypress Hill frontman B-Real handled much of the album's

CYPRESS HILL

production with contributions from Pete Rock, Mike Shinoda of Linkin Park, Jake One, and several others.

Debuting at #19 on the *Billboard* 200, *Rise Up* would spawn the singles "Armada Latina," which featured Pitbull and Marc Anthony and reached #25 on the Rap chart; "Get 'Em Up"; "It Ain't Nothin'," featuring Young De; and the title track, which featured Tom Morello of Rage Against the Machine. Other guests on *Rise Up* included Daron Malakian of System of a Down, Everlast, Evidence, and the Alchemist.

APRIL 27

B.o.B. releases *B.o.B. Presents: The Adventures of Bobby Ray* on Atlantic.

After releasing several mixtapes since 2006, the debut studio album from Georgia rapper and producer B.o.B. debuted at #1 on the *Billboard* 200. The multi-platinum album featured an impressive cast of guest artists that included Rivers Cuomo, Janelle Monáe, T.I., Lupe Fiasco, Bruno Mars, Eminem, and Hayley Williams.

Three of the highly successful album's singles became top ten hits on the *Billboard* Hot 100: #2 "Airplanes," featuring Hayley Williams; the multi-platinum #1 "Nothin' on You," featuring Bruno Mars; and the multi-platinum #10 "Magic," featuring Rivers Cuomo.

MAY 4

Big K.R.I.T. releases *K.R.I.T. Wuz Here* mixtape on Nature Sounds.

Although the Mississippi rapper had been releasing mixtapes since 2005, *K.R.I.T. Wuz Here* was the rapper's breakthrough mixtape, earning him critical acclaim and eventually leading to the rapper's deal with Def Jam.

The set included appearances from Curren$y, Wiz Khalifa, and Devin the Dude and yielded one single: "Country Shit," which cracked the top twenty of the Rap chart. A remix of the song featuring Ludacris and Bun B was released in 2011.

JUNE 8

Plies releases his fourth album *Goon Affiliated* on Slip-n-Slide.

Reaching #5 on the *Billboard* 200 and topping the Rap and R&B/Hip-Hop charts, the Florida street rapper's latest was the first that featured guest appearances. It spawned the hit singles "She Got It Made," featuring Bei Maejor, which reached #17 on the Rap chart, and J.R. Rotem–produced "Becky," which reached #32 on the R&B chart. Fabolous and Young Jeezy guested on the track "Look Like" and Trey Songz was featured on the cut "Kitty Kitty." Producers on *Goon Affiliated* included J.U.S.T.I.C.E. League, Fatboi, J.R. Rotem, and Zaytoven among others.

JUNE 15

Drake releases his debut album *Thank Me Later* on Young Money.

The highly anticipated release, which debuted at #1 on the *Billboard* Hot 100, combined hip-hop with R&B and a small touch of reggae. The introspective lyrics about fame and self-examination on the chart-topping, multi-platinum album caused many to compare him to Kid Cudi and Kanye West.

The blockbuster set featured the hits "Find Your Love," which reached #5 on the *Billboard* Hot 100; the gold-selling "Miss Me," featuring Lil Wayne; "Fireworks," featuring Alicia Keys; "Up All Night," featuring Nicki Minaj; the Grammy-nominated "Fancy," featuring T.I. and Swizz Beatz; and "Over," which topped the Rap chart. Other guests included Jay Z, Young Jeezy, and The-Dream. Some of the producers on the Toronto MC's long awaited full-length release included Kanye West, Swizz Beatz, Timbaland, Noah "40" Shebib, and Boi-1da.

JUNE 18

Eminem releases his seventh album *Recovery* on Shady/Aftermath.

The Grammy-winning *Recovery* is a sort of thematic sequel to Eminem's 2009 *Relapse* and featured a

DRAKE

BUN B

plethora of hot producers including Alex da Kid, Dr. Dre, Boi-1da, Just Blaze, Emile, Havoc of Mobb Deep, Mr. Porter, Jim Jonsin, DJ Khalil, Script Shepherd, Supa Dups, as well as Slim Shady himself.

The critically acclaimed set featured the Grammy-winning, diamond-selling "Not Afraid"; the chart-topping "Love the Way You Lie," featuring Rihanna; the gold-selling "Spacebound"; and the platinum-selling "No Love," featuring Lil Wayne. Although "Won't Back Down," featuring Pink, was not released as an official single, it managed to chart on four national charts.

JUNE 22

The Roots release their ninth studio album *How I Got Over* on Def Jam.

The Grammy-nominated, politically charged set debuted at #6 on the *Billboard* 200. Beloved by critics, the album contained the singles "The Fire," featuring John Legend; the title track featuring Dice Raw; and a remake of the Monsters of Folk track "Dear God," renamed "Dear God 2.0," with the Monsters joining the Philly hip-hop band on the updated version.

Other guests on *How I Got Over* included Truck North, P.O.R.N., STS, Peedi Peedi, Joanna Newsom, Blu, Phonte, Patty Crash, and Amber Coffman, Angel Deradoorian, and Haley Dekle from the rock group Dirty Projectors.

JULY 5

Big Boi releases his debut solo album *Sir Lucious Left Foot: The Son of Chico Dusty* on Def Jam.

Debuting at #3 on the *Billboard* 200, Big Boi's long-awaited first solo album came four years after Outkast's last official release, 2006's *Idlewild*. With production by André 3000, Lil Jon, Organized Noize, Malay, Scott Storch, and Royal Flush, the lyrically dexterous set featured appearances from Sleepy Brown, Yelawolf, T.I., B.o.B., and Gucci Mane, among others.

Critically acclaimed, the funky, inventive album's lead single, "Shutterbug," featuring Cutty, was nominated for a Grammy for best rap performance by a duo or group.

JULY 20

Rick Ross releases his fourth album *Teflon Don* on Def Jam.

Debuting at #2 on the *Billboard* 200, the gold-selling album spawned the hits "Aston Martin Music," which featured Drake and Chrisette Michele and reached #30 on the *Billboard* Hot 100; "Super High," featuring Ne-Yo; and "B.M.F. (Blowin' Money Fast)" featuring Styles P.

Featuring all-star production from the likes of Lex Luger, No I.D., Kanye West, J.U.S.T.I.C.E. League, and the Inkredibles, the well-reviewed set included guest appearances by Diddy, Raphael Saadiq, Jay Z, John Legend, Gucci Mane, Erykah Badu, Trey Songz, Kanye West, Jadakiss, and Cee-Lo Green.

AUGUST 2

Chuck D of Public Enemy releases his second solo album *Don't Rhyme for the Sake of Riddlin'* on Slam Jamz.

Fellow PE member Professor Griff appears on the album as does Chuck's fellow Confrontation Camp cohort Kyle "Ice" Jason. Other guests included Heet Mob, Jahi, Fine Arts Militia and longtime Strong Island musical soldier, Johnny "Juice" Rosado. Fan favorites on the thoughtful set include "I Rap Black," "I Hate Hate," "This Bit of Earth," and "Tear Down That Wall."

AUGUST 3

Bun B releases his third solo album *Trill OG* on Universal.

Debuting at #4 on the *Billboard* 200, *Trill OG* was the former UGK rapper's first album for Universal. The album spawned several singles, including "Countin' Money," which featured Yo Gotti and Gucci Mane, the DJ Premier–produced "Let 'Em Know," and "Trillionaire," which featured T-Pain.

Other guests on the album include Trey Songz, Drake, Young Jeezy, and a posthumous appearance by Pimp C and 2Pac. *Trill OG* featured production by DJ Premier, Drumma Boy, Steve Below, Boi-1da, Big E, DJ B-Do, 40, as well as Play-N-Skillz.

AUGUST 5

Wyclef Jean files for candidacy in the 2010 Haitian presidential election.

In the wake of the Caribbean country's disastrous earthquake near the capital city of Port-au-Prince, Wyclef Jean filed to run for president. Many thought a highly unlikely victory for Jean would bring some political transparency to Haiti, which has long been embroiled in political and economic controversy and strife. However, Haiti's electoral commission ruled that Jean was ineligible because he had not met the country's requirement for residency for five years.

AUGUST 17

Lil Wayne releases the single "Right Above It" on Young Money.

Off Wayne's album *I Am Not a Human Being*, "Right Above It" featured Drake and was produced by Kane Beatz. The multi-platinum song topped the Rap chart and peaked at #6 on the *Billboard* Hot 100, giving the New Orleans rapper his fourth top ten hit.

OCTOBER 5

Waka Flocka Flame releases his debut studio album, *Flockaveli*, on 1017 Brick Squad.

Debuting at #6 on the *Billboard* 200, the crunk-inspired, intense album from the 1017 Brick Squad member was mainly produced by Lex Luger and also featured production by Drumma Boy, Southside, and others.

Flockaveli featured the hit singles, "Hard in da Paint"; "Grove St. Party," featuring Kebo Gotti; "Oh Let's Do It," featuring Cap and whose remix featured Rick Ross, Diddy, and Gucci Mane; and the smash "No Hands," featuring Roscoe Dash and Wale, which reached #13 on the *Billboard* Hot 100.

Other guests on *Flockaveli* included French Montana, Cartier Kitten, Mouse, YG Hootie, Joe Moses, Big Deal, Suge Gotti, Baby Bomb, RA Diggs, Uncle Murda, Popa Smurf, Ice Burgandy, Pastor Troy, Slim Dunkin, and Gudda Gudda.

CHUCK D:

People might criticize his style but Waka Flocka certainly got something out of the "less is more" rhyme style. Critics often forget nowadays that it is visual if not more so than audio this artist exemplifies. Style and sight as much as story and sound.

NOVEMBER 9

Kid Cudi releases second studio album *Man on the Moon II: The Legend of Mr. Rager* on Universal.

Kid Cudi's second album fared slightly better on the charts than his acclaimed debut album, peaking at #3 on the *Billboard* 200. The gold-selling set spawned two singles: the platinum-selling "Erase Me," which featured Kanye West and reached #22 on the *Billboard* Hot 100, and "Mr. Rager." Mary J. Blige, Cee-Lo Green, St. Vincent, and Chip tha Ripper appear as featured artists on the album. Jim Jonsin, Dot da Genius, Chuck Inglish, and Plain Pat all contributed production to the album.

NOVEMBER 19

Nicki Minaj releases her debut album *Pink Friday* on Universal.

The highly anticipated album from the Trinidadian New York-based artist debuted at #2 on the *Billboard* 200. Including both rapid-fire rapping and singing, the multi-platinum set featured a slew of singles, including Minaj's first top twenty hit on the *Billboard* Hot 100, "Your Love," which topped the Rap chart; "Check It Out," featuring will.i.am; and the Grammy-nominated, platinum-selling "Moment 4 Life," featuring Drake, which reached #13 on the *Billboard* Hot 100. The album also featured guest appearances from Eminem, Natasha Bedingfield, Kanye West, and Rihanna.

Nicki Minaj garnered four Grammy nominations in 2012, including best new artist and best rap album. A deluxe version of the album was released in the summer of 2011. That version included "Super Bass," the multi-platinum blockbuster that reached #3 on the *Billboard* Hot 100.

CHUCK D:

"I'm the Best" is the first track off Minaj's debut. The production is tight and her flow is just as tight. "I'm the Best" displays confidence, strength, and power the young girls and women who are listening to it are looking for. Confidence. Strength. Power—not just on display on this opening track, throughout the entire album.

NOVEMBER 22

Kanye West releases his sixth album *My Beautiful Dark Twisted Fantasy* on Roc-A-Fella.

The Grammy Award–winning, platinum-selling chart-topper is considered by many as Kanye's most creative, artistic, and diverse set to date. Debuting at #1 on the *Billboard* 200, the album was praised for its musical diversity, incorporating different influences like classical, electro, and soul all backed by hip-hop.

Exploring themes like fame, drugs and alcohol, ego, love, and self-reflection, the blockbuster featured production by West along with some of the hottest producers in the industry including the RZA, Jeff Bhasker, Bink!, No I.D., Mike Dean, Emile, DJ Frank E, Mike Caren, Kyambo Joshua, S1, and Lex Luger.

My Beautiful Dark Twisted Fantasy contained the smash hit singles, "All of the Lights," featuring Rihanna; the gold-selling "Runaway," featuring Pusha T; the platinum-selling "Monster," featuring Jay Z; Rick Ross, Nicki Minaj, and Bon Iver; and the Grammy-nominated "Power." Other guests on *My Beautiful Dark Twisted Fantasy* included John Legend, Kid Cudi, Cyhi the Prynce, and Raekwon of the Wu-Tang Clan.

DECEMBER 7

Redman releases his seventh album *Reggie* on Def Jam.

Redman, using the alter ego Reggie after his own birth name Reggie Noble, told the press prior to the release of the set that he was using an alter ego for the album's more "pop-oriented" approach as opposed to his more rugged style.

Featuring production from Ty Fyffe, Rockwilder, the Audibles, DJ Khalil, Tone Mason, and several others, the album did not feature longtime collaborator Erick Sermon. Cracking the *Billboard* 200, the set contained the singles "Def Jammable" and "Rockin' wit da Best," featuring Kool Moe Dee. Other guests on *Reggie* included DJ Kool, Pooh Bear, Ready Roc, Saukrates, Runt Dawg, Method Man, Bun B, Melanie Rutherford, and Faith Evans.

DECEMBER 21

Ghostface Killah releases his ninth solo album *Apollo Kids* on Def Jam.

Featuring production by Pete Rock, Scram Jones, Jake One, and Sean C & LV, the gritty set featured guest appearances by Busta Rhymes, The Game, Joell Ortiz, Trife Diesel, Jim Jones, Sheek Louch of the L.O.X., Black Thought of the Roots, Shawn Wiggs, Sun God, Redman, as well as fellow Wu-bangers Method Man, U-God, the GZA, Cappadonna, and Killah Priest. Reaching #10 on the Rap chart, the well-reviewed album spawned the fan favorites "How You Like Me Baby" and "Superstar."

DECEMBER 21

Mann releases the remix to his hit single, "Buzzin'," on Beluga Heights.

The original version, released two months prior, was on the LA rapper's debut album *Mann's World*, released in the summer of 2011. The "Buzzin'" remix, a hit single in the US and the UK, featured 50 Cent.

2011

NATE DOGG

JANUARY 11

Lecrae releases his fifth album *Rehab: The Overdose* on Reach.

The Christian rapper's album is sort of a coda to his previous Grammy-nominated set *Rehab*, released just five months prior, which was a collection of songs that dealt with battling addictions and overcoming drug abuse, while this set dealt with more biblical themes such as love of Christ, hope, and peace.

Debuting at #15 on the *Billboard* 200 and #4 on the Rap chart, the album featured guest appearances by J. Paul, Canon, Swoope, Suzy Rock, and Thi'sl.

FEBRUARY 1

Chris Brown releases the single "Look at Me Now" on Jive.

The Grammy-nominated single, featuring Lil Wayne and Busta Rhymes, is from Brown's album *F.A.M.E.* Reaching #6 on the *Billboard* Hot 100 and topping the Rap and R&B/Hip-Hop charts, the Dirty South–inspired single was on many critics' best-of-the-year lists.

MARCH 7

Lupe Fiasco releases his third studio album *Lasers* on Atlantic.

Debuting at #1 on the *Billboard* 200, Lupe Fiasco's third studio album featured production from the Neptunes, Alex da Kid, Kane Beatz, and King David. Although the album represented the peak of Lupe Fiasco's mainstream popularity, the record and release were fraught with tension. When Atlantic delayed releasing the album, Lupe's fans protested and signed petitions, which helped solidify the release date.

The album's multi-platinum lead single "The Show Goes On" was nominated for two Grammys and is the rapper's second top ten *Billboard* Hot 100. Skylar Grey, Trey Songz, and John Legend all appear as featured artists on the album.

CHUCK D:

After the talk of fan-organized protests, behind alleged foot-dragging by his label, Lupe Fiasco promoted yet another evolution in the rap game: How fan-driven, Internet-girded revolutions—even rumored ones—support an artist. Whether crowd sourcing an album or making damn sure an anticipated one hits, this event signaled the influence of audiences.

MARCH 15

Nate Dogg passes away at the age of forty-one.

The Long Beach rapper died after suffering a series of strokes. Nate Dogg was best known for his work alongside pioneering early '90s Los Angeles artists like Dr. Dre, Warren G, and Snoop Dogg. The rapper played a large part in the development of early '90s G-Funk.

MARCH 15

Action Bronson releases his debut album *Dr. Lecter* on Fine Fabric.

Produced by Tommy Mas, the debut by the Queens rapper was named after the Hannibal Lecter character in the book and movie *The Silence of the Lambs*. His high-pitched delivery led to numerous comparisons to Ghostface Killah. The fun set from the former chef featured numerous references to food.

MARCH 29

Wiz Khalifa releases his third album *Rolling Papers* on Atlantic.

Debuting at #2 on the *Billboard* 200, the multi-platinum album spawned several singles, including the Grammy-nominated "Black and Yellow," which gave the rapper his first #1 on the *Billboard* Hot 100.

Other singles included "Roll Up," which reached #13 on the *Billboard* Hot 100; "No Sleep," which reached #6 on the *Billboard* Hot 100; and the platinum-selling "On My Level," featuring Too $hort.

The album featured production from Stargate, Jim Jonsin, Benny Blanco, and Lex Luger, among others. Too $hort, Curren$y, and Chevy Woods appear on *Rolling Papers* as featured artists.

MARCH 29

Mac Miller releases his debut EP *On and On and Beyond* on Rostrum.

The Pittsburgh rapper made his name releasing mixtapes and videos, which led to the release of his major label debut. Debuting at #55 on the *Billboard* 200, the EP contained the previously released tracks "In the Air," "Another Night," "Life Ain't Easy," and "Live Free." The new tracks on *On and On and Beyond* included, "Put It On" and the title track.

The tracks on the EP were produced by Jay Fish, Matt Grover, Kalvin & HOBBS, Ritz Reynolds, I.D. Labs, and Andrew Dawson.

MARCH 29

Snoop Dogg releases his eleventh album *Doggumentary* on Priority.

Debuting at #8 on the *Billboard* 200, *Doggumentary* featured an array of producers including Battlecat, Meech Wells, Kanye West, Scott Storch, David Guetta, and several others.

Guest appearances included Bootsy Collins, Mr. Porter, Uncle Chucc, LaToiya Williams, John Legend, Gorillaz, Too $hort, Daz Dillinger, Wiz Khalifa, Marty James, Goldie Loc, Kobe, Devin the Dude, Traci Nelson, E-40, Young Jeezy, and country music legend Willie Nelson.

Doggumentary spawned the hit singles "Boom" featuring T-Pain and "Wet," which reached #25 on the Rap chart.

APRIL 5

Jim Jones releases his fifth solo album *Capo* on Epic.

The catchy lead single for the set, "Perfect Day," which reached #67 on the *Billboard* Hot 100, featured LOGiC and Chink Santana, who also produced the track. Some of the other producers on *Capo* included Lex Luger, Wyclef Jean, and Drumma Boy. Guests included Ashanti, the Game, Sen City, Aaron LaCrate, Lloyd Banks, Raekwon, Cam'ron, Nicole Wray, Lady H, Rell, Mel Matrix, and Prodigy of Mobb Deep.

APRIL 5

Nicki Minaj releases the single "Super Bass" on Young Money.

Produced by Kane Beatz, "Super Bass" would become Minaj's first-ever top five hit on the *Billboard* Hot 100. The multi-platinum song, included on the deluxe rerelease of her debut studio album *Pink Friday*, was a top twenty hit in more than ten countries.

APRIL 27

Beastie Boys release *Hot Sauce Committee Part Two* on Capitol.

Debuting at #2 on the *Billboard* 200 and topping the R&B/Hip-Hop and Rap charts, the Beastie Boys' first album of original lyrics since 2004 would end up being the group's final studio album.

The critically acclaimed album in their signature style spawned four singles: "Lee Majors Come Again"; the Grammy-nominated "Too Many Rappers," which featured Nas and reached the *Billboard* Hot 100; "Make Some Noise"; and "Don't Play No Game That I Can't Win," featuring Santigold, which reached #80 on the R&B/Hip-Hop chart.

Adam "MCA" Yauch had been diagnosed with cancer two years before the album's release, and would die the following year.

ACTION
BRONSON

MAY 3

Bad Meets Evil release the hit single "Fast Lane," on Shady.

Produced by Mr. Porter, JG, and Eminem, the gold-selling single by the Motor City superstar duo of Eminem and Royce da 5'9", from their debut EP *Hell: The Sequel*, reached #32 on the *Billboard* Hot 100. Their EP, released on June 14, debuted at #1 on the *Billboard* 200.

MAY 10

Tyler, the Creator releases his major label debut *Goblin* on XL.

The gold-selling "Yonkers," with its provocative lyrics and music video, is considered to be the rapper's breakthrough single. Its success helped garner interest for Tyler's debut self-produced set, which debuted at #5 on the *Billboard* 200. The grim set from the leader of the Los Angeles rap crew Odd Future Wolf Gang Kill Them All featured guest appearances by Frank Ocean, Syd tha Kyd, Taco Bennett, Jasper Dolphin, Domo Genesis, Hodgy Beats, and Mike G.

JUNE 17

Pitbull releases his sixth album *Planet Pit* on J Records.

Pitbull's last set for J Records before it folded, the gold-selling album featured the multi-platinum, chart-topping "Give Me Everything," featuring Ne-Yo, Afrojack, and Nayer; "International Love," which featured Chris Brown and reached #13 on the *Billboard* Hot 100; "Rain Over Me," which featured Marc Anthony and charted on both the English and Spanish language charts in the US; and "Hey Baby (Drop It on the Floor)," which featured T-Pain and reached #7 on the *Billboard* Hot 100. Other guests included Enrique Iglesias, Kelly Rowland, Jamie Drastik, Vein, David Rush, and Jamie Foxx.

Debuting at #7 on the *Billboard* 200 and topping the R&B/Hip-Hop charts, the set included meringue, Miami bass, freestyle, and reggae elements with production by David Guetta, Redfoo, DJ Frank E, and Dr. Luke, among others.

JUNE 28

Big Sean releases his major label debut *Finally Famous* on Def Jam.

After releasing a trilogy of mixtapes over four years, *Finally Famous* served as the Detroit rapper's debut studio release. Debuting at #3 on the *Billboard* 200 and executively produced by Kanye West, the album spawned three top forty *Billboard* Hot 100 singles: "My Last," which featured Chris Brown and also topped the Rap chart; "Marvin & Chardonnay," which featured Kanye West and Roscoe Dash; and the platinum-selling "Dance (A$$)," which reached #2 on the Rap chart. Other guest appearances included Lupe Fiasco, John Legend, Chiddy Bang, and The-Dream.

JUNE 29

Lil B releases his fifth album *I'm Gay (I'm Happy)* on Amalgam Digital.

The politically charged set, which reached #56 on the R&B/Hip-Hop charts, tackled issues as diverse as poverty, racism, and the law. A day after the release of "I'm Gay (I'm Happy)," the Berkeley MC offered it for free via a link on his Facebook page for fans who couldn't afford to pay.

The album's title was meant as a show of support to the LBGTQ community and the challenges and discrimination they face in everyday life. The album's cover art is a reference to the 1976 set *I Want You* by Marvin Gaye. Many in the gay community applauded Lil B's gesture of solidarity, while the rapper fought off death threats from others over the album's title.

JULY 2

Kendrick Lamar releases debut album *Section.80* on Top Dawg.

Peaking at #13 on the Rap chart, Kendrick Lamar's debut studio album was released after the West Coast rapper released a series of mixtapes and a debut studio EP in 2009. The album is a loose concept record that traces the hard lives of two characters named Tammy and Keisha.

The album's lead single "HiiiPoWer" was produced by J. Cole and was well reviewed by a number of publications. Other producers that worked on the album include Terrace Martin, THC, Tommy Black, and Sounwave.

JULY 8

Sony Pictures Classics release the documentary film *Beats, Rhymes & Life: The Travels of a Tribe Called Quest* in US theaters.

The film, which premiered at the Sundance Film Festival six months earlier, was directed by actor and hip-hop fan Michael Rapaport, who was also a fan of the group.

The film followed their various breakups and reunions, as well as the diabetes and kidney disease that affected group member Phife Dawg.

In addition to interviewing and following group members Q-Tip, Ali Shaheed Muhammad, and Jarobi White, the film also featured interviews with Questlove of the Roots, the Beastie Boys, Ludacris, Mos Def, Mary J. Blige, De La Soul, DJ Red Alert, the Jungle Brothers, the Beatnuts, and an endless list of the who's who in hip-hop.

JULY 19

DJ Khaled releases *We the Best Forever* on Universal Motown.

Debuting at #5 on the *Billboard* 200, DJ Khaled's fifth studio album featured an extensive array of A-list guests that included Drake, Lil Wayne, Rick Ross, Ludacris, Mary J. Blige, Jadakiss, Fabolous, Chris Brown, Ne-Yo, the Game, Busta Rhymes, Birdman, T-Pain, Akon, B.o.B., and Jeezy.

The album's second single, "I'm on One," which featured Drake, Rick Ross, and Lil Wayne, became a top ten single on the *Billboard* Hot 100, DJ Khaled's first ever. The album included additional production from Boi-1da, Lex Luger, and 40.

JULY 26

Jay Rock releases his debut solo album *Follow Me Home* on Top Dawg Records.

The thoughtful set about urban life by the Black Hippy member featured the hit singles "All My Life (In the Ghetto)," featuring Lil Wayne and will.i.am and "Hood Gone Love It," featuring fellow Black Hippy member Kendrick Lamar.

Reaching #10 on the Rap chart, *Follow Me Home* featured guest appearances by Ab-Soul, Chris Brown, Tech N9ne, Krizz Kaliko, J. Black, Schoolboy Q, Rick Ross, and BJ the Chicago Kid. Some of the producers on the well-reviewed set include Cool & Dre, Dae One, Focus..., and J.U.S.T.I.C.E. League.

AUGUST 8

Kanye West and Jay Z release *Watch the Throne* on Def Jam.

The first-ever full-length collaboration between Kanye West and Jay Z, *Watch The Throne* debuted at #1 on the *Billboard* 200 and received seven Grammy nominations. The platinum-selling set sampled a wide range of artists including Otis Redding, Audio Two, Nina Simone, James Brown, Curtis Mayfield, and Quincy Jones and spawned a number of singles, including the Grammy-winning "No Church in the Wild"; the Grammy-winning "Otis"; and the top five hit "Niggas in Paris," which won two Grammys for best rap performance and best rap song, sold more than five million copies in its first three years, and charted in more than a dozen countries.

Beyoncé, Frank Ocean, and The-Dream all appear as featured artists on the album. Jay Z and Kanye West followed the album with an extensive world tour that would become the highest-grossing hip-hop tour of all time.

AUGUST 29

Lil Wayne releases his ninth studio album *Tha Carter IV* on Young Money.

Debuting at #1 on the *Billboard* 200, the multi-platinum album spawned four top forty singles on the *Billboard* Hot 100: "6 Foot 7 Foot, " which featured Cory Gunz; "John," which featured Rick Ross; "How to Love," which also reached #2 on the R&B/Hip-Hop and Rap charts; and "She Will," which featured Drake. Other guests on the album included T-Pain, John Legend, Jadakiss, Nas, Bun B, and Busta Rhymes.

Tha Carter IV included production from Cool & Dre, T-Minus, Mr. Bangladesh, and Willy Will.

SEPTEMBER 16

Kirko Bangz releases the single "Drank in My Cup" on Warner Bros.

The song from the Houston rapper's mixtape *Progression 2: A Young Texas Playa* would become the biggest single of his career, peaking at #28 on the *Billboard* Hot 100. Produced by the Houston production duo Sound M.O.B., the platinum-selling single's official remix included guest appearances from J. Cole, Juelz Santana, and 2 Chainz.

SEPTEMBER 27

J. Cole releases his debut studio album *Cole World: The Sideline Story* on Columbia.

The introspective studio release from the North Carolina rapper spawned four singles, including the platinum-selling lead "Work Out," which was J. Cole's first top twenty on the *Billboard* Hot 100 and "Can't Get Enough," which featured Trey Songz and reached #5 on the Rap chart.

Debuting at #1 on the *Billboard* 200 and topping the R&B/Hip-Hop and Rap charts, the platinum-selling set was mainly self-produced and included guest appearances from Jay Z, Drake, and Missy Elliott. Jay Z, who signed J. Cole to his Roc Nation label, served as executive producer on the album.

OCTOBER 7

Rick Ross releases the single "You the Boss," on Maybach.

"You the Boss," produced by K.E. and featuring Nicki Minaj, was originally intended as the first single off Ross's fifth album, *God Forgives, I Don't*, but was eventually removed from the album's track list altogether. The gold-selling track reached #5 on the R&B chart and #10 on the Rap chart.

OCTOBER 11

Snoop Dogg and Wiz Khalifa release the single "Young, Wild & Free" on Atlantic.

Produced by the Smeezingtons, the lead single from the soundtrack to *Mac & Devin Go to High School* featured an appearance by Bruno Mars. The Grammy-nominated, multi-platinum track reached #7 on the *Billboard* Hot 100.

OCTOBER 11

DJ Drama releases his third album *Third Power* on eOne.

Peaking at #6 on the Rap chart, the gold-selling set from the Philly hip-hop artist would spawn the hit singles "Undercover," featuring Chris Brown and J. Cole; "Ain't No Way Around It," featuring Future; and the #1 smash "Oh My," featuring Wiz Khalifa, Fabolous, and Roscoe Dash. The "Oh My" remix, which was also featured on the album, contained guest appearances by 2 Chainz, Big Sean, and Trey Songz.

Other guests on *Third Power* included Young Jeezy, Freddie Gibbs, Maino, Meek Mill, Freeway, Young Chris, Ya Boy, Akon, B.o.B., Crooked I, French Montana, Pusha T, Gucci Mane, Red Café, Yo Gotti, Wale, and Talia Coles and featured production by Drumma Boy, Lex Luger, Akon, Jim Jonsin, Cardiak, Mike Dean, Don Cannon, Boi-1da, and others.

NOVEMBER 1

Wale releases his second studio album *Ambition* on Warner Bros.

Debuted at #2 on the *Billboard* 200 and topping the R&B/Hip-Hop and Rap charts, the gold-selling set earned Wale his first top forty *Billboard* Hot 100 single with the Grammy-nominated "Lotus Flower Bomb," which featured Miguel.

The second studio album from the DC rapper also featured guest appearances from Kid Cudi, Jeremih, Rick Ross, Meek Mill, Ne-Yo, Big Sean, and Lloyd. Diplo, T-Minus, Lex Luger, and DJ Toomp all contributed production to *Ambition*.

NOVEMBER 15

Drake releases his second studio album *Take Care* on Young Money.

Drake's second introspective chart-topping set, which won the Grammy for best rap album, featured a slew of hit singles, including "Take Care," which featured Rihanna and reached #9 on the *Billboard* Hot 100; "HYFR," featuring Lil Wayne; the gold-selling "Marvins Room"; "Headlines"; "Make Me Proud," which featured Nicki Minaj and topped the R&B and Rap charts; and the multi-platinum anthem "The Motto."

Other guests on the multi-platinum album include Rick Ross, The Weeknd, André 3000, Birdman, and Kendrick Lamar and producers include 40, Just Blaze, Jamie XX, The Weeknd, Supa Dups, and Boi-1da.

NOVEMBER 15

Betty Wright and the Roots release the album *Betty Wright: The Movie* on S-Curve.

The soul legend, who rose to fame in 1972 with the million-selling "Clean Up Woman" on Alston Records, produced *Betty Wright: The Movie* with the Roots drummer Questlove. Guests on this set included Joss Stone, Snoop Dogg, Robert "the Messenger" Bozeman, and Lenny Williams. The critically acclaimed album also produced the hit single "Grapes on a Vine," featuring Lil Wayne.

DECEMBER 2

The Roots release their tenth studio album *Undun* on Def Jam.

Undun is a concept album centered on the life of fictional character, Redford Stevens. Reaching #2 on the Rap chart, the innovative set received much critical acclaim for its existential qualities. *Undun* produced the hit single "Make My," featuring Big K.R.I.T. & Dice Raw. Other guests on *Undun* included Truck North, Bilal, Phonte, Greg Porn, and Just Blaze. The album featured several coproducers all overseen by drummer, group leader, and musical director Questlove.

DECEMBER 5

***T.I. & Tiny: The Family Hustle* premieres on VH1.**

The reality show, starring rap superstar T.I. and his wife Tameka "Tiny" Cottle of R&B group Xscape, featured the couple at home with their six children. The show explored their family life as well as their entertainment careers.

DECEMBER 20

Young Jeezy releases his fourth album *TM: 103 Hustlerz Ambition* on Def Jam.

The third and final installment in the Thug Motivation series, after being delayed for close to two years, was finally released to an eagerly awaiting fan base. The gold-selling set debuted at #3 on the *Billboard* 200.

Among the hit singles released on the album were "Leave You Alone" featuring Ne-Yo, "F.A.M.E." featuring T.I., and "I Do," featuring Jay Z and André 3000. The deluxe edition of the album featured the hit songs "Ballin'" featuring Lil Wayne and the Grammy-nominated "Lose My Mind" featuring Plies.

Other guests on *Hustlerz Ambition* included Trick Daddy, Fabolous, Jadakiss, Snoop Dogg, Mitchelle'l, Devin the Dude, Future, Jill Scott, and 2 Chainz. The album featured an array of producers, including Drumma Boy, J.U.S.T.I.C.E. League, Warren G, Midnight Black, and others.

CHUCK D:

I often see ATL superstar Young Jeezy as probably one of hip-hop's most serious dudes. He invited me to participate in his black president videos but I had previous commitments. Still, I was honored to be asked. Young Jeezy's blueprint is out of the Ice Cube mode, which I overstand quite well. Simply a straight rhyming cat that brought the South some lyrical muscle.

2012

JANUARY 10

Yo Gotti releases his third studio album *Live from the Kitchen* on RCA.

Producers on the Memphis native's hit album included Drumma Boy, Shawty Redd, Big K.R.I.T., and others.

Debuting at #12 on the *Billboard* 200, *Live from the Kitchen* spawned the hit singles, "We Can Get It On," which reached #22 on the Rap chart; "5 Star," which featured Gucci Mane, Trina, and Nicki Minaj and cracked the *Billboard* Hot 100; and "Single," featuring Stuey Rock.

Other guests on *Live from the Kitchen* included Rick Ross, Big Sean, Wiz Khalifa, 2 Chainz, Nicki Minaj, Gucci Mane, Trina, Wale, and Jadakiss.

JANUARY 13

Tyga releases the smash hit "Faded" on Young Money Records.

Reaching #6 on the Rap chart, "Faded," which also featured Lil Wayne, is from Tyga's sophomore album *Careless World: Rise of the Last King*, released later the same year.

JANUARY 14

Schoolboy Q releases his second studio album *Habits & Contradictions* on Top Dawg via iTunes.

The well-received set from the Black Hippy musical collective member featured guest appearances from Jay Rock, Jhené Aiko, Dom Kennedy, Curren$y, Ab-Soul, and Kendrick Lamar. Peaking at #16 on the Rap chart, the eighteen-track set included the Best Kept Secret–produced single "Hands on the Wheel," with A$AP Rocky that cracked the R&B/Hip-Hop charts. Other producers who worked on the album included Lex Luger, the Alchemist, Mike Will Made it, and Sounwave.

MARCH 11

Chief Keef releases his debut single "I Don't Like" on Interscope.

Produced by Young Chop, the debut label single from the teenage Chicago rapper featured Lil Reese and was a top twenty hit on the Rap chart. The song eventually served as the lead single to Chief Keef's debut album *Finally Rich*.

MARCH 24

Future releases the hit single "Same Damn Time" on Epic.

Reaching #12 on the R&B/Hip-Hop chart, the infectious "Same Damn Time," produced by Sonny Digital, was from Future's debut album *Pluto* released the same year. A remix featured Diddy and Ludacris and another featured Rick Ross, Gunplay, and Meek Mill.

APRIL 2

Nicki Minaj releases her second studio album *Pink Friday: Roman Reloaded* on Young Money.

Minaj's multi-platinum second set featured appearances from Cam'ron, Rick Ross, 2 Chainz, Lil Wayne, Young Jeezy, Nas, Drake, and Beenie Man.

Debuting at #1 on the *Billboard* 200, the album's lead single, "Starships," reached #5 on the *Billboard* Hot 100. The album's other singles were "Right by My Side" with Chris Brown; "Beez in the Trap" which featured 2 Chainz and reached #7 on the Rap chart; "Pound the Alarm"; and "Va Va Voom," which reached #22 on the *Billboard* Hot 100.

RedOne, Alex da Kid, Kane Beatz, Dr. Luke, Alex P, T-Minus, Rico Beats, and Hit-Boy all contributed production to *Pink Friday: Roman Reloaded*.

2012

NICKI MINAJ

APRIL 3

Chance the Rapper self-releases his debut mixtape *10 Day*.

Recorded during the Chicago rapper's ten-day high school suspension, Chance the Rapper's debut set became one of the most widely praised of the year. The mixtape featured appearances from Chicago artists Vic Mensa, Alex Wiley, Nico Segal, and Lili K. and production from Flying Lotus, Lex Luger, Chuck Inglish, and THEMpeople.

APRIL 14

The Beastie Boys are inducted into the Rock & Roll Hall of Fame.

LL Cool J and Chuck D inducted the group, with Mike D and King Ad-Rock accepting honor in a ceremony at Public Hall in Cleveland, Ohio. MCA was admitted into New York-Presbyterian Hospital the same day after battling cancer of the lymph nodes for the past three years. He would tragically pass away less than a month later, on May 4.

CHUCK D:

Inducting the Beastie Boys into the Rock & Roll Hall of Fame was an extremely honorable and bittersweet event. Adam MCA Yauch, who clearly was a hero of mine at that point, asked me first, and then Adam Horovitz and Mike Diamond. MCA was ill and later couldn't make the ceremony. LL Cool J presented them with me in Cleveland. Def Jam—the Beastie Boys were major for bringing me there. They put us on our first tour with *License to Ill*. They exposed our music via DJ Hurricane on national TV before we were anywhere. We watched these guys grow and transcend beyond their beginnings to make a musical pattern to follow. Innovate, never repeat yourself twice. Root yourself in the pioneering blue and black print of hip-hop, no matter how high you go. Be a tight group until death do you part. The Beasties were and are always saluting the elements whenever you hear, see, or read 'em. This is why it's so hard to duplicate them.

Mike D and Ad-Rock did not perform but a supergroup of Black Thought and Questlove of the Roots, Kid Rock, and Travie McCoy performed Beastie classics like "No Sleep 'Til Brooklyn," "The New Style," "Sabotage," and "So What'cha Want."

APRIL 15

A hologram of Tupac performs at Coachella.

During their headlining Coachella performance, Dr. Dre and Snoop Dogg debuted a hologram of Tupac, which performed a brief four-song set that included "California Love" and "Hail Mary."

Although the performance spawned rumors of a posthumous Tupac tour, the hologram, which was actually an advanced optical illusion using CGI graphics, was developed exclusively for the Coachella performance.

Tupac's performance came during Dr. Dre and Snoop Dogg's greatest hits set that also featured appearances from 50 Cent, Wiz Khalifa, Kendrick Lamar, and Eminem.

MAY 1

B.o.B. releases his sophomore album *Strange Clouds* on Grand Hustle.

Peaking at #5 on the *Billboard* 200 and topping the R&B/Hip-Hop and Rap charts, the platinum-selling set contained the hit singles "Out of My Mind," featuring Nicki Minaj; the multi-platinum "So Good," which featured Ryan Tedder of OneRepublic; "Both of Us," which featured Taylor Swift and reached #18 on the *Billboard* Hot 100; and the multi-platinum title track, which featured Lil Wayne and reached #7 on the *Billboard* Hot 100.

Other guests on *Strange Clouds* included Trey Songz, Chris Brown, T.I., Lauriana Mae, Playboy Tre, and legendary actor Morgan Freeman and an array of producers including Mike Will Made It, Dr. Luke, Unik, Billboard, Frequency, and Stargate, among others.

THE BEASTIE BOYS

MAY 15

Killer Mike releases his sixth album *R.A.P. Music* on Williams Street.

The "R.A.P." in the album's title was an acronym for "Rebellious African People." Produced by El-P, the critically acclaimed set by the Outkast colleague contains the singles, "Don't Die"; "Untitled," featuring Scar; and "Big Beast," featuring Bun B, T.I., and Trouble.

Reaching #12 on the R&B/Hip-Hop chart and #8 on the Rap chart, the politically charged *R.A.P. Music* also featured Emily Panic on the cut "Anywhere But Here" and scratching throughout by DJ Abilities.

JUNE 19

Juvenile releases his tenth album *Rejuvenation* on Rap-A-Lot.

Rejuvenation saw the Big Easy MC reunite with producer Mannie Fresh to rehash their days of the late 1990s at Cash Money Records. Reaching #39 on the R&B/Hip-Hop chart, the album's single, "Power," featured Rick Ross.

Other producers contributing to *Rejuvenation* included Drumma Boy, Sinista, S-8ighty, C. Smith, and Bass Heavy. Guests on the set included UTP, Z-Ro, Trae tha Truth, Young Juve, and Skip.

JULY 3

Prodigy releases his third solo album *H.N.I.C. 3* on Infamous.

The third installment of the Mobb Deep member's H.N.I.C. series, which reached #15 on the Rap chart, featured production by the Alchemist, Ty Fyffe, S.C., Sid Roams, Beat Butcha, Young L, and T.I., who also appeared on the track "What's Happening." Other guest appearances on *H.N.I.C. 3* include Esther, Willie Taylor of Day26, Vaughn, Boogz Boogetz, Wiz Khalifa, and Prodigy's Mobb Deep partner Havoc.

JULY 13

Nas releases his eleventh studio album *Life Is Good* on Def Jam.

The New York rapper's fifth #1 album on the *Billboard* 200, and his third consecutive #1 since his *Hip Hop Is Dead,* featured production from Boi-1da, 40, Swizz Beatz, Salaam Remi, Da Internz, and No I.D. Anthony Hamilton, Miguel, Mary J. Blige, Rick Ross, and Swizz Beatz all appear on *Life Is Good* as featured artists.

The introspective album, written after Nas's divorce from the singer Kelis, was nominated for four Grammys in 2013, including best rap album. The singles "Daughters" and "Cherry Wine," which featured vocals from Amy Winehouse, were responsible for Nas's three other Grammy nominations.

JULY 17

Masta Ace releases his eighth album *MA_DOOM: Son of Yvonne* on M3.

With beats on the set taken from MF Doom's Special Herbs series of instrumental mixtapes, Ace pays tribute in lyrical dexterity to his mother Yvonne, who brought him up on her own. Outside of MF Doom's approval to use the tracks, the two artists did not work directly together, outside of his guesting with Big Daddy Kane on the track "Think I Am." Other guests on the album included Reggie B, Milani the Artist, and Pav Bundy.

JULY 30

Rick Ross releases his fifth album *God Forgives, I Don't* on Def Jam.

Debuting at #1 on the *Billboard* 200, the ambitious set was nominated for best rap album at the 2013 Grammys. *God Forgives, I Don't* featured appearances from Dr. Dre, Jay Z, Ne-Yo, André 3000, and Meek Mill, and spawned several singles, two of which, "Touch'N You" featuring Usher and "Diced Pineapples" featuring Wale and Drake, became top twenty hits on the R&B/Hip-Hop and Rap charts. Pharrell Williams, Jake One, Cool & Dre, and Rico Love all contributed production, with DJ Khaled serving as coexecutive producer.

AUGUST 14

2 Chainz releases his debut album *Based on a T.R.U. Story* on Def Jam.

The Grammy-nominated platinum-selling debut from the Georgia rapper debuted at #1 on the *Billboard* 200. The set yielded three top ten singles on the Rap chart: "No Lie" featuring Drake, "Birthday Song" featuring Kanye West, and "I'm Different."

Other guests on the album included Lil Wayne, Nicki Minaj, The-Dream, John Legend, Mike Posner, and Scarface and production by Drumma Boy, Mike Posner, The-Dream, Mr. Bangladesh, Mike Will Made It, DJ Mustard, and Kanye West.

SEPTEMBER 11

Juicy J releases the single "Bandz a Make Her Dance" on Columbia.

Produced by Mike Will Made It, the platinum-selling song featured Lil Wayne and 2 Chainz. "Bandz a Make Her Dance" peaked at #29 on the *Billboard* Hot 100 and reached #6 on the R&B/Hip-Hop chart and #5 on the Rap chart. The song's remix featured French Montana, B.o.B., LoLa Monroe, and Wiz Khalifa.

SEPTEMBER 14

G.O.O.D. Music releases its debut *Cruel Summer* on G.O.O.D. Music Records.

G.O.O.D. Music, a label launched by Kanye West, stands for "Getting Out Our Dreams." The collective was comprised of Kanye West, Big Sean, and Pusha T.

Debuting at #2 on the *Billboard* 200, the set featured a number of charting singles, including the multi-platinum, Grammy-nominated "Mercy," which featured 2 Chainz and reached #13 on the *Billboard* Hot 100; "Cold" featuring DJ Khaled; "New God Flow," with Pusha T and Kanye West; and "Clique," with Kanye West, Jay Z, and Big Sean, which reached #12 on the *Billboard* Hot 100.

Producers included Hit-Boy, Illmind, Mannie Fresh, Young Chop, Lifted, Mike Will Made It, Hudson Mohawke, Mike Dean, and Kanye West.

SEPTEMBER 24

Wiz Khalifa releases "Remember You" on Atlantic.

Reaching #15 on the R&B/Hip-Hop chart, the platinum-selling single, which featured The Weeknd, is from Wiz Khalifa's album *O.N.I.F.C.* It was nominated for a Grammy for best rap/sung collaboration.

SEPTEMBER 27

Lil Wayne passes Elvis Presley for most appearances on the *Billboard* Hot 100.

Lil Wayne's appearance on The Game's single "Celebration" gave the New Orleans rapper the highest number of appearances on the *Billboard* Hot 100 for a single artist since the chart was debuted in 1958. Of his 109 appearances on the *Billboard* Hot 100, 42 of the instances featured Lil Wayne as the lead artist.

OCTOBER 9

Macklemore & Ryan Lewis release their debut studio album *The Heist* on Macklemore LCC.

The self-produced, recorded, and released album from the Seattle duo turned into a chart-topping and platinum-selling smash. *The Heist,* which won the Grammy for best rap album, contained three hit singles dating back two years prior to the album's release: 2010's "My Oh My"; 2011's gold-selling "Wing$"; and 2011's chart-topping, multi-platinum "Can't Hold Us," featuring Ray Dalton. Other singles included the 2012 Grammy-winning, multi-platinum "Thrift Shop," featuring Wanz and the Grammy-nominated, multi-platinum "Same Love," featuring Mary Lambert.

Other guests on *The Heist* included Ab-Soul, Allen Stone, Buffalo Madonna, The Teaching, Schoolboy Q, Hollis, Evan Roman, Eighty4 Fly, and Ben Bridwell of Band of Horses, most of which were from the Seattle area.

CHUCK D:

Mac has been doing it quite for some time now. I had been getting his music and playing it since I started my *AndYouDontStop!* RAPstation .com radio show on 99.5 WBAI in NYC. He hails from the Seattle area and our show producer Baird Flatline Warnick is from there as well. His independent drive, skill, knowledge, and confidence have gotten my full support and attention. No fluke here.

OCTOBER 22

Kendrick Lamar releases his sophomore album *Good Kid, M.A.A.D. City* on Top Dawg.

The platinum-selling, Grammy-nominated album tells the story of Lamar's upbringing in the gang-infested streets of Compton, California. Beloved by fans and critics alike, it spawned five hit singles: the gold-selling "Poetic Justice," featuring Drake; the gold-selling "Swimming Pools (Drank)"; "Bitch, Don't Kill My Vibe"; "The Recipe," featuring Dr. Dre; and "Backseat Freestyle."

Debuting at #2 on the *Billboard* 200, it featured guest appearances by Jay Rock, MC Eiht, Mary J. Blige, Anna Wise, Kent Jamz, Black Hippy, and Jay Z and featured production by Dr. Dre, DJ Khalil, Pharrell Williams, Just Blaze, Scoop DeVille, T-Minus, and several others.

DECEMBER 18

T.I. releases his eighth studio album *Trouble Man: Heavy Is the Head* on Atlantic.

Debuting at #2 on the *Billboard* 200, the set featured production from T.I.'s longtime collaborator DJ Toomp along with Pharrell Williams, Lil C, Rico Love, and No I.D. Singles included the gold-selling "Ball," which featured Lil Wayne, and "Hello," featuring Cee-Lo Green. Other guests on the gold-selling album include Meek Mill, A$AP Rocky, André 3000, Lil Wayne, Pink, R. Kelly, and Akon.

2013

JANUARY 15

A$AP Rocky releases his debut album *Long.Live. A$AP* on RCA.

Peaking atop the *Billboard* 200, the platinum-selling debut from the Harlem rapper produced four singles, the Hit-Boy produced "Goldie"; the Skrillex produced "Wild for the Night," which reached #19 on the Rap chart; "Fashion Killa" which reached #46 on the R&B/Hip-Hop chart; and the multi-platinum "Fuckin' Problems," which featured Kendrick Lamar, 2 Chainz, and Drake and was nominated for a Grammy for best rap song in 2014.

Other producers and guests on the album include A$AP Yams, 40, Danger Mouse, Clams Casino, Jim Jonsin, Rico Love, T-Minus, Schoolboy Q, Santigold, Joey Bada$$, Yelawolf, Danny Brown, Action Bronson, and Big K.R.I.T.

JANUARY 18

Lil Wayne releases the single "Love Me" on Young Money.

"Love Me," which featured Drake and Future, is from Lil Wayne's *I Am Not a Human Being II.* Peaking at #9 on the *Billboard* Hot 100, the multi-platinum song was coproduced by Mike Will Made It and A+.

JANUARY 29

Ace Hood releases the single "Bugatti" on Cash Money Records.

"Bugatti," which was from Hood's fourth album *Trials & Tribulations*, was produced by Mike Will Made It. Featuring guest appearances by Rick Ross and Future, the platinum-selling single reached #8 on the Rap chart.

Remixes for "Bugatti" featured guest appearances by 2 Chainz, Wiz Khalifa, French Montana, T.I., and Meek Mill.

FEBRUARY 5

Wale releases the single "Bad" on Rick Ross's Maybach Music.

Reaching #21 on the *Billboard* Hot 100, the multi-platinum single off Wale's third album *The Gifted* featured a guest appearance by Tiara Thomas, who also coproduced the track with Kelson Camp.

A remix of "Bad" was later released by Maybach featuring superstar Rihanna.

MARCH 12

Rich Gang release the single "Tapout" on Cash Money.

Rich Gang is a supergroup comprised of the Cash Money and Young Money Millionaires artists Lil Wayne, Nicki Minaj, Mack Maine, Future, and Birdman. Produced by Southside, TM88, and Detail, the gold-selling single, which reached #44 on the *Billboard* Hot 100, is from the supergroup's self-titled debut album released the same year.

MARCH 21

Sage the Gemini releases the hit single "Gas Pedal" on Black Money.

"Gas Pedal," from the California MC's debut album *Remember Me*, was produced by Dominic Wynn Woods aka Sage the Gemini. Reaching #29 on the *Billboard* Hot 100 and #6 on the R&B/Hip-Hop chart, the multi-platinum hyphy single featured Iamsu! on the original release and Justin Bieber on the remix.

APRIL 9

Tyga releases his third album *Hotel California* on Young Money.

Debuting at #7 on the *Billboard* 200, *Hotel California* included production from Cool & Dre, Lil' C, Mars, DJ Mustard, Detail, the Olympicks, among others.

The fan favorite set spawned the singles "Dope," which featured Rick Ross and reached #15 on the Rap chart; "For the Road," featuring Chris Brown; and

A$AP ROCKY

J. COLE

"Show You," featuring Future. Other guests on *Hotel California* included The Game, 2 Chainz, Wiz Khalifa, Jadakiss, Cedric Gervais, and Lil Wayne.

APRIL 30

Chance the Rapper self-releases his second mixtape *Acid Rap*.

Chance the Rapper's second mixtape is one of the most critically acclaimed rap mixtapes of 2013. Despite being distributed exclusively online for free, the mixtape reached #63 on the R&B/Hip-Hop chart. Chance the Rapper created the mixtape, which includes elements of jazz, gospel, blues, and soul, largely while under the influence of acid.

The set included appearances from Chance the Rapper's Chicago collaborators like Vic Mensa, Saba, BJ the Chicago Kid, and Lili K., as well as Ab-Soul, Action Bronson, Childish Gambino, and Twista.

MAY 21

French Montana releases his debut solo album *Excuse My French* on Coke Boys, Bad Boy, Maybach, and Interscope.

The debut set by the Moroccan-American rapper reached #4 on the *Billboard* 200 and topped the Rap and R&B/Hip-Hop charts. The album's profile was raised by its guests, which included Chef Raekwon, Ne-Yo, Max B, C.A.S.H., Birdman, DJ Khaled, Mavado, Ace Hood, Snoop Dogg, Scarface, Diddy, Jeremih, and The Weeknd.

Excuse My French also featured a plethora of hot producers including Mike Will Made It, Cardiak, Lex Luger, Lee on the Beats, Rico Love, Harry Fraud, Young Chop, and Jahlil Beats.

Excuse My French contained the hit singles "Pop That," which featured Drake, Rick Ross, and Lil Wayne and reached #2 on the Rap and R&B/Hip-Hop charts; "Freaks," featuring Nicki Minaj; and "Ain't Worried About Nothin'," which reached #14 on the Rap chart.

JUNE 11

Action Bronson releases his first major label release, *Saaab Stories*, on Vice.

Peaking at #6 on the Rap chart, Bronson's dark debut EP, produced by Brooklyn's Harry Fraud, spawned the underground hit single "Strictly 4 My Jeeps." Big Body Bes appeared on the track "72 Virgins," Wiz Khalifa on the cut "The Rockers," and Prodigy of Mobb Deep and Raekwon of the Wu-Tang Clan on "Seven Series Triplets."

JUNE 18

J. Cole releases his sophomore album *Born Sinner* on Roc Nation.

Reaching the top of the *Billboard* 200 and R&B/Hip-Hop charts, the self-reflective, platinum-selling album was produced by Cole along with Christian Rich, Jake One, Elite, Syience, and others. The set contained a number of hit singles including the platinum-selling "Crooked Smile," which featured TLC and reached #27 on the *Billboard* Hot 100; the Grammy-nominated, platinum-selling "Power Trip," featuring Miguel; "She Knows," featuring Amber Coffman and Cults; and "Forbidden Fruit" featuring Kendrick Lamar. The album cut "Let Nas Down" was written in response to hearing that his idol didn't like the J. Cole's single "Work Out."

CHUCK D:

J. Cole created his own niche while being supported by a major machine has always seemed to be very, as they say, underground. In hip-hop, it is always important to have the next selects coming from the anointed greats. J. Cole is no exception. That particular album is one of the selects from Dr. Dre himself, whatever Kendrick Lamar is to the West Coast; J. Cole is that East Coast component. J. Cole is an heir apparent and this record exemplifies it. His spit and lyricism is a great signifier for the next decade in hip-hop and rap.

JUNE 18

Kanye West releases his sixth album *Yeezus* on Roc-A-Fella.

The album's minimalist concept was influenced by French artist Charles-Édouard Jeanneret-Gris aka Le Corbusier, whom West learned about while visiting the Louvre in Paris. West even employed famed producer and Def Jam founder Rick Rubin to come in two weeks before the album's release to contribute to the set's clean style. Other producers on *Yeezus* included 88-Keys, Daft Punk, No I.D., Mike Dean, Carlos Broady, and Lupe Fiasco.

The chart-topping, eclectic set would be nominated for two Grammy Awards including best rap album. Hit singles off *Yeezus* included the platinum-selling "Bound 2," which featured Charlie Wilson of the Gap Band and reached #3 on the Rap and R&B/Hip-Hop charts; the platinum-selling "Black Skinhead," which reached #15 on the Rap charts; and the gold-selling "Blood on the Leaves" which sampled Nina Simone's "Strange Fruit."

JUNE 25

Wale releases the third studio album *The Gifted* on Atlantic.

Debuting at #1 on the *Billboard* 200, the gold-selling set from the DC rapper is packed with prodigious rhymes and guest appearances, including Rihanna on his multi-platinum remix of "Bad," which reached #21 on the *Billboard* Hot 100; Juicy J and Nicki Minaj on "Clappers," which hit #37 on the R&B/Hip-Hop chart; and Sam Dew on "LoveHate Thing." Other guests included Cee-Lo Green, Meek Mill, Ne-Yo, Rick Ross, Wiz Khalifa, 2 Chainz, and weirdly comedian Jerry Seinfeld.

JULY 2

Far East Movement release the single "The Illest" on Cherrytree.

"The Illest" was produced by Ricky Reed of Wallpaper and featured Houston MC Riff Raff. Reaching #18 on the Rap chart, the single from the Asian-American pop-rap group was featured on the group's EP *Dirty Bass*, released six months later.

JULY 4

Jay Z releases his twelfth album *Magna Carta Holy Grail* on Roc-A-Fella.

The ambitious set was initially offered as a free digital download for Samsung customers via the Magna Carta app and then released to traditional retailers four days later. Due to a large buy from Samsung, *Magna Carta Holy Grail* was certified platinum on the day of its release to traditional retail, a record. The album has since gone multi-platinum.

Debuting at #1 on the *Billboard* 200, *Magna Carta Holy Grail* spawned the Grammy-nominated, gold-selling "Part II (On the Run)," featuring his wife Beyoncé; the Grammy-nominated "Tom Ford," which reached #8 on the Rap chart; and the Grammy-winning "Holy Grail," featuring Justin Timberlake. Other guests on set included Frank Ocean and Rick Ross.

The album featured production by Timbaland and J-Roc, along with a host of others, including Mike Dean, Pharrell Williams, Mike Will Made It, Swizz Beatz, Travis Scott, Boi-1da, and The-Dream.

JULY 30

Tech N9ne releases his thirteenth album *Something Else* on RBC.

Debuting at #4 on the *Billboard* 200, the potent set, broken into portions titled Earth, Wind, and Fire, had a unique sound and somewhat experimental direction. The critically acclaimed album was supported by two singles "So Dope (They Wanna)," featuring Wrekonize, Snow Tha Product, and Twisted Insane and "Fragile," featuring Kendrick Lamar, ¡Mayday!, and Kendall Morgan and included the interesting "Strange 2013," which featured the remaining members of the Doors and a Jim Morrison sample.

Other guests on *Something Else* included B.o.B., Wiz Khalifa, T-Pain, Krizz Kaliko, Serj Tankian, Big Scoob, Red Café, Trae tha Truth, Scoop DeVille, Big K.R.I.T., Kutt Calhoun, Cee-Lo Green, The Game, Angel Davenport, Tyler Lyon, and Liz Suwandi, as well as production by Seven, Drumma Boy, Young Fyre, Fredwreck, and others.

AUGUST 13

Big Sean releases the single "Control" on Def Jam.

Produced by No I.D., the critically acclaimed song by Big Sean is best known for guest Kendrick Lamar's legendary verse, in which the Compton rapper challenged a dozen fellow rappers saying he was the best freestyle lyricist in rap. Some of the rappers Lamar name-checked included Big K.R.I.T., J. Cole, Meek Mill, Drake, Mac Miller, Pusha T, and A$AP Rocky.

The song sparked a number of response tracks from rappers like A$AP Ferg, Lupe Fiasco, Meek Mill, and Big K.R.I.T.

SEPTEMBER 10

2 Chainz releases his second studio album *B.O.A.T.S. II: Me Time* on Def Jam.

Debuting at #3 on the *Billboard* 200, the second set from the Georgia rapper was kicked off with the Pharrell-produced "Feds Watching," which reached #12 on the Rap chart and "Used 2," which was produced and cowritten by Mannie Fresh. Other guests and producers on the album include Fergie, Drake, T-Pain, Lil Wayne, Rich Homie Quan, Lloyd, and Ma$e.

SEPTEMBER 24

Drake releases his third studio album *Nothing Was the Same* on Young Money.

Fueled by the multi-platinum, Grammy-nominated single "Started from the Bottom," the Canadian rapper's third set debuted atop the *Billboard* 200. The second multi-platinum single "Hold on, We're Going Home," which featured the duo Majid Jordan, reached #4 on the *Billboard* Hot 100. The Grammy-nominated, self-reflective album featured guest appearances from Jay Z, Sampha, Detail, and production by Noah "40" Shebib, Dre Moon, Hagler, Jake One, Mike Zombie, Boi-1da, and Nineteen85, among others.

NOVEMBER 5

Eminem releases his eighth studio album *The Marshall Mathers LP 2* on Interscope.

The Grammy-winning, multi-platinum album, coexecutive produced by Dr. Dre and Rick Rubin, generated five singles, four of which were in the top twenty on the *Billboard* Hot 100: "Berzerk," "Survival," "Rap God," "Headlights," and "The Monster," which featured Rihanna and won the Grammy for best rap/sung collaboration.

Debuting at #1 on the *Billboard* 200, the critically acclaimed, lyrically agile set featured appearances from Kendrick Lamar, Nate Ruess, and Skylar Grey and production by Alex da Kid, Jeff Bhasker, and DJ Khalil.

DECEMBER 10

Childish Gambino releases *Because the Internet* on Glassnote.

Debuting at #7 on the *Billboard* 200, the second studio album from actor-singer Donald Glover featured appearances from Chance the Rapper, Jhené Aiko, and Azealia Banks, with additional vocals from Kai and Mystikal. Singles for the set include "3500," which reached #64 on the *Billboard* Hot 100, and "Crawl" which reached #28 on the R&B/Hip-Hop chart.

The critically acclaimed, gold-selling album, produced mainly by Gambino and Ludwig Göransson, was nominated for best rap album at the 2014 Grammys.

CHUCK D:

Like his song says...because the Internet is what it is, it is a brilliant platform if well used. Rap artists like Glover can create phenomena, split its personality into two or three separate revenue streams, and gather a fan base from each one.

DECEMBER 10

Problem releases his debut EP *Understand Me* on Diamond Lane.

Peaking at #44 on the R&B/Hip-Hop chart, the debut EP by the German-born and Compton-raised MC followed the release of a slew of mixtapes dating back to 2006.

Understand Me contained the singles "Say That Then," featuring Glasses Malone and the previously released "Like Whaaat," featuring Bad Lucc. Mars also guested on the track "Stop Playin'." Producers on *Understand Me* included Iamsu!, P-Lo, Mars, League of Starz, and Yung JR.

DECEMBER 17

Mac Miller releases the live album *Live from Space* on Rostrum.

Live from Space was recorded during Miller's Space Migration Tour during the summer of 2013. Reaching #23 on the R&B/Hip-Hop chart, the concert album featured performances of some of his biggest hits including "S.D.S." and "Watching Movies" from his second album *Watching Movies with the Sound Off* released that same summer.

2014

JANUARY 14

Macklemore beats Kendrick Lamar for best rap album at the Grammys.

Macklemore's pop smash *The Heist* beat out Kendrick Lamar's *good kid, m.A.A.d. City,* an album that was near universally lauded as one of the best records of the year, for the best rap album Grammy.

Macklemore fueled controversy by making public the apology text he had sent to Lamar after winning the award. "You got robbed. I wanted you to win," wrote the Seattle rapper.

JANUARY 29

Young Thug and Bloody Jay release *Black Portland* mixtape.

Black Portland was the first of six mixtapes Young Thug released in 2014. The critically acclaimed set, his first full-length collaboration with Atlanta rapper Bloody Jay, was named one of *Rolling Stone*'s 50 Best Albums of 2014.

FEBRUARY 17

Iggy Azalea releases "Fancy" single.

Iggy Azalea's breakthrough hit, which featured pop singer Charli XCX, topped the *Billboard* Hot 100 for seven weeks. The multi-platinum song was the biggest crossover rap hit of 2014, topping the charts in several countries.

FEBRUARY 25

Migos release their *No Label 2* mixtape.

Migos's critically acclaimed mixtape would be rereleased as a proper studio album in June 2014. The rereleased album included "New Atlanta," a new single featuring Jermaine Dupri, Young Thug, and Rich Homie Quan.

Featuring production from Metro Boomin, Zaytoven, and TM88, along with a host of others, the mixtape from the Georgia group included guest verses from Meek Mill and Rich Homie Quan. The Stack Boy Twaun–produced single "Fight Night" reached #17 on the Rap chart.

FEBRUARY 25

Schoolboy Q releases his major label debut *Oxymoron* on Top Dawg/Interscope.

Debuting at #1 on the *Billboard* 200, the Grammy-nominated aggressive album yielded five singles: "Collard Greens," "Man of the Year," "Break the Bank," "Studio," and "Hell of a Night," all of which reached the top fifty in the R&B/Hip-Hop chart. "Studio" became Schoolboy Q's highest-charting single of his career, landing at #38 on the Hot 100.

Schoolboy Q's major label debut featured an impressive roster of guest rappers like Kendrick Lamar, 2 Chainz, Tyler, the Creator, and Raekwon. The platinum-selling *Oxymoron* was the product of extensive collaboration with producers like Mike Will Made It, Pharrell, Clams Casino, DJ Dahi, Boi-1da, and more.

MARCH 3

Pharrell releases his second studio album *Girl* on Columbia.

Debuting at #2 on the *Billboard* 200, the upbeat *Girl* was nominated for a total of four Grammys, including an album of the year nomination. "Happy," the album's lead single (originally released on the soundtrack of *Despicable Me 2*), became one of the bestselling international songs of all time and was nominated for an Academy Award. It won two Grammys for best pop solo performance and best music video.

Pharrell enlisted a wide range of A-list musicians for the recording of *Girl*, including Justin Timberlake, Daft Punk, Miley Cyrus, and Alicia Keys.

MARCH 3

Rick Ross releases his sixth studio album *Mastermind* on Def Jam.

Debuting at #1 on the *Billboard* 200 and selling close to 200,000 copies in its first week alone, *Mastermind* featured executive production credits from Ross, DJ Khaled, and Puff Daddy, and included additional production from a long list of collaborators including DJ Mustard, The Weeknd, Kanye West, Boi-1da, and J-Roc.

Singles from the album included the gold-selling "The Devil Is a Lie," featuring Jay Z, which reached #16 on the Rap chart and "Thug Cry," featuring Lil Wayne, which reached #37 on the R&B charts. Other guests on the set included Kanye West, Meek Mill, Big Sean, French Montana, and Jeezy.

MARCH 18

Freddie Gibbs and Madlib release *Piñata* on Madlib's label Madlib Invazion.

Piñata, the first collaborative album between rapper Freddie Gibbs and musician Madlib, also featured guest verses from rappers like Danny Brown, Raekwon, and Earl Sweatshirt.

Despite peaking at #39 on the *Billboard* 200, the self-produced album was hailed by a number of publications as one of the best rap albums of 2014.

Piñata was recorded over the course of three years, and the album was released after Gibbs left his deal with Young Jeezy's Corporate Thugz Entertainment.

MARCH 18

YG releases his debut studio album *My Krazy Life* on Def Jam.

Debuting at #2 on the *Billboard* 200, the gold-selling set from the Compton rapper featured high-profile collaborators like Jeezy, Drake, Kendrick Lamar, Rich Homie Quan, Ty Dolla $ign, Schoolboy Q, and Jay Rock.

The album was largely produced by DJ Mustard and also featured tracks from Ty Dolla $ign, Terrace Martin, and Metro Boomin.

The album spawned the multi-platinum single "My Nigga," which featured Jeezy and Rich Homie Quan and reached #19 on the *Billboard* Hot 100; "Left, Right"; the platinum-selling "Who Do You Love?" featuring Drake; and "Do It to Ya."

APRIL 11

Outkast perform their first reunion show at Coachella.

In January 2014, it was announced that Outkast would be headlining Coachella in the spring, marking the starting date of the band's first tour in more than ten years. The sold-out show featured performances of the hits, such as "Hey Ya!" and "Ms. Jackson," as well as some fan favorites like "Hootie Hoo" and "Skew It on Bar-B."

APRIL 22

Future releases his second studio album *Honest* on Epic.

Debuting at #2 on the *Billboard* 200, Future's sophomore set was executive produced by Mike Will Made It and includes a slew of high-profile guests including Kanye West, Pharrell, Drake, André 3000, Wiz Khalifa, and Pusha T.

The well-reviewed album from the Atlanta rapper includes the lead single "Karate Chop (Remix)," which featured Lil Wayne and reached #19 on the Rap chart, followed by "Honest," which reached #18 on the R&B/Hip-Hop chart and the love song "Real and True" with Miley Cyrus and Mr Hudson.

APRIL 22

Fetty Wap self-releases the "Trap Queen" single.

Fetty Wap self-released his breakthrough hit in April and it was rereleased by 300 Entertainment in December. By the spring of 2015 the infectious single had reached #2 on the *Billboard* Hot 100, topping the R&B/Hip-Hop chart for three weeks in April, and was nominated for two Grammys in 2016.

A number of artists released unofficial remixes of "Trap Queen," some including verses from Fabolous, French Montana, and Rick Ross. The official remix featured Quavo and Gucci Mane.

FETTY WAP

CHUCK D:

Rap music has evolved from GMFFF telling us "It's like a jungle sometimes..." to another generation describing their own versions of said jungle in entirely unique ways. Another telling example of the digital age: How Fetty Wap could maneuver around all the traditional platforms for record promotion—including radio play to see a track go viral—first locally and then rival label–promoted cuts toe-to-toe.

APRIL 22

Iggy Azalea releases her debut album *The New Classic* on Def Jam.

The Australian rapper's debut was one of the biggest crossover albums in years, selling more than a million records and earning Azalea four Grammy nominations, including best new artist and record of the year for "Fancy."

In addition to the chart-topping "Fancy," *The New Classic* spawned the hits "Black Widow," Azalea's duet with Rita Ora, and the platinum-selling "Work," both of which reached #3 on the *Billboard* Hot 100.

The well-reviewed album was coexecutive produced by T.I., who appeared on the gold-selling "Change Your Life," and also featured production credits from Norwegian pop producers Stargate.

MAY 6

Atmosphere releases their eighth studio album *Southsiders* on Rhymesayers.

Minneapolis rap duo eighth's set debuted at #8 on the *Billboard* 200, which reached #3 on the R&B/Hip-Hop chart. Rapper Slug and producer Ant created an emotionally resonant album that included fan favorites such as "Bitter," "Flicker," and "The World Might Not Live Through the Night."

MAY 19

The Roots release their eleventh album *...And Then You Shoot Your Cousin* on Def Jam.

Debuting at #11 on the *Billboard* 200, the ambitious concept album examined violence and other self-destructive behaviors in society. It featured samples from singers Nina Simone and Mary Lou Williams as well as avant-garde electronic artist Michel Chion. The album's title was a reference to KRS-One's 1997 single "Step into a World."

JUNE 3

50 Cent releases his fifth studio album *Animal Ambition* on G Unit.

Debuting at #4 on the *Billboard* 200 and topping the R&B/Hip-Hop chart, the album's eleven tracks were all released as singles, including the hit "Pilot" which reached #20 on the Rap chart and the Dr. Dre–produced "Smoke," which featured Trey Songz. Other guests on the set include Yo Gotti, Prodigy, Styles P, and Jadakiss. Jake One, Frank Dukes, and longtime collaborator Dawaun Parker all contributed production. 50 Cent made news when he announced that he would become the first major artist to accept Bitcoin payments for purchases of *Animal Ambition*.

IGGY AZALEA

JUNE 5

Rich Gang release the single "Lifestyle" on Cash Money.

Featuring Young Thug and Rich Homie Quan, the platinum-selling "Lifestyle" was produced by London on da Track. Reaching #16 on the *Billboard* Hot 100 and #4 on the R&B/Hip-Hop chart, the somewhat unintelligible single was remixed by Lil Boosie and Waka Flocka Flame.

JUNE 18

Rae Sremmurd release their debut single "No Flex Zone" on Interscope.

The platinum-selling debut by the Mississippi duo reached #36 on the *Billboard* Hot 100 and #8 on both the R&B/Hip-Hop and Rap charts. The song was produced by Mike Will Made It, who signed the group to his EarDrummers Entertainment, which would release their album *SremmLife* in 2015. The official remix of "No Flex Zone" featured Nicki Minaj and Pusha T, but a variety of artists would end up remixing the hit song.

JULY 22

Common releases his tenth studio album *Nobody's Smiling* on Def Jam.

Debuting at #6 on the *Billboard* 200 and topping the R&B/Hip-Hop chart, the thoughtful album addresses violence and poverty in Common's hometown of Chicago.

While the album was produced by Common's longtime collaborator No I.D., a wide range of collaborators worked with Common on the album, including Jhené Aiko, Big Sean, Vince Staples, and Dreezy.

JULY 25

Bobby Shmurda releases his debut single "Hot Nigga" on Epic.

Reaching #6 on the *Billboard* Hot 100, the platinum-selling single is a freestyle over a Jahlil Beats track originally used on Lloyd Banks's 2012 song "Jackpot." The song spawned the Shmoney dance, a viral craze inspired by the song's music video.

A remix of the song featured Chris Brown, Jadakiss, Fabolous, Yo Gotti, Busta Rhymes, and Rowdy Rebel.

AUGUST 4

Nicki Minaj releases the single "Anaconda" on Young Money.

The lead single to Minaj's third album, *The Pinkprint*, which reached #2 on the *Billboard* Hot 100 charts, topping the R&B/Hip-Hop chart, is one of the biggest singles of Minaj's career and her highest charting US single to date. The song extensively samples Sir Mix-A-Lot's multi-platinum 1992 hit "Baby Got Back."

Several weeks later, Minaj released the video for "Anaconda," which broke the record for most streams in its first twenty-four hours, with close to twenty million views.

AUGUST 11

DJ Mustard releases his debut studio album *10 Summers* on Republic.

Produced exclusively by the California producer, the debut set featured artists that included Lil Wayne, Wiz Khalifa, YG, Rick Ross, and Fabolous. Reaching #20 on the R&B/Hip-Hop chart, the party-anthem packed album included the single "Down on Me," featuring 2 Chainz and Ty Dolla $ign.

AUGUST 19

Wiz Khalifa releases his fifth album *Blacc Hollywood* on Atlantic.

Debuted at #1 on the *Billboard* 200, the gold-selling set brings together artists like Nicki Minaj and Juicy J for featured guest vocals. The album featured two singles, the DJ Mustard–produced, gold-selling "You and Your Friends," which featured Snoop Dogg and Ty Dolla $ign and the Grammy-nominated, platinum-selling "We Dem Boyz," which reached #4 on the Rap chart. It was later released with a remix that featured Nas, Rick Ross, and Schoolboy Q. Other producers included I.D. Labs, Stargate, Dr. Luke, Kane Beatz, among others.

WIZ KHALIFA

Khalifa also recorded songs with pop stars Adele and Miley Cyrus during the *Blacc Hollywood* sessions, but the songs were never released.

SEPTEMBER 1

ILoveMakonnen releases his debut single "Tuesday" on Warner.

Produced by Sonny Digital and Metro Boomin, the platinum-selling song from the Atlanta rapper featured Drake and became a crossover hit, reaching #12 on the *Billboard* Hot 100 and #2 on the R&B/Hip-Hop chart. The Grammy-nominated hit appeared on his EP *ILoveMakonnen*.

SEPTEMBER 9

Lecrae releases his seventh album *Anomaly* on Reach.

Christian rapper Lecrae's seventh album was his most commercially successful to date. With *Anomaly*, Lecrae became the first-ever artist to top both the *Billboard* 200 and the Gospel albums chart. Working with producers that included Gawvi, Tyshane, Ace Harris, and Alex Medina, the self-reflective set, which touches on a number of personal issues, was certified gold in 2016.

The track "Messengers," which featured For King & Country, won a 2015 Grammy for best contemporary Christian music performance/song. The album's third single, "All I Need Is You," was nominated for a best rap performance Grammy.

SEPTEMBER 23

Kendrick Lamar releases the single "i" on Interscope.

The Grammy-winning "i," which was produced by Rahki, was written by Lamar as a way to help him ward off depression. The song, which samples 1973's "That Lady" by the Isley Brothers, is the first song from Lamar's third album *To Pimp a Butterfly*, which was released the following year. The album version of "i" is a different recording than the single.

OCTOBER 21

T.I. releases his ninth album *Paperwork* on Columbia.

T.I.'s ninth album, inspired by turn-of-the-century classics like Jay Z's *The Blueprint* and Outkast's *Aquemini*, debuted at #2 on the *Billboard* 200. The biggest single, the platinum-selling "No Mediocre" which featured T.I. protégée Iggy Azalea, reached #33 on the *Billboard* Hot 100. Another hit was the gold-selling "About the Money," which featured fellow Atlanta rapper Young Thug.

Paperwork was executive produced by Pharrell with additional work by producers that included DJ Mustard, The-Dream, DJ Toomp, Tricky Stewart, Tommy Brown, and London on da Track. The album's roster of featured artists included Usher, The-Dream, Chris Brown, and Jeezy.

OCTOBER 24

Run the Jewels release their second studio album *Run the Jewels 2* on Mass Appeal.

The critically acclaimed follow-up to *Run the Jewels* was the second full-length collaboration from Killer Mike and El-P. The duo formed the group in part as an homage to classic rap groups like Run-D.M.C., Geto Boys, and N.W.A.

The explosive set, which reached #50 on the *Billboard* 200 and #6 on the Rap chart, featured the singles "Blockbuster Night, Pt. 1," "Oh My Darling Don't Cry," and "Close Your Eyes (And Count to Fuck)." The album featured an eclectic group of special guests including Gangsta Boo, Travis Barker, Zack de la Rocha, Diane Coffee, and Boots. A number of music publications, including *Complex* and *Pitchfork*, named *Run the Jewels 2* on their "best album of 2014" lists.

NOVEMBER 6

Azealia Banks releases her debut album *Broke with Expensive Taste* on Prospect Park.

Released after her mixtape *Fantasea*, the Harlem rapper's debut album incorporated elements of dance, rap, and pop music. It spawned four singles, including "Chasing Time."

Reaching #30 on the *Billboard* 200, *Broke with Expensive Taste* was recorded over a period of several years, after early versions of the album were rejected by Banks's initial label, Interscope Records. The critically acclaimed set featured production from Apple Juice Kid, AraabMuzik, and J. Cole.

NOVEMBER 10

Big K.R.I.T. releases his second solo studio album *Cadillactica* on Def Jam.

The Mississippi rapper's second set, which debuted at #5 on the *Billboard* 200, is an Afrofuturist concept record that incorporated elements of roots and country music. The album featured production from Terrace Martin, Alex da Kid, DJ Dahi, Jim Jonsin, and DJ Khalil, but was predominantly produced by Big K.R.I.T.

Singles from the critically acclaimed album included "Soul Food," featuring Raphael Saadiq, "Pay Attention," featuring Rico Love, and the title track. Other guests who appeared on the album included Lupe Fiasco, E-40, Wiz Khalifa, Bun B, and Devin the Dude. On the album's deluxe version, A$AP Ferg appeared on the track "Lac Lac."

NOVEMBER 25

***Nellyville*, a reality show about Nelly, premieres on BET.**

Nelly's reality show, which chronicled the single father's relationship with his two children, niece, and nephew, ran for two seasons on BET.

DECEMBER 2

Wu-Tang Clan release their sixth album *A Better Tomorrow* on Warner Bros.

The legendary Staten Island rap group's first studio release in seven years debuted at #29 on the *Billboard* 200. The album, which was produced largely by RZA, had a long, conflicted origin, with RZA and Raekwon publicly disagreeing about the direction of the album for years before its release. Singles include the Rick Rubin–produced "Ruckus in B Minor" and "Keep Watch," which featured Nathaniel, GZA, Method Man, Cappadonna, and Inspectah Deck.

DECEMBER 9

Ghostface Killah releases his eleventh studio album *36 Seasons* on Tommy Boy.

Just a week after Wu-Tang released their reunion album, Wu-Tang rapper Ghostface Killah released his eleventh studio album, which he claimed was recorded in eleven days.

Reaching #10 on the R&B/Hip-Hop chart, the concept album traces Ghostface Killah's alter ego Tony Starks's return to his Staten Island hometown after being in jail for nine years. Mainly produced by the Revelations, along with Fizzy Womack, Malik Adbul-Rahmaan, and the 45 King, the well-received set featured guest appearances by Kool G Rap, AZ, Pharoahe Monch, among others.

DECEMBER 9

J. Cole releases his third studio album *2014 Forest Hills Drive* on Roc Nation and Columbia Records.

Debuting at #1 on the *Billboard* 200, the North Carolina rapper's platinum-selling set was named for his home address in Fayetteville, North Carolina, where he lived during his teenage years.

2014 Forest Hills Drive was largely produced by J. Cole, who also worked with producers like Illmind, Phonix Beats, Willie B, and Vinylz on a number of tracks. The album's four singles, "Apparently," "Wet Dreamz," "No Role Modelz," and "Love Yourz" all reached the top forty on the Hip-Hop/R&B chart.

The album was nominated for several awards, including the 2016 Grammy for best rap album, and won the 2015 BET Award for album of the year.

DECEMBER 15

Nicki Minaj releases her third studio album *The Pinkprint* on Young Money.

Debuting at #2 on the *Billboard* 200, Minaj's blockbuster album spawned several hit singles, including the multi-platinum "Anaconda"; the Grammy-nominated "Truffle Butter," which featured Drake and Lil Wayne; the platinum-selling "The Night Is Still Young"; and "Only," which also featured Drake and Lil Wayne and a chorus by Chris Brown and topped the R&B/Hip-Hop chart. Other guests included Beyoncé, Drake, Lil Wayne, Meek Mill, Ariana Grande, Jessie Ware, and Chris Brown.

Without any of Minaj's many alter egos present on the collection of songs, *The Pinkprint* was Minaj's most personal album to date. The Grammy-nominated album, which featured production from pop A-listers like Dr. Luke and will.i.am, was executive produced by Birdman and Lil Wayne as well as Cash Money founder Ronald Williams.

2015

JANUARY 6

Rae Sremmurd release their debut studio album *Sremmlife* on Interscope Records.

The majority of the songs on the Mississippi duo's infectious debut are produced by Mike Will Made It, with additional work by Sonny Digital, Young Chop, Soundz, PackPack, Marz, Honorable C.N.O.T.E., and A+.

Debuting at #5 on the *Billboard* 200 and topping the Rap and R&B/Hip-Hop charts, the platinum-selling *Sremmlife* spawned five singles, including "No Flex Zone"; the multi-platinum "No Type," which reached #16 on the *Billboard* Hot 100; and "Throw Sum Mo," which featured Nicki Minaj and Young Thug and reached #30 on the *Billboard* Hot 100. They are also featured on the remix of "No Flex Zone."

JANUARY 7

Hip-hop drama *Empire* premieres on Fox.

The wildly successful primetime drama, which was nominated for three Emmys in its first two years, became one of the biggest mainstream moments for rap music in 2015.

The season one soundtrack debuted at #1 on the *Billboard* 200 when it was released in March, and featured original songs performed by Juicy J, Jennifer Hudson, and Mary J. Blige. Timbaland served as the executive producer and musical supervisor for the first two seasons of the show.

JANUARY 18

A$AP Yams dies of an accidental drug overdose at the age of twenty-six.

A$AP Yams was the coowner of the A$AP Worldwide record label and a close collaborator and partner of A$AP Rocky. A$AP Yams was one of the preeminent tastemakers, bloggers, and executives in New York rap during the late aughts and early teens.

JANUARY 20

Lupe Fiasco releases his fifth studio album *Tetsuo & Youth* on his label 1st & 15th Entertainment.

Debuting at #14 on the *Billboard* 200 and making several publications lists for best rap albums of 2015, the innovative set is the Chicago rapper's final album in his contentious deal with Atlantic Records. With production mainly by DJ Dahi, S1, and VohnBeatz, the thoughtful album included the single "Mission" about cancer survivors and featured the Gap Band's Charlie Wilson, who had survived cancer himself.

JANUARY 30

Kid Ink releases his third studio album *Full Speed* on RCA.

On his third album, Kid Ink enlisted pop stars on the songs that were released as singles, such as Usher and Tinashe on "Body Language" and R. Kelly and frequent collaborator Chris Brown on "Dolo." Other guests in the all-star-packed set included Migos, Trey Songz, Young Thug, and Dej Loaf.

The Los Angeles rapper topped the R&B/Hip-Hop chart with *Full Speed* and peaked at #14 on the *Billboard* 200. The catchy album featured production from Metro Boomin, DJ Mustard, Stargate, DJ Dahi, and Key Wane.

FEBRUARY 12

Drake releases *If You're Reading This It's Too Late* on Republic.

While Drake referred to the collection as a mixtape, *If You're Reading This It's Too Late* was officially released via Drake's label and ended up debuting at #1 on the *Billboard* 200. Drake surprise-released the seventeen-song album with a twelve-minute film accompanying his song "Jungle." Other singles on the well-reviewed album included "Preach," which reached #27 on the R&B/Hip-Hop chart and the multi-platinum "Energy," which reached #26 on the *Billboard* Hot 100.

The Grammy-nominated, multi-platinum set featured Lil Wayne and Travis Scott and included extensive production from Boi-1da and PartyNextDoor.

FEBRUARY 20

Chris Brown and Tyga release their debut studio album *Fan of a Fan: The Album* on RCA.

After releasing a mixtape *Fan of a Fan* in 2010, *Fan of a Fan: The Album* served as singer Chris Brown and rapper Tyga's proper collaborative debut release. Debuting at #7 on the *Billboard* 200 and topping the R&B/Hip-Hop chart, the album featured guest appearances from 50 Cent, Pusha T, Ty Dolla $ign, and Schoolboy Q. The album's lead single, "Ayo," became an international hit, charting in more than a dozen countries.

FEBRUARY 22

Common and John Legend win an Oscar for best original song for their song "Glory."

The original song, written for the movie *Selma*, also won a Golden Globe and Grammy and reached #11 on the Rap chart. At the Academy Awards, Common and John Legend, backed by a full gospel choir, delivered a moving rendition of the spiritual protest anthem, which references the Civil Rights movement and Black Lives Matter protests in Ferguson.

TYGA

KENDRICK LAMAR

FEBRUARY 24

Big Sean releases his third studio album *Dark Sky Paradise* on Def Jam.

Recorded entirely in his home studio, Big Sean's platinum-selling album debuted at #1 on the *Billboard* 200 and yielded five singles: the multi-platinum "I Don't Fuck with You," which featured E-40 and reached #11 on the *Billboard* Hot 100; the gold-selling "Paradise"; the multi-platinum "Blessings," which featured Drake and reached #9 on the R&B/Hip-Hop charts; the Grammy-nominated "One Man Can Change the World," which featured John Legend and Kanye West; and the gold-selling "Play No Games," which featured Chris Brown and Ty Dolla $ign.

Kanye West and Big Sean coexecutive produced the album, which also featured production from DJ Dahi, Mike Will Made It, DJ Mustard, Boi-1da, Metro Boomin, and Key Wane.

MARCH 10

Wiz Khalifa and Charlie Puth release their single "See You Again" on Atlantic.

Written for the soundtrack to *Furious 7* as a tribute to the late actor Paul Walker, Wiz Khalifa's duet with pop singer Charlie Puth was a massive crossover success, sitting at #1 on the *Billboard* Hot 100 for three months. The multi-platinum "See You Again" had the most digital sales of any song globally in 2015. Puth and Khalifa were nominated for three Grammys for their collaboration.

MARCH 15

Kendrick Lamar releases his third studio album *To Pimp a Butterfly* on Top Dawg/Aftermath/Interscope.

To Pimp a Butterfly debuted at #1 on the *Billboard* 200 and went on to be the most critically acclaimed album of 2015. The Grammy-winning album featured an extensive list of collaborators, producers, and jazz musicians including Thundercat, Kamasi Washington, Flying Lotus, Pharrell Williams, Snoop Dogg, James Fauntleroy, and Bilal.

To Pimp a Butterfly, which was executive produced by Dr. Dre and Anthony "Top Dawg" Tiffith, tackles a number of political and personal issues. The platinum-selling set spawned three Grammy-winning singles: "i," "These Walls," and "Alright," which became an anthem for the Black Lives Matter movement.

CHUCK D:

His subject matter is obviously revolutionary, not just subject wise but sonically also. Kendrick Lamar is hip-hop's hashtag challenge, because there are moments in *TPAB* when you can see him challenging himself. You see the revolutionary but also a black man who struggles with his imperfections. Listening to the remixed Tupac interview that he used on *TPAB* shows his innovative mind at work. On this, he brings forth the pure spirit of two of our greatest groundbreakers, by starting with George Clinton and rounding it out with Pac on "Mortal Man."

MARCH 23

Action Bronson releases his second studio album *Mr. Wonderful* on Atlantic.

On his sophomore release, the Queens rapper worked with producers Mark Ronson, 40, and the Alchemist, and enlisted guests Party Supplies and Big Body Bes, among others, for guest appearances. Four singles were released for the fun set, including "Baby Blue," which featured Chance the Rapper and cracked the *Billboard* Hot 100. Debuting at #7 on the *Billboard* 200, the album featured more singing and live instrumentation than previous Action Bronson albums and sampled artists like Billy Joel and the Emotions.

MARCH 23

Earl Sweatshirt releases *I Don't Like Shit, I Don't Go Outside* on Columbia.

Debuting at #12 on the *Billboard* 200, *I Don't Like Shit* was Earl Sweatshirt's second solo album after the rapper came to prominence as a member of the Odd Future collective.

Vince Staples, Dash, Na'kel, and Wiki all made guest appearances on the dark set, which was coproduced by Left Brain and Thebe Kgositsile (who is Earl Sweatshirt). The critically acclaimed album made many publications' year-end lists for album of the year.

MARCH 31

Ludacris releases his ninth album *Ludaversal* on Def Jam.

The Atlanta rapper's ninth album, his first in more than five years, was produced in part by Mike Will Made It, Da Internz, Rico Love, and Giorgio Tuinfort. The album debuted at #3 on the *Billboard* 200, making it Ludacris's eighth overall top five-charting album. The album included "Ocean Skies," a tribute to the rapper's late father that featured Monica and the lead single "Good Lovin'," which featured Miguel and reached #30 on the R&B/Hip-Hop chart. Other guests on the album included Usher, Big Sean, and Big K.R.I.T., as well as Rick Ross and John Legend on the deluxe edition.

MARCH 31

Wale releases his fourth studio album *The Album About Nothing* on Atlantic.

Debuting at #1 on the *Billboard* 200, R&B/Hip-Hop and rap charts, *The Album About Nothing* yielded two singles: "The Body," which featured Jeremih and reached #26 on the R&B/Hip-Hop chart, and "The Matrimony," which featured Usher and reached #17 on the R&B/Hip-Hop chart. Other guests on the album included J. Cole and SZA, as well as production by Soundz, Jake One, DJ Khalil, DJ Dahi, J Gramm, among others.

At the time of its release, Wale called *The Album About Nothing* the most personal record of his career. The album's title, which dates back to Wale's 2008 mixtape *The Mixtape About Nothing*, was inspired by the '90s sitcom *Seinfeld*, known as "the show about nothing." Jerry Seinfeld served as a mentor to Wale on the album, visiting the rapper in the studio during recording sessions.

APRIL 13

Tyler, the Creator releases *Cherry Bomb* on Odd Future.

Debuting at #4 on the *Billboard* 200, the album incorporates a wide range of the rapper's eclectic influences, including N.E.R.D., Joy Division, and Ronnie McNeir. *Cherry Bomb* was coproduced by Tyler, the Creator and Incubus guitarist Mike Einziger and featured guest appearances from Pharrell, Kanye West, Lil Wayne, and Schoolboy Q.

"Smuckers," which featured Kanye West and Lil Wayne, was originally intended to be a song for Jay Z and Kanye West's collaborative 2011 album *Watch the Throne.*

APRIL 17

Young Thug releases his *Barter 6* mixtape on Atlantic.

The mixtape, which featured guests T.I., Birdman, and Boosie Badazz, was largely produced by Wheezy and London on da Tracks, with Young Thug serving as executive producer. Peaking at #22 on the *Billboard* 200 and #5 on the R&B/Hip-Hop chart, the mixtape spawned two singles: "Check" and "Constantly Hating," which featured Birdman. Other guests on the set included Duke, Boosie Badazz, Young Dolph, and Jacquees, among others.

Young Thug originally planned to call the album *Carter 6*, in reference to Lil Wayne's *Tha Carter* albums, but after a public feud between the two rappers, the name was changed to *Barter 6* for legal reasons.

TYLER, THE CREATOR

APRIL 27

Yelawolf releases his second studio album *Love Story* on Shady/Interscope.

The Alabama rapper's second set, which debuted at #3 on the *Billboard* 200 and topped the R&B/Hip-Hop and Rap charts, was executive produced by Eminem, who also guested on the track "Best Friend." The emotional album sampled a variety of artists including Outkast, Snoop Dogg and Dr. Dre, and Patsy Cline.

Yelawolf wrote "Have a Great Flight" about the death of his grandmother. At the time of the album's release, Yelawolf said it's the only song he's ever written by himself on guitar.

APRIL 28

Raekwon releases his sixth studio album *Fly International Luxurious Art* on Caroline.

The Wu-Tang Clan rapper's sixth solo album, which reached #6 on the Rap charts, yielded three singles: "All About You," which featured Estelle; "Somebody Kill It," which featured Melanie Fiona; and "Wall to Wall," which featured French Montana and Busta Rhymes.

The stylish album featured a deep list of guest artists that included A$AP Rocky, Rick Ross, Snoop Dogg, 2 Chainz, and Ghostface Killah and producers included Jerry Wonda, Scram Jones, S1, and Swizz Beatz, among others.

MEEK MILL

MAY 5

Silentó releases his debut single "Watch Me (Whip/Nae Nae)" on Capitol.

With its accompanying dance, Silentó's debut single became a crossover hit, reaching #3 on the *Billboard* Hot 100. Several months after the song debuted, seventeen-year-old rapper Silentó released a music video for the multi-platinum song, which went on to amass more than 1.2 billion views on YouTube.

MAY 12

Snoop Dogg releases his thirteenth studio album *Bush* on Columbia.

Artists ranging from Kendrick Lamar to Gwen Stefani to Rick Ross all appeared on the album, with Pharrell Williams serving as executive producer and providing backup vocals. Reaching #14 on the *Billboard* 200 and topping the R&B/Hip-Hop charts, the album served as a reunion for Snoop and Pharrell, who had collaborated on a series of hits like "Beautiful" and "Drop It Like It's Hot" that rejuvenated Snoop Dogg's career in the early aughts. The album yielded three singles: "Peaches N Cream" which featured the Gap Band's Charlie Wilson; "So Many Pros"; and "California Roll," which featured Stevie Wonder and reached #15 on the R&B/Hip-Hop charts.

MAY 18

Nicki Minaj and Beyoncé release "Feeling Myself" video.

Nicki Minaj and Beyoncé cowrote this song off Minaj's *The Pinkprint* alongside SZA and Hit-Boy. Reaching #12 on the R&B charts and #39 on the *Billboard* Hot 100. The video, which included footage of Minaj and Beyoncé partying at Coachella, was released exclusively on Tidal.

MAY 26

A$AP Rocky releases his second studio album *At. Long. Last. A$AP* on RCA.

Debuting at #1 on the *Billboard* 200, the ambitious album featured a slew of special guests, including Future, M.I.A., Kanye West, and Lil Wayne.

The album's second single, the gold-selling "Everyday," featured Miguel, Mark Ronson, and a notable vocal sample from Rod Stewart, who was credited on the track as a featured artist. In addition to Rod Stewart, the album featured samples from unlikely sources such as Leonard Cohen and Lucero. The video for the gold-selling single "L$D" was nominated for a Grammy Award.

Danger Mouse, Juicy J, A$AP Rocky, and A$AP Yams, who had died just a few months earlier, all served as executive producers, with Kanye West, DJ Khalil, Jim Jonsin, and Hudson Mohawke, among others, contributing production.

CHUCK D:

As a fresh voice in the rap game Rocky, along with his Harlemesque/Houstonized crew, have taken a hip-hop spoon and mixed Midwest and East Coast sonics with rock and blues flavors. His rap collaboration combos are turning out songs that many are calling experimental, but it's actually magical when an album can mix in Lil Wayne with Rod Stewart. I've always favored groups over solos especially in the second decade of the millennium, so the A$AP collective movement is no doubt very interesting to me to watch. Thus it was cool collaborating with his partner A$AP Ferg.

MAY 26

Boosie Badazz releases his sixth studio album *Touch Down 2 Cause Hell* on Atlantic.

Debuting at #3 on the *Billboard* 200, the Louisiana rapper's well-received set was released just a year after he was released from prison for drug possession. The rapper wrote more than five hundred songs while in jail. The visceral album spawned three singles: "On That Level," featuring Webbie, "Like a Man," featuring Rich Homie Quan, and "Retaliation."

Touch Down 2 Cause Hell featured guest appearances from artists like Young Thug, T.I., Jeezy, J. Cole, Rick Ross, and Chris Brown.

JUNE 20

Vince Staples releases his debut album *Summertime '06* on Def Jam.

The critically acclaimed album from the California rapper is his full-length label release, following his 2014 EP *Hell Can Wait.* The album, which collected stories from the rapper's violent Long Beach upbringing, harkened back to the SoCal gangsta rap of the early '90s.

Reaching #39 on the *Billboard* 200, Staples's debut album featured guest appearances from Jhené Aiko, Joey Fatts, and Daley and spawned three singles: "Señorita"; "Get Paid," which featured Desi Mo; and "Norf Norf." The inventive album was mainly produced by No I.D., with additional work from DJ Dahi, Clams Casino, Mikky Ekko, and Christian Rich.

JUNE 28

P. Diddy leads Bad Boy reunion at BET Awards with Lil' Kim, 112, French Montana, the L.O.X., Faith Evans, and Ma$e.

To celebrate the twentieth anniversary of his Bad Boy label, P. Diddy led the Bad Boy family through a ten-song, ten-minute medley at the awards show. They performed hits like "Peaches and Cream," and "I Need a Girl Pt. 2," debuted a new song with Pharrell, and paid tribute to the Notorious B.I.G. The BET Awards performance inspired the label to reunite during the summer of 2016 for a twenty-four-date Bad Boy Family Reunion tour.

JUNE 29

Meek Mill releases his second studio album *Dreams Worth More Than Money* on Dream Chasers.

With Rick Ross serving as executive producer, *Dreams Worth More Than Money* featured a star-studded list of guests, including The Weeknd, Puff Daddy, Future, and Jeremih.

Debuting at #1 on the *Billboard* 200, the gold-selling album yielded three singles: "Check"; the platinum-selling "All Eyes on You," featuring Chris Brown and Nicki Minaj; and the platinum-selling "R.I.C.O." featuring Drake.

Shortly after the album's release, Meek Mill began an ongoing feud with Drake by suggesting on Twitter that the reason Drake didn't promote Meek Mill's album was because Drake didn't write his own raps.

JULY 4

Lil Wayne releases *Free Weezy Album* on Young Money/Republic.

Free Weezy Album, which sampled James Brown and the Animals, was released exclusively on Tidal, where it was streamed more than ten million times in its first week.

The album-mixtape featured Wiz Khalifa and Jeezy, with production from London on da Track, Kane Beatz, and longtime collaborator Infamous, among others.

The set was released six months after the New Orleans rapper sued Bryan "Birdman" Williams for $51 million over withheld money. The lawsuit also involved Lil Wayne's ongoing struggle with Young Money Entertainment over the release of his *Tha Carter V* album.

JULY 17

Future releases his third album *DS2* on Epic.

Debuting at #1 on the *Billboard* 200, the platinum-selling, emotionally charged album yielded three singles, including the platinum-selling "Fuck Up Some Commas"; "Where Ya At," featuring Drake; and "Stick Talk." *DS2 (Dirty Sprite 2)* was the follow-up to Future's 2011 debut mixtape, *Dirty Sprite.*

Produced largely by Metro Boomin and Southside, *DS2* was one of the most critically acclaimed rap albums of the year, making a number of publications' year-end lists for best albums.

JULY 31

Migos releases their debut album *Yung Rich Nation* on 300 Entertainment.

The creative debut from the Georgia rap trio of Quavo, Offset, and Takeoff featured production from Zaytoven, Murda Beatz, and Honorable C.N.O.T.E. and guest appearances from Young Thug and Chris Brown. The Deko-produced club hit "One Time" reached #34 on the R&B/Hip-Hop chart.

Debuting at #17 on the *Billboard* 200 and peaking at #3 on the Rap chart, the album was released just months after two-thirds of the group was arrested on drug and gun charges during a show in Georgia.

JULY 31

Drake releases "Hotline Bling" single on OVO Sound.

Drake's crossover, multi-platinum hit was produced and cowritten by Nineteen85. The lead single to Drake's 2016 album *Views* was released in July, but didn't reach #2 on the *Billboard* Hot 100 until the song's video was released in October. The "Hotline Bling" video was financed entirely by Apple, and was released initially as an Apple Music exclusive. The "Hotline Bling" video was heavily influenced by the light installations of American spatial artist James Turrell.

Several artists, including Lil Wayne and Erykah Badu, released their own versions of the song in 2015.

AUGUST 6

***Hamilton* opens on Broadway.**

The Broadway play, which was created by and starred Lin-Manuel Miranda, dramatized the life of founding father Alexander Hamilton. Performed entirely in rap verse, it provided Broadway with its first mainstream hip-hop musical. Miranda, a diehard fan, littered the play with allusions to his favorite rappers, like Notorious B.I.G., Lauryn Hill, and Eminem.

Hamilton's Broadway cast included Daveed Diggs, Leslie Odom Jr., and Christopher Jackson. The play's original cast recording, released a month after the play debuted on Broadway, eventually reached #3 on the *Billboard* 200. *Hamilton* has won 11 Tonys, a Grammy, and an NAACP Image Award.

CHUCK D:

Hip-hop and rap is a tool that can verbally transmit information of any kind, whether history, street life, poli-tricks, or anything else that's current. The fact that mainstream USA has a new successful vehicle running that uses it to tell us something relevant, proves that. I had a ball playing the soundtrack on *...And You Don't Stop!* show.

AUGUST 7

Dr. Dre releases his third studio album *Compton* on Apple Music.

Dr. Dre's long-awaited gold-selling set was his first full-length release in sixteen years, serving as the follow-up to the rapper's genre-defining classic *2001*. The release of *Compton* coincided with, and was inspired by, the release of the 2015 film *Straight Outta Compton*, a hip-hop biopic about N.W.A. It was originally released on Apple Music and the iTunes store, with a wider release on August 21.

Debuting at #2 on the *Billboard* 200, the ambitious and critically acclaimed *Compton* featured guest appearances from Eminem, Snoop Dogg, Ice Cube, Kendrick Lamar, Xzibit, and Anderson .Paak.

AUGUST 14

Universal Pictures's *Straight Outta Compton* opens in theaters.

The acclaimed movie, which traces the rise of N.W.A, was directed by F. Gary Gray and coproduced, in part, by Dr. Dre and Ice Cube. *Straight Outta Compton* grossed more than $200 million at the box office and was nominated for an Academy Award for best original screenplay.

Apart from Dr. Dre's *Compton* album, the official soundtrack to the film, featuring the music of N.W.A, Eazy-E, Ice Cube, Dr. Dre, and Snoop Dogg, debuted at #2 on the *Billboard* 200.

The movie was filmed in Compton, and starred Jason Mitchell as Eazy-E, Corey Hawkins as Dr. Dre, and O'Shea Jackson Jr., Ice Cube's son, as Ice Cube.

AUGUST 27

Macklemore & Ryan Lewis release the single "Downtown" featuring Melle Mel, Kool Moe Dee, and Grandmaster Caz.

"Downtown" was the lead single from *This Unruly Mess I've Made*, Macklemore's follow-up album to their breakthrough crossover success *The Heist.* For the song, the duo recruited pioneering late '70s/ early '80s hip-hop legends Melle Mel, Kool Moe Dee, and Grandmaster Caz. The song provided the three rappers with their greatest bout of exposure in decades. Reaching #12 on the *Billboard* Hot 100, the song has been certified platinum.

AUGUST 30

Nicki Minaj performs with Taylor Swift at the VMAs.

Minaj's high-profile performance with Taylor Swift at the 2015 VMAs came after the two had created a mild controversy the previous month arguing about VMA nominations on Twitter. After Minaj opened the show with a performance of "Trini Dem Girls," Swift joined the rapper for Minaj's "The Night Is Still Young" and a brief snippet of Swift's "Bad Blood."

SEPTEMBER 5

Travis Scott releases his debut studio album *Rodeo* on Epic.

The Texas rapper's debut reached #3 on *Billboard* 200 and topped the Rap chart in its first week. The album spawned two singles: the gold-selling "3500," which featured Future and 2 Chainz and reached #25 on the R&B/Hip-Hop chart, and the double platinum "Antidote," which reached #16 on the *Billboard* Hot 100. Other high-profile guests on the gold-selling album included Juicy J, Kanye West, Justin Bieber, Chief Keef, The Weeknd, and Young Thug.

Scott handled most of the production on the set with help from Metro Boomin, DJ Dahi, Kanye West, Pharrell Williams, Noah Goldstein, Terrace Martin, The Weeknd, and Zaytoven.

SEPTEMBER 11

Jay Rock's second album *90059* is released on Top Dawg.

90059 was Jay Rock's first studio album in four years since his 2011 debut *Follow Me Home*. Debuting at #16 on the *Billboard* 200 and topping the Rap chart, the SoCal rapper's sophomore set featured guest appearances from Kendrick Lamar, Busta Rhymes, and SZA.

The album yielded three singles: "Money Trees Deuce," which served as a sequel to Kendrick Lamar's *good kid, m.A.A.d. city* album track "Money Trees"; "Gumbo"; and "90059," featuring Lance Skiiiwalker.

SEPTEMBER 18

Mac Miller releases his third studio album *GO:OD AM* on Warner Bros.

Debuting at #4 on the *Billboard* 200, the Pennsylvania rapper's major label debut dealt with a number of personal topics and produced two singles: "100 Grandkids," which reached #100 on the *Billboard* Hot 100 and "Weekend," featuring Miguel. Other guests on the album included Lil B, Chief Keef, and Ab-Soul, as well as production by Tyler, the Creator, Thundercat, DJ Dahi, I.D. Labs, and Sounwave.

SEPTEMBER 20

Drake and Future release *What a Time to Be Alive* on Young Money.

The inaugural mixtape from Drake and Future, which debuted at #1 on the *Billboard* Hot 100, was primarily produced by noted hip-hop producer Metro Boomin. The two rappers had regularly collaborated in the studio over the years, and had toured together earlier in the year.

The album spawned the multi-platinum single "Jumpman," which reached #12 on the *Billboard* Hot 100.

SEPTEMBER 25

Fetty Wap releases his self-titled debut on his own label RGF Productions.

Fetty Wap's debut album became one of the surprise blockbuster releases of 2015, topping the *Billboard* 200 and R&B/Hip-Hop chart and going platinum in 2016. The album spawned four *Billboard* Hot100 top ten singles, including "679," "My Way," "Again," and "Trap Queen," which earned Fetty Wap two Grammy nominations. The album extensively featured Fetty Wap's Paterson, New Jersey, rap trio Remy Boyz, which also included rappers P-Dice and Monty.

OCTOBER 9

The Game releases his sixth studio album *Documentary 2* on eOne.

Debuting at #2 on the *Billboard* 200, the highly anticipated set was a sequel to the LA rapper's debut album *The Documentary*, released a decade earlier in 2005.

Documentary 2 featured a who's who of West Coast rap, including Kendrick Lamar, Snoop Dogg, Dr. Dre, and Ice Cube. Other guests include Drake, will.i.am, Future, Q-Tip, Dej Loaf, and Kanye West, who appeared on the lead single "100," which reached #25 on the R&B/Hip-Hop chart. Producers included will.i.am, DJ Premier, Boi-1da, Kanye West, and Mike Will Made It.

OCTOBER 13

Flo Rida releases the single "My House" on Atlantic.

Reaching #4 on the *Billboard* Hot 100, the multi-platinum single was the third from Flo Rida's *My House* EP. "My House" gave Flo Rida his eleventh top ten single in the United States.

OCTOBER 23

DJ Khaled releases his eighth album *I Changed a Lot* on his own label We the Best.

Like his previous sets, DJ Khaled's album was a star-studded collection of collaborations. The album yielded four singles: "They Don't Love You No More," which featured Jay Z, Meek Mill, Rick Ross, and French Montana; the gold-selling "Hold You Down," featuring Chris Brown, August Alsina, Future, and Jeremih, which reached #10 on the R&B/Hip-Hop chart; the gold-selling "How Many Times," featuring Chris Brown, Lil Wayne, and Big Sean; and "Gold Slugs," which featured Chris Brown, August Alsina, and Fetty Wap. Other guests including Usher, John Legend, Fabolous, Lil Wayne, and Future also appeared on the album, which debuted at #12 on the *Billboard* Hot 100. DJ Khaled produced a number of the tracks, along with others, including Mike Zombie, the Beat Bully, Lee on the Beats, and Danja.

NOVEMBER 13

Logic releases his second studio album *The Incredible True Story* on Def Jam.

The Maryland rapper's sophomore set debuted at #3 on the *Billboard* 200, topped the R&B/Hip-Hop and Rap charts, and was certified gold. The experimental album's eighteen tracks outlined an ambitious, imaginative storyline set a hundred years in the future. *The Incredible True Story* sampled tracks from a wide range of artists, including Travis Scott, Grizzly Bear, and Mayer Hawthorne. Two songs from the album "Fade Away" and "I Am the Greatest" hit #44 and #50 on the R&B/Hip-Hop chart respectively.

NOVEMBER 13

Ty Dolla $ign releases his debut studio album *Free TC* on Atlantic Records.

Ty Dolla $ign's anticipated full-length studio debut came after the rapper spent several years releasing mixtapes and EPs. The album's name refers to the rapper's brother, Gabriel "TC" Griffin, who at the time of the album's release had been incarcerated for eleven years. A year later, the rapper released a short documentary about his brother's case also titled *Free TC*.

Debuting at #14 on the *Billboard* 200, the critically acclaimed album produced a number of singles, including the platinum-selling "Blasé," which featured Future and Rae Sremmurd and reached #20 on the R&B/Hip-Hop chart. Other guests included Kendrick Lamar, Kanye West, Wiz Khalifa, Diddy, Fetty Wap, Babyface, Trey Songz, E-40, R. Kelly, and Jagged Edge. The ambitious set includes production from high-profile talent like Babyface, Benny Blanco, DJ Mustard, Stargate, and Metro Boomin.

NOVEMBER 13

Jeezy releases his sixth studio album *Church in These Streets* on Def Jam.

Debuting at #4 on the *Billboard* 200, the latest set from the Atlanta rapper spawned four singles: "God," "Church in These Streets," "Gold Bottles," and "Sweet Life." The latter single featured Janelle Monáe. Monica appeared on the album's final track, "Forgive Me." The album included production by talent that included Zaytoven, London on da Track, TM88, and Southside.

NOVEMBER 20

Jadakiss releases his fourth studio album *Top 5 Dead or Alive* on Def Jam.

Debuting at #4 on the *Billboard* 200 and topping the R&B/Hip-Hop chart, Jadakiss's critically acclaimed set featured Future, Lil Wayne, Jeezy, Wiz Khalifa, Puff Daddy, Nas, Akon, and Ne-Yo, among others.

Swizz Beatz, who appeared on the track "Jason," also contributed production, along with producers including Rico Beats, Scram Jones, and Just Blaze.

DECEMBER 6

Desiigner releases his single "Panda" on Def Jam.

The debut single from the eighteen-year-old Brooklyn rapper Desiigner became a massive crossover success, topping the *Billboard* Hot 100 charts the following spring. The triple-platinum hit inspired a number of remixes by artists like Lupe Fiasco, T-Pain, Meek Mill, and Lil' Kim. The song was sampled by Kanye West on his 2016 album *The Life of Pablo*.

DECEMBER 12

Rick Ross releases his eighth studio album *Black Market* on Def Jam.

Black Market, the rapper's fourth studio album over a two-year stretch, detailed Ross's brief time spent behind bars on album tracks like "Foreclosure."

Debuted at #6 on the *Billboard* 200, the set included guest appearances by a number of artists including Mariah Carey, Mary J. Blige, Nas, Future, Cee-Lo Green, John Legend, and Chris Brown, who appeared on the single "Sorry," which reached #32 on the R&B/Hip-Hop chart. The album included production from DJ Mustard, DJ Khaled, Jahlil Beats, and Jake One.

2016

JANUARY 15

Anderson .Paak releases his second album *Malibu* on Steel Wool.

Malibu was released following Anderson .Paak's extensive collaboration on Dr. Dre's album *Compton*, released the previous year. One of the most stylistically diverse rap albums of the year, blending soul, gospel, funk, R&B, jazz, and rock, the album included production from Madlib, DJ Khalil, Kaytranada, and 9th Wonder. The Grammy-nominated album, which reached #9 on the R&B/Hip-Hop chart, included the single "Am I Wrong?" featuring Schoolboy Q and "Room in Here" featuring Sonyae Elise and The Game.

FEBRUARY 5

Young Thug releases the mixtape *I'm Up* on Atlantic.

Debuting at #22 on the *Billboard* 200, the Georgia rapper's latest release featured production from Wheezy, Mike Will Made It, London on da Track, and Metro Boomin. *I'm Up* was the first of several mixtapes Young Thug released throughout 2016. Guests on the mixtape included two members of Migos, Quavo and Offset, along with Lil Durk, Ralo, Solo Lucci, and Young Butta.

CHUCK D:

Like many of his notable predecessors, Young Thug knows how to mix his videos and his music's messages into that hyped hip-hop animation that makes the visual age such a valuable tool for explaining even the most complex and socially challenging issues.

FEBRUARY 6

Future releases his fourth studio album *Evol* on Epic.

Debuting at #1 on the *Billboard* 200, the well-reviewed, gold-selling set was Future's third #1 album in just seven months. Shortly before its release, Future explained that the album's title was the word "love" spelled backward. Just weeks before *Evol*, Future released his *Purple Reign* mixtape.

Future coexecutive produced the album alongside Metro Boomin. The only guest on the album is The Weeknd on the multi-platinum single "Low Life," which reached #18 on the *Billboard* Hot 100.

FEBRUARY 14

Kanye West releases his seventh studio album *Life of Pablo* on Roc-A-Fella.

The gospel-inspired ambitious album, which debuted at #1 on the *Billboard* 200, West's seventh consecutive #1, featured collaborations with Chance the Rapper, Kirk Franklin, Desiigner, Rihanna, Kid Cudi, Chris Brown, Frank Ocean, The Weeknd, Kendrick Lamar, and André 3000. The album spawned the singles the Grammy-nominated "Famous," "Father Stretch My Hands," and "Fade."

Kanye West produced the Grammy-nominated album alongside a host of coproducers including Rick Rubin, Chance the Rapper, Mike Dean, Noah Goldstein, and Hudson Mohawke.

The critically acclaimed set was debuted a few days before its release at Madison Square Garden during West's Yeezy Season Three fashion show. West continued working on and altering the album even once it was released as an exclusive stream on Tidal, changing the track list and tinkering with the mixes of several songs long after it was available for public consumption.

FEBRUARY 15

Grammy-winner Kendrick Lamar performs "The Blacker the Berry" and "Alright" at the awards show.

Performing in a shackled chain gang with his band behind bars on a prison stage set, Lamar's controversial performance provided one of the highlights of the evening. Lamar led all artists by winning Grammys that night, including for best rap album. Lamar was also nominated for album and song of the year.

FEBRUARY 19

Yo Gotti releases his fifth studio album *The Art of Hustle* on Epic Records.

The Art of Hustle debuted at #4 on the *Billboard* 200, giving the veteran Memphis rapper his highest charting album to date. The well-reviewed set came after a particularly prolific period for Yo Gotti, who released five mixtapes the previous year. The album spawned two singles: "Down in the DM," which reached #13 on the *Billboard* Hot 100 and the gold-selling "Law," which featured E-40 and reached #29 on the R&B/Hip-Hop charts. Other guests on the album included Lil Wayne, Future, and Timbaland, who also produced a track. Other producers included Kane Beatz, Street Symphony, Drumma Boy, Bangladesh, and Neenyo.

FEBRUARY 26

Macklemore & Ryan Lewis release their second studio album *This Unruly Mess I've Made* on Macklemore LLC.

Macklemore's highly anticipated follow-up to their blockbuster album *The Heist* debuted at #4 on the *Billboard* 200 and topped the R&B/Hip-Hop charts. On the song "White Privilege," Macklemore addresses his position in rap as a highly successful white rapper. Elsewhere on the album, he deals with his struggles with success and addiction.

The set featured an eclectic group of guests from various genres, including Ed Sheeran, Chance the Rapper, DJ Premier, Leon Bridges, YG, Anderson .Paak, KRS-One, Melle Mel, Kool Moe Dee, and Grandmaster Caz.

MARCH 2

Fat Joe and Remy Ma release the single "All the Way Up" featuring French Montana on RNG/Empire.

The song, which was Fat Joe's most successful single in a decade, was seen as a major comeback for the New York rapper. The platinum-selling track reached #27 on the *Billboard* Hot 100 and broke the top ten on the R&B/Hip-Hop chart.

"All the Way Up" updates Fat Joe's retro leanings for contemporary pop audiences with its mix of horns and modern drum programming. A remix to the single was released in May featuring a high-profile guest verse from Jay Z.

MARCH 4

2 Chainz releases *ColleGrove* on Def Jam.

Debuting at #4 on the *Billboard* 200, the album was initially set to be a joint release between Lil Wayne and 2 Chainz and the title is a mashup of the hometowns of Lil Wayne and 2 Chainz, Hollygrove in New Orleans, and College Park, Georgia. Due to contractual issues, the album is a 2 Chainz release, with Lil Wayne appearing on all but three tracks.

Production credits on the lyrically dexterous set include Mannie Fresh, London on da Track, Metro Boomin, TM88, and Mike Will Made It.

MARCH 4

Kendrick Lamar releases *untitled unmastered* on Top Dawg/Aftermath/Interscope.

The album was a collection of previously unreleased outtakes and demos from the sessions for Lamar's 2015 opus *To Pimp a Butterfly*. Lamar had performed several of *untitled unmastered*'s songs on television before the album's release. The album, which debuted at #1 on the *Billboard* 200, was surprise-released with no promotion or announcement barely a year after the release of *To Pimp a Butterfly*. The critically acclaimed album featured instrumentation and vocals from collaborators Thundercat, SZA, Cee-Lo Green, Robert Glasper, Jay Rock, and Terrace Martin.

MARCH 11

Flatbush Zombies self-release *3001: A Laced Odyssey* on Glorious Dead Records.

Despite being released without any label, the debut studio album from the independent Brooklyn rap trio debuted at #10 on the *Billboard* 200 and #2 on the R&B/Hip-Hop chart. On the album, the group, comprised of Meechy Darko, Zombie Juice, and Erick "the Architect" Elliott, offered their own psychedelic take on an otherwise throwback '90s New York rap sound.

APRIL 1

Big Sean and Jhené Aiko release *Twenty88* on Def Jam.

Big Sean and Jhené Aiko's debut collaborative album debuted at #5 on the *Billboard* 200. Calling themselves Twenty88, the Los Angles singer and Detroit rapper had collaborated several times before on previous Big Sean albums. 1990s R&B duo K-Ci & JoJo appeared on the track "2 Minute Warning."

APRIL 8

N.W.A is inducted into the Rock & Roll Hall of Fame.

Ice Cube, Dr. Dre, MC Ren, and DJ Yella accepted the award on stage alongside Kathie Wright, the mother of late rapper Eazy-E. The group was inducted by Kendrick Lamar, who introduced them with a personal speech honoring the rap outfit known as "the world's most dangerous group."

N.W.A did not perform at the event, but their memorable induction speech included Ice Cube's impassioned definition of rock 'n' roll. "Rock 'n' roll is not conforming to the people who came before you, but creating your own path in music and in life," he said. "That is rock 'n' roll, and that is us."

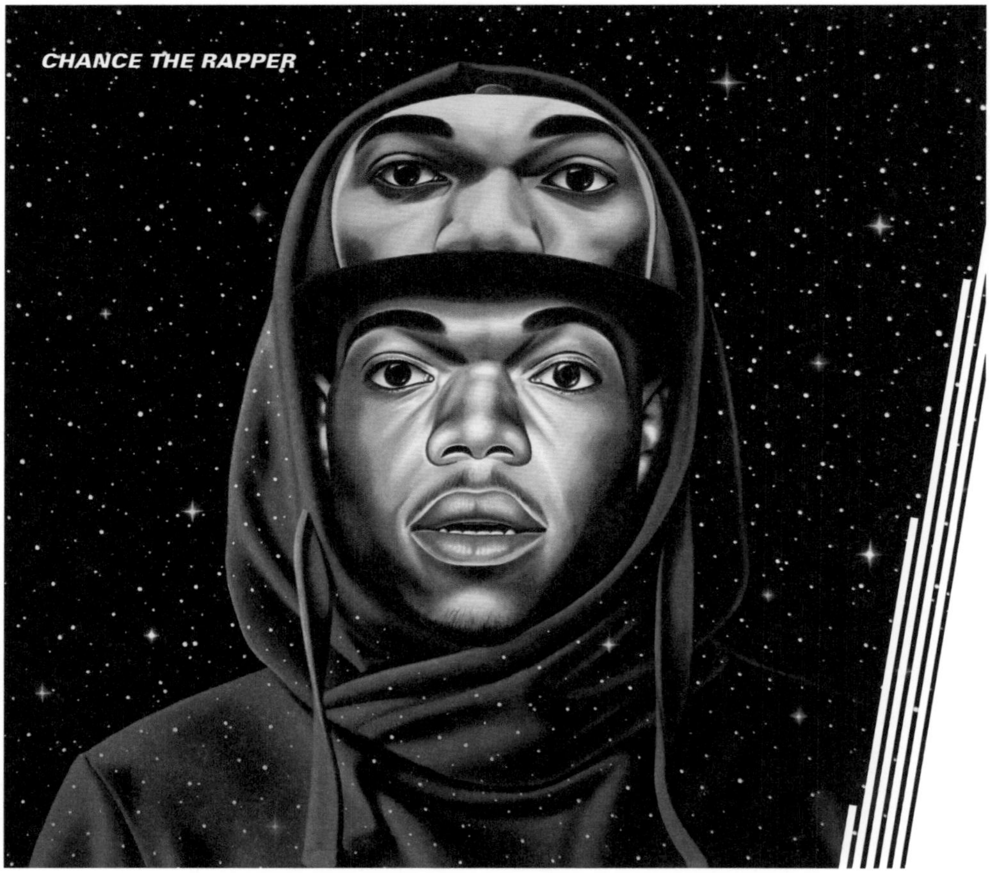

APRIL 15

J Dilla's posthumous *The Diary* is released on Mass Appeal.

Originally recorded in 2001 and 2002, *The Diary* was legendary rapper and producer J Dilla's last planned release before he died in 2006 of a blood disease. Reaching #5 on the Rap chart and #6 on the R&B/Hip-Hop chart, the album featured J Dilla's vocals and production, and included vocals from rappers including Snoop Dogg, Kokane, and Bilal.

APRIL 22

A$AP Ferg releases his second studio album *Always Strive and Prosper* on RCA.

One of the eclectic album's central themes is family, with several songs directly addressing specific family members, such as his uncle and grandmother. The New York rapper's grandmother delivers spoken word at one point on the album. Debuting at #8 on the *Billboard* 200, the album featured two singles: the gold-selling "New Level," which featured Future and reached #30 on the R&B/Hip-Hop chart and "Back Hurt," featuring Migos.

The impressive cast of featured artists on the ambitious set included Missy Elliott, Skrillex, Chuck D, Schoolboy Q, Rick Ross, Chris Brown, Big Sean, and Ty Dolla $ign. The record's stellar production included tracks from Clams Casino, DJ Khalil, No I.D., Stargate, TM88, and DJ Mustard.

APRIL 29

Drake releases *Views* on Young Money.

With a cover image of Drake sitting on top of Toronto's CN Tower, the multi-platinum *Views* also topped the charts for ten weeks at #1 on the *Billboard* 200.

The blockbuster album featured several hits including the Grammy-winning "Hotline Bling"; the multi-platinum, chart-topping "One Dance," featuring Wizkid and Kyla; and the platinum-selling "Controlla," as well as high-profile collaborations with Future and Rihanna. Although it didn't appear on the album version, the Grammy-nominated "Pop Style" also featured a guest appearance from Kanye West and Jay Z (as "The Throne").

The album was executive produced by Drake and 40 and included additional production from Kanye West, Nineteen85, Jordan Ullman, and Maneesh Bidaye.

MAY 6

D.R.A.M. releases the single "Broccoli" featuring Lil Yachty on Atlantic.

Virginia rapper D.R.A.M. had his breakthrough single with "Broccoli," which became one of the biggest crossover rap successes of 2016. The multi-platinum single featured Lil Yachty, a nineteen-year-old Atlanta rapper who made his name in 2016 through his work with Chance the Rapper and Kanye West. D.R.A.M. was first introduced to Lil Yachty through Rick Rubin. "Broccoli" served as the lead single to *Big Baby D.R.A.M.*, D.R.A.M.'s studio debut.

MAY 12

Young M.A self-releases her hit single "Ooouuu."

The Brooklyn rapper's breakthrough single was produced by U-Dub, and later remixed by Remy Ma and French Montana. The song reached #9 on the R&B/Hip-Hop chart and #19 on the *Billboard* Hot 100, making it one of the most successful rap singles during the summer of 2016. The official remix featured 50 Cent.

MAY 13

Chance the Rapper self-releases his third mixtape *Coloring Book*.

Chance the Rapper's third free mixtape reached #8 on the *Billboard* Hot 100 based on streaming numbers alone. The Grammy-winning *Coloring Book* featured an impressive list of guests including Lil Wayne, Kanye West, 2 Chainz, Justin Bieber, Future, Jeremih, Ty Dolla $ign, and Young Thug.

Like *The Life of Pablo*, Chance the Rapper's album, which featured gospel choirs and deeply religious lyrics, was directly inspired by gospel and roots music. *Coloring Book* served as Chance the Rapper's pop breakthrough success, earning him a Grammy for best new artist.

Many of the songs on *Coloring Book* were produced by the Social Experiment, a band of Chicago musicians and producers that includes Chance the Rapper.

CHUCK D:

When a Rap MC can rise up out of the chaos of Chi-Town and without trumpets or traditional platforms become a hip-hop success, it's incredible. Without actually releasing his project officially, he defied common moves and carved him a niche his own way. Chance is part of a new generation of wordsmiths that moves beyond one-dimensional hip-hop caricatures. I ran into him doing his thing in 2016 in the studio and I was like, "this dude is so nontraditional that I know the studio is *inside him.*"

JUNE 17

YG releases his second studio album *Still Brazy* on Def Jam.

Debuting at #6 on the *Billboard* 200, YG's album was largely inspired by sociopolitical issues, including the racially motivated presidential campaign of Donald Trump. The album included the single "FDT" (Fuck Donald Trump), and YG spent much of 2016 on his headlining Fuck Donald Trump tour.

Several tracks on the album, which featured big-name collaborations from Drake and Lil Wayne, were inspired by police shootings, such as "Black & Brown" and "Police Get Away wit Murder." *Still Brazy* featured production from Terrace Martin, Ty Dolla $ign, Hit-Boy, and P-Lo.

JUNE 17

The Game releases *Streets of Compton* on eOne Music.

Debuting at #25 on the *Billboard* 200, the Game's album served as a soundtrack to his three-part A&E documentary about Compton, which aired in June 2016. The soundtrack featured guest appearances by Problem, Boogie, J3, AD, Micah, Payso, and AV and spawned the single"Roped Off."

JUNE 26

Beyoncé and Kendrick Lamar perform "Freedom" at the BET Awards.

Kendrick Lamar and Beyoncé delivered the most talked-about performance at the 2016 BET Awards with their rendition of Beyoncé's *Lemonade* single "Freedom." The duo's politically charged performance, complete with audio snippets of Martin Luther King Jr., served as the opening to the awards show.

JULY 1

Snoop Dogg releases his fourteenth album *Coolaid* on eOne Music.

Debuting at #40 on the *Billboard* 200, the well-received album was largely seen by critics as a return to form for the Los Angeles rapper. The album yielded two singles: "Kush Ups" which featured Wiz Khalifa and reached #50 on the R&B charts and "Point Seen Money Gone," featuring Jeremih. Snoop Dogg's fourteenth album featured guests including Trick Trick, Suga Free, and E-40, with production from all-star talent like Swizz Beatz, Timbaland, and Just Blaze.

JULY 8

Schoolboy Q releases his fourth album *Blank Face LP* on Interscope.

With credits from producers like DJ Dahi, Metro Boomin, Swizz Beatz, and Tyler, the Creator, *Blank Face LP* included three singles, one of which, "THat Part," cracked the *Billboard* Hot 100, making it Schoolboy Q's most successful single to date. The song "Str8 Ballin" shares the same title as Tupac's 1994 song, which Schoolboy Q has called his all-time favorite Tupac song.

Debuting at #2 on the *Billboard* 200 and topping the R&B chart, the critically acclaimed album featured appearances from Kanye West, Vince Staples, Jadakiss, Anderson .Paak, SZA, and Miguel. Accompanying the album is a series of short films, one of which was codirected by Kendrick Lamar.

2016

SCHOOLBOY Q

DJ KHALED

JULY 20

Drake and Future begin their Summer Sixteen Tour in Austin, Texas.

Drake and Future's extensive tour spanned four months and more than fifty dates where they performed many of their joint songs, such as "Jumpman" and "Big Rings."

Special guests on the tour, which stopped at high-profile venues like Madison Square Garden, included Kanye West, Cam'ron, Juelz Santana, Fat Joe, Remy Ma, T.I., J. Cole, Eminem, Gucci Mane, 2 Chainz, Rihanna, Lil Wayne, YG, Snoop Dogg, and Ty Dolla $ign.

JULY 22

Gucci Mane releases his ninth studio album *Everybody Looking* on Atlantic.

Peaking at #2 on the *Billboard 200, Everybody Looking* was released just a few months after the Atlanta rapper served a two-year jail sentence for firearm possession. Gucci Mane recorded the album, his first in five years, in just six days.

The well-received album includes guest appearances from Drake, Kanye West, and Young Thug, with production credits from Mike Will Made It, Zaytoven, Boi-1da, and Drumma Boy.

JULY 29

DJ Khaled releases his ninth album *Major Key* on Epic.

The producer's first release since his rise to fame through the social media platform Snapchat, *Major Key* debuted at #1 on the *Billboard* 200, giving the Miami producer the highest charting record of his career.

Once again, Khaled's gold-selling album featured an extensive, wide-ranging list of guests that included Nas, Kendrick Lamar, J. Cole, Nicki Minaj, Rick Ross, YG, Busta Rhymes, Fat Joe, Wale, Wiz Khalifa, and Jadakiss, to name a few. Platinum-selling singles on the blockbuster set included "For Free," which reached #13 on the *Billboard* Hot 100 and "I Got the Keys," which featured Jay Z and Future and reached #9 on the R&B chart.

CHUCK D:

The Lyricist. The Storyteller. The Technical Rapper. The Party Rapper. The Conscious Rapper. The Political Rapper. These are six kinds of different rappers. It's a phenomenal feat when any producer-DJ decides to put together an album with more than one type of rapper from this list. DJ Khaled did just that in *Major Key*. One gets the sense that Khaled, with each track is building to something. The last track, "Progress" featuring Jamaican artist, Mavado makes the purpose of the album is clear. This is Khaled's ode to hip-hop and going back to its Jamaican heritage with "Progress" really seals the deal.

AUGUST 12

***The Get Down* premieres on Netflix.**

The Netflix series, a musical drama about the beginnings of hip-hop in the 1970s Bronx, was created by noted director Baz Luhrmann and includes Nas, Rahiem, and Grandmaster Flash as producers.

The Get Down soundtrack, released the same day as the show premiered, included a mix of classic songs and original material from Miguel, Raury, Leon Bridges, Grandmaster Flash, Donna Summer, Christina Aguilera, Teddy Pendergrass, Janelle Monáe, and Jaden Smith.

AUGUST 12

Rae Sremmurd releases *Sremmlife 2.*

Debuting at #7 on the *Billboard* 200, the club-friendly *Sremmlife 2* spawned three singles: "By Chance," "Look Alive," which reached #26 on the R&B chart, and "Black Beatles," which topped the charts, the group's fourth top forty single.

Sremmlife 2 featured appearances from Lil Jon, Gucci Mane, Juicy J, and Kodak Black, and shows the group exploring a more mature, adventurous sound than on their debut.

AUGUST 25

Kanye West's Saint Pablo Tour begins in Indianapolis.

West spent all of the fall of 2016 on tour promoting his album *The Life of Pablo*. One of the most successful of 2016, the tour, which did not have an opening act, featured an innovative stage production in which West performed on a suspended stage over the main floor of the crowd.

AUGUST 26

De La Soul releases their ninth studio album *and the Anonymous Nobody...* on A.O.I.

The New York rap trio's reunion album was funded in part through crowdsourcing. Debuting at #12 on the *Billboard* 200 and topping the Rap chart, it was the group's first studio album in four years.

Executive produced by Jordan Katz, the Grammy-nominated album featured artists ranging from Snoop Dogg to Usher to David Byrne to Jill Scott to Damon Albarn.

AUGUST 26

Young Thug releases the mixtape *Jeffery* on Atlantic Records.

Young Thug's third mixtape of 2016, which reached #8 on the *Billboard* 200, incorporated reggae and dancehall influences and featured guest appearances by Travis Scott, Gucci Mane, Wyclef Jean, Quavo, and Offset.

Shortly before the release of *Jeffery*, Young Thug's label head Lyor Cohen announced that Young Thug would no longer be going by the name Young Thug and would, instead, be known as "No, My Name Is Jeffery."

SEPTEMBER 2

Isaiah Rashad releases his debut album *The Sun's Tirade* on Top Dawg.

After releasing a debut EP in 2014, *The Sun's Tirade* served as the Tennessee rapper's debut album. *The Sun's Tirade* came after a several-year period in which Rashad struggled from addiction to Xanax and alcohol.

Critically acclaimed, it included appearances from label mates Kendrick Lamar, SZA, and Jay Rock. After Rashad's lead single "Free Lunch" premiered a few weeks before the album's release, *The Sun's Tirade* debuted at #17 on the *Billboard* 200 and #4 on the R&B/Hip-Hop chart.

SEPTEMBER 2

Travis Scott releases his second album *Birds in the Trap Sing McKnight* on Epic.

Debuting at #1 on the *Billboard* 200, the album yielded three singles: "wonderful," featuring The Weeknd; the platinum-selling "pick up the phone," which featured Young Thug and reached #12 on the R&B chart; and the gold-selling "goosebumps" which featured Kendrick Lamar and reached #21 on the R&B chart.

One of many artists who contributed guest vocals to the gold-selling album was Kid Cudi, who Travis Scott has called one of his greatest inspirations. Other artists guesting on the album included Quavo, Cassie, Blac Youngsta, and 21 Savage.

SEPTEMBER 27

Danny Brown releases his fourth album *Atrocity Exhibition* on Warp.

Peaking at #77 on the *Billboard* 200, Danny Brown's critically acclaimed and lyrically dexterous fourth album was on many critics' best-of lists.

The Detroit rapper's grim and anxious album, primarily produced by Paul White, spawned three singles: "When It Rain"; "Pneumonia," featuring Schoolboy Q; and "Really Doe," which featured vocals from Kendrick Lamar, Earl Sweatshirt, and Ab-Soul.

NOVEMBER 11

A Tribe Called Quest releases *We Got It from Here... Thank You 4 Your Service* on Epic.

The comeback album from the pioneering rap group is their first since 1998's *The Love Movement*. The genesis for the group's reunion came after they reunited for a twenty-fifth anniversary performance on *The Tonight Show*.

We Got It from Here... Thank You 4 Your Service was the last-ever studio album to feature all the original members of A Tribe Called Quest, as Phife Dawg died a few months before the album's release.

Debuting at #1 on the *Billboard* 200, the critically acclaimed album featured appearances by André 3000, Kendrick Lamar, Kanye West, Anderson. Paak, Talib Kweli, Elton John, and Jack White, as well as longtime collaborator Busta Rhymes. The politically charged single "We the People..." reached #23 on the Rap chart.

DECEMBER 2

***The Hamilton Mixtape* is released on Atlantic.**

Produced in part by Questlove, the album, which debuted at #1 on the *Billboard* 200, is a collection of covers and interpretations of Lin-Manuel Miranda's hip-hop musical *Hamilton*. The various artists who contributed songs for the album included Ja Rule, Ashanti, the Roots, Nas, Usher, Watsky, Alicia Keys, Wiz Khalifa, John Legend, Common, and Chance the Rapper.

INDEX

Page numbers in **bold** refer to images on respective pages.

A

B

C

D

E

F

G

H

I

J

K

N

O

P

Q

R

S

T

U

V

W

X

Y

Z

ARTIST CREDITS

Special shout out to all the artists who contributed their work to the book.

—Salute,

ASKEM: The Creator of Art You Hear: 9, 11, 14, 17, 26, 27, 31, 34, 38, 39, 46, 47, 59, 63, 64, 72, 73, 76, 79, 86, 93, 103, 106, 121, 122, 123, 137, 152, 153, 172, 175, 188, 191, 201, 210, 213, 225, 237, 255, 258, 264, 304, 312

Amy Cinnamon Art: 6, 10, 13, 21, 58, 67, 69, 89, 96, 98, 110, 145, 156, 167, 183, 237

André LeRoy Davis: 48, 54, 116, 151, 163, 178, 181, 195, 226

Shepard Fairey: vii

Shepard Fairey based on a photograph by Glen E. Friedman: 22, 37, 45, 278

Darren Holtom: 51, 164, 166

Andrew J. Katz: 56, 68, 243

Timothy McAuliffe, Gold Van: 267, 276

Scared of Monsters: 141, 184, 198, 207, 217, 218, 247, 250, 275, 285, 286, 294, 295, 303, 308, 321, 322

Rinat Shingareev: 132, 229, 241, 257, 297, 307, 318

Marco Ventura: 83 (*Rolling Stone*, 2005), 192 (*GQ*, 2000)

Piero F. Giunti

Both as a solo artist and as the leader of the groundbreaking hip-hop group Public Enemy (which was inducted into the Rock & Roll Hall of Fame in 2013), Chuck D helped pave the way for political, social, and culturally conscious hip-hop. Public Enemy's albums remain among the most critically acclaimed works in the genre, including *It Takes a Nation of Millions to Hold Us Back* and *Fear of a Black Planet*. He is on the road three weeks out of each month touring with Public Enemy and his supergroup Prophets of Rage which includes members of Cypress Hill and Rage Against the Machine. Or you can find him speaking at tech and music conferences around the world. A visionary in digital entertainment, Chuck D helped lead the file-sharing movement, launched one of the first online entertainment websites, Rapstation.com, and digital-only record labels, the SpitSlam Record Label Group. Public Enemy was the second act to ever release an album in MP3 format. Chuck D splits his days off among Long Island, Atlanta, and Southern California.